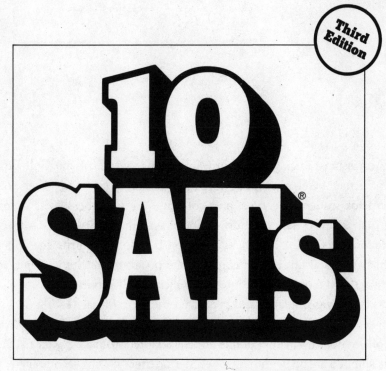

Third Edition

10 SATs

PLUS ADVICE FROM THE COLLEGE BOARD ON HOW TO PREPARE FOR THEM

COLLEGE ENTRANCE EXAMINATION BOARD
NEW YORK

The Admissions Testing Program (ATP) is a program of the College Board, a nonprofit membership organization that provides tests and other educational services for students, schools, and colleges. The membership is composed of more than 2,500 colleges, schools, school systems, and education associations. Representatives of the members serve on the Board of Trustees and advisory councils and committees that consider the programs of the College Board and participate in the determination of its policies and activities.

This book was prepared and produced by Educational Testing Service (ETS), which develops and administers the tests of the Admissions Testing Program for the College Board. The text of this book is adapted from *Taking the SAT*, a booklet that is shipped at the beginning of each academic year to secondary schools for free distribution to students who plan to register for the SAT. (Copies of *Taking the SAT* can be purchased for $4.00 each; 50 or more, $2.00 each.)

The College Board and Educational Testing Service are dedicated to the principle of equal opportunity, and their programs, services, and employment policies are guided by that principle.

Contents

Introduction

The College Board knows that some people are uncomfortable with the prospect of taking any test, but that there is even greater anxiety before taking national standardized tests such as the Scholastic Aptitude Test (SAT). One reason that people worry about how they will do on the SAT is that they don't know what the test will be like, what it measures, or how the results will be used.

This book helps students to become better acquainted with the SAT and, therefore, reduce some of that anxiety. The following topics are included:

- What the SAT measures
- The format of the test as a whole
- The kinds of questions on the test
- How to mark the answer sheet
- How each question is scored
- Rules of good test-taking practice
- How scores are reported and used
- How to use sample tests for practice and self-scoring

This information and one sample test are also available in the booklet *Taking the SAT*, which students who plan to take the test receive free of charge from their schools. *Taking the SAT* and the *Registration Bulletin* (see page 7) are revised annually and contain the most up-to-date information about the SAT and testing procedures.

In addition, the College Board makes public five editions of the SAT each year as part of its ongoing program to provide full public information about these tests. Ten of these editions, all of which have been administered in the past few years, are included in this book. Other than to help students become familiar with the test, use of all 10 tests in preparing for the SAT probably will be of limited value. These tests illustrate the range of questions and topics on any SAT test; however, research offers no evidence that extensive drill or practice on these particular tests will increase scores significantly. The soundest preparation for the SAT continues to be serious application to regular school studies, with emphasis on academic courses and plenty of outside reading.

Although this book has been written for students and others who are planning to take the SAT, it also may be useful to parents, teachers, and individuals who have an interest in the SAT and who use its results.

If you want to write or call . . .	**Address**	**Phone Numbers (Monday-Friday)**	
	College Board ATP	Princeton, NJ	Bay Area Office, CA
	P.O. Box 6200	8:30 a.m. to 9:30 p.m. Eastern time	8:15 a.m. to 4:30 p.m.
	Princeton, NJ 08541-6200	(609) 771-7588 Registration	Pacific time
		(609) 771-7600 Score Reports	(415) 654-1200
		(609) 771-7435 General Information	

How the Tests Are Developed

Many people are involved in the development of every new edition of the Scholastic Aptitude Test (SAT) and the Test of Standard Written English (TSWE). Questions are written by high school and college teachers and by test specialists at Educational Testing Service. Questions then are placed in an equating section of the SAT to be tried out under standard testing conditions by representative samples of students. The responses to each question are then analyzed statistically. Satisfactory questions become part of a pool of questions from which new editions of the SAT are assembled.

In developing a new edition of the SAT, test specialists and test editors review each question and reading selection on which questions are based for accuracy and to ensure balanced content of the test as a whole. Each reviewer prepares a list of answers that is compared with other reviewers' lists to verify agreement on the correct answer for each question. In addition, trained "sensitivity" reviewers eliminate any references in the test material that might be unfair or offensive to some student groups because of stereotyping, sex bias, or content that could produce negative feelings.

After the new edition has been assembled, the SAT and TSWE Committees, composed of high school teachers, college faculty, and educational administrators, review the test a final time before it is given to students. In addition to reviewing all new tests, these committees also are responsible for determining overall test specifications, recommending related research, and advising the College Board on policy matters related to the tests.

SAT Committee 1987-88

Paul M. Pressly, The Savannah Country Day School, Savannah, Georgia, *Chair*

John A. Blackburn, University of Virginia, Charlottesville, Virginia

Diane Briars, Pittsburgh Public Schools, Pittsburgh, Pennsylvania

Jim Cox, Anaheim Union School District, Anaheim, California

Dorothy H. Dillon, Kent Place School, Summit, New Jersey

Karl Furstenberg, Wesleyan University, Middletown, Connecticut

Jean Lockhart, John Foster Dulles High School, Sugarland, Texas

Jose P. Mestre, University of Massachusetts, Amherst, Massachusetts

Jacqueline H. Simmons, Paul Robeson High School, Chicago, Illinois

Frank B. Womer, University of Michigan, Ann Arbor, Michigan

TSWE Committee 1987-88

Jacqueline J. Royster, Spelman College, Atlanta, Georgia, *Chair*

Jeanette P. Morgan, University of Houston, Houston, Texas

Aida M. Ortiz-Ruiz, Hostos Community College/CUNY, Bronx, New York

Gregory L. Rubano, Toll Gate High School, Warwick, Rhode Island

William H. Thomas, Mt. Diablo Unified School District, Concord, California

About the Test

The SAT

The SAT is a multiple-choice test made up of verbal and math sections. The verbal questions test your vocabulary, verbal reasoning, and understanding of what you read. The math questions test your ability to solve problems involving arithmetic, elementary algebra, and geometry. These verbal and mathematical abilities are related to how well you will do academically in college. The SAT does not measure other factors and abilities—such as creativity, special talents, and motivation—that may also help you do well in college.

SAT scores are useful to college admissions officers in comparing the preparation and ability of applicants from different high schools which may vary widely in their courses and grading standards. Colleges also consider your high school record and other information about you in making admissions decisions. Your high school record is probably the best single indicator of how you will do in college, but a combination of your high school grades and test scores is an even better indicator. ✧

The TSWE

The TSWE (Test of Standard Written English) is a multiple-choice test given at the same time as the SAT, but it has a different purpose. The TSWE is intended to be used to help the college you attend choose an English course appropriate for your ability. The questions in it measure your ability to recognize standard written English, the language that is used in most college textbooks and that you will probably be expected to use in the papers you write in college.

How the Test Is Organized

The SAT and TSWE are included in the same test book. Each test book is divided into six sections:

- 2 SAT-verbal sections
- 2 SAT-math sections
- 1 TSWE section
- 1 section of equating questions (verbal, math, or TSWE)

The questions in the equating section do not count toward your score. They are used for two purposes: First, representative questions from earlier editions are given again in order to set the SAT on the 200 to 800 scale. Repeating these questions makes it possible to compare scores earned at different administrations. Second, the equating section is used to try out questions for future use in the SAT. Trying out questions in advance makes it possible to assemble each edition of the SAT with the same mix of easy and hard questions. Thus, the unscored equating section is used to assemble SATs of comparable difficulty so that college admissions officers can compare SAT scores equitably.

You will be given 30 minutes to work on each section. The six sections are not in the same order in every test book. On the following pages you will find detailed explanations of each type of question as well as tips on how to make the best use of the testing time.

How to Register

The *Registration Bulletin* contains a registration form and directions on how to register for the test and how to have your scores reported. The *Bulletin* also describes other tests and services of the Admissions Testing Program (ATP), such as the Achievement Tests, the Student Descriptive Questionnaire (SDQ), and the Student Search Service (SSS).

The SAT is administered on a regular schedule (six times a year in most states) at thousands of test centers throughout the world. To avoid late fees, you must send in your registration form at least five weeks before the test date you have chosen. Registration schedules and test fees are listed in the *Registration Bulletin*.

A supply of the *Registration Bulletin* is sent to all high schools each year. High school students can pick up a copy of the *Bulletin* at their school guidance or counseling office. Test candidates who are not currently in high school may obtain a copy by writing to the address on page 5.

Preparing for the SAT

Keep Things in Perspective

In many ways, you have been preparing for the SAT during your entire school career. Doing well on the SAT is a natural result of hard work in academic courses in school and a strong interest in reading and other mentally challenging activities. If you are reading this book, chances are that you are seriously considering going to college. For many students, taking the SAT is one of the first steps in the college admission process and, logically, you want to do your best when you take the test. But getting ready for the SAT should be only one part of your overall plan to gain admission to college.

Surveys by major national educational organizations show that most colleges are likely to view your high school record—the courses you have taken and your rank in class or grade average—as most important. Usually this record is viewed along with your SAT scores. Indications of personal qualities such as motivation, initiative, and leadership ability may also influence colleges' decisions.

Even though SAT scores are seldom the most important factor in admissions decisions, they do carry weight, in varying degrees, with many colleges. For that reason, you should be as well prepared as possible to show your skills when you take the SAT.

You Can Prepare for the SAT: Here's How and Why

Over the long term, a good selection of solid academic courses, wide reading, and consistent hard work on your studies are the best strategies. In the short run, you should be sure that you know the format of the test:

How it is organized,
The kinds of questions it asks,
The terms and concepts it uses,
How it is timed, and how it is scored.

You should also know some basic rules of test-taking strategy, including when and why to guess, how to pace yourself, and so on. If you do not have this information you may be at a disadvantage in taking the test. *Taking the SAT* provides this information. Students who have read it carefully and taken the full practice test that it contains have reported greater confidence, less anxiety, and more familiarity with the test than students who did not use the booklet.

Just how much practice you may need to feel comfortable is a decision you must make. For those who want to practice with more than one sample SAT, the College Board publishes several books of sample tests, which are available from your school guidance office, your school or local library, and in bookstores. Remember, though, that practice is not likely to improve your scores dramatically. If you are nervous about taking tests, it can help you relax. But simply drilling on hundreds of questions cannot do much to help you develop the skills in verbal and mathematical reasoning that the test measures.

What About Coaching Courses?

There is a bewildering array of courses, books, and computer software programs available to help you prepare for the SAT. Some of them do no more than provide the familiarization and practice that is described in the previous section. Others are intended to help you develop your mathematical and verbal skills. These are often called "coaching" courses and we are often asked whether they work.

The vast majority of coaching courses are conducted in school, during class time or after hours, at little or no cost to students. A few commercial coaching courses are elaborate and costly. Some require as much time and effort as you might spend in a full semester course in school.

Some students may improve their scores by taking these courses, while others may not. Unfortunately, despite decades of research, it is still not possible to predict ahead of time who will improve, and by how much—and who will not. For that reason, the College Board cannot recommend coaching courses, especially if they cost a lot or require a lot of time and effort that could be spent on schoolwork or other worthwhile activities.

We are not saying they don't work. We just can't say with certainty whether a particular program or activity will work for you. We can suggest some questions to ask in deciding whether to take a coaching course, but we cannot tell you what your decision should be.

First, how much time should you devote to this activity? Your SAT scores may help distinguish you from other applicants. But so may success in an especially rigorous course, involvement in school or community activities, or demonstrating an outstanding special talent.

It is important to know that most students who take the SAT a second time have not been coached. Yet, most of these students show growth the second time—on average, 15-20 points on verbal and 15-20 points on math. Out of every 100 students who repeat the test, five will show a gain of 100 points or more on verbal or math, while one will show a drop of 100 points or more.

How much improvement beyond normal growth may result from coaching? The best available research suggests that short-duration (20 hours or so) familiarization courses improve scores on the average about 10 points on the verbal section and about 15 points on the math section. Studies of some longer-duration (40 hours or so) courses that stress work to develop the underlying skills measured by the test suggest average gains of 15-20 points on the verbal section and 20-30 points on the math section.

Keep in mind these are averages; some students improve their scores dramatically, while others show little or no gain. Some scores even go down.

Very much larger gains than these are claimed by some commercial coaching courses. Some appear based only on the scores of students who have improved dramatically on retaking the test. It is not always clear whether the reported gains are for verbal and math separately or added together. It is also not clear whether scores that drop are included in these claims.

Finally, are there tricks you can learn to beat the SAT? Some commercial coaching courses claim to teach them. Many are not tricks at all, but legitimate pieces of advice that all test takers should know and that are provided free in *Taking the SAT*. On the rare occasions that a useful trick has surfaced, the test developers who write the SAT immediately have changed the test so that the trick would no longer help. It is risky business to rely on tricks instead of using the strategies suggested in *Taking the SAT* and thinking carefully about the questions.

Our Recommendations

The College Board believes that the coaching that works best is the coaching that is most like hard schoolwork. If that is so, you should ask yourself whether you can't do just as much by studying harder and taking more demanding courses.

You can, and should, ask for advice from your parents, counselors, and teachers. Talk with your friends, too. But don't rely too heavily on anecdotal evidence, especially if it is second- or third-hand.

If you decide to consider a course, investigate it carefully. Examine carefully and ask for verification of all claims of results. Weigh the investment—both in time and in money. Be sure you know what is available from your school before you decide to pay for a commercial course.

And above all, ask what you can do in your regular schoolwork, in your leisure time on your own, or working with fellow students or adults to prepare for the SAT without distracting from other things that are important to your education and your college aims.

Know What to Expect

The best way to prepare for the test is to know what will be expected of you on the test day. To make sure you are prepared for the test, you should:

- **Read this book and *Taking the SAT*.** They have the information you will need to become familiar with all aspects of the test. Be sure you understand how the test is organized and how it will be scored. The information in these books will help you learn the answers to such questions as "Should I guess?" "Do difficult questions get more credit than easy ones?" "Should I memorize mathematical formulas?"

- **Study the sample questions and explanations.** The sample questions that begin on page 12 will give you a good idea of the kinds of questions on the test. The more familiar you are with the sample questions, the more comfortable you'll feel when you see the questions in your test book on the day of the test.

- **Study and understand the test directions.** The directions for answering the questions in this book are exactly the same as those in the test book. If you study the directions now, you will spend less time reading and figuring them out on the test day and will have more time for answering the questions.

- **Take at least one sample test, score it, and review the questions you missed.** Try to take a practice test under conditions similar to those of the test day. (Suggestions for doing so are on page 34, just before the first sample test.) Make sure you use one of the answer sheets provided. That way you'll already have been through a dry run before you take the test.

The Day Before the Test

Learn as much as you can about the test well before you plan to take it. Following are some suggestions for activities the day or evening before the test:

- **Review briefly the sample questions, explanations, and test directions in this book.** Hours of intense study the night before probably will not help your performance on the test and might even make you more anxious. But a short review of the information you studied earlier probably will make you feel more comfortable and better prepared.

- **Get your testing materials together and put them in a place that will be convenient for you in the morning.** Use this checklist:
  - ✓ Admission Ticket
  - ✓ Acceptable identification (You won't be admitted to the test center without it. See the *Registration Bulletin* for specific examples.)
  - ✓ Two No. 2 (soft-lead) pencils with erasers
  - ✓ Directions to the test center, if you need them
  - ✓ All the materials you will need to register as a standby, if you have not preregistered (See the *Registration Bulletin*.)

- **Spend the evening relaxing.** You'll accomplish little by worrying about the test. Read a book or watch TV, or do anything else you find relaxing.

- **Get a good night's sleep.** You'll want to feel your best when you take the test, so try to be well rested and refreshed. Get to bed early, set your alarm early enough to avoid having to rush, and feel satisfied that you've prepared yourself well for the test day.

Test-Taking Tips

Here are some specific test-taking tips that will help when you actually take the test.

✓ Within each group of questions of the same type, the easier questions are usually at the beginning of the group and the more difficult ones are at the end. (The reading comprehension questions are an exception. The reading passages are usually ordered easiest to hardest, but the questions that follow each passage are ordered according to the logic and organization of the passage.)

✓ If you're working on a group of questions and find that the questions are getting too difficult, quickly read through the rest of the questions in that group and answer only those you think you know. Then go on to the next group of questions in that section. (Again, this advice does not necessarily apply to the questions immediately following a reading passage, in which case a difficult reading comprehension question might be followed by an easier one.)

✓ You get just as much credit for correctly answering easy questions as you do for correctly answering hard ones. So answer all the questions that seem easy before you spend time on those that seem difficult.

✓ You get one point for each question you answer correctly. You lose a *fraction* of a point for each question you answer incorrectly. You neither gain nor lose credit for questions you omit. (See page 65 for more detailed information on scoring.)

✓ You don't have to answer every question correctly to score well. In fact, many students who answer only 40-60 percent of the questions correctly receive average or slightly above-average scores.

✓ You *can* guess. If you know that one or more answer choices for a question are definitely wrong, then it's generally to your advantage to guess from the remaining choices. But because of the way the test is scored, random guessing is unlikely to increase your score.

✓ You *can* omit questions. Many students who do well on the SAT omit some questions. You can always return to questions you've omitted if you finish before time is up for that section.

✓ If you do not respond to any SAT-verbal, SAT-math, or TSWE questions, you will receive the minimum score for that part.

✓ Use the test book for scratchwork and to mark questions you omitted, so you can go back to them if you have time. You will not receive credit for any responses written in the test book. You must mark all your responses to test questions on the separate answer sheet before time is up on each section.

✓ Do *not* make extra marks on the answer sheet. They may be misread as answers by the scoring machine. If the scoring machine reads what looks like two answers for one question, that will be considered an omitted question. So it's in your best interest to keep your answer sheet free of any stray marks.

✓ Any four-choice mathematics question (see page 61) for which you mark the fifth answer oval, E, will be treated as an omitted question. You will not receive credit for that response.

✓ Mark only one answer for each question. To be certain that your answer will be read by the scoring machine, make sure your mark is dark and completely fills the oval, as shown in the first example below.

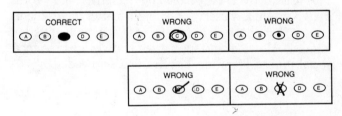

Sample Questions and Explanations

Following are sample questions and explanations for each type of question that appears on the SAT. Become familiar with the directions. You'll see them again on the test you will take.

Verbal Sections of the SAT

The verbal sections of the SAT contain four types of questions:

- 25 antonyms
- 20 analogies
- 15 sentence completions
- 25 questions based on reading passages

The antonyms usually take the least time per question, followed by analogies, sentence completion questions, and, finally, the reading comprehension questions. Individual students spend varying amounts of time working on the different types of questions. Some students can answer two or three antonyms a minute, but the same students may take more than seven minutes to read a 400-word passage and answer five questions on it.

Your answers to the 85 questions in the verbal sections make up your total verbal score. (See page 66.) The score report you receive will also show two subscores: (1) a vocabulary subscore, based on the antonym and analogy questions, and (2) a reading subscore, based on the sentence completions and the questions on the reading passages.

A careful balance of reading materials and words drawn from a variety of subject-matter fields helps ensure that the test is fair to students with different interests. However, no specialized knowledge in science, social studies, literature, or other fields is needed.

Antonyms (opposites) ■■■■■■■

Antonym questions primarily test the extent of your vocabulary. The vocabulary used in the antonym questions includes words that you are likely to come across in your general reading, although some words may not be the kind you use in everyday speech.

Directions: Each question below consists of a word in capital letters, followed by five lettered words or phrases. Choose the word or phrase that is most nearly <u>opposite</u> in meaning to the word in capital letters. Since some of the questions require you to distinguish fine shades of meaning, consider all the choices before deciding which is best.

EXAMPLE:
GOOD: (A) sour (B) bad (C) red
(D) hot (E) ugly

Ⓐ ● Ⓒ Ⓓ Ⓔ

You can probably answer this example without thinking very much about the choices. However, most of the antonyms in the verbal section require more careful analysis. When you work on antonym questions, remember that:

1. Among the five choices offered, you are looking for the word that means the *opposite* of the given word. Words that have exactly the same meaning as the given word are not included among the five choices.

2. You are looking for the *best* answer. Read all of the choices before deciding which one is best, even if you feel sure you know the answer. For example:

   SUBSEQUENT: (A) primary (B) recent
   (C) contemporary (D) prior (E) simultaneous

   Subsequent means "following in time or order; succeeding." Someone working quickly might choose (B) *recent* because it refers to a past action and *subsequent* refers to an action in the future. However, choice (D) *prior* is the best answer. It is more nearly the opposite of *subsequent* than is *recent*.

3. Few words have exact opposites, that is, words that are opposite in all of their meanings. You should find the word that is *most nearly* opposite. For example:

   FERMENTING: (A) improvising (B) stagnating
   (C) wavering (D) plunging (E) dissolving

   Even though *fermenting* is normally associated with chemical reactions, whereas *stagnating* is normally associated with water, *fermenting* means "being agitated," and *stagnating* means "being motionless." Therefore, choice (B) *stagnating* is the best of the five choices.

4. You need to be flexible. A word can have several meanings. For example:

DEPRESS: (A) force (B) allow (C) clarify (D) elate (E) loosen

The word *depress* can mean "to push down." However, no word meaning "to lift up" is included among the choices. Therefore, you must consider another meaning of *depress*, "to sadden or discourage." Option (D) *elate* means "to fill with joy or pride." The best answer is (D) *elate*.

5. You'll often recognize a word you have encountered in your reading but have never looked up in the dictionary. If you don't know the dictionary meaning of a word but have a sense of how the word should be used, try to make up a short phrase or sentence using the word. This may give you a clue as to which choice is an opposite, even though you may not be able to define the word precisely.

INCUMBENT: (A) conscious (B) effortless (C) optional (D) improper (E) irrelevant

You may remember *incumbent* used in a sentence such as, "It is incumbent upon me to finish this." If you can think of such a phrase, you may be able to recognize that *incumbent* means "imposed as a duty" or "obligatory." Of the five choices, (A), (B), and (D) are in no way opposites of *incumbent* and you can easily eliminate them. Choice (E) means "not pertinent" and choice (C) means "not compulsory." Although choice (E) may look attractive, choice (C) *optional* is more nearly an exact opposite to *incumbent*. Choice (C), therefore, is the answer.

Some General Tips for Answering Antonym Questions

Answering antonyms depends on knowing the uses as well as the meanings of words, so just memorizing word lists is probably of little value. You're more likely to improve your performance on antonyms and other kinds of verbal questions by doing things that help you to think about words and the way they are used. So, it would be a good idea to:

✓ Read books or magazines on subjects with which you're not already familiar. This will give you an idea of how familiar words can have different meanings in different contexts.

✓ Use a dictionary when you come across words that you don't understand. This will help to broaden your vocabulary and could improve your performance on the tests.

Analogies

Analogy questions test your ability to see a relationship in a pair of words, to understand the ideas expressed in the relationship, and to recognize a similar or parallel relationship.

> **Directions: Each question below consists of a related pair of words or phrases, followed by five lettered pairs of words or phrases. Select the lettered pair that best expresses a relationship similar to that expressed in the original pair.**
>
> **EXAMPLE:**
> **YAWN : BOREDOM : : (A) dream : sleep (B) anger : madness   (C) smile : amusement (D) face : expression   (E) impatience : rebellion**
> Ⓐ Ⓑ ● Ⓓ Ⓔ

The first step in answering an analogy question is to establish a precise relationship between the original pair of words (the two capitalized words). In the example above, the relationship between *yawn* and *boredom* can best be stated as "(first word) is a physical sign of (second word)," or "(first word) is a facial expression of (second word)." The second step in answering an analogy question is to decide which of the five pairs given as choices best expresses a similar relationship. In the example above, the answer is choice (C): a (smile) is a physical sign of (amusement), or a (smile) is a facial expression of (amusement). None of the other choices shares a similar relationship with the capitalized pair of words: a *dream* is something that occurs when you are asleep, but it is not usually thought of as being a sign of *sleep* as, for example, closed eyes or a snore might be; *anger* denotes strong displeasure and *madness* can refer to rage or insanity, but neither word is a physical sign of the other; an *expression* is something that appears on a *face*, but a *face* is not a sign of an *expression*; *impatience* may lead to *rebellion* or be characteristic of a rebellious person, but *impatience* is not a physical sign of *rebellion*.

For the analogy below, state the relationship between the original pair of words and then decide which pair of words from choices (A) to (E) has a similar or parallel relationship.

SUBMISSIVE : LED : : (A) wealthy : employed (B) intolerant : indulged   (C) humble : humiliated (D) incorrigible : taught (E) inconspicuous : overlooked

The relationship between *submissive* and *led* can be expressed as "to be submissive is to be easily led." Only choice (E) has the same relationship: "to be inconspicuous is to be easily overlooked." To be *intolerant* is not to be easily *indulged*, to be *humble* is not to be easily *humiliated,* and to be *incorrigible* (or incapable of being reformed) is not to be easily *taught.* With regard to choice (A), the statement "to be wealthy is to be easily employed" is an expression of opinion and not an expression of the relationship between the words according to their dictionary meanings.

Practice describing verbal relationships. Below are some examples of the kinds of relationships that could be used.

SONG : REPERTOIRE : : (A) score : melody
(B) instrument : artist   (C) solo : chorus
(D) benediction : church   (E) suit : wardrobe

The best answer is choice (E). The relationship between the words can be expressed as "several (first word) make up a (second word)." Several (songs) make up a (repertoire) as several (suits) make up a (wardrobe).

REQUEST : ENTREAT : : (A) control : explode
(B) admire : idolize   (C) borrow : steal
(D) repeat : plead   (E) cancel : invalidate

The best answer is choice (B). Although both of the capitalized words have similar meanings, they express different degrees of feeling; to (entreat) is to (request) with strong feeling as to (idolize) is to (admire) with strong feeling. To answer analogy questions, you must think carefully about the precise meanings of words. For instance, if you thought the word "entreat" meant only "to ask" instead of "to ask urgently," you would have trouble establishing the correct relationship between *request* and *entreat.*

FAMINE : STARVATION : : (A) deluge : flood
(B) drought : vegetation   (C) war : treaty
(D) success : achievement   (E) seed : mutation

The best answer is choice (A). The relationship can be stated as (famine) results in (starvation) as a (deluge) results in a (flood). None of the other pairs of words expresses a causal relationship. Choice (C) is close, since a *treaty* often follows after a *war,* but we do not think of a war "causing" a treaty in the same way that a famine "causes" starvation.

AMPLIFIER : HEAR : : (A) turntable : listen
(B) typewriter : spell   (C) platter : eat
(D) camera : feel   (E) microscope : see

The best answer is choice (E). An (amplifier) magnifies in order to help a person (hear) in the same way that a (microscope) magnifies in order to help a person (see). Note that, in (A), while a *turntable* is part of a larger mechanism that allows a person to *listen,* the choice is not as good an answer as (E) because a *turntable* does not magnify anything. Choice (D) is also wrong for a similar reason: a *camera* produces pictures that may make a person *feel* something, but a *camera* does not magnify in order to help a person to *feel.*

Some choices may have relationships that are close but not parallel to the relationship in the original pair. However, the correct answer has *most nearly* the same relationship as the original pair. Look at the following example.

KNIFE : INCISION : : (A) bulldozer : excavation
(B) tool : operation   (C) pencil : calculation
(D) hose : irrigation   (E) plow : agriculture

On the most general level, the relationship between *knife* and *incision* is that the object indicated by the first word is used to perform the action indicated by the second word. Since "a (knife) is used to make an (incision)," "a (bulldozer) is used to make an (excavation)," and "a (hose) is used for (irrigation)," there appear to be two correct answers. You need to go back and state the relationship more precisely. Some aspect of the relationship between the original pair exists in only one of the choices. A more precise relationship between *knife* and *incision* could be expressed as: "a knife cuts into something to make an incision" and "a bulldozer cuts into something to make an excavation." This relationship eliminates *hose : irrigation* as a possible answer. The best answer is choice (A).

Remember that a pair of words can have more than one relationship. For example:

PRIDE : LION : : (A) snake : python   (B) pack : wolf
(C) rat : mouse   (D) bird : starling   (E) dog : canine

A possible relationship between *pride* and *lion* might be that "the first word describes a characteristic of the second (especially in mythology)." Using this reasoning, you might look for an answer such as *wisdom : owl,* but none of the given choices has that kind of relationship. Another relationship between *pride* and *lion* is "a group of lions is called a pride"; therefore, the answer is (B) *pack : wolf,* since "a group of wolves is called a pack."

Some General Tips for Answering Analogy Questions

✓ State the relationship between the two capitalized words in a sentence or phrase as clearly as you can. Next, find the pair of words that has the most similar or parallel relationship. Don't be misled by choices that merely suggest a vague association. Be sure that you can identify a specific relationship.

✓ Always compare the relationship between the <u>pair</u> of capitalized words with the relationship between the <u>pair</u> of words in each of the choices. Don't try to set up a relationship between the first word in the original pair and the first word in each of the five choices.

✓ Think carefully about the meanings of words. The words in analogy questions are used according to their dictionary definitions or meanings closely related to their dictionary definitions. The better you know the precise meanings of words, the less trouble you'll have establishing the correct relationships between them.

✓ Don't be misled by relationships that are close but not parallel to the relationship in the original pair. The correct answer has a relationship that is <u>most nearly parallel</u> to the relationship between the capitalized words.

Sentence Completion Questions ▪▪▪▪▪▪

Sentence completion questions test your ability to recognize relationships among parts of a sentence. Each question has a sentence with one or two words missing. Below the sentence, five words or pairs of words are given. You must choose the word or set of words that best fits with the other parts of the sentence. In sentence completion questions, you have to know the meanings of the words offered as choices and you also have to know how to use those words properly in the context of a sentence. The sentences are taken from published material and cover a wide variety of topics. You'll find that, even if you're not familiar with the topic of a sentence, there's enough information in the sentence for you to find the correct answer from the context of the sentence itself.

<u>Directions:</u> Each sentence below has one or two blanks, each blank indicating that something has been omitted. Beneath the sentence are five lettered words or sets of words. Choose the word or set of words that, when inserted in the sentence, <u>best</u> fits the meaning of the sentence as a whole.

EXAMPLE:
Although its publicity has been ----, the film itself is intelligent, well-acted, handsomely produced, and altogether ----.
  (A) tasteless . . respectable (B) extensive . . moderate
   (C) sophisticated . . amateur (D) risqué . . crude
    (E) perfect . . spectacular

⬤ Ⓑ Ⓒ Ⓓ Ⓔ

The word *although* suggests that the publicity gave the wrong impression of the movie, so look for two words that are more or less opposite in meaning. Also, the second word has to fit in with "intelligent, well-acted, handsomely produced." Choices (D) and (E) are not opposites. The words in choice (B) are somewhat opposite in meaning, but do not logically fulfill the expectation set up by the word *although*. Choice (C) can't be the correct answer, even though *sophisticated* and *amateur* are nearly opposites, because an "intelligent, well-acted, handsomely produced" film isn't amateurish. Only

choice (A), when inserted in the sentence, makes a logical statement.

For a better understanding of sentence completion questions, read the following sample questions and explanations.

Nearly all the cultivated plants utilized by the Chinese have been of ---- origin; even rice, though known in China since Neolithic times, came from India.
  (A) foreign (B) ancient (C) wild (D) obscure
   (E) common

To answer this question, you need to consider the entire sentence—the part that comes after the semicolon as well as the part that comes before it. If you only consider the first part of the question, all five choices seem plausible. The second part of the sentence adds a specific example—that rice came to China from India. This idea of origin supports and clarifies the "origin" mentioned in the first part of the sentence and eliminates (C), (D), and (E) as possible answers. The mention of Neolithic times makes (B) harder to eliminate, but the sentence is not logical when (B) is used to fill in the blank because the emphasis in the second part of the sentence—country of origin—is inconsistent with that in the first—age. Only choice (A) produces a sentence that is logical and consistent.

The excitement does not ---- but ---- his senses, giving him a keener perception of a thousand details.
  (A) slow . . diverts (B) blur . . sharpens
   (C) overrule . . constricts (D) heighten . . aggravates
    (E) forewarn . . quickens

Since the sentence has two blanks to be filled, you must make sure that both words make sense in the sentence. If you look for grammatical clues within the sentence, you will see that the word *but* implies that the answer will involve two words that are more or less opposite in meaning. If you keep this in mind, you can eliminate all of the choices except for (B) *blur . . sharpens*. Only the words in choice (B) imply opposition. Also, "sharpens his senses" is consistent with the notion that he has a "keener perception of a thousand details."

They argue that the author was determined to ---- his own conclusion, so he ---- any information that did not support it.
  (A) uphold . . ignored (B) revise . . destroyed
   (C) advance . . devised (D) disprove . . distorted
    (E) reverse . . confiscated

The logic of the sentence makes it fairly easy to eliminate choices (B), (D), and (E). The first word in choice (A), *uphold,* and the first word in (C), *advance,* seem all right. However, the second word in choice (C), *devised,* does not make sense in the sentence. Why would an author who wished to advance his theory devise information that did not support it? Only choice (A) makes a logically consistent sentence.

She is a skeptic, ---- to believe that the accepted opinion of the majority is generally ----.

    (A) prone . . infallible   (B) afraid . . misleading
      (C) inclined . . justifiable   (D) quick . . significant
        (E) disposed . . erroneous

The words to be inserted in the blank spaces in the question above must result in a statement that is consistent with the definition of a skeptic. Since a skeptic would hardly consider the accepted opinion of the majority as *infallible*, *justifiable*, or *significant*, you can eliminate choices (A), (C), and (D). A skeptic would not be afraid that the accepted opinion of the majority is *misleading*; a skeptic would believe that it was. Therefore, choice (B) is not correct. Only choice (E) *disposed . . erroneous* makes a logical sentence.

Some General Tips for Answering Sentence Completion Questions ▬▬▬▬

✓ Read the entire sentence carefully; make sure you understand the ideas being expressed.

✓ Don't select an answer simply because it is a popular cliché or "sounds good."

✓ In a question with two blanks, the right answer must correctly fill <u>both</u> blanks. A wrong answer choice often includes one correct and one incorrect word.

✓ After choosing an answer, read the entire sentence to yourself and make sure that it makes sense.

✓ Consider all the choices; be sure you haven't overlooked a choice that makes a better and more accurate sentence than your choice does.

Reading Comprehension Questions ▬▬▬▬

The reading comprehension questions on the SAT test your ability to read and understand a passage. The test generally will have one passage taken from each of the following six categories:

Narrative:	novels, short stories, biographies, essays
Biological Science:	medicine, botany, zoology
Physical Science:	chemistry, physics, astronomy
Humanities:	art, literature, music, philosophy, folklore
Social Studies:	history, economics, sociology, government
Argumentative:	the presentation of a definite point of view on some subject

Each passage contains all the information you'll need to answer the questions that follow it.

Several types of questions are asked about the passage. Some ask about the main idea of a passage. Some ask about those ideas that are stated directly in the passage. Some ask you to recognize applications of the author's principles or opinions. In some questions you must make an inference from what you have read. And in others you must evaluate the way the author develops and presents the passage.

Following are a sample passage, sample questions, and explanations of each of the questions.

> <u>Directions:</u> Each passage below is followed by questions based on its content. Answer the questions following each passage on the basis of what is <u>stated</u> or <u>implied</u> in that passage.

Any survey of medieval town life delights in the color of guild organizations: the broiders and glovers, the shipwrights and upholsters, each with its guild hall, its distinctive livery, and its elaborate set of rules. But if life in the guilds and at the fairs provides a sharp contrast with the stodgy life on the manor, we must not be misled by surface resemblances into thinking that guild life represented a foretaste of modern life in medieval dress. It is a long distance from guilds to modern business firms, and it is well to fix in mind some of the differences.

In the first place, the guild was much more than just an institution for organizing production. Whereas most of its regulations concerned wages and conditions of work and specifications of output, they also dwelt at length on noneconomic matters: on a member's civic role, on his appropriate dress, and even on his daily deportment. Guilds were the regulators not only of production but of social conduct.

Between guilds and modern business firms there is a profound gulf. Unlike modern firms, the purpose of guilds was not first and foremost to make money. Rather, it was to preserve a certain orderly way of life—a way which envisaged a decent income for the master craftsmen but which was certainly not intended to allow any of them to become "big" businessmen. On the contrary, guilds were specifically designed to ward off any such outcome of an uninhibited struggle among their members. The terms of service and wages were fixed by custom. So, too, were the terms of sale: a guild member who cornered the supply of an item or bought wholesale to sell at retail was severely punished. Competition was strictly limited and profits were held to prescribed levels. Advertising was forbidden, and even technical progress in advance of one's fellow guildsmen was considered disloyal.

Surely the guilds represent a more "modern" aspect of feudal life than the manor, but the whole temper of guild life was still far removed from the goals and ideals of modern business enterprise. There was no free competition and no restless probing for advantage. Existing on the margin of a relatively moneyless society, the guilds were organizations that sought to take the risks out of their slender enterprises. As such, they were as drenched in the medieval atmosphere as the manors.

Following are sample questions about this passage. You may be asked to identify the main idea or primary focus of the passage. For example:

1. The author is primarily concerned with

   (A) analyzing the origins of the guild system
   (B) explaining the relationship between manors, fairs, and modern business firms
   (C) depicting the weaknesses of the guilds' business practices
   (D) stressing the historical evolution of guilds to modern business firms
   (E) discussing some differences between medieval and modern business practices

The answer to the question is (E). The passage compares medieval business practices, as represented by the guilds, with modern business practices. The author describes the guilds and suggests some ways in which they differ from contemporary business organizations. The most concise statement of what the author intends to discuss in the passage is made at the end of the first paragraph in lines 8-10. Choice (A) is incorrect because the passage does not mention the origins of the guild system. Choice (B) is unacceptable because the author's main comparison is not between manors, fairs, and modern business firms, even though all are mentioned in the passage. Choices (C) and (D) are slightly harder to eliminate. Readers who think that the author is criticizing the guilds by pointing out the ways in which they differ from modern business enterprise are mistaken; there is no evidence in the passage to suggest that the author wants either to praise or to criticize the guilds. Choice (D) mentions the author's main concerns—guilds and modern business firms—but is incorrect because the passage does not deal with the evolution from medieval to modern practices.

Another type of question asks about details stated in the passage. Sometimes this type of question asks about a particular phrase or line; at other times, the part or parts of the passage referred to are not as precisely identified. For example:

2. According to the passage, modern business enterprises, compared to the medieval guilds, are

   (A) more concerned with increasing profits
   (B) influenced more by craftsmen than by tradesmen
   (C) more subordinate to the demands of consumers
   (D) less progressive in financial dealings
   (E) less interested in quantity than quality

To answer this question, locate the parts of the passage that compare guilds and modern business—the beginnings of the third and fourth paragraphs. Lines 19-20 suggest that the foremost purpose of modern firms is to make money. Lines 34-37 indicate that "free competition" and "restless probing for advantage" are central to modern business enterprise. Choice (A) is the most appropriate answer among the choices given. There is no justification in the passage for any of the other choices. Some people might argue from their own experience or opinion that (C) is a possible answer. However, since the question says, "According to the passage . . .," the answer must be based on what is stated in the passage.

Some questions ask you to make inferences based on the passage. For example:

3. It can be inferred that the guilds were organized as they were because

   (A) life on the manors was boring and drab
   (B) technical improvements were still improbable
   (C) they stressed preservation and stability, not progress
   (D) people in medieval times were interested in advancing individual liberty
   (E) social status was determined by income

This question is not answered simply and directly in the passage itself, but the passage gives you information to draw on. In the third paragraph, the author notes that the purpose of guilds "was to preserve a certain orderly way of life" and that guilds were specifically designed "to ward off . . . uninhibited struggle among their members." In the fourth paragraph, the author states that the guilds "were organizations that sought to take the risks out of their slender enterprises." From these statements and the comparisons between guilds and modern business firms that the author makes elsewhere in the passage, choice (C) is the most reasonable conclusion to draw. Choice (A) is stated in the passage, but is not related to the purpose of the organization of the guilds. The statement about technical progress made in lines 31-32 weakens the plausibility of the inference in (B). The passage doesn't provide enough information to justify the inferences made in (D) and (E). This is a fairly easy and straightforward inference question. You may be asked others that will require somewhat more sophisticated reasoning processes.

Other types of questions ask you to apply information in the passage to situations that are not specifically mentioned in the passage or to evaluate the author's logic, organization, attitude, tone, or language. Following is an example of one type of question that asks you to apply information given in the passage.

4. According to the passage, which of the following would LEAST likely be found in a guild handbook?

   (A) The fees a master guildsman should charge
   (B) The bonus a member would receive for record sales
   (C) The maximum number of hours a guildsman would be expected to work
   (D) The steps a new shipwright would follow to become a master craftsman
   (E) The organizations to which a member should contribute as an upstanding citizen

To answer this question, you must decide which of the five choices is least likely to have been included in a guild handbook. The passage does not mention a handbook, but it does provide enough information about the areas of business and personal life that the guilds attempted to regulate to enable you to make reasoned judgments. The passage suggests that (A), (C), and (E) would definitely be included in such a handbook and that (D) would be a logical area of concern and regulation for a guild. Choice (B) seems to be the least likely area of regulation and is, therefore, the correct answer. In fact, the statements made in the passage about the purpose of the guilds—to enable all master craftsmen to earn a decent income and to discourage ruthless competition among members—suggest that offering a bonus for record sales would indeed be an unlikely activity for a guild to engage in.

The question below is another type of evaluation question.

5. With which of the following statements concerning modern business firms would the author be most likely to agree?

   (A) They make rules concerning appropriate business practices for employees.
   (B) They permit the free play of price in terms of service and sales.
   (C) Their main concern is the stability of profit levels.
   (D) Their aim is to discourage competition among independent manufacturers.
   (E) They are organized in such a way that cooperating monopolies will develop.

Paragraphs three and four provide information about the author's characterization of modern business practices and support choice (B) as the correct response. Choices (A), (C), and (D) are more true of guilds than of modern business firms. There is little or nothing in the passage to support (E) as the answer; the author stresses the competition rather than cooperation of modern businesses. When answering such questions, remember to read the question carefully and to look for evidence in the passage to support your choice. In this question, for example, you are not asked which of the statements about modern business is true or which of the statements you agree with, but which one the author is most likely to agree with based on what he or she has written in the passage. Sometimes questions that ask for the most likely or least likely answer require you to make careful distinctions between choices that are partly correct and those that are more complete or more accurate.

Some General Tips for Answering Reading Comprehension Questions

✓ Read each passage carefully. Follow the author's reasoning. Notice attitude, tone, and general style.

✓ You may want to mark an important fact or idea, but don't waste too much time underlining or making notes in the margin of the test book. Try to get a sense of the principal ideas, facts, and organization of the passage.

✓ A passage with a subject that is familiar to you or in which you are interested may be easier for you. If a passage seems too difficult, you might want to skip it and go on. You would be omitting only a few questions and saving yourself time. You can always return to that passage if you finish before time is up for that section of the test.

✓ You might want to read the questions before you read the passage so that you have a sense of what to look for. But if the content of the passage is familiar, looking at the questions before you read the passage might be a waste of time. Try both methods when taking a sample test in this book and see if one approach is more helpful than the other.

✓ Answer questions on the basis of what is *stated* or *implied* in the passage. Don't answer questions on the basis of your personal opinion or knowledge.

✓ Read all of the choices before you choose your answer.

✓ Answer the question that is asked. Don't pick one of the choices simply because you know it's a true statement.

✓ Make sure the answer you choose is the best among the choices given. Don't be misled by choices that are partially true.

✓ In answering main idea questions, don't be distracted by statements that are true according to the passage but that are secondary to the central point.

Mathematical Sections of the SAT

Some questions in the mathematical sections of the SAT are like the questions in your math textbooks. Other questions ask you to do original thinking and may not be as familiar to you. The questions are designed for students who have had a year of algebra and some geometry. Many of the geometric ideas involved are usually taught in the elementary and junior high years, but a few of the questions involve topics that are first taught in high school geometry. Most of the questions are classified as arithmetic, algebra, or geometry, and there is approximately an equal number of each type.

When you take the SAT, remember to use the available space in the test book for scratchwork. You are not expected to do all the reasoning and figuring in your head.

Following is a review of some specific words, phrases, and concepts you should know. Sample questions and explanations follow the review. The two types of questions that appear in the mathematical sections are explained separately.

Mathematics Review ■■■■■

Some Mathematical Concepts with Which You Should Be Familiar

Arithmetic—simple addition, subtraction, multiplication, and division; percent; average; odd and even numbers; prime numbers; divisibility (for example, 24 is divisible by 8 but not by 5)

Algebra—negative numbers; simplifying algebraic expressions; factoring; linear equations; inequalities; simple quadratic equations; positive integer exponents; roots

Geometry—area (square, rectangle, triangle, and circle); perimeter of a polygon; circumference of a circle; volume of a box and cube; special properties of isosceles, equilateral, and right triangles; 30°-60°-90° and 45°-45°-90° triangles; properties of parallel and perpendicular lines; locating points on a coordinate grid

Words and Phrases You Should Know

When You See:	Think:
Positive Integers	$1, 2, 3, 4, \ldots$
Negative Integers	$-1, -2, -3, -4, \ldots$
Integers	$\ldots, -4, -3, -2, -1, 0, 1, 2, 3, 4, \ldots$
Odd Numbers	$\pm 1, \pm 3, \pm 5, \pm 7, \pm 9, \ldots$
Even Numbers	$0, \pm 2, \pm 4, \pm 6, \pm 8, \ldots$
Consecutive Integers	$n, n + 1, n + 2, \ldots$ (n = an integer)
Prime Numbers	$2, 3, 5, 7, 11, 13, 17, 19, \ldots$

Arithmetic and Algebraic Concepts You Should Know

Odd and Even Numbers

Addition:	Multiplication:
even + even = even	even × even = even
odd + odd = even	even × odd = even
even + odd = odd	odd × odd = odd

Percent

Percent means hundredths or number out of 100, so that $\frac{40}{100} = 40$ percent and 3 is 75 percent of 4 (because $\frac{3}{4} = \frac{75}{100} = 75$ percent).

Some Percent Equivalents:

$\frac{1}{10} = 0.1 = 10\%$

$\frac{1}{5} = 0.2 = 20\%$

$\frac{1}{2} = 0.5 = 50\%$

$\frac{1}{1} = 1.0 = 100\%$

$\frac{2}{1} = 2.0 = 200\%$

Note: To convert a fraction or decimal to a percent, multiply by 100.

General Method of Converting a Fraction $\frac{a}{b}$ to a Percent:

$\frac{a}{b} = \frac{x}{100}$

$x = 100 \left(\frac{a}{b}\right)$

Example: $\frac{3}{4} = \frac{x}{100}$

Therefore, $x = 100 \left(\frac{3}{4}\right) = 75$

$\frac{3}{4} = \frac{75}{100} = 75\%$

Percents Greater Than 100

Problem: 5 is what percent of 2?

Solution 1: $\dfrac{5}{2} = \dfrac{x}{100}$

$$x = \dfrac{500}{2} = 250$$

Therefore, 5 is 250 percent of 2.

Solution 2: "5 is what percent of 2?" is equivalent to

$$5 = \dfrac{x}{100} \cdot 2 = \dfrac{2x}{100}$$

$$500 = 2x$$

$$x = 250$$

This solution is a fairly direct translation of the question into an algebraic statement as follows:

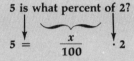

Note that saying 5 is 250 percent of 2 is equivalent to saying that 5 is $2\frac{1}{2}$ times 2.

Problem: Sue earned $10 on Monday and $12 on Tuesday. The amount earned on Tuesday was what percent of the amount earned on Monday?

An equivalent question is "$12 is what percent of $10?"

Solution: $\dfrac{12}{10} = \dfrac{x}{100}$

$$x = \dfrac{1,200}{10} = 120$$

So, $\dfrac{12}{10} = \dfrac{120}{100} = 120\%$

Percents Less Than 1

Problem: 3 is what percent of 1,000?

Solution: $\dfrac{3}{1,000} = 0.003 = 0.3\%$ or $\dfrac{3}{10}$ of 1 percent

Problem: Socks are $1.00 a pair or 2 pairs for $1.99. The savings in buying 2 pairs is what percent of the total cost at the single pair rate?

Solution: At the single pair rate, 2 pairs would cost $2.00, so the savings is only $0.01. Therefore, you must answer the question "$0.01 is what percent of $2.00?" Because $\dfrac{0.01}{2.00} = \dfrac{0.5}{100}$, the savings is 0.5% or $\dfrac{1}{2}$ of 1 percent.

Average

The most common mathematical meaning of the word *average* is the arithmetic mean. The average (arithmetic mean) of a set of n numbers is the sum of the numbers divided by n. For example, the average of 10, 20, and 27 is

$$\dfrac{10 + 20 + 27}{3} = \dfrac{57}{3} = 19$$

Unless otherwise indicated, the term *average* will be used on the mathematical portion of the SAT to denote the arithmetic mean. Questions involving the average can take several forms. Some of these are illustrated below.

Finding the Average of Algebraic Expressions

Problem: Find the average of $(3x + 1)$ and $(x - 3)$.

Solution: $\dfrac{(3x + 1) + (x - 3)}{2} = \dfrac{4x - 2}{2} = 2x - 1$

Finding a Missing Number if Certain Averages Are Known

Problem: The average of a set of 10 numbers is 15. If one of these numbers is removed from the set, the average of the remaining numbers is 14. What is the value of the number removed?

Solution: The sum of the original 10 numbers is $10 \cdot 15 = 150$. The sum of the remaining 9 numbers is $9 \cdot 14 = 126$. Therefore, the value of the number removed must be $150 - 126 = 24$.

Finding a Weighted Average

Problem: In a group of 10 students, 7 are 13 years old and 3 are 17 years old. What is the average of the ages of these 10 students?

Solution: The solution is *not* the average of 13 and 17, which is 15. In this case the average is

$$\dfrac{7\,(13) + 3\,(17)}{10} = \dfrac{91 + 51}{10} = 14.2 \text{ years}$$

The expression "weighted average" comes from the fact that 13 gets a weight factor of 7 whereas 17 gets a weight factor of 3.

Problem: Jane traveled for 2 hours at a rate of 70 kilometers per hour and for 5 hours at a rate of 60 kilometers per hour. What was her average speed for the 7-hour period?

Solution: In this situation, the average speed is:

$$\frac{\text{Total Distance}}{\text{Total Time}}$$

The total distance is $2(70) + 5(60) = 440$ km. The total time is 7 hours. Thus, the average speed was $\frac{440}{7} = 62\frac{6}{7}$ kilometers per hour. Note that in this example the average speed, $62\frac{6}{7}$, is not the average of the two separate speeds, which would be 65.

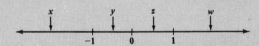

n	1	2	3	4	5	6	7	8	9	10	11	12
n^2	1	4	9	16	25	36	49	64	81	100	121	144

n	-1	-2	-3	-4	-5	-6	-7	-8	-9	-10	-11	-12
n^2	1	4	9	16	25	36	49	64	81	100	121	144

positive $\times$ positive = positive
negative $\times$ negative = positive
negative $\times$ positive = negative
$-(a - b) = b - a$
$(-x)^2 = x^2$
If $x < 0, x^2 > 0$

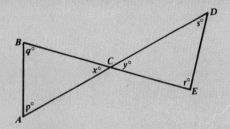

On the number
line above: $x < y$
      $y^2 > 0$ For example, $-2 < -\frac{1}{2}$

      $z^2 < z$ For example, $(\frac{1}{2})^2 < \frac{1}{2}$

      $x^2 > z$ For example, $(-2)^2 > \frac{1}{2}$

      $z^2 < w$
      $x + z < 0$
      $y - x > 0$

Note: Unless otherwise indicated, in all questions involving number lines, the numbers on the number line increase from left to right. Similarly, in questions involving the x and y axes, numbers to the right of the y axis are positive and numbers above the x axis are positive.

$x^2 + 2x = x(x + 2)$
$x^2 - 1 = (x + 1)(x - 1)$
$x^2 + 2x + 1 = (x + 1)(x + 1) = (x + 1)^2$
$x^2 - 3x - 4 = (x - 4)(x + 1)$

Geometric Figures

Figures that accompany problems on the test are intended to provide information useful in solving the problems. They are drawn as accurately as possible EXCEPT when it is stated in a particular problem that the figure is not drawn to scale. The following examples illustrate the way figures can be interpreted.

Example 1

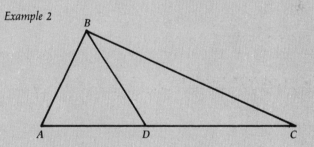

Since AD and BE are line segments, ACB and DCE are vertical angles, and you can conclude that $x = y$. You should NOT assume that $AC = CD$, that $p = 60$, or that the angle at vertex E is a right angle even though they might appear that way.

Example 2

Note: Figure not drawn to scale.

Although the note indicates that $\triangle ABC$ is not drawn to scale, you may assume that:

(1) ABD and DBC are triangles.
(2) D is between A and C.
(3) ADC is a straight line.
(4) Length $AD <$ length AC
(5) Measure $\angle ABD <$ measure $\angle ABC$

You may **not** assume the following:

(1) Length $AD <$ length DC
(2) Measure $\angle BAD =$ measure $\angle BDA$
(3) Measure $\angle DBC <$ measure $\angle ABD$
(4) $\angle ABC$ is a right angle.

Example 3

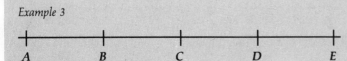

Note: Figure not drawn to scale.

Given: $AC = 10$, $AE = 18$, $BC = 6$

The figure above is not drawn to scale. However, the lengths of three of the line segments are given, and these lengths can be used to determine the lengths of certain other segments. For example,

$$AB = AC - BC = 10 - 6 = 4$$

$$CE = AE - AC = 18 - 10 = 8$$

However, from the information given, it is not possible to determine the length of either *CD* or *DE*.

In general, even when figures are not drawn to scale, the relative positions of points and angles may be assumed to be in the order shown. Also, line segments that extend through points and appear to lie on the same line may be assumed to be on the same line, as illustrated in the three figures above. The note that a figure is not drawn to scale is used when specific lengths and degree measures may not be accurately shown.

Geometric Skills and Concepts

Properties of Parallel Lines

1. If two parallel lines are cut by a third line, the alternate interior angles are equal.
   For example:

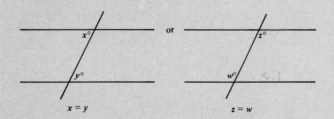

2. If two parallel lines are cut by a third line, the corresponding angles are equal.
   For example:

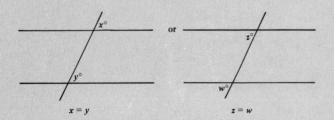

Note: Words like "alternate interior" or "corresponding" are generally **not** used on the test, but you do need to know which angles are equal.

Angle Relationships

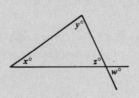

$x + y + z = 180$
(Because the sum of the interior angles of a triangle is 180°)

$z = w$
(When two straight lines intersect, vertical angles are equal.)

$y = 70$
(Because x is equal to y and $60 + 50 + x = 180$)

$y = 30$
(Because a straight angle is 180°, $y = 180 - 150$)

$x = 80$
(Because $70 + 30 + x = 180$)

$x = 10$
(Because $4x + 5x = 90°$) Also, the length of side AC is greater than the length of side BC (Because $\angle B$ is greater than $\angle A$)

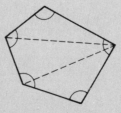

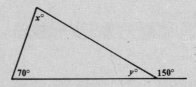

The sum of all angles of the polygon above is $3 (180°) = 540°$ because it can be divided into 3 triangles, each containing 180°.

If AB is parallel to CD, then $x + y = 180$ (Because $x + z = 180$ and $y = z$)

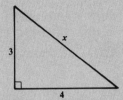

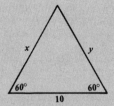

$x = 5$
(By the
Pythagorean
Theorem,
$x^2 = 3^2 + 4^2$
$x^2 = 9 + 16$
$x^2 = 25$
$x = \sqrt{25} = 5$)

$x = y = 10$
(Because the un-
marked angle is
$60°$, all angles of
the triangle are
equal, and, there-
fore, all sides of
the triangle are
equal)

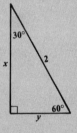

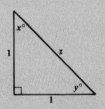

$y = 1$
(Because the
length of the side
opposite the $30°$
angle in a right
triangle is half
the length of the
hypotenuse)

$x = \sqrt{3}$
(By the Pythagorean
Theorem,
$x^2 + 1^2 = 2^2$
$x^2 = 3$
$x = \sqrt{3}$)

$x = y = 45°$
(Because two
sides are equal,
the right triangle
is isosceles and
angles x and y are
equal. Also, $x + y =$
90 which makes both
angles $45°$)

$z = \sqrt{2}$
(Because $1^2 + 1^2 = z^2$)

Area of a rectangle = length × width = $L × W$
Perimeter of a rectangle = $2(L + W)$
Examples:

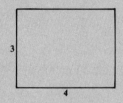

Area = 12

Perimeter = 14

Area = $(x - 3)(x + 3) =$
$x^2 - 9$

Perimeter = $2[(x + 3) + (x - 3)]$
$= 2(2x) = 4x$

Area of a circle = πr^2 (where r is the radius)
Circumference of a circle = $2\pi r = \pi d$ (where d is the diameter)
Examples:

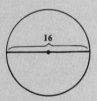

Area = $\pi(3^2) = 9\pi$
Circumference = $2\pi(3)$
$= 6\pi$

Area = $\pi(8^2) = 64\pi$
Circumference = $\pi(16) = 16\pi$

Area of a triangle = $\frac{1}{2}$ (base × altitude)

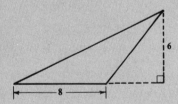

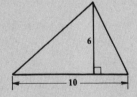

Area = $\frac{1}{2} \cdot 8 \cdot 6 = 24$

Area = $\frac{1}{2} \cdot 10 \cdot 6 = 30$

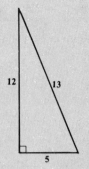

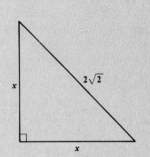

$$\text{Area} = \frac{1}{2} \cdot 5 \cdot 12 = 30$$

$$\text{Perimeter} = 12 + 5 + 13 = 30$$

$x = 2$
(Because $x^2 + x^2 = (2\sqrt{2})^2$
$2x^2 = 4 \cdot 2$
$x^2 = 4$
$x = 2$)

$$\text{Area} = \frac{1}{2} \cdot 2 \cdot 2 = 2$$

$$\text{Perimeter} = 2 + 2 + 2\sqrt{2}$$
$$= 4 + 2\sqrt{2}$$

Volume of a Rectangular Solid (box)

Volume of a box = length × width × height = L · W · H
Examples:

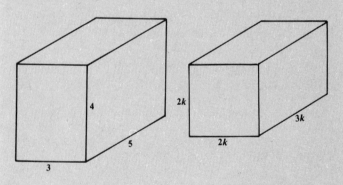

Volume = $5 \cdot 3 \cdot 4 = 60$ Volume = $(3k)(2k)(2k) = 12k^3$

Standard Multiple-Choice Questions ▬▬▬

Directions: In this section solve each problem, using any available space on the page for scratchwork. Then decide which is the best of the choices given and fill in the corresponding oval on the answer sheet.

The following information is for your reference in solving some of the problems.

Circle of radius *r*:
Area = πr^2;
Circumference = $2\pi r$
  The number of degrees of arc in a circle is 360.
  The measure in degrees of a straight angle is 180.

Triangle: The sum of the measures in degrees of the angles of a triangle is 180.

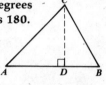

If $\angle CDA$ is a right angle, then
(1) area of $\triangle ABC =$
$$\frac{AB \times CD}{2}$$
(2) $AC^2 = AD^2 + DC^2$

Definitions of symbols:

= is equal to	≤ is less than or equal to
≠ is unequal to	≥ is greater than or equal to
< is less than	‖ is parallel to
> is greater than	⊥ is perpendicular to

Note: Figures that accompany problems in this test are intended to provide information useful in solving the problems. They are drawn as accurately as possible EXCEPT when it is stated in a specific problem that its figure is not drawn to scale. All figures lie in a plane unless otherwise indicated. All numbers used are real numbers.

Two types of multiple-choice questions are used in the mathematical sections of the SAT:

1. Standard multiple-choice questions (approximately two-thirds of the math questions)

2. Quantitative comparison questions (approximately one-third of the math questions)

The formulas and symbols given in the directions that follow appear in the test book. Learning them now will help you when you take the actual test.

The problems that follow will give you an idea of the type of mathematical thinking required. First, try to answer each question yourself. Then read the explanation, which may give you new insights into solving the problem or point out techniques you'll be able to use again. Note that the directions indicate that you are to select the *best* of the choices given.

1. If $2a + b = 5$, then $4a + 2b =$
   (A) $\frac{5}{4}$ (B) $\frac{5}{2}$ (C) 10 (D) 20 (E) 25

This is an example of a problem that requires realizing that $4a + 2b = 2(2a + b)$. Therefore, $4a + 2b = 2(2a + b) = 2(5) = 10$. The correct choice is (C).

2. If $16 \cdot 16 \cdot 16 = 8 \cdot 8 \cdot P$, then $P =$

   (A) 4 (B) 8 (C) 32 (D) 48 (E) 64

This question can be solved by several methods. A time-consuming method would be to multiply the three 16s and then divide the result by the product of 8 and 8. A quicker approach would be to find what additional factors are needed on the right side of the equation to match those on the left side. These additional factors are two 2s and a 16, the product of which is 64. Yet another method involves solving for P as follows:

$$P = \frac{\overset{2}{\cancel{16}} \cdot \overset{2}{\cancel{16}} \cdot 16}{\cancel{8} \cdot \cancel{8}} = 2 \cdot 2 \cdot 16 = 64$$

The correct choice is (E).

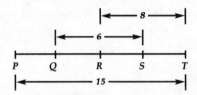

Note: Figure not drawn to scale.

3. In the figure above, if R is the midpoint of QS, then $PQ =$

   (A) 1 (B) 2 (C) 3 (D) 4 (E) 5

The figure for this question is not drawn to scale so it is important to solve the problem using the given information rather than estimating lengths visually. It may be helpful in questions like this to write lengths you have determined on the figure. Since R is given as the midpoint of QS and the figure shows the length of QS to be 6, we know that $QR = RS = 3$, so the length of ST will equal 5 as shown in the following figure.

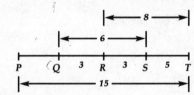

Since $QT = 11$, subtracting 11 from the total length of 15 gives the length of PQ as 4. The correct choice is (D).

4. If the average of seven x's is 7, what is the average of fourteen x's?

   (A) $\frac{1}{7}$ (B) $\frac{1}{2}$ (C) 1 (D) 7 (E) 14

Don't get caught up in the wording of this problem, which might lead you to choose (E) 14. The average of any number of equal numbers such as x is always x. Since you are given that the average of seven x's is 7, it follows that $x = 7$ and that the average of fourteen x's is also 7. The correct choice is (D).

5. The town of Mason is located on Eagle Lake. The town of Canton is west of Mason. Sinclair is east of Canton, but west of Mason. Dexter is east of Richmond, but west of Sinclair and Canton. Assuming all these towns are in the United States, which town is farthest west?

   (A) Mason (B) Dexter (C) Canton
   (D) Sinclair (E) Richmond

For this kind of problem, drawing a diagram may help. In this case, a line can be effectively used to locate the relative position of each town. Start with the statement "The town of Canton is west of Mason" and, using abbreviations, draw the following:

From the remaining information, place the other towns in their correct order:

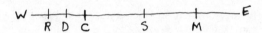

The final sketch shows that the town farthest west is Richmond (R) and the correct choice is (E).

6. If the symbol ∇ between two expressions indicates that the expression on the right exceeds the expression on the left by 1, which of the following is (are) true for all real numbers x?

   I. $x(x + 2) \nabla (x + 1)^2$
   II. $x^2 \nabla (x + 1)^2$
   III. $\frac{x}{y} \nabla \frac{x + 1}{y + 1}$

   (A) None (B) I only (C) II only
   (D) III only (E) I and III

This kind of problem involves working with a newly defined symbol. One approach is to check the statements one at a time. Statement I reduces to $x^2 + 2x \nabla x^2 + 2x + 1$, so the expression on the right does exceed the expression on the left by 1. Therefore, statement I is true. Statement II reduces to $x^2 \nabla x^2 + 2x + 1$, so the right expression exceeds the left expression by $2x + 1$, which is not equal to 1 except when $x = 0$. This makes statement II false. Statement III is more difficult to check, but you can verify by subtraction or by substituting numbers (for example, $x = 3$, $y = 5$) that the expression on the right does not exceed the expression on the left by 1. Therefore, statement III is false. The only true statement is I, so the correct choice is (B).

In a problem of this kind, if you are able to decide about only one or two statements, you can still eliminate some choices and guess among those remaining. For example, if you can conclude that I is true, then the correct choice is either (B) or (E) because these choices contain statement I.

7. If a car travels X kilometers of a trip in H hours, in how many hours can it travel the next Y kilometers at this rate?

(A) $\dfrac{XY}{H}$ (B) $\dfrac{HY}{X}$ (C) $\dfrac{HX}{Y}$ (D) $\dfrac{H+Y}{X}$ (E) $\dfrac{X+Y}{H}$

You can solve this problem by using ratios or by using the distance formula.

Using the ratio method, X kilometers is to H hours as Y kilometers is to $\square$ hours, where $\square$ represents the amount of time required to travel Y kilometers:

$$\frac{X}{H} = \frac{Y}{\square}$$

$$X\,\square = HY$$

$$\square = \frac{HY}{X}$$

The correct choice is (B).

8. If 90 percent of P is 30 percent of Q, then Q is what percent of P?

(A) 3% (B) 27% (C) 30% (D) 270% (E) 300%

Writing an algebraic equation for this percent problem not only simplifies the work, it also helps you organize your thoughts. "90 percent of P is 30 percent of Q" can be written as $0.90P = 0.30Q$ (or $\frac{9}{10}P = \frac{3}{10}Q$).

"Q is what percent of P" tells you to find $\frac{Q}{P}$ and express it as a percent. $\frac{Q}{P} = 3$ and, therefore, Q is 300 percent of P and the correct choice is (E). (See pages 19-20 for a review of percent.)

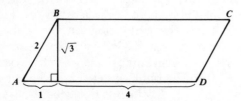

9. The figure above shows a piece of paper in the shape of a parallelogram with measurements as indicated. If the paper is tacked at its center to a flat surface and then rotated about its center, the points covered by the paper will be a circular region of diameter

(A) $\sqrt{3}$ (B) 2 (C) 5 (D) $\sqrt{28}$ (E) $\sqrt{39}$

The first step in solving the problem is to realize that the center of the parallelogram is the point of intersection of the two diagonals; thus, the diameter you are looking for is the length of the longer diagonal AC. One way to find AC is to think of the additional lines drawn as shown in the following figure.

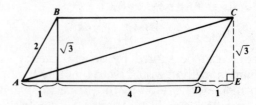

The triangles at each end are congruent (equal in size and shape), so the lengths of DE and CE are 1 and $\sqrt{3}$, respectively. AEC is a right triangle; therefore, the Pythagorean Theorem can be used in solving the problem:

$$AC^2 = CE^2 + AE^2$$
$$AC^2 = (\sqrt{3})^2 + (6)^2 = 3 + 36 = 39$$

The diameter AC is $\sqrt{39}$ and the correct choice is (E).

10. A number is divisible by 9 if the sum of its digits is divisible by 9. Which of the following numbers is divisible by 45?

(A) 63,345
(B) 72,365
(C) 99,999
(D) 72,144
(E) 98,145

It would be very time-consuming to divide each choice by 45. In order for a number to be divisible by 45 it must be divisible by both 9 and 5. Choices (A), (B), and (E) are divisible by 5, but choices (C) and (D) are not. So you can eliminate choices (C) and (D) immediately. You are given that a number is divisible by 9 if the sum of its digits is divisible by 9. The sum of the digits in choices (A), (B), and (E) are 21, 23, and 27, respectively.

Of these choices only 27 is divisible by 9. The correct choice is (E). Your scratchwork for this problem might appear as follows:

(A) 63,345 ~~21~~
(B) 72,365 ~~23~~
(C) ~~99,999~~
(D) ~~72,144~~
(E) 98,145 ㉗

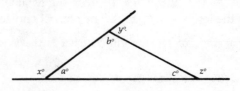

11. In the figure above, $x + y + z - (a + b + c) =$

(A) 360
(B) 180
(C) 90
(D) 0
(E) −90

It may first appear that the correct answer cannot be determined from the information given. However, since each pair of adjacent angles forms a 180° angle (for example, $x° + a° = 180°$), the sum of all lettered angles is $3 \cdot 180°$, or $540°$. This means that

$$x + y + z + (a + b + c) = 540.$$

Since a, b, and c are the degree measures of the angles in a triangle, their sum must be 180. Therefore,

$$x + y + z + 180 = 540$$
$$\text{so that } x + y + z = 360$$

The desired result is then obtained as follows:

$$x + y + z - (a + b + c) = 360 - 180 = 180$$

The correct choice is (B) 180.

Quantitative Comparison Questions ▬▬▬

Quantitative comparison questions emphasize the concepts of equalities, inequalities, and estimation. They generally involve less reading, take less time to answer, and require less computation than regular multiple-choice questions. Quantitative comparison questions may not be as familiar to you as other types of questions. Therefore, understand the directions ahead of time. Be careful not to mark answer option E when responding to the four-choice quantitative comparison questions.

Directions: Each of the following questions consists of two quantities, one in Column A and one in Column B. You are to compare the two quantities and on the answer sheet fill in oval

  A if the quantity in Column A is greater;
  B if the quantity in Column B is greater;
  C if the two quantities are equal;
  D if the relationship cannot be determined from the information given.

AN E RESPONSE WILL NOT BE SCORED.

Notes: 1. In certain questions, information concerning one or both of the quantities to be compared is centered above the two columns.

  2. In a given question, a symbol that appears in both columns represents the same thing in Column A as it does in Column B.

  3. Letters such as x, n, and k stand for real numbers.

EXAMPLES				Explanations:
	Column A	Column B	Answers	
E1.	2×6	$2 + 6$	●ⒷⒸⒹⒺ	(The answer is A because 12 is greater than 8.)
E2.	$180 - x$	y	ⒶⒷ●ⒹⒺ	(The answer is C because $x + y = 180$, thereby making $180 - x$ equal to y.)
E3.	$p - q$	$q - p$	ⒶⒷⒸ●Ⓔ	(The answer is D because nothing is known about either p or q.)

In E2, the figure above the columns shows angles $x°$ and $y°$ on a line.

To solve a quantitative comparison problem, you compare the quantities in the two columns and decide whether one quantity is greater than the other, whether the two quantities are equal, or whether the relationship cannot be determined from the information given. Remember that your answer should be:

A if the quantity in Column A is greater;
B if the quantity in Column B is greater;
C if the two quantities are equal;
D if the relationship cannot be determined from the information given.

Problems are clearly separated and the *quantities to be compared are always on the same line as the number of the problem.* (See example 2 on page 28.) Figures and additional information provided for some problems appear *above* the quantities to be compared. The following are some practice problems with explanations to help you understand this type of question.

	Column A	Column B
1.	$(37)(\frac{1}{43})(58)$	$(59)(\frac{1}{43})(37)$

Because the numbers in this problem are fairly large, it may save time to study the multipliers first before attempting the calculations. Note that (37) and $(\frac{1}{43})$ appear in both quantities; thus, the only numbers left for you to compare are 58 and 59. Since $59 > 58$, the quantity on the right is greater and the correct choice is (B).

Figures are also included in some questions that appear in the quantitative comparison format.

Column A	Column B

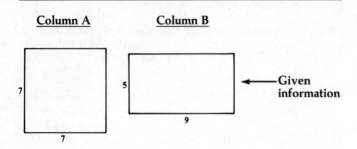

← Given information

| 2. The perimeter of the square | The perimeter of the rectangle | ← Quantities to be compared |

It can be assumed that the units used to indicate measures in a given problem are the same in all figures in that problem unless otherwise stated. The correct choice is (C) because the perimeter of the square is $4 \cdot 7 = 28$ units and the perimeter of the rectangle is $(2 \cdot 5) + (2 \cdot 9) = 28$ units.

Column A	Column B

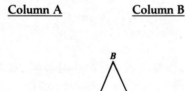

$AB = BC$

| 3. | x | y |

Since $AB = BC$, the angles opposite AB and BC are equal and, therefore, $x = y$. The correct choice is (C).

Column A	Column B
4.	$\sqrt{2} - 1$	$\sqrt{3} - 1$

For any positive number x, the symbol $\sqrt{x}$ denotes the positive square root of x. The fact that $\sqrt{3} > \sqrt{2}$ leads to the conclusion that $\sqrt{3} - 1 > \sqrt{2} - 1$. The correct choice is (B). Note that $x^2 = 9$ has two solutions, $x = 3$ or $x = -3$. However, $\sqrt{9} = 3$, not ± 3.

Column A	Column B
5.	$x + 1$	$2x + 1$

Because both expressions contain a "1," the problem is one of comparing x with $2x$. When you compare algebraic expressions, a useful technique is to consider zero and negative numbers for possible values of the unknown.

$2x > x$ for positive values of x
$2x = x$ for $x = 0$
$2x < x$ for negative values of x

The correct choice is (D), as the relationship cannot be determined from the information given. If you had been given that x was positive (that is, $x > 0$), the correct choice would have been (B) because $2x$ would be greater than x.

Column A	Column B

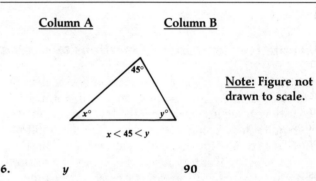

Note: Figure not drawn to scale.

$x < 45 < y$

| 6. | y | 90 |

Because the sum of the angles of a triangle is 180, $x + y + 45 = 180$ or $x + y = 135$. Since $x < 45$, it follows that $y > 90$. The answer is (A). In this problem you should not try to determine the answer from the appearance of the figure because the note indicates that the figure is not drawn to scale.

Column A	Column B

$x \neq 1$

| 7. | $\dfrac{x^2 - 1}{x - 1}$ | x |

The condition $x \neq 1$ (read x is not equal to 1) is given because the algebraic fraction in Column A is not defined for $x = 1$ (the denominator becomes zero). The solution of this problem involves simplifying the fraction in Column A as follows:

$$\frac{x^2 - 1}{x - 1} = \frac{(x + 1)(x - 1)}{x - 1} = x + 1$$

Therefore, the quantity in Column A is equal to $x + 1$. Since $x + 1$ is always greater than x, the answer is (A).

Column A	Column B
8. Area of a triangle with altitude 4	Area of a triangle with base 5

To answer this question, you need to know how to find the area of a triangle. To find the area of a triangle, you need to know the length of a base and the altitude to that base. You can't find the "area of a triangle with altitude 4" without knowing the base, so the area of such a triangle could be any number depending on the length of the base. Likewise, you can't find the "area of a triangle with base 5" without knowing the length of the altitude. Since you can't tell anything about the two areas, the correct choice is (D).

The Test of Standard Written English

The questions on the TSWE measure skills that are important to the kind of writing you will do in most college courses. In particular, the questions test your ability to recognize the kind of language essential to a finished piece of writing—writing that would be considered acceptable by most educated readers and writers of American English.

The TSWE is made up of 50 questions of two types: usage questions and sentence correction questions. The test is arranged in the following way:

- 25 usage questions
- 15 sentence correction questions
- 10 more usage questions

The questions in the TSWE ask you to recognize several different types of language problems.

Use of basic grammar—for example, subject-verb agreement, agreement of pronouns with the nouns to which they refer, and the correct use of verb tense.

Sentence structure—for example, distinguishing between complete and incomplete sentences and recognizing when the connections between parts of a sentence are clear and when they are not.

Choice of words—for example, recognizing when words or phrases should be revised to make the meaning of a sentence clear or to make the language consistent with what is normally expected of educated writers.

The questions do not ask you to define or to use grammatical terms nor do they test spelling or capitalization. In a few questions, punctuation marks like the semicolon or apostrophe are important in arriving at the correct answer, but these questions primarily test the structure in which the punctuation appears.

The best way to prepare for the TSWE is to get regular practice in writing and rewriting your own prose, paying particular attention to clarity and effectiveness of expression. You should also try to gain experience in reading the prose of skilled writers on a variety of subjects, noticing especially how the writers use language to create meaning. As with the SAT, reading the sample questions and explanations and taking the first sample test provided in this book will help you prepare for the TSWE. After you've taken and scored the sample test, look carefully at the questions you missed. Talk over those questions with your teachers and other students and look up the portions of your textbooks that discuss the problems in wording and sentence structure that were most difficult for you.

Usage Questions

The questions in this section measure skills that are important to writing well. In particular, they test your ability to recognize and use language that is clear, effective, and correct according to the requirements of standard written English, the kind of English found in most college textbooks.

Directions: The following sentences contain problems in grammar, usage, diction (choice of words), and idiom.

Some sentences are correct.

No sentence contains more than one error.

You will find that the error, if there is one, is underlined and lettered. Assume that elements of the sentence that are not underlined are correct and cannot be changed. In choosing answers, follow the requirements of standard written English.

If there is an error, select the one underlined part that must be changed to make the sentence correct and fill in the corresponding oval on your answer sheet.

If there is no error, fill in oval Ⓔ.

EXAMPLE: SAMPLE ANSWER
                                            Ⓐ Ⓑ ● Ⓓ Ⓔ

The region has a climate so severe that plants
                              A
growing there rarely had been more than twelve
      B   C
inches high. No error
      D   E

As you can see from the example, a usage question consists of a sentence in which four short portions of the sentence are underlined and lettered, and a fifth underline, "No error," follows. Sometimes the underlined portion of the sentence is only a single word, as in (D) above. In other cases it is a group of words or a phrase, as in (A), (B), and (C).

For each question, you must decide whether one of the underlined portions must be changed to make the sentence acceptable in standard written English. In the example above, the underlined portion lettered (C) must be changed because the verb *has* earlier in the sentence leads the reader to expect *are* or possibly *have been*. The tense of the verb at (C) must be changed to be consistent with the tense of *has*. Therefore, the correct answer to the example is (C).

It is true that changes could be made in the other underlined portions of the sentence in the example, but none of those changes is necessary to make the sentence acceptable. It is also true that the sentence could be corrected by changing *has* in the first part of the sentence to *had*, but in this type of question the change must be made in a portion of the sentence that is underlined. Notice that if none of the underlined portions needed to be changed, the correct answer would be (E). By choosing (E) as the answer, you would be indicating that the sentence was correct as written.

Most usage questions test your ability to recognize problems in basic grammatical structure or in choice of words. A few usage questions also test problems in sentence structure. To give you a better sense of the variety of problems tested by usage questions, a few more sample questions follow. Keep in mind the following suggestions as you work through the sample questions.

✓ For each question, read the entire sentence carefully but quickly.

✓ Go back over the sentence, looking at each underlined portion to see whether anything needs to be changed to make the sentence correct.

✓ If you find an error, mark the oval on your answer sheet with the same letter as the underlined portion with the error.

✓ If you don't find an error, don't waste time searching for one. Mark the oval for (E), No error, on your answer sheet to indicate that you believe the sentence is correct as written.

✓ In general, you should be able to move quickly through the usage questions on the test, since they do not involve much reading. Put a mark next to any usage question you want to return to and move on to the next question. That way you will probably have enough time for the sentence correction questions, which usually require more time per question.

The four sample questions that follow originally appeared in the TSWE. They are arranged in order of increasing difficulty. Together, the example question and the four samples should give you a sense of the difficulty level of the questions you will be asked.

1. One of the <u>goals of</u> women's organizations
$$\text{A}$$
<u>is to encourage</u> projects that will <u>make</u> life <u>easier for</u>
$$\text{B}\text{C}\text{D}$$
working mothers. <u>No error</u>
$$\text{E}$$

Probably the first impression you get from reading the sentence is that nothing is really wrong with it. But before you make a final decision, you should look at the sentence again, especially at the underlined portions. The (A) portion, *goals of*, seems correct; *of* is the appropriate preposition for the context. The (B) portion, *is to encourage*, is a little more complicated but also seems correct; *is* is the appropriate verb to use with *one* and *to encourage* is all right following *is*, even though *encouraging* might be nearly as good. In (C), *make* is appropriate with the subject *projects* and is idiomatic in the expression *make life easier*. In (D), *easier* is a comparative form of *easy* and is used correctly, and *for* is the preposition that should follow it for the meaning intended.

Even though your analysis probably would not be as extensive as this, you should do something fairly similar, quickly checking each underlined portion of the sentence to make sure that each is acceptable as written. For some portions, you might have been able to think of another way of writing the sentence, even a way of improving it a little, but you probably decided that no changes were necessary in the underlined portions. At this point, you should have been able to decide on (E), <u>No error</u>, as the correct answer. Keep in mind that some usage questions are correctly answered with (E).

2. <u>Probably</u> the best-known baseball player <u>of all time</u>,
$$\text{A}\text{B}$$
Babe Ruth established a record for lifetime home runs

that has <u>only recently</u> <u>been</u> <u>broke</u>. <u>No error</u>
$$\text{C}\text{D}\text{E}$$

You may have noticed when you read the question for the first time that *broke* in (D) should be changed to *broken*. But if you didn't see the error immediately, or if you were not sure of it, you should have looked at the sentence again, especially at the underlined portions. In (A), *probably* is the appropriate adverb, in (B) *of all time* is an acceptable idiom and is used correctly, and in (C) the adverbs *only* and *recently* are acceptable together, with *only* modifying *recently*. But in (D), *broke* is clearly incorrect and needs to be changed to make the sentence acceptable in standard written English. The complete and correct verb for this part of the sentence is *has been broken.* With *has been,* the only possible form of the verb *break* that can be used is *broken.* The correct choice is (D).

3. Many travelers claim <u>having seen</u> the Abominable
                       A

   Snowman, <u>but</u> no one has proved that
           B

   <u>such a creature</u> <u>actually</u> exists. <u>No error</u>
      C   D   E

The answer is (A). In the context of this sentence, the verb *claim* requires the expression *to have seen; claim having seen* is not idiomatic in American English and is therefore not acceptable. The word *but* at (B) provides a link between the two major parts of the sentence and appropriately suggests a contrast between the ideas they present. The expression at (C), *such a creature,* and the adverb *actually* at (D) are correct, although other expressions and adverbs could be substituted.

4. The administration's statements <u>on</u> economic policy
                             A

   <u>indicates</u> that the <u>elimination of</u> hunger <u>will be given</u> first
     B   C   D
   priority. <u>No error</u>
          E

This question is more difficult than any of the others, so you may not immediately see the error in it. For a question as difficult as this one, you should be sure to look carefully at the underlined portions when you reread the sentence. In (A), *on* is correct and idiomatic, though the word *about* could possibly be substituted. Similarly, the preposition *of* is idiomatic with *elimination* in (C), and *elimination* is itself the right word for the meaning implied by the rest of the sentence. In (D), *will be given* is correct in tense and uses the correct form of the verb *give.* But *indicates* at (B) is incorrect; it is a singular verb and should not be used with the plural subject *statements.* The singular noun *policy* before (B) may appear at first to be the subject of the sentence, but a good writer would eventually see that the real subject *statements* is plural and therefore requires the plural verb *indicate.* The correct choice is (B).

Sentence Correction Questions

> **Directions:** In each of the following sentences, some part or all of the sentence is underlined. Below each sentence you will find five ways of phrasing the underlined part. Select the answer that produces the most effective sentence, one that is clear and exact, without awkwardness or ambiguity, and fill in the corresponding oval on your answer sheet. In choosing answers, follow the requirements of standard written English. Choose the answer that best expresses the meaning of the original sentence.
>
> Answer (A) is always the same as the underlined part. Choose answer (A) if you think the original sentence needs no revision.
>
> EXAMPLE: SAMPLE ANSWER
>   Ⓐ ● Ⓒ Ⓓ Ⓔ
>
> Laura Ingalls Wilder published her first book <u>and she was sixty-five years old then.</u>
>
> (A) and she was sixty-five years old then
> (B) when she was sixty-five years old
> (C) at age sixty-five years old
> (D) upon reaching sixty-five years
> (E) at the time when she was sixty-five

Sentence correction questions present you with a sentence and four possible revisions of it—(B), (C), (D), or (E). The (A) version is always a repetition of the underlined portion of the original sentence. The underline in the original sentence tells you how much of the sentence will be revised in the other versions that are presented to you.

The example question above is a sentence in which the connection between the two major ideas is weak. The use of *and* to join the two clauses suggests that the ideas are of equal importance in the sentence, but the wording and the ideas in the clauses themselves suggest that the first idea should actually be the major point of the sentence and that the second should be secondary to it. Versions (B), (C), (D), and (E) all begin with more appropriate connecting words, but (B) is the only one in which the second idea of the sentence is clearly, concisely, and idiomatically expressed. Therefore, (B) is the correct choice.

The directions for the sentence correction questions tell you to look for the most effective sentence. In some questions you may find a version of the original sentence that has no grammatical errors, but that does not express the ideas of the sentence as effectively as another version. For other questions you may be able to think of a version you consider better than any of the choices given. In either case, you should select the version that is the best of those presented.

Sentence correction questions are primarily concerned with problems of sentence structure. But you'll also need to consider basic principles of grammar and word choice to decide which of the versions makes the clearest and most effective sentence. For example, some versions will be grammatically incorrect or the ideas in the sentence will be presented so awkwardly or imprecisely that they cannot be considered acceptable. You'll get a sense of the problems tested in the sentence correction questions from the discussion of the sample questions provided here. You'll also have an idea of the range of difficulty found in the questions, since the sample questions given here are arranged in order of increasing difficulty. To learn as much as possible from the sample questions, read carefully the directions that precede the example question above and approach the questions with the following suggestions in mind.

✓ In each question, read the original sentence carefully but quickly. Note the underlined portion of the sentence because that is the portion that may need to be revised. Remember that the portion with no underline stays the same.

✓ Keep in mind the portion of the original sentence that stays the same when you read through each of the versions presented.

✓ Decide which version seems best. If you can't decide between two choices, go back and read each version you have chosen in the context of the entire sentence.

✓ If you still feel uncertain about your answer, put a mark next to that question in your test book and note which versions you thought might be correct. You can return to the question later if you have time.

1. **Althea Gibson was the first Black American to win major tennis championships and played in the 1950s.**

    (A) Althea Gibson was the first Black American to win major tennis championships and played in the 1950s.
    (B) Althea Gibson, being the first Black American to win major tennis championships, and playing in the 1950s.
    (C) Althea Gibson, playing in the 1950s, being the first Black American to win major tennis championships.
    (D) Althea Gibson, who played in the 1950s, was the first Black American to win major tennis championships.
    (E) Althea Gibson played in the 1950s, she was the first Black American to win major tennis championships.

Here the original sentence is entirely underlined, so you can expect the versions that follow to be revisions of the whole sentence.

This question is fairly easy. You may have been able to decide which version of the sentence was best simply by reading through all of the choices. However, to help you feel more certain of your choice and to help you under-

stand more fully how the decision can be made, it's worth looking separately at each version. The (A) version, the same as the original sentence, has a problem similar to the one in the boxed example: *and* does not adequately convey the relationship between the two clauses in the sentence. The (B) version has the same problem and an additional one: the use of *being* and *playing* makes it an incomplete sentence. In the (C) version, *playing* seems at first to have corrected the original problem of relationship between parts of the sentence, but the use of *being* gives the second idea no more importance than the first and also makes this version an incomplete sentence. In (E), you can see that a comma is used improperly as a means of connecting two independent clauses. Thus, (D) is the only acceptable version. In (D), the major point appears in the main part of the sentence and receives most emphasis, while the less important point appears in the *who* clause and so is emphasized less.

You won't need to analyze most of the sentence correction questions in this much detail. You'll be able to decide by reading through each version and looking closely at one or two of them. But you should use this approach for the questions that are most difficult for you, especially the ones you miss on the sample TSWE.

2. **After placing the meatballs in a pan, the cook sautéed them until they were brown and then let them simmer in the sauce.**

    (A) and then let them simmer
    (B) then they were simmered
    (C) and then simmering it
    (D) then letting them simmer
    (E) and then the simmering was done

You should have read the original sentence quickly, noting that the portions not underlined will remain the same in all versions of the sentence. The original sentence and choice (A) may have seemed plausible, but you should have gone on to the other versions before making a final decision. In the (B) version, the unexpected shift from the *cook* as subject to *they* (the meatballs) is awkward and somewhat confusing. The (C) version uses *simmering* where *simmered* is needed to parallel *sautéed*. Furthermore, the pronoun *it* does not seem to refer back to anything named earlier in the sentence. In the (D) version, the use of *letting* rather than *let* again neglects the parallel with *sautéed*. The (E) version is wordy and, like the (B) version, involves a shift in which a passive construction replaces a more appropriate active one and in which the action is described without reference to the person responsible for it. Therefore, the best version of the sentence in this case is the original one, so the correct choice is (A).

3. <u>Being as it was a full moon</u>, the tides were exceptionally high when the storm struck.

   (A) Being as it was a full moon
   (B) With the moon as full
   (C) Due to there being a full moon
   (D) The moon was full
   (E) Because the moon was full

The problems most immediately apparent in this question are problems in wording. The (A) version, like the underlined portion in the original sentence, uses *Being as*, an expression that is not considered acceptable in standard written English. In addition, the indirect *it was* construction introduces unnecessary wordiness. The (B) version seems acceptable in itself, but leads the reader to expect a construction ("as it was") different from the one that follows in the rest of the sentence. In the (C) version, *due to* is used in a manner that is generally considered unacceptable usage, and *there being* introduces unnecessary wordiness. The (D) version is acceptable in its wording but, when combined with the rest of the sentence, results in the unacceptable joining of two independent clauses with a comma. What is needed in this sentence is an expression that is acceptable in good written English and that accurately reflects the relationship between the first and second parts of the sentence. Version (E) solves the problem—the word *because* indicates that the fullness of the moon was causally related to the high tides described in the second part of the sentence. Therefore, (E) is the correct choice.

4. The Dutch had been trading with the Orient since the sixteenth <u>century, their ships have visited</u> Persia and Japan.

   (A) century, their ships have visited
   (B) century while their ships had visited
   (C) century, but their ships had been visiting
   (D) century, when their ships visited
   (E) century, where their ships were visiting

The original sentence and the (A) version present two problems. First, two independent statements are joined by a comma, with no indication of the relationship between them. Second, the tense of the verb *have visited* is not consistent with the tense of *had been trading* earlier in the sentence. The (B) version may appear to be acceptable, but the relationship between the ideas in the sentence is not the one implied by *while* and the use of *while* makes the sentence illogical. Similarly, the (C) version appears plausible, but the contrast implied by *but* is not appropriate to the relationship between the two parts of the sentence. The (D) version corrects both of the problems presented in the original sentence and is more logical than either (B) or (C). Notice that the tense of *visited* is consistent with the earlier verb *had been trading*. It suggests that Dutch ships had traveled to Persia and Japan in the sixteenth century, and that such travel was part of a process of Dutch trade with the Orient that continued until some later, unspecified time. Version (E) resembles (D), except that *where* is substituted for *when* and *were visiting* for *visited*. Since the connection with *century* is clearly one of time rather than place, the use of *where* is not appropriate. Furthermore, the use of *were visiting* would imply emphasis on visits occurring over a period of time. Such emphasis is not called for, because the purpose in this part of the sentence is to describe the point at which the Dutch began trading with the Orient. Therefore, (D) expresses most effectively the ideas in the two parts of the sentence as well as the relationship between them. The correct choice is (D).

The Sample Tests

The first SAT in this book (pages 37-64) was given on May 2, 1987 (except for section 3, the TSWE, which was given on June 6, 1981). The equating section has been omitted because it contains questions that may be used in future editions of the test. The sample test will be most helpful if you take it under conditions as close as possible to those of the test:

- To complete the first sample test in one sitting, you will need two and one-half hours because this test has a TSWE as well as two verbal and two math sections. The other sample tests omit the TSWE; therefore, allow only two hours for them.

- Sit at a desk or table that has been cleared of any other papers or books. You can't take a calculator, a dictionary, books, or notes into the test room.

- Allow yourself only 30 minutes for each section of the test. Have a kitchen timer or clock in front of you for timing yourself on the sections.

- Tear out the sample answer sheet on page 35 and fill it in just as you will on the day of the test.

- Read the instructions on page 37. They are reprinted from the back cover of the test book. When you take the test, you will be asked to read them before you begin answering questions. Don't start timing the first section of the test until you have completed reading these instructions.

- After you finish the practice test, read "How To Score the Sample Test," on page 65.

Reviewing Your Performance

Although you're probably most interested in your scores, you should spend some time after you take a practice test reviewing your mistakes on questions and also your overall approach to the test. Ask yourself these questions:

- Did you finish most of the questions in each section? Although the last few questions in each section usually are very difficult and are omitted by many students, you might want to adjust your pacing if you didn't get to a large number of questions at the end of each section.

- Did you make a lot of careless mistakes? Perhaps you were rushing and should slow your pace.

- Did you spend too much time on particular questions? Perhaps you should have moved on after marking them in your test book (not the answer sheet) and returned to them if you had time at the end of the section.

- Did you guess after you had eliminated some of the choices but still weren't sure of the answer? (Remember, although wild guessing probably won't affect your scores, you shouldn't be too cautious either.)

- Were there particular types of questions that gave you more difficulty than others? If so, you might want to review the descriptions of those questions in the beginning of this book and then practice again on one of the other sample tests in this book.

- Did you spend so much time reading directions that you took time away from answering questions? If you become thoroughly familiar with the test directions printed in this book, you won't have to spend as much time reading them when you take the actual test.

- Look at the specific questions you missed. Did you get caught by a choice that was only partly correct? Figure out what step you overlooked in your reasoning.

For most students, practice on one or two sample tests is enough. However, if you still feel uneasy about a particular type of question (or if you happen to enjoy taking tests), you can work on some of the other tests in this book. Whatever you do, don't memorize answers. It's highly unlikely that any of these questions will be on a test you will take. But whenever you run across a word or an idea that's new to you, be sure you learn what it means and how to use it.

IMPORTANT: The following codes are unique to your testbook. Copy them on your answer sheet exactly as shown.

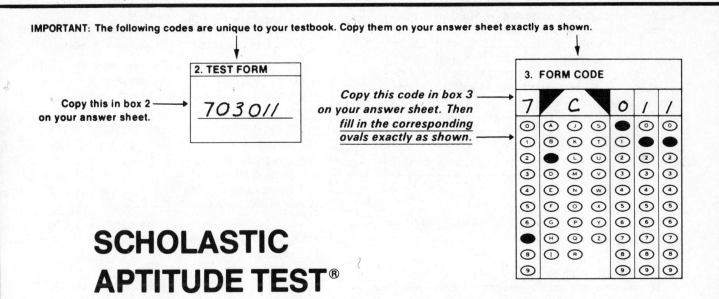

Copy this in box 2 on your answer sheet. →

2. TEST FORM

703011

Copy this code in box 3 on your answer sheet. Then *fill in the corresponding ovals exactly as shown.* →

3. FORM CODE

7   C   0   1   1

SCHOLASTIC APTITUDE TEST®

and Test of Standard Written English

You will have three hours to work on the questions in this test book, which is divided into six 30-minute sections. The supervisor will tell you when to begin and end each section. If you finish before time is called, you may check your work on that section, but you are <u>not to work on any other section.</u>

Do not worry if you are unable to finish a section or if there are some questions you cannot answer. Do not waste time puzzling over a question that seems too difficult for you. You should work as rapidly as you can without sacrificing accuracy.

Students often ask whether they should guess when they are uncertain about the answer to a question. Your test scores will be based on the number of questions you answer correctly minus a fraction of the number you answer incorrectly. Therefore, it is improbable that random or haphazard guessing will change your scores significantly. If you have some knowledge of a question, you may be able to eliminate one or more of the answer choices as wrong. It is generally to your advantage to guess which of the remaining choices is correct. Remember, however, not to spend too much time on any one question.

Mark all your answers on the separate answer sheet. Mark only one answer for each question. Since the answer sheet will be machine scored, be sure that each mark is dark and that it completely fills the oval. In each section of the answer sheet, there are spaces to answer 50 questions. When there are fewer than 50 questions in a section of your test, use only the spaces that correspond to the question numbers. Do not make stray marks on the answer sheet. If you erase, do so completely, because an incomplete erasure may be scored as an intended response.

You may use the test book for scratchwork, but you will not receive credit for anything written there.

(The passages for this test have been adapted from published material. The ideas contained in them do not necessarily represent the opinions of the College Board or Educational Testing Service.)

DO NOT OPEN THIS BOOK UNTIL THE SUPERVISOR TELLS YOU TO DO SO.

TEST 1—FORM CODE 7C

<table>
<tr><td>SECTION 1</td><td>Time—30 minutes
45 Questions</td><td>For each question in this section, choose the best answer and fill in the corresponding oval on the answer sheet.</td></tr>
</table>

Each question below consists of a word in capital letters, followed by five lettered words or phrases. Choose the word or phrase that is most nearly <u>opposite</u> in meaning to the word in capital letters. Since some of the questions require you to distinguish fine shades of meaning, consider all the choices before deciding which is best.

Example:

GOOD: (A) sour   (B) bad   (C) red
(D) hot   (E) ugly

Ⓐ ● Ⓒ Ⓓ Ⓔ

1. GRITTY: (A) smooth and soft
   (B) cold and silent   (C) bright and colorful
   (D) healthy   (E) elongated

2. RESOLVE: (A) willingness   (B) indecision
   (C) dependency   (D) reliability   (E) irrelevance

3. OPAQUE: (A) impoverished   (B) brittle
   (C) spiked   (D) transparent   (E) noisy

4. DEGRADATION:
   (A) saturation
   (B) elevation
   (C) perturbation
   (D) fascination
   (E) procrastination

5. CRINGE: (A) wait impatiently
   (B) react quickly   (C) treat kindly
   (D) fold neatly   (E) stand boldly

6. UNWARY: (A) alert   (B) sad
   (C) angry   (D) eager   (E) dutiful

7. HAMPER: (A) ogle   (B) clarify
   (C) assist   (D) uncover   (E) ventilate

8. DISCREPANCY: (A) expansion
   (B) correspondence   (C) consequence
   (D) lack of judgment   (E) increase in worth

9. GAUNT: (A) rotund   (B) garish
   (C) nervous   (D) stylish   (E) valiant

10. MORATORIUM:
    (A) period of activity
    (B) arrogant behavior
    (C) picturesque scene
    (D) successful contestant
    (E) unexpected response

11. CASTIGATE: (A) collect
    (B) hesitate   (C) salute
    (D) deteriorate   (E) mobilize

12. ABSTEMIOUS: (A) proud   (B) overindulgent
    (C) undervalued   (D) easily overtaken
    (E) having many talents

13. WHET: (A) evade   (B) ingest
    (C) solidify   (D) deaden   (E) reap

14. ANTEDILUVIAN: (A) homemade
    (B) jingoistic   (C) newfangled
    (D) well-balanced   (E) sweet-scented

15. RIFE: (A) rare   (B) weak   (C) progressive
    (D) adaptable   (E) enjoyable

GO ON TO THE NEXT PAGE

Each sentence below has one or two blanks, each blank indicating that something has been omitted. Beneath the sentence are five lettered words or sets of words. Choose the word or set of words that, when inserted in the sentence, best fits the meaning of the sentence as a whole.

Example:

Although its publicity has been ----, the film itself is intelligent, well-acted, handsomely produced, and altogether ----.

(A) tasteless. .respectable (B) extensive. .moderate
(C) sophisticated. .amateur (D) risqué. .crude
(E) perfect. .spectacular ●ⒷⒸⒹⒺ

16. As the Jacksons cheerfully poured forth a stream of personal revelations, it soon became evident that ---- was not the distinguishing characteristic of this couple.

(A) volubility (B) discursiveness (C) shyness
(D) enthusiasm (E) gaiety

17. Laboratories have been warned that provisions for animal protection that in the past were merely ---- will now be mandatory; ---- of this policy will lose their federal research grants.

(A) comprehensive. .adversaries
(B) nominal. .advocates
(C) disregarded. .proponents
(D) recommended. .violators
(E) compulsory. .resisters

18. Because the increase in the birth rate during that decade was dramatic and unprecedented, demographers judged that this rise was ---- and that the birth rate would gradually ----, but they were surprised by yet another increase.

(A) characteristic. .flourish
(B) enduring. .rebound
(C) recurrent. .terminate
(D) temporary. .diminish
(E) beneficial. .deviate

19. To Judith, traveling was ----; her sister, however, looked upon each trip as an ---- experience.

(A) confusing. .unnerving
(B) joyous. .exciting
(C) exhilarating. .interminable
(D) stupefying. .unhappy
(E) tiring. .exhausting

20. The film ---- to present a believable portrait of life because it ---- the seemingly insignificant details that give each person's experience its unique nature.

(A) seeks. .deletes   (B) refuses. .supplies
(C) manages. .ignores   (D) fails. .omits
(E) contrives. .distorts

21. The project's objective is to find and map every remaining example of these medieval earthworks before they are ---- by modern agricultural machinery.

(A) superseded   (B) stabilized   (C) disclosed
(D) replicated   (E) obliterated

22. If society is to make creative use of its internal tensions, we need to see differences as ---- rather than mutually threatening.

(A) illusory   (B) ominous   (C) coercive
(D) detrimental   (E) complementary

23. The revised 1983 edition of Colish's pathfinding study, first published in 1968, incorporates her valuable scholarship of the ---- years and thereby reflects the ---- of the author's thoughts.

(A) culminating. .preparation
(B) intervening. .refinement
(C) following. .stagnation
(D) intermittent. .chronology
(E) final. .immaturity

24. At its best, scientific investigation is a ---- activity; researchers know that their work will be open to general scrutiny, and so they ---- their arguments in defense of their positions.

(A) careful. .neglect   (B) secret. .strengthen
(C) tedious. .invent   (D) public. .marshal
(E) scholarly. .denounce

25. Novelist Jeffery Paul Chan is committed to ---- the myth of an exotic Chinatown, a myth that he believes has been an impediment to the development of a more positive identity for young Chinese-Americans.

(A) disseminating   (B) debunking   (C) forging
(D) condoning   (E) romanticizing

GO ON TO THE NEXT PAGE ➡

Each passage below is followed by questions based on its content. Answer the questions following each passage on the basis of what is stated or implied in that passage.

An observer watching the sky on any clear moonless night can easily observe streaks of light flashing across it every now and then. The ancients interpreted these flashes as "falling stars," and this name is still used by many people in referring to such phenomena. This colorful description gives an entirely wrong impression of the flashes. They are actually caused by meteors, often not much larger nor more massive than grains of sand, which enter the Earth's atmosphere at a speed of about 20 miles per second. Most meteors are disintegrated by the intense heat generated by friction with the air. The temperature of the meteor and of the air surrounding it increases to a few thousand degrees as the kinetic energy of the meteor is quickly transformed into heat; one then sees a sudden luminous streak across the sky whose length, duration, and brightness depend on the size, mass, and speed of the meteor. If it were not for the deceleration resulting from the Earth's atmosphere, many meteoric particles striking the Earth would have an impact greater than that of a .45-caliber bullet and would be very destructive. The number of meteors that enter the Earth's atmosphere in a single 24-hour period and are bright enough to be seen is extremely large. In fact, these meteors are the source of the several tons of meteoric or cosmic dust that are added to the Earth and its atmosphere every day.

Since the debris that separates from the head of a comet continues to move as a stream of matter in the orbit of the comet, a much larger number of meteors is observed when the Earth passes close to such an orbit. In fact, one then observes what is called a meteor shower, with all the meteors in the shower appearing to diverge from, or converge to, a single point in the sky. This phenomenon is illusory; the meteors are really traveling parallel to each other, but they seem to converge to or diverge from a point in the sky because parallel lines seem to intersect at infinity. During the Leonid shower—one whose apparent convergence point was in the constellation of Leo—that occurred on November 13, 1833, meteors were so abundant that many thousands were seen at some observing stations. Such rich showers, however, are rare. Twelve distinct meteor showers, almost one a month, occur every year, but most of them are not very impressive. Each of these is associated with the orbit of a comet.

26. According to the passage, the intensity of the streak caused by a meteor is influenced by which of the following?

   I. The dimensions of the meteor
   II. The origin of the meteor
   III. The velocity of the meteor

   (A) I only
   (B) I and II only
   (C) I and III only
   (D) II and III only
   (E) I, II, and III

27. Which of the following statements about the kinetic energy of a meteor traveling through the Earth's atmosphere can be accurately inferred from the passage?

   (A) It increases the closer the meteor gets to the Earth's surface.
   (B) It serves to neutralize the atmosphere's effect on the meteor.
   (C) It is partially converted into light.
   (D) It is not sufficient to make the meteor visible.
   (E) It cannot be precisely calculated.

28. According to the author, a meteor shower results when

   (A) the Earth passes near the path of a comet
   (B) a massive comet begins to disintegrate
   (C) meteor clusters collide and break up
   (D) the kinetic energy of a meteor is transformed into heat
   (E) meteors converge to a single point in the sky

29. With which of the following statements concerning meteors would the author be most likely to agree?

   (A) Meteors can alter the surface of a planet without an atmosphere.
   (B) Meteors diverge from a single point in the sky.
   (C) Meteors converge to a single point in the sky.
   (D) The speed of a meteor determines its mass.
   (E) The brightness of a meteor indicates its distance from Earth.

30. The author does all of the following in developing the passage EXCEPT

   (A) refute a mistaken notion
   (B) use an illustrative analogy
   (C) explain an optical illusion
   (D) refer to a historical event
   (E) present a personal anecdote

GO ON TO THE NEXT PAGE

In certain non-Western societies, a scholar once suggested, the institution of communal music "gives to individuals a solid center in an existence that seems to be almost chaos, and a continuity in their being that would
Line
(5) otherwise too easily dissolve before the calls of the implacable present. Through its words, people who might be tempted to give in to the malice of circumstances find their old powers revived or new powers stirring in them, and through these life itself is sustained."
(10) This, I think, sums up the role played by song in the lives of Black American slaves. Songs of the years before Emancipation supply abundant evidence that in the structure of the music, in the survival of oral tradition, and in the ways the slaves expressed their Christianity,
(15) important elements of their common African heritage became vitally creative aspects of their Black American culture.

Although it was once thought that Africans newly arrived in America were passive recipients of European
(20) cultural values that supplanted their own, most African slaves in fact were so isolated from the larger American society beyond the plantation that European cultural influence was no more than partial. Through necessity they drew on and reestablished the only cultural frame
(25) of reference that made any sense to them, that of cultures in which they had been raised, and thus passed on distinctly African cultural patterns to slaves born and raised in America. One example of the process of cultural adjustment is the response to Christianity,
(30) valued by American-born slaves not as an institution imported intact from another culture but as a spiritual perception of heroic figures and demonstration of divine justice that they could use to transcend the bonds of their condition through the culturally significant
(35) medium of song. Earlier historians frequently failed to perceive the full importance of this because they did not take seriously enough the strength of feeling represented in the sacred songs. A religion that was a mere anodyne imposed by an oppressing culture could never have
(40) inspired a music as forceful and striking to all who witnessed it as the religious music of the American slaves. Historians who have tried to argue that these people did not oppose the institution of slavery in any meaningful collective way reason from a narrowly
(45) twentieth-century Western viewpoint. Within the frame of reference inherited from African cultures in which the functions of song included criticism and mockery of rulers, there were meaningful methods of opposition to authority and self-assertion so foreign to most Western
(50) historians as to be unrecognizable. Modern Americans raised in a wholly Western culture need to move mentally outside their own culture, in which music plays only a peripheral role, before they can understand how American-born slaves put to use the functions music had had for their African ancestors.

31. Which of the following statements best expresses the main idea of the passage?

  (A) Communal song was a vital part of the heritage of American-born slaves.
  (B) Communal music was primarily important as a recreational pastime.
  (C) Communal song had several functions in ancient African cultures.
  (D) Non-Western cultures give Western historians insights into elements of their own culture.
  (E) Songs prized by American slaves reminded them of their legendary homelands.

32. Underlying the scholar's description of communal music (lines 2-9) is the assumption that human existence

  (A) presents a rich variety of subjects for popular songs
  (B) sometimes reveals profound artistic truths
  (C) often seems bewildering and hopeless
  (D) crushes the spirit of even the most resourceful artist
  (E) rarely encourages artistic expression

33. The passage suggests that the "strength of feeling" (line 37) expressed in the slaves' religious music was a direct reflection of which of the following?

  (A) The use of religion to distract people from present problems
  (B) The sense of injustice as inevitable and inescapable
  (C) The perception of Christianity as a distinctly foreign institution
  (D) The role of song as a vehicle for social commentary
  (E) The importance of music to Western society

GO ON TO THE NEXT PAGE

34. The sentence that begins "A religion that was . . ." (lines 38-42) makes all of the following points EXCEPT:

    (A) Christianity had important spiritual significance for Black American slaves.
    (B) People who have assumed that slaves considered Christianity only a superficial, alien institution are mistaken.
    (C) The power of the slaves' religious music indicates how deeply they felt what they sang.
    (D) The slaves' religious music provided a moving experience for the listeners as well as the singers.
    (E) The religious music of American-born slaves made only indirect use of Christian figures.

35. The author states that historians have sometimes misunderstood the music of American slaves for which of the following reasons?

    I.   They could not personally observe the music being sung by American slaves.
    II. Some historians interpreted the significance of this music within the wrong cultural context.
    III. Many Western historians felt uncomfortable with the presentation of religious stories through art.

    (A) I only
    (B) II only
    (C) III only
    (D) I and II
    (E) I and III

Each question below consists of a related pair of words or phrases, followed by five lettered pairs of words or phrases. Select the lettered pair that best expresses a relationship similar to that expressed in the original pair.

Example:

YAWN:BOREDOM :: (A) dream:sleep
(B) anger:madness   (C) smile:amusement
 (D) face:expression   (E) impatience:rebellion

Ⓐ Ⓑ ● Ⓓ Ⓔ

---

36. LEOTARD : DANCER ::
    (A) apron : chef   (B) badge : detective
    (C) baton : conductor   (D) hammer : carpenter
     (E) microscope : scientist

37. SHRUG : SHOULDERS ::   (A) grin : jokes
    (B) hug : friends   (C) frown : lines
    (D) bite : food   (E) nod : head

38. TRUNK : AUTOMOBILE ::   (A) pilot : airplane
    (B) passenger : train   (C) elevator : building
     (D) closet : house   (E) gear : transmission

39. BASKETBALL : BASKET ::   (A) football : foot
    (B) soccer : goal   (C) baseball : stadium
    (D) bowling : gutter   (E) tennis : racket

40. EPIC : LITERATURE ::
    (A) plot : fiction
    (B) etching : frame
    (C) symphony : music
    (D) blueprint : construction
    (E) accompaniment : ballet

41. INTEREST : OBSESSION ::
    (A) confidence : conceit   (B) gasp : terror
     (C) intelligence : talent   (D) trust : suspicion
     (E) punishment : crime

42. CORRODED : METAL ::   (A) diseased : antibody
    (B) erased : mistake   (C) intended : action
     (D) implied : opinion   (E) corrupted : integrity

43. DEPOSE : RULER ::   (A) unfrock : priest
    (B) assassinate : politician   (C) delegate : emissary
    (D) renounce : authority   (E) challenge : rival

44. PALISADE : STAKES ::   (A) dike : ocean
    (B) lawn : grass   (C) moat : castle
    (D) hedge : shrubs   (E) garden : plants

45. EGOIST : ALTRUISM ::
    (A) sluggard : energy   (B) antagonist : pain
    (C) glutton : food   (D) masochist : pleasure
     (E) philanthropist : generosity

SECTION 2 Time—30 minutes
25 Questions

In this section solve each problem, using any available space on the page for scratchwork. Then decide which is the best of the choices given and fill in the corresponding oval on the answer sheet.

The following information is for your reference in solving some of the problems.

Circle of radius r: Area = πr^2; Circumference = $2\pi r$
  The number of degrees of arc in a circle is 360.
The measure in degrees of a straight angle is 180.

Definitions of symbols:
= is equal to
≠ is unequal to
< is less than
> is greater than
≦ is less than or equal to
≧ is greater than or equal to
‖ is parallel to
⊥ is perpendicular to

Triangle: The sum of the measures in degrees of the angles of a triangle is 180.
If $\angle CDA$ is a right angle, then

(1) area of $\triangle ABC = \dfrac{AB \times CD}{2}$

(2) $AC^2 = AD^2 + DC^2$

Note: Figures that accompany problems in this test are intended to provide information useful in solving the problems. They are drawn as accurately as possible EXCEPT when it is stated in a specific problem that its figure is not drawn to scale. All figures lie in a plane unless otherwise indicated. All numbers used are real numbers.

1. If $n + n + n = n + 10,$ then $n =$

(A) 5
(B) 10
(C) 15
(D) 20
(E) 30

Skirt Size	Skirt Length
2	$20\frac{1}{2}$ inches
4	22 inches
6	x inches
8	25 inches
10	$26\frac{1}{2}$ inches
12	28 inches

2. In the table above, if the difference in skirt lengths between any skirt size and the next larger size is constant, what is the value of x?

(A) $22\frac{1}{2}$

(B) 23

(C) $23\frac{1}{2}$

(D) 24

(E) $24\frac{1}{2}$

3. Widgets are packed exactly $\frac{1}{2}$ dozen to a carton, and extras are left for the next packing. If a batch of 103 widgets is ready to be packed and if there are enough cartons, how many widgets will be left for the next packing?

(A) 1
(B) 2
(C) 3
(D) 4
(E) 5

4. If a, b, and c are integers, the expression $a(b + c)$ is always equal to each of the following EXCEPT

(A) $(a + b)c$
(B) $a(c + b)$
(C) $(b + c)a$
(D) $(c + b)a$
(E) $ab + ac$

GO ON TO THE NEXT PAGE

5. If $2y = 3$, then $3(2y)^2 =$

(A) $\dfrac{27}{4}$

(B) 18

(C) $\dfrac{81}{4}$

(D) 27

(E) 81

6. Which of the following is equal to 0.00238×10^2?

(A) 2.38
(B) 0.238
(C) 0.0238
(D) 0.000238
(E) 0.0000238

Questions 7-8 refer to the following definition.

$$\frac{a \mid b}{c} = \frac{a \cdot b}{c} + \frac{b \cdot c}{a} + \frac{c \cdot a}{b} \quad \text{for all nonzero } a,$$

b, and c.

For example,

$$\frac{2 \mid 4}{6} = \frac{2 \cdot 4}{6} + \frac{4 \cdot 6}{2} + \frac{6 \cdot 2}{4} = \frac{4}{3} + 12 + 3 = 16\frac{1}{3}$$

7. $\dfrac{3 \mid 12}{4} =$

(A) 1
(B) 9
(C) 10
(D) 16
(E) 26

8. If $x \neq 0$, $\dfrac{x \mid x^2}{x^3} =$

(A) $x^6 + x^4 + x^2$

(B) $x^5 + x + \dfrac{1}{x}$

(C) $x^4 + x^3 + 1$

(D) $x^4 + x^2 + 1$

(E) $x^2 + x + 1$

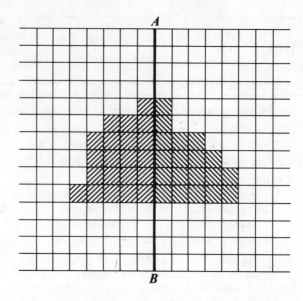

9. What is the least number of additional squares that must be shaded in the figure above to make the shaded region symmetric about the line AB?

(A) One
(B) Two
(C) Three
(D) Four
(E) Five

10. The number $n - 3$ is how much less than $n + 3$?

(A) 3
(B) 6
(C) $n - 6$
(D) $n - 3$
(E) $2n$

11. How many odd positive integers are less than 36?

(A) 16
(B) 17
(C) 18
(D) 19
(E) 35

GO ON TO THE NEXT PAGE ⇒

12. The ratio of the lengths of the sides of two squares is 1:3. What is the ratio of their areas?

  (A) 1:9
  (B) 1:6
  (C) 1:4
  (D) 1:3
  (E) 2:3

13. If Joe picks strawberries at an average rate of m quarts per hour, approximately how many quarts does he pick in h hours, in terms of m and h?

  (A) $\dfrac{m}{h}$

  (B) $\dfrac{h}{m}$

  (C) $m - h$

  (D) $m + h$

  (E) mh

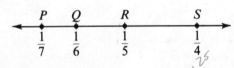

14. On the number line above, where does the number 0.13 lie?

  (A) To the right of point S
  (B) Between points R and S
  (C) Between points Q and R
  (D) Between points P and Q
  (E) To the left of point P

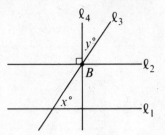

Note: Figure not drawn to scale.

15. In the figure above, line ℓ_2 is parallel to line ℓ_1 and is perpendicular to ℓ_4. B is a point on lines ℓ_2, ℓ_3, and ℓ_4. If $x = y$, what is the value of x?

  (A) 15
  (B) 30
  (C) 45
  (D) 50
  (E) 60

16. Of seven consecutive integers in increasing order, if the sum of the first three integers is 33, what is the sum of the last three integers?

  (A) 36
  (B) 39
  (C) 42
  (D) 45
  (E) 48

GO ON TO THE NEXT PAGE

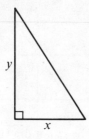

Note: Figure not drawn to scale.

17. In the right triangle above, if x and y are integers and $x + y = 8$, what is the value of x for which the area of the triangle is maximum?

(A) 1
(B) 2
(C) 4
(D) 6
(E) 7

18. In a 3-drawer chest, Ira has 30 percent of his shirts in drawer A, 25 percent in drawer B, and the rest in drawer C. What is the fewest number of shirts he could have in drawer C?

(A) 1
(B) 4
(C) 9
(D) 10
(E) 20

19. If $af = 6$, $fg = 1$, $ag = 24$, and $a > 0$, then $afg =$

(A) $\dfrac{3}{2}$

(B) 4

(C) 6

(D) 12

(E) 144

20. In the figure above, a cubic box with edge of length x inches is tied with a string 106 inches long. The string crosses itself at right angles on the top and bottom of the box. If the bow required 10 inches of string, what is the maximum number of inches x could be?

(A) 12
(B) 13
(C) 16
(D) 17
(E) 18

21. If x, $\dfrac{1}{x}$, y, $\dfrac{1}{y}$, z, and $\dfrac{1}{z}$ are integers, which of the following could NOT be a value of $x + y + z$?

(A) 4
(B) 3
(C) 1
(D) −1
(E) −3

GO ON TO THE NEXT PAGE

22. If $x - y$ is positive, which of the following could be true about x and y ?

    I. $y < x < 0$

    II. $0 < y < x$

    III. $x < y < 0$

  (A) I only
  (B) II only
  (C) III only
  (D) I and II
  (E) I and III

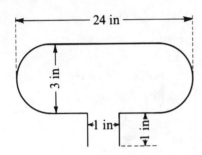

Note: Figure not drawn to scale.

23. The figure above represents a television antenna made completely of wire. The rounded sections of the antenna are semicircles. How many inches of wire are in the part of the antenna shown?

  (A) $40 + 3\pi$
  (B) $43 + 3\pi$
  (C) $43 + 6\pi$
  (D) $44 + 3\pi$
  (E) $48 + 3\pi$

24. In January Ms. Walker spent $\frac{1}{4}$ of the money in her savings account. The following month she spent $\frac{1}{5}$ of the remainder. If she then had $3,000 left, how much was in her savings account originally?

  (A) $4,500
  (B) $5,000
  (C) $5,500
  (D) $6,000
  (E) $7,500

25. In $\triangle ABC$, D is the midpoint of AC , and another point, E , is on AC such that $BE \perp AC$. Which of the following must be true?

  (A) $\angle ABD = \angle DBC$

  (B) $\angle EBD = \frac{1}{4} \angle ABC$

  (C) $\angle BAD = \angle BDA$

  (D) The length of AC > the length of BC

  (E) The length of BD > the length of BE

IF YOU FINISH BEFORE TIME IS CALLED, YOU MAY CHECK YOUR WORK ON THIS SECTION ONLY. DO NOT TURN TO ANY OTHER SECTION IN THE TEST.   **S T O P**

SECTION **3**   Time—30 minutes
                50 Questions

The questions in this section measure skills that are important to writing well. In particular, they test your ability to recognize and use language that is clear, effective, and correct according to the requirements of standard written English, the kind of English found in most college textbooks.

Directions: The following sentences contain problems in grammar, usage, diction (choice of words), and idiom.

Some sentences are correct.
No sentence contains more than one error.

You will find that the error, if there is one, is underlined and lettered. Assume that elements of the sentence that are not underlined are correct and cannot be changed. In choosing answers, follow the requirements of standard written English.

If there is an error, select the one underlined part that must be changed to make the sentence correct and fill in the corresponding oval on your answer sheet.

If there is no error, fill in oval Ⓔ.

EXAMPLE:

The region has a climate so severe that plants
                                A
growing there rarely had been more than twelve
        B   C
inches high. No error
        D   E

SAMPLE ANSWER

Ⓐ Ⓑ ● Ⓓ Ⓔ

1. A few scientists claim that food additives not only
                                                 A
improve the quality of foods but also made them
              B   C   D
safer. No error
        E

2. It is rumored that the names of them to be promoted
        A   B   C
will be announced tomorrow, but I believe the

choices have not been made yet. No error
       D   E

3. In 1957, the appearance of the first Soviet satellite
                              A
has created a panic in the United States that con-
   B
tinued for nearly a decade. No error
        C   D   E

4. In appreciation about her work, the committee
                       A
presented its retiring director with, among other
         B   C
gifts, a plaque describing her accomplishments.
                D
No error
   E

5. For many people, hang-gliding, an increasingly
       A   B
popular sport, seems satisfying the urge to fly.
                     C   D
No error
   E

6. Despite much research, there are still certain
   A   B
elements in the life cycle of the cicada that are
          C
not fully understood. No error
       D   E

7. Louise's fair skin was sunburned so badly that she
                       A   B
looked as if she had fell into a bucket of red paint.
       C   D
No error
   E

8. Whenever we hear of a natural disaster, even in a
   A   B
distant part of the world, you feel sympathy for the
                           C   D
people affected. No error
                     E

GO ON TO THE NEXT PAGE ⟹

48

9. Late in the war, the Germans, <u>retreating in haste</u>,
                                    A   B
<u>left many</u> of <u>their</u> prisoners go free. <u>No error</u>
    C   D   E

10. In many states, there <u>seems</u> to be a belief, <u>openly</u>
       A   B   C
expressed by educators, that the methods of teaching

reading should be <u>changed</u>. <u>No error</u>
                     D   E

11. Throughout the Middle Ages women <u>work</u> <u>beside</u>
    <u>   </u>   B   C
    A
men, knowing that the efforts of men and women

alike were <u>essential to survival</u>. <u>No error</u>
              D   E

12. <u>Without hardly</u> a doubt, the novels of Thomas
       A
Pynchon <u>are</u> <u>more complex</u> than the novels of
           B   C
<u>many other</u> contemporary writers. <u>No error</u>
    D   E

13. The leading roles in the <u>widely acclaimed</u> play, a
                                A
<u>modern</u> version of an Irish folktale, <u>were performed</u>
    B   C
by Jessica and <u>he</u>. <u>No error</u>
                  D   E

14. In the reserve section of the library, <u>there is</u> two
                                              A
<u>volumes</u> of essays by James Baldwin <u>on</u> the relation
    B   C
of the Black artist and intellectual <u>to</u> society.
                                        D
<u>No error</u>
    E

15. Many studies have <u>tried to</u> determine <u>whether or not</u>
                         A   B
seeing violence on television <u>makes</u> children behave
                                 C
<u>more violent</u>. <u>No error</u>
    D   E

16. Between ten <u>and</u> twenty per cent of the textbook
                  A
<u>appears to be</u> new; <u>the rest</u> is a <u>revision</u> of the
    B   C   D
previous edition. <u>No error</u>
                       E

17. Some people seem <u>remarkably</u> insensitive to physical
                        A
pain, <u>and</u> this insensitivity <u>does not mean</u> that
        B   C
they are able to endure other kinds of pain.
<u>   </u>
D
<u>No error</u>
    E

18. During the meeting, Congresswoman Barbara Jordan
    <u>   </u>
    A
<u>stressed that</u> educators and legislators must cooper-
    B
ate <u>where</u> the goal of equal opportunity <u>is</u> to be
       C   D
reached. <u>No error</u>
             E

19. The population of American alligators, <u>dangerously</u>
                                              A
small a few years ago, <u>are</u> now estimated at
                          B   C
<u>more than one million</u>. <u>No error</u>
    D   E

20. <u>Such novels as</u> *Heidi* and *Little Women*
    A
have long been considered by young and old <u>alike</u> to
                                              C
be <u>a classic</u> of children's literature. <u>No error</u>
    D   E

21. <u>Anyone who</u> gathers mushrooms for the purpose of
    A
eating <u>them</u> must distinguish <u>carefully</u> <u>between</u>
          B   C   D
poisonous and nonpoisonous species. <u>No error</u>
                                         E

22. <u>In regards to</u> the energy crisis, the President <u>urged</u>
    A   B
all homeowners <u>to keep</u> <u>their</u> thermostats at sixty-
                  C   D
five degrees in winter. <u>No error</u>
                            E

23. Long ago, well before the <u>invention of</u> the printing
                                 A   B
press, poets often <u>sung</u> <u>their</u> poetry to small,
                      C   D
interested audiences. <u>No error</u>
                          E

24. <u>Because of</u> extreme weather conditions, starvation
    A
<u>exists</u> in some countries where they must <u>struggle</u>
    B   C
every day <u>to stay alive</u>. <u>No error</u>
              D   E

25. The energy question, along with <u>several other</u> issues,
                                       A
<u>are going</u> to be <u>discussed</u> <u>at</u> the next meeting of the
    B   C   D
state legislature. <u>No error</u>
                       E

GO ON TO THE NEXT PAGE

Directions: In each of the following sentences, some part or all of the sentence is underlined. Below each sentence you will find five ways of phrasing the underlined part. Select the answer that produces the most effective sentence, one that is clear and exact, without awkwardness or ambiguity, and fill in the corresponding oval on your answer sheet. In choosing answers, follow the requirements of standard written English. Choose the answer that best expresses the meaning of the original sentence.

Answer (A) is always the same as the underlined part. Choose answer (A) if you think the original sentence needs no revision.

EXAMPLE:

Laura Ingalls Wilder published her first book and she was sixty-five years old then.

(A) and she was sixty-five years old then
(B) when she was sixty-five years old
(C) at age sixty-five years old
(D) upon reaching sixty-five years
(E) at the time when she was sixty-five

SAMPLE ANSWER

Ⓐ ● Ⓒ Ⓓ Ⓔ

---

26. Freud's complex theory based on the death instinct is, for most people, one that is with difficult understanding.

    (A) with difficult understanding
    (B) difficult to understand
    (C) to understand difficultly
    (D) having difficulty being understood
    (E) difficult for understanding

27. In the nineteenth century, trains were more than machines they were expressions of the greatness of the United States.

    (A) machines they were
    (B) machines and were
    (C) machines; they were
    (D) machines, although they were
    (E) machines, but were

28. In the sunlight, the cherry blossoms that burst out everywhere, like foam on breaking waves.

    (A) blossoms that burst
    (B) blossoms bursting
    (C) blossoms, which are bursting
    (D) blossoms burst
    (E) blossoms, which burst

29. When Dorothy Richardson decided to become a novelist, she knew that her writing would leave her little time for other work.

    (A) When Dorothy Richardson decided to become
    (B) After the decision was made by Dorothy Richardson to become
    (C) After the decision by Dorothy Richardson to become
    (D) When Dorothy Richardson decides to become
    (E) When Dorothy Richardson decided about becoming

30. The difference between the twins is that one is humorous; the other, serious.

    (A) one is humorous; the other, serious
    (B) of one being humorous, the other is serious
    (C) one is humorous; the other being serious
    (D) one is humorous, although the other is more serious
    (E) of a humorous one and one that is serious

31. The United States did not go on the gold standard until 1900, it went off it thirty-three years later.

    (A) until 1900, it went off it thirty-three years later
    (B) until 1900; however, going off after thirty-three years
    (C) until 1900, although going off in thirty-three years
    (D) until 1900, it was thirty-three years later when it went off it
    (E) until 1900 and went off it thirty-three years later

32. Many memos were issued by the director of the agency that had an insulting tone, according to the staff members.

    (A) Many memos were issued by the director of the agency that
    (B) Many memos were issued by the director of the agency who
    (C) The issuance of many memos by the director of the agency which
    (D) The director of the agency issued many memos that
    (E) The director of the agency, who issued many memos that

GO ON TO THE NEXT PAGE

33. The widespread slaughter of buffalo for their skins profoundly shocked and angered Native Americans.

(A) shocked and angered Native Americans
(B) shocked Native Americans, angering them
(C) shocked Native Americans, and they were also angry
(D) was a shock and caused anger among Native Americans
(E) was shocking to Native Americans, making them angry

34. Consumers are beginning to take notice of electric cars because they are quiet, cause no air pollution, and gasoline is not used.

(A) cause no air pollution, and gasoline is not used
(B) air pollution is not caused, and gasoline is not used
(C) cause no air pollution, and use no gasoline
(D) causing no air pollution and using no gasoline
(E) air pollution is not caused, and no gasoline is used

– ended here –

35. Because she was a woman was why Sharon Frontiero, a lieutenant in the United States Air Force, felt that she was being treated unfairly.

(A) Because she was a woman was why Sharon Frontiero, a lieutenant in the United States Air Force, felt that she was being treated unfairly.
(B) Sharon Frontiero, a lieutenant in the United States Air Force, felt that she was being treated unfairly because she was a woman.
(C) Because she was a woman, Sharon Frontiero felt that this was why she was being treated unfairly as a lieutenant in the United States Air Force.
(D) Sharon Frontiero, a lieutenant in the United States Air Force, feeling that she was being treated unfairly because she was a woman.
(E) A woman, Sharon Frontiero, felt that because she was a lieutenant in the United States Air Force, that she was being treated unfairly.

36. A major difference between people and apes is brain size, a person's brain is three times as large as the brain of an ape.

(A) size, a person's brain is
(B) size, with a person's brain being
(C) size; a person's brain is
(D) size; a person's brain, it is
(E) size, in that it is

37. The process of how European immigrant groups being absorbed into American society is complex.

(A) of how European immigrant groups being absorbed
(B) for European immigrant groups being absorbed
(C) where European immigrant groups were absorbed
(D) by which European immigrant groups have been absorbed
(E) whereby the absorption of European groups has been

38. Mr. Howe's class has organized a special program for our school; the purpose being to help us increase our understanding of Japanese culture.

(A) school; the purpose being to
(B) school and the purpose is to
(C) school, the purpose is to
(D) school, being to
(E) school to

39. Light reaching earth from the most distant stars originated billions of years ago.

(A) reaching earth from the most distant stars
(B) which reaching earth from the most distant stars
(C) from the most distant stars reaching earth
(D) that is from the most distant stars and reaches earth
(E) reaching earth which is from stars that are most distant

40. Joseph Conrad was born and educated in Poland and he wrote all of his novels in English.

(A) Joseph Conrad was born and educated in Poland and he
(B) Joseph Conrad, being born and educated in Poland,
(C) Although being born and educated in Poland, Joseph Conrad
(D) Although Joseph Conrad was born and educated in Poland, he
(E) Being from Poland, where he was born and educated, Joseph Conrad

GO ON TO THE NEXT PAGE

Note: The remaining questions are like those at the beginning of the section.

Directions: For each sentence in which you find an error, select the one underlined part that must be changed to make the sentence correct and fill in the corresponding oval on your answer sheet.

If there is no error, fill in oval Ⓔ .

EXAMPLE:

The region has a climate so severe that plants
                          A
growing there rarely had been more than twelve
        B   C
inches high. No error
        D   E

SAMPLE ANSWER

Ⓐ Ⓑ ● Ⓓ Ⓔ

41. If you find that it is difficult to concentrate
        A   B
in noisy surroundings, one should try to find a
        C   D
quiet place to study. No error
                      E

42. The speaker claimed that no other modern

nation devotes so small a portion of its wealth
        A   B   C
to public assistance and health as the United States
                              D
does. No error
      E

43. The thought of trying to persuade their three-year-
                    A   B
old to sit in a high chair did not appeal to either the
    C
mother nor the father. No error
        D   E

44. The bright fiberglass sculptures of Luis Jiménez
        A
has received critical acclaim not only in his home
    B   C
state, New Mexico, but also in New York. No error
                              D   E

45. Doctors see a connection between increased amounts
                    A   B
of leisure time spent sunbathing and the increased
                              C
number of cases of skin cancer. No error
    D   E

46. Whether or not credit card companies should prevent
        A
their customers to acquire substantial debts was the
    B   C
issue discussed at the meeting. No error
    D   E

47. The board's final recommendations included hiring
                              A
additional personnel, dismissing the head of research,
    B   C
and a reorganized marketing division. No error
    D   E

48. Some people prefer attending movies to television
                A   B
because they dislike the frequent interruptions of
        C   D
programs for commercials. No error
                          E

49. Like many factory workers of a century ago,
    A   B
women today are developing organizations to
        C
represent their interests. No error
    D   E

50. In a prominent city newspaper, they claim that the
                              A
number of unregistered participants in this year's
    B   C
marathon was half that of last year's. No error
                D   E

IF YOU FINISH BEFORE TIME IS CALLED, YOU MAY CHECK YOUR WORK ON
THIS SECTION ONLY. DO NOT TURN TO ANY OTHER SECTION IN THE TEST.

S T O P

SECTION 5 Time—30 minutes 40 Questions

For each question in this section, choose the best answer and fill in the corresponding oval on the answer sheet.

Each question below consists of a word in capital letters, followed by five lettered words or phrases. Choose the word or phrase that is most nearly <u>opposite</u> in meaning to the word in capital letters. Since some of the questions require you to distinguish fine shades of meaning, consider all the choices before deciding which is best.

Example:

GOOD: (A) sour (B) bad (C) red (D) hot (E) ugly

Ⓐ ● Ⓒ Ⓓ Ⓔ

1. UNCORK: (A) reform (B) empty (C) seal (D) dry out (E) blend in

2. FRAUDULENCE: (A) truthfulness (B) prosperity (C) melancholy (D) composure (E) potency

3. WITHSTAND: (A) learn from (B) copy from (C) add to (D) show to (E) yield to

4. ARCHAIC: (A) minor (B) modern (C) flattened (D) unique (E) urban

5. WISPY: (A) substantial (B) frigid (C) conventional (D) colorful (E) odorless

6. MYRIAD: (A) personal taste (B) accurate image (C) loud group (D) small number (E) nearby place

7. PONTIFICATE: (A) idolize (B) persist (C) speak modestly (D) investigate promptly (E) drive carelessly

8. NEFARIOUS: (A) adroit (B) dapper (C) serious (D) virtuous (E) eloquent

9. BILLOWING: (A) drooping (B) liberated (C) distant (D) silent (E) enthusiastic

10. MAGNANIMOUS: (A) dainty (B) latent (C) vengeful (D) conspicuous (E) compatible

Each sentence below has one or two blanks, each blank indicating that something has been omitted. Beneath the sentence are five lettered words or sets of words. Choose the word or set of words that, when inserted in the sentence, <u>best</u> fits the meaning of the sentence as a whole.

Example:

Although its publicity has been ----, the film itself is intelligent, well-acted, handsomely produced, and altogether ----.

(A) tasteless. .respectable (B) extensive. .moderate (C) sophisticated. .amateur (D) risqué. .crude (E) perfect. .spectacular

● Ⓑ Ⓒ Ⓓ Ⓔ

11. Because of improvements made in the microscope, organisms that heretofore were ---- are now easily studied.

(A) unavoidable (B) indistinguishable (C) inactive (D) intolerable (E) inconsequential

12. I found that the writer's ideas were sufficiently ---- to make me bear with his ---- language.

(A) intriguing. .skill with (B) interesting. .abuses of (C) humble. .mastery of (D) shallow. .errors in (E) misguided. .style of

13. Paradoxically, this successful entrepreneur is sometimes ---- and at other times reclusive.

(A) autonomous (B) dispassionate (C) solitary (D) unthinking (E) gregarious

GO ON TO THE NEXT PAGE

5

14. Rice has been referred to as a nearly perfect food, in that one can ---- with rice as the major part of one's diet without any ---- physical effects.

    (A) survive. .salutary
    (B) languish. .harmful
    (C) subsist. .deleterious
    (D) decline. .deteriorating
    (E) thrive. .benign

15. The speaker ---- his initial indiscriminate generalizations by ---- that each segment of the Hispanic population in the United States is a distinct group with its own identity and values.

    (A) renounced. .denying
    (B) reiterated. .assuming
    (C) qualified. .emphasizing
    (D) minimized. .doubting
    (E) verified. .insisting

Each question below consists of a related pair of words or phrases, followed by five lettered pairs of words or phrases. Select the lettered pair that best expresses a relationship similar to that expressed in the original pair.

Example:

YAWN:BOREDOM :: (A) dream:sleep (B) anger:madness (C) smile:amusement (D) face:expression (E) impatience:rebellion

Ⓐ Ⓑ ● Ⓓ Ⓔ

16. HEIGHT : MOUNTAIN :: (A) ray : sun (B) length : width (C) peak : valley (D) depth : sea (E) weight : scale

17. RING : BOXER :: (A) grandstand : racehorse (B) stage : actor (C) track meet : runner (D) box office : ticket (E) airport : plane

18. STUDY : KNOWLEDGE ::
    (A) accomplishment : incentive
    (B) exercise : strength
    (C) reality : wish
    (D) cookbook : food
    (E) time : growth

19. SAND : HOURGLASS :: (A) liquid : bottle (B) strap : wristwatch (C) battery : flashlight (D) line : ruler (E) mercury : thermometer

20. STATUE : SCULPTOR ::
    (A) fire : firefighter (B) paint : painter (C) medicine : doctor (D) law : lawyer (E) suit : tailor

21. LAMENTATION : SORROW ::
    (A) instigation : plot
    (B) reassurance : anxiety
    (C) exclamation : surprise
    (D) resistance : futility
    (E) interruption : occurrence

22. ACQUIRE : STEAL :: (A) capture : interrogate (B) impress : influence (C) testify : perjure (D) denounce : insult (E) frighten : tremble

23. EXCERPT : BOOK :: (A) swatch : fabric (B) revision : manuscript (C) review : film (D) fringe : shawl (E) chapter : index

24. SUPPLANT : REPLACEMENT ::
    (A) terrorize : protection
    (B) obliterate : destruction
    (C) implant : extraction
    (D) infiltrate : discovery
    (E) supplement : inadequacy

25. MAELSTROM : WATER :: (A) blizzard : wind (B) rock slide : earth (C) tornado : air (D) tidal wave : ocean (E) plateau : land

GO ON TO THE NEXT PAGE →

Each passage below is followed by questions based on its content. Answer the questions following each passage on the basis of what is <u>stated</u> or <u>implied</u> in that passage.

As soon as cable service was restored after the earthquake, Baron Okura replied to architect Frank Lloyd Wright's inquiry with a message of congratulation: HOTEL STANDS UNDAMAGED AS MONUMENT OF YOUR GENIUS. HUNDREDS OF HOMELESS PROVIDED FOR BY PERFECTLY MAINTAINED SERVICE. CONGRATULATIONS, OKURA.

Never one to display undue reticence in such matters, Wright speedily convened a press conference at which he said nothing to dissuade reporters from drawing the inference that the Imperial Hotel was the only building in Tokyo that had remained standing through the disaster. In fact, however, hundreds of other solid masonry buildings in both Tokyo and Yokohama also withstood the quake—most notably those of British architect Josiah Condor, whose numerous structures suffered considerably less damage than Wright's. Nonetheless, the Imperial Hotel's thoroughly undeserved fame as the only building that had stood up through the great Tokyo quake was to prove far more unshakable than the edifice itself; and Wright's renown as the man who had designed and built it flourished accordingly. While by no means wholly responsible for the architectural revolution that was to revitalize the world's cities during the next four decades, the worldwide repute of Wright's Imperial Hotel was to facilitate and hasten its progress. By the time this famous edifice was demolished in 1967, the great earthquake had been instrumental in altering not only the appearance of Tokyo but also that of many of the other great cities in the world.

26. The primary purpose of the passage is to

   (A) outline some of Wright's failings as an architect
   (B) describe the architectural revolution brought about by Wright
   (C) explain how Wright increased his fame and helped change the world's architecture
   (D) attack Wright's architectural abilities and his greed for world renown
   (E) compare the historical significance of Wright's work to that of Josiah Condor

27. The passage suggests that Josiah Condor was not as famous as Wright because Condor

   (A) was not an innovative architect
   (B) did not take advantage of publicity
   (C) did not design buildings especially to withstand earthquakes
   (D) did not realize the extent of the damages caused by the Tokyo quake
   (E) had stopped designing new buildings by the time the architectural revolution took place

28. In developing the passage, the author does all of the following EXCEPT

   (A) offer a comparison
   (B) make use of historical facts
   (C) refer to a written document
   (D) rely on recollected private experience
   (E) point out a cause and effect relationship

GO ON TO THE NEXT PAGE

In any part of the world where there are pronounced seasonal changes in climate, organisms appear and disappear at particular times with uncanny precision. Biologists have long wondered how they do it, and the answer to this question is even now not entirely clear.

As the Earth spins through its seasonal cycle, several environmental parameters change on an annual basis. Temperatures fluctuate, periods of high and low precipitation alternate, and day length increases and decreases. Like temperature, the time and amount of precipitation in most parts of the world is highly unpredictable on a week-to-week basis, even though seasonal averages may not fluctuate significantly. Unlike temperature and precipitation, however, day length repeats itself with monotonous precision year in and year out; it is not particularly surprising, therefore, that many organisms respond to this parameter.

Response to day length, or photoperiodism, among most groups of higher organisms is well known. However, the most detailed studies have been done with flowering plants and insects—partially because they are readily handled in large numbers under laboratory conditions, and partially because many of them have sufficiently short life cycles that their response to photoperiod is quickly evident and hence accessible to experimentation. In insects the most carefully studied phenomenon is entry into diapause, a dormant state that occurs in different insects at very different developmental stages, from the egg through adulthood. In flowering plants the phenomenon subjected to closest analysis has been the transformation from vegetative to reproductive growth—the initiation and development of flowers—although it has been demonstrated that other phenomena, such as the onset of autumn coloration and entrance into winter dormancy, are also responses to day length.

29. The passage is best described as which of the following?

   (A) A response to a controversial theory of ecological relationships
   (B) An explanation of a newly discovered cycle of growth
   (C) An account of climatic events in different parts of the world
   (D) A list of observations made during the course of one year
   (E) An inquiry into possible causes of certain biological phenomena

30. The author cites all of the following as responses to photoperiodism EXCEPT

   (A) insect entry into diapause
   (B) development of flowers
   (C) short life cycles of plants and insects
   (D) onset of winter dormancy in plants
   (E) start of autumn coloration in leaves

31. According to the passage, the phenomenon of diapause is accurately characterized as which of the following?

   I.   A state of inactivity
   II. A response to a change in the number of daylight hours
   III. An effect produced primarily through artificial laboratory conditions

   (A) I only
   (B) II only
   (C) III only
   (D) I and II only
   (E) I, II, and III

GO ON TO THE NEXT PAGE

Isabel had never met a person having less of that fault which is the principal obstacle to friendship—the air of reproducing the more tiresome, the stale, the too-
Line familiar parts of one's own character. The gates of
(5) Isabel's confidence were opened wider than they had ever been; she said things to this amiable auditor that she had not yet said to anyone. Sometimes she took alarm at her candor: it was as if she had given to a comparative stranger the key to her cabinet of jewels. Afterwards,
(10) however, she always remembered that one should never regret a generous error and that if Madame Merle had not the merits she attributed to her, so much the worse for Madame Merle.

There are many amiable people in the world, and
(15) Madame Merle was far from being vulgarly good-natured and restlessly witty. She knew how to think and she had thought to very good purpose. Of course, too, she knew how to feel; Isabel couldn't have spent a week with her without being sure of that. This was indeed
(20) Madame Merle's most perfect gift. Life had told upon her; it was part of the satisfaction to be taken in her society that when Isabel talked of what she was pleased to call serious matters Madame Merle understood her so easily and quickly. Emotion, it is true, had become with
(25) Madame Merle rather historic; she made no secret of the fact that the fount of passion, thanks to having been rather violently tapped at one period, didn't flow quite so freely as of yore.

32. The primary purpose of this passage is to

(A) contrast Madame Merle's worldliness with Isabel's naïveté
(B) investigate Madame Merle's idiosyncratic character
(C) illustrate by example the ideal friendship between women
(D) describe the reasons for Isabel's attraction to Madame Merle
(E) emphasize Madame Merle's coarseness by describing Isabel's sophistication

33. It can be inferred from the passage that the "generous error" in line 11 refers to Isabel's

(A) willingness to believe Madame Merle worthy of her confidence
(B) careless freedom with her personal jewelry
(C) reluctance to be critical of Madame Merle's behavior
(D) acceptance of Madame Merle as an equal
(E) desire to give Madame Merle financial assistance

34. The author's attitude toward "many amiable people" (line 14) is best expressed by which of the following?

(A) They represent a majority of the population.
(B) They are boisterous but sensitive and able to think to good purpose.
(C) They are prone to be high-spirited more often than they are amiable.
(D) They deserve the praise and admiration of others.
(E) They are often forced and excessive in their friendliness.

35. With which of the following observations concerning friendship would Isabel most likely agree?

(A) Sympathetic understanding is not absolutely essential to a strong friendship.
(B) A friendship is difficult with a person who echoes the wearisome aspects of one's own character.
(C) One must avoid expressing confidences to new friends.
(D) People should never reveal more of their feelings to friends than those friends share in return.
(E) One should always be careful not to attribute merits to a friend before they have been proven.

GO ON TO THE NEXT PAGE

5

(This passage was written in 1960.)

Where government has entered directly into the field of art, the experience has too often been disheartening. Political influences have exerted themselves. The standards of the artist and the critic have been ignored or, *Line* where these have been permitted a measure of authority, (5) the tendency has been for an artistic clique to entrench itself. The art that has been encouraged under official auspices has almost always favored the less adventurous and the more classically hidebound schools.

(10) From this experience, leading figures in the art world have drawn the conclusion that anything is better than the intrusion of government. It may be questioned, however, whether such individuals in the United States are not thinking too narrowly as professionals, without an (15) adequate understanding of the governmental methods and institutions that in other fields, no less delicate than art, have permitted our political system to act with detachment and a regard for the highest and most sophisticated standards.

(20) The functions performed by the National Institute of Health and the National Science Foundation are, to take two modern examples, quite as complex as the encouragement of art; they are performed with a high level of competence and professional skill. Certainly we should be (25) capable of devoting as much ingenuity to the creation of adequate processes for the nurturing of art as we have for promoting health or science.

It may be argued that, although public officials may not think of themselves as experts on health or science, (30) they may assume they know what is good in art. There is a need for widespread acceptance of the idea that art has its own standards, irrespective of one's personal preferences; that it is professional, disciplined, and subject to the rational and informed judgments of the critics. Unless (35) these principles are accepted, it is perhaps impossible to hope that government can promote art without debasing it. But even that is not reason to despair. There already exist precedents of high officials upholding the verdicts of juries whose views on art differed admittedly from their (40) own. There are also notable examples of government cultural activity successfully protected from political pressure. The Freer Gallery and the National Gallery of Art remind us how private and public efforts can combine to produce results of highest excellence.

36. The passage as a whole is concerned primarily with which of the following questions?

(A) Why is the government interested in promoting art?
(B) Should the government have a role in supporting the arts?
(C) How much influence does the government have over artistic standards?
(D) Why have artists not been more involved in government-sponsored art projects?
(E) How have political influences affected artistic standards in the United States?

37. The author indicates that the art sponsored by governments has tended to be

(A) unpopular   (B) grandiose
(C) conventional   (D) unrealistic   (E) exotic

38. Why does the author criticize those art experts who believe the government should not enter into the field of art?

(A) They do not know enough about the successful functioning of governmental institutions in other fields.
(B) They have disapproved of art that was encouraged under official auspices.
(C) They have established impossible standards for government-sponsored art.
(D) They have placed too much trust in politicians' ability to evaluate art.
(E) They are reluctant to speak out in defense of artistic standards.

39. The author mentions the National Gallery of Art chiefly as an example of

(A) successful government involvement with art
(B) government cultural activity affected by political pressure
(C) an institution similar in organization to the National Institute of Health
(D) the entrenchment of an artistic clique in a government project
(E) an institution uninfluenced by the opinions of experts

40. Which of the following does the author include among the "principles" mentioned in line 35?

(A) Only an artist can properly evaluate his or her own work.
(B) The government can support art without devaluating artistic standards.
(C) There are critical standards by which judgments about art can be made.
(D) The appreciation of art is a matter of subjective preference.
(E) Public officials can best determine the proper allocation for government funds in the field of art.

SECTION **6**   Time—30 minutes   In this section solve each problem, using any available space on the page for scratchwork. Then decide which is the best of the choices given and fill in the corresponding oval on the answer sheet.
35 Questions

The following information is for your reference in solving some of the problems.

Circle of radius r: Area $= \pi r^2$; Circumference $= 2\pi r$
  The number of degrees of arc in a circle is 360.
The measure in degrees of a straight angle is 180.

Definitions of symbols:
$=$ is equal to $\leq$ is less than or equal to
$\neq$ is unequal to $\geq$ is greater than or equal to
$<$ is less than $\parallel$ is parallel to
$>$ is greater than $\perp$ is perpendicular to

Triangle: The sum of the measures in degrees of the angles of a triangle is 180.
If $\angle CDA$ is a right angle, then

(1) area of $\triangle ABC = \dfrac{AB \times CD}{2}$

(2) $AC^2 = AD^2 + DC^2$

Note: Figures that accompany problems in this test are intended to provide information useful in solving the problems. They are drawn as accurately as possible EXCEPT when it is stated in a specific problem that its figure is not drawn to scale. All figures lie in a plane unless otherwise indicated. All numbers used are real numbers.

1. If the ratio of a to b is $\dfrac{7}{3}$, then the ratio of $2a$ to b is

(A) $\dfrac{7}{6}$

(B) 2

(C) $\dfrac{7}{3}$

(D) 3

(E) $\dfrac{14}{3}$

2. On any given day, 8:30 a.m. is how many minutes past 7:15 a.m. ?

(A) 15
(B) 45
(C) 75
(D) 105
(E) 115

3. If $x + y = 8$ and $xy = 15$, then $x - y$ could equal

(A) 2
(B) 4
(C) 6
(D) 7
(E) 9

4. $\dfrac{1}{5} - \dfrac{2}{10} + \dfrac{3}{15} - \dfrac{4}{20} =$

(A) $-\dfrac{2}{5}$

(B) $-\dfrac{1}{5}$

(C) 0

(D) $\dfrac{2}{5}$

(E) $\dfrac{1}{2}$

GO ON TO THE NEXT PAGE

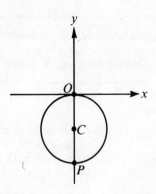

5. In the figure above, the circle with center C has radius 5 and passes through O. The coordinates (x, y) of point P are

(A) $(-10, 0)$
(B) $(-5, 0)$
(C) $(-5, 5)$
(D) $(0, -5)$
(E) $(0, -10)$

$$
\begin{array}{r}
37 \\
\times\ 2F \\
\hline
H4G \\
74 \\
\hline
88G
\end{array}
$$

6. If F, G, and H each represent a different digit in the correctly worked multiplication problem above, what digit does F represent?

(A) 3
(B) 4
(C) 5
(D) 6
(E) 7

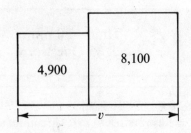

7. The figure above is composed of two squares with areas as shown. What is the value of v?

(A) 60
(B) 65
(C) 130
(D) 160
(E) 650

GO ON TO THE NEXT PAGE

Questions 8-27 each consist of two quantities, one in Column A and one in Column B. You are to compare the two quantities and on the answer sheet fill in oval

- A if the quantity in Column A is greater;
- B if the quantity in Column B is greater;
- C if the two quantities are equal;
- D if the relationship cannot be determined from the information given.

AN E RESPONSE WILL NOT BE SCORED.

EXAMPLES

	Column A	Column B	Answers
E1.	2×6	$2 + 6$	● Ⓑ Ⓒ Ⓓ Ⓔ

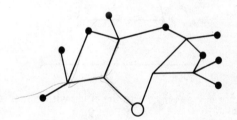

	Column A	Column B	Answers
E2.	$180 - x$	y	Ⓐ Ⓑ ● Ⓓ Ⓔ
E3.	$p - q$	$q - p$	Ⓐ Ⓑ Ⓒ ● Ⓔ

Notes:

1. In certain questions, information concerning one or both of the quantities to be compared is centered above the two columns.
2. In a given question, a symbol that appears in both columns represents the same thing in Column A as it does in Column B.
3. Letters such as x, n, and k stand for real numbers.

	Column A	Column B
8.	$1 + 11 + 111 + 1{,}111$	$9 + 99 + 999$
9.	$\dfrac{20}{35}$	$\dfrac{40}{70}$

$$x = 24 - y$$
$$y - 6 = 7$$

	Column A	Column B
10.	x	y

$$50\% \text{ of } z = 90$$

	Column A	Column B
11.	z	45

DISTRIBUTION OF TIME FOR ACTIVITIES OVER A 24-HOUR PERIOD

	Column A	Column B
12.	The number of hours available for "Other Activities"	12 hours

Column A **Column B**

A "tripath" is a path along exactly three connected line segments from ○ to any point marked ●.

	Column A	Column B
13.	The number of different tripaths possible	9

$$x > 0$$

	Column A	Column B
14.	The average (arithmetic mean) of x, $2x$, and 30	The average (arithmetic mean) of x and $2x$

GO ON TO THE NEXT PAGE ⟶

Column A	Column B

Questions 15-16 refer to the following graph.

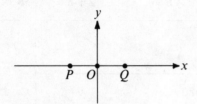

15. x-coordinate of point P x-coordinate of point Q

16. y-coordinate of point P y-coordinate of point Q

$$2 + r < s$$

17. r s

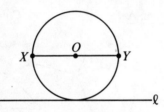

Line ℓ is tangent to the circle with center O.
$$XY = 9$$

18. The distance from O to   4
any point on ℓ

$$m > 0$$
$$n > 0$$

19. $m + n$ mn

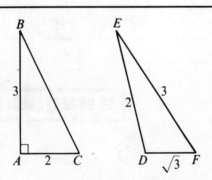

Note: Figures not drawn to scale.

20. Perimeter of $\triangle ABC$ Perimeter of $\triangle DEF$

Column A	Column B

Three line segments with a common end point form three angles of measures $x°$, $y°$, and $z°$.

21. The value of $x + y$ 180

$$p < 0$$

22. $p^2 + p^3 + p^4 + p^5$ 0

$$(x + 5)(x - 3) = 0$$

23. x 5

$$\frac{6}{25} + \frac{6}{25} + \frac{6}{25} = \frac{x}{75}$$

24. x 36

An isosceles right triangle has area 18.

25. The length of its $6\sqrt{2}$
hypotenuse

A bicyclist traveled 19 kilometers in n hours at an average speed of 32 kilometers per hour.

26. n $\frac{2}{3}$

Of 100 freshmen, 30 are taking history but not calculus and 50 are taking calculus but not history.

27. The number of freshmen   19
taking both history and
calculus

GO ON TO THE NEXT PAGE ⇨

Solve each of the remaining problems in this section using any available space for scratchwork. Then decide which is the best of the choices given and fill in the corresponding oval on the answer sheet.

28. The sum of two consecutive positive integers is never divisible by

(A) 2
(B) 3
(C) 5
(D) 7
(E) 9

29. Equal amounts of peanuts, cashews, and almonds are packed separately in bags. If 3 bags, one of each kind, cost a total of $3.00 and 2 bags of peanuts and 2 bags of cashews cost a total of $3.50, how much does 1 bag of almonds cost?

(A) $1.25
(B) $1.50
(C) $1.75
(D) $2.00
(E) $2.25

30. If A, B, C, and D are four distinct points on a circle such that the four chords AB, BC, CD, and DA are of equal length, the diameter of the circle is equal to the length of which of the following?

(A) AD

(B) AC

(C) CD

(D) $\dfrac{AD + BC}{2}$

(E) $\dfrac{AB + BD}{2}$

31. If $\dfrac{x}{3} = x^2$, the value of x can be which of the following?

I. $-\dfrac{1}{3}$

II.   0

III. $\dfrac{1}{3}$

(A) I only
(B) II only
(C) III only
(D) II and III only
(E) I, II, and III

32. Jean uses the symbol above to indicate that a circle of radius X can be drawn in the interior of a square with side of length Y without touching the sides of the square. Which of the following is correct?

(A)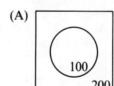
(B)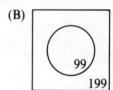
(C)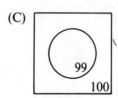
(D)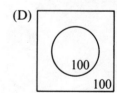
(E)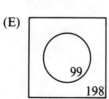

GO ON TO THE NEXT PAGE

63

33. If the average (arithmetic mean) of six numbers is −6, and the sum of four of the numbers is 20, what is the average of the other two numbers?

    (A)   7
    (B)   8
    (C) −8
    (D) −28
    (E) −32

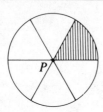

34. The circle above with center *P* is divided into 6 equal regions. If the area of the circle is 36π, what is the perimeter of the shaded region?

    (A) 12π + 6
    (B) 6π + 12
    (C) 6π + 6
    (D) 2π + 36
    (E) 2π + 12

35. A 2-cup mixture consists of $\frac{1}{3}$ flour and $\frac{2}{3}$ corn-meal. If 1 cup of flour is added to make a 3-cup mixture, approximately what percent of the 3-cup mixture is flour?

    (A) 65%
    (B) 55%
    (C) 50%
    (D) 45%
    (E) 35%

IF YOU FINISH BEFORE TIME IS CALLED, YOU MAY CHECK YOUR WORK ON THIS SECTION ONLY. DO NOT TURN TO ANY OTHER SECTION IN THE TEST.   **S T O P**

How to Score the Sample Test

Before you can find out what your scores are on the College Board 200 to 800 scale, you need to determine your verbal, mathematical, and TSWE raw scores. The steps for doing so for each section of the test and a scoring worksheet are provided below and on page 66. Use the table on page 67 to determine your correct and incorrect answers for each section.

Determining Your Raw Scores

SAT-Verbal Sections 1 and 5

Step A: Count the number of correct answers for section 1 and record the number in the space provided on the worksheet. Then do the same for the incorrect answers. (Do not count omitted answers.) To determine subtotal A, use the formula:

$$\text{number correct} - \frac{\text{number incorrect}}{4} = \text{subtotal A}$$

Step B: Count the number of correct answers and the number of incorrect answers for section 5 and record the numbers in the spaces provided on the worksheet. To determine subtotal B, use the formula:

$$\text{number correct} - \frac{\text{number incorrect}}{4} = \text{subtotal B}$$

Step C: To obtain C, add subtotal A to subtotal B, keeping any decimals. Enter the resulting figure on the worksheet.

Step D: To obtain D, your raw verbal score, round C to the nearest whole number. (For example, any number from 44.50 to 45.49 rounds to 45.) Enter the resulting figure on the worksheet.

SAT-Mathematical Sections 2 and 6

Step A: Count the number of correct answers and the number of incorrect answers for section 2 and record the numbers in the spaces provided on the worksheet. To determine subtotal A, use the formula:

$$\text{number correct} - \frac{\text{number incorrect}}{4} = \text{subtotal A}$$

Step B: Count the number of correct answers and the number of incorrect answers for the *five-choice questions (questions 1 through 7 and 28 through 35)* in section 6 and record the numbers in the spaces provided on the worksheet. To determine subtotal B, use the formula:

$$\text{number correct} - \frac{\text{number incorrect}}{4} = \text{subtotal B}$$

Step C: Count the number of correct answers and the number of incorrect answers for the *four-choice questions (questions 8 through 27)* in section 6 and record the numbers in the spaces provided on the worksheet. To determine subtotal C, use the formula:

$$\text{number correct} - \frac{\text{number incorrect}}{3} = \text{subtotal C}$$

<u>Note:</u> **Do not count any E responses to questions 8 through 27 as correct or incorrect. Because these four-choice questions have no E answer choices, E responses to these questions are treated as omits.**

Step D: To obtain D, add subtotal A, subtotal B, and subtotal C, keeping any decimals. Enter the resulting figure on the worksheet.

Step E: To obtain E, your raw mathematical score, round D to the nearest whole number. (For example, any number from 44.50 to 45.49 rounds to 45.) Enter the resulting figure on the worksheet.

TSWE: Section 3

Step A: Count the number of correct answers for section 3 and record the number in the space provided on the worksheet. Then do the same for the incorrect answers. (Do not count omitted answers.) To determine your unrounded raw score, use the formula:

$$\text{number correct} - \frac{\text{number incorrect}}{4} = \begin{array}{l}\text{total unrounded}\\ \text{raw score}\end{array}$$

Step B: To obtain B, your raw TSWE score, round A to the nearest whole number. (For example, any number from 34.50 to 35.49 rounds to 35.) Enter the resulting figure on the worksheet.

SCORING WORKSHEET
FOR THE SAMPLE TEST

SAT-Verbal Sections

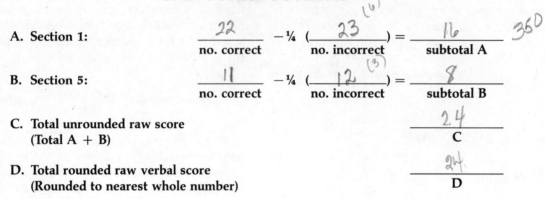

A. Section 1: $\dfrac{22}{\text{no. correct}}$ — ¼ ($\dfrac{23^{(6)}}{\text{no. incorrect}}$) = $\dfrac{16}{\text{subtotal A}}$ 350

B. Section 5: $\dfrac{11}{\text{no. correct}}$ — ¼ ($\dfrac{12^{(3)}}{\text{no. incorrect}}$) = $\dfrac{8}{\text{subtotal B}}$

C. Total unrounded raw score
   (Total A + B) $\dfrac{24}{\text{C}}$

D. Total rounded raw verbal score
   (Rounded to nearest whole number) $\dfrac{24}{\text{D}}$

SAT-Mathematical Sections

A. Section 2: $\dfrac{}{\text{no. correct}}$ — ¼ ($\dfrac{}{\text{no. incorrect}}$) = $\dfrac{}{\text{subtotal A}}$

B. Section 6:
   Questions 1 through 7 and $\dfrac{7}{\text{no. correct}}$ — ¼ ($\dfrac{0}{\text{no. incorrect}}$) = $\dfrac{7}{\text{subtotal B}}$
   28 through 35 (5-choice)

C. Section 6:
   Questions 8 through 27 $\dfrac{11}{\text{no. correct}}$ — ⅓ ($\dfrac{7^{(2.3)}}{\text{no. incorrect}}$) = $\dfrac{8.77}{\text{subtotal C}}$
   (4-choice)

D. Total unrounded raw score
   (Total A + B + C) $\dfrac{}{\text{D}}$

E. Total rounded raw math score
   (Rounded to nearest whole number) $\dfrac{}{\text{E}}$

TSWE

47

A. Section 3: Total $\dfrac{22}{\text{no. correct}}$ — ¼ ($\dfrac{8^{(2)}}{\text{no. incorrect}}$) = $\dfrac{20}{\text{A}}$
   unrounded raw score

B. Total rounded raw TSWE score
   (Rounded to nearest whole number) $\dfrac{20}{\text{B}}$

ANSWERS TO SAMPLE TEST QUESTIONS AND PERCENTAGE OF STUDENTS ANSWERING EACH QUESTION CORRECTLY

Section 1 — Verbal			Section 2 — Mathematical			Section 3 — TSWE			Section 5 — Verbal			Section 6 — Mathematical		
Question number	Correct answer	Percentage of students answering the question correctly	Question number	Correct answer	Percentage of students answering the question correctly	Question number	Correct answer	Percentage of students answering the question correctly	Question number	Correct answer	Percentage of students answering the question correctly	Question number	Correct answer	Percentage of students answering the question correctly
1	A	93%	1	A	91%	1	C	86%	1	C	95%	1	E	93%
2	B	89	2	C	89	2	B	91	2	A	88	2	C	84
3	D	77	3	A	86	3	B	81	3	E	77	3	A	89
4	B	68	4	A	79	4	A	84	4	B	63	4	C	80
5	E	64	5	D	76	5	C	87	5	A	42	5	E	66
6	A	66	6	B	79	6	E	90	6	D	33	6	B	78
7	C	53	7	E	82	7	D	77	7	C	26	7	D	64
8	B	34	8	D	59	8	C	78	8	D	24	8	A	96
9	A	29	9	D	65	9	C	71	9	A	36	9	C	84
10	A	36	10	B	72	10	E	78	10	C	11	10	B	70
11	C	22	11	C	73	11	B	82	11	B	94	11	A	69
12	B	28	12	A	66	12	A	74	12	B	61	12	B	67
13	D	23	13	E	56	13	D	73	13	E	56	13	A	68
14	C	23	14	E	62	14	A	91	14	C	28	14	D	37
15	A	7	15	C	59	15	D	50	15	C	21	15	B	59
16	C	81	16	D	45	16	E	68	16	D	91	16	C	73
17	D	82	17	C	45	17	B	60	17	B	89	17	B	67
18	D	94	18	C	28	18	C	57	18	B	92	18	A	63
19	C	74	19	D	23	19	B	65	19	E	86	19	D	57
20	D	76	20	A	36	20	D	52	20	E	84	20	A	68
21	E	70	21	A	22	21	E	79	21	C	54	21	D	45
22	E	47	22	D	24	22	A	44	22	C	33	22	D	21
23	B	40	23	B	15	23	C	62	23	A	40	23	B	65
24	D	44	24	B	19	24	C	39	24	B	35	24	A	47
25	B	24	25	E	18	25	B	67	25	C	32	25	C	29
26	C	72				26	B	94	26	C	56	26	B	37
27	C	43				27	C	68	27	B	67	27	D	21
28	A	56				28	D	83	28	D	70	28	A	52
29	A	56				29	A	79	29	E	61	29	A	40
30	E	71				30	A	50	30	C	41	30	B	38
31	A	51				31	E	65	31	D	40	31	D	26
32	C	32				32	D	63	32	D	45	32	B	34
33	D	23				33	A	82	33	A	53	33	D	16
34	E	32				34	C	69	34	E	24	34	E	17
35	B	30				35	B	90	35	B	38	35	B	12
36	A	85				36	C	54	36	B	34			
37	E	89				37	D	70	37	C	36			
38	D	79				38	E	40	38	A	31			
39	B	74				39	A	60	39	A	51			
40	C	59				40	D	44	40	C	25			
41	A	53				41	D	76						
42	E	39				42	E	70						
43	A	21				43	D	68						
44	D	10				44	B	59						
45	A	11				45	E	59						
						46	C	53						
						47	D	62						
						48	B	50						
						49	E	46						
						50	A	45						

Notes: The percentages for the SAT-verbal and SAT-mathematical sections are based on the analysis of the answer sheets for a random sample of juniors and seniors who took this test in May 1987 and whose mean scores were 435 on the SAT-verbal sections and 483 on the SAT-mathematical sections.

The percentages for TSWE are based on the analysis of the answer sheets for a random sample of all students who took this test in June 1981 and whose mean score was 43.

SCORE CONVERSION TABLE
Sample SAT and TSWE

| Raw Score | College Board Scaled Score | | Raw Score | College Board Scaled Score | | Raw Score | College Board Scaled Score |
	SAT-Verbal	SAT-Math		SAT-Verbal	SAT-Math		TSWE
85	800		40	460	600		
84	780		39	450	590		
83	760		38	450	580		
82	750		37	440	570		
81	740		36	430	560	50	60+
80	730		35	430	550	49	60+
79	720		34	420	540	48	60+
78	720		33	410	530	47	60+
77	710		32	410	520	46	59
76	700		31	400	510	45	58
75	690		30	390	510	44	57
74	690		29	390	500	43	56
73	680		28	380	490	42	55
72	670		27	370	480	41	54
71	660		26	370	470	40	53
70	660		25	360	460	39	52
69	650		24	350	450	38	51
68	640		23	340	440	37	50
67	630		22	340	430	36	49
66	630		21	330	420	35	48
65	620		20	320	410	34	47
64	610		19	310	400	33	46
63	600		18	300	390	32	45
62	600		17	300	380	31	44
61	590		16	290	370	30	43
60	580	800	15	280	370	29	42
59	580	780	14	270	360	28	41
58	570	760	13	270	350	27	40
57	560	750	12	260	340	26	39
56	560	740	11	250	330	25	38
55	550	730	10	250	320	24	37
54	540	720	9	240	310	23	36
53	540	710	8	230	300	22	35
52	530	700	7	230	300	21	34
51	530	690	6	220	290	20	33
50	520	680	5	220	280	19	32
49	510	670	4	210	270	18	31
48	510	660	3	200	260	17	30
47	500	660	2	200	260	16	29
46	490	650	1	200	250	15	28
45	490	640	0	200	240	14	27
44	480	630	−1	200	230	13	26
43	480	620	−2	200	220	12	25
42	470	610	−3	200	210	11	24
41	460	600	−4 or below	200	200	10	22
						9	21
						8 or below	20

Finding Your College Board Scores

Use the table on page 68 to find the College Board scores that correspond to your raw scores on this edition of the SAT. For example, if you received a raw verbal score of 32 on this edition of the test, your College Board score would be 410. If your raw mathematical score were 22, your College Board score would be 430 for this edition. If your raw TSWE score were 31, your College Board score would be 44 for this edition.

Because some editions of the SAT may be slightly easier or more difficult than others, statistical adjustments are made in the scores to ensure that each College Board score indicates the same level of performance, regardless of the edition of the SAT you take. A given raw score will correspond to different College Board scores, depending on the edition of the test taken. A raw score of 40, for example, may convert to a College Board score of 460 on one edition of the SAT, but might convert to a College Board score of 480 on another edition of the test. When you take the SAT, your score is likely to differ somewhat from the score you obtained on the sample test. People perform at different levels at different times, for reasons unrelated to the test itself. The precision of any test is also limited because it represents only a sample of all the possible questions that could be asked.

Reviewing Your Performance on the Sample Test

After you have scored your sample test by following the directions on page 65 and above, analyze your performance.

Asking yourself these questions and following the suggestions can help:

- Did you omit questions because you ran out of time before you reached the end of a section? Reread pages 12 through 33. The suggestions in them may help you pace yourself better.

- Did you spend so much time reading directions that you took time away from answering questions? If you become thoroughly familiar with the test directions printed in this book, you won't have to spend as much time reading them when you take the actual test.

- Look at the specific questions you missed. Did you get caught by a choice that was only partly correct? Figure out what step you overlooked in your reasoning.

How Difficult Were the Questions?

The table on page 67 gives the percentages of a sample of students who chose the correct answer for each question. (These students obtained a mean SAT-verbal score of 435, mean SAT-mathematical score of 483, and mean TSWE score of 43.) These percentages will give you an idea of how difficult each question was.

For example, 64 percent of this group of students answered question 5 in verbal section 1 correctly. However, only 36 percent selected the correct answer for question 10 in section 1. In other words, question 5 was easier than question 10 for the students who took this edition of the SAT.

After the Test

Receiving Your Score Report

About six weeks after you take the SAT and TSWE, you will receive your College Planning Report, which will include your scores, your percentile ranks, and interpretive information. With this report, you'll receive a booklet, *Using Your College Planning Report*, which provides advice on how to use your scores and other information to help you with your college planning.

SAT Question-and-Answer Service

If you take the SAT on one of the dates for which the SAT Question-and-Answer Service is available, you may order the service when you register for the test or anytime up to five months after the test. You will receive a copy of your test questions and answer sheet, a list of the correct answers, and scoring instructions. See the *Registration Bulletin* or *Using Your College Planning Report* for additional information on how to order. (This service does not apply to the TSWE.)

A Sample Score Report

A sample score report for a fictional student is provided on pages 72-73. The report has six major parts:

1. Identification Information
   This is the information that will be used to identify your record, which is stored at Educational Testing Service. If you have any questions about your report, call or write to the College Board's Admissions Testing Program at the address given on page 5.

2. Test Scores
   The next section shows your most recent test scores. SAT scores are shown both as specific numbers and as score ranges to help illustrate that the test cannot measure your abilities with perfect accuracy (see "How Precise Are Your Scores?" below).

3. Summary of Test Scores
   This section summarizes your test scores and includes all of your scores from any Admissions Testing Pro-gram tests (SAT or Achievement Tests) that you have taken at any time while in high school.

4. Educational Background
   This information comes from the Student Descriptive Questionnaire (SDQ), which you fill out when you register to take the test. It describes your high school course work, summarizes your grades, and gives your grade point average and class rank.

5. Plans for College
   This section includes information about your plans for future study that you reported in the Student Descriptive Questionnaire.

6. Colleges and Scholarship Programs That Received a Score Report
   This information about the institutions to which you have your scores sent includes addresses, telephone numbers, application and financial aid deadlines, and the basis for admissions decisions.

SAT and TSWE Scores

SAT scores are reported on a scale of 200 to 800. You receive separate scores for the verbal and math sections of the SAT. SAT-verbal subscores (reading comprehension and vocabulary) are on a scale of 20 to 80. TSWE scores are reported from 20 to 60 +. The tests have no passing or failing scores, and they are not scored on a curve—that is, the scores of other students who took the test with you had no effect on your score.

What Do Your Percentile Ranks Mean?

The percentile ranks on your score report allow you to compare your scores with those of other students. A percentile rank tells you the percentage of students in a given group whose scores were below yours. Remember that the same score can have a different percentile rank for different groups, depending on the ability of the group. (For example, a runner whose time ranks in the 80th percentile when compared with the junior varsity track team might rank in the 50th percentile when compared with the varsity team, which usually has faster runners.)

Percentile ranks on your score report compare your scores with those of "College-bound Seniors/National": all seniors who took the test any time while in high school, and with "College-bound Seniors/State": all seniors in your state who took the test any time while in high school.

How Precise Are Your Scores?

When you consider your scores, keep in mind that no test can measure your abilities with perfect accuracy. If you took a different edition of a test or the same edition on different days, your score probably would be different each time. If you were to take a test an infinite number of times, your scores would tend to cluster about an average value. Testing specialists call this average your "true score," the score you would get if a test could measure your ability with perfect accuracy. To measure how much students' obtained scores vary from their true scores, an index called the standard error of measurement (SEM) is used.

For the SAT, the SEM is about 30 points. About two-thirds of those taking the test score within 30 points (or one SEM) of their true score. If your true score is 430, for example, the chances are about 2 out of 3 that you will score between 400 and 460 (430 plus or minus 30).

You should think of your scores in terms of score ranges rather than precise measurements—a 400 SAT score, for example, should be thought of as being in the 370 to 430 range. This will help you realize that a small difference between your score and another student's on the same test does not indicate any real difference in ability. College admissions officers also are advised to look at scores this way.

Will Your Scores Go Up if You Take the Test Again?

As indicated above, you are not likely to get exactly the same score on a test twice. Improving your score a great deal also is unlikely. Some students who repeat tests do improve their scores, but, on the average, these increases are small.

The *average* increase for a junior who takes the SAT again when a senior is about 15-20 points for the verbal score and 15-20 points for the math score. About two out of three students who retake the test improve their scores, but the scores of about one student in three go down. About one student in 20 gains 100 or more points, and about one in 100 loses 100 or more points. Students whose first SAT scores are low are more likely to achieve score gains. Students whose initial scores are high are less likely to achieve score gains.

If you repeat a test, your earlier scores will still appear on your score report. Colleges evaluate multiple scores on the same test in different ways. Some look at all the scores on your report; others use just the highest, most recent, or an average.

Who Receives Your Scores?

A score report will be sent to your high school if you provide your high school code number when you register for the test. Reports also will be sent to all colleges and scholarship programs whose code numbers you give.

The College Board may use your scores and descriptive information for research, but no information that can be identified with you is ever released without your consent.

How Do Colleges Use Your Score Report?

Your SAT scores give college admissions officers an idea of how well you have developed some of the abilities you will need to do well in college courses. The scores also help them to compare you with students from schools with different grading standards. Admissions people know that although your high school grades are the best *single* indicator of your readiness to do college work, a combination of your high school grades and your SAT scores provides a better indicator than either one alone.

Some colleges also use Achievement Tests in making admissions decisions or for course placement, or both. The TSWE is a placement test designed to identify students who may need help in developing their writing skills. Your college may use it to help place you in the freshman English course that is right for you.

Colleges vary in the way they use test scores, but few, if any, make admissions decisions based on scores alone. Therefore, low or high scores should neither discourage you nor make you overconfident. Admissions officers usually consider the descriptive information on your score report as well as other information sent by you and your school.

Different colleges value different qualities in applicants: One college may be looking for leadership potential, while another may place more weight on various extracurricular activities. Some colleges have open admissions policies and admit almost all applicants. Some will admit students who have particular qualities, even if the students' grades and scores indicate they will have to make an extra effort. Whatever your scores, remember that probably there are many colleges that could meet your needs and where you would be happy.

ADMISSIONS TESTING PROGRAM
The College Board

COLLEGE PLANNING REPORT

SCORE REPORT FOR **MARGARET   K WRIGHT**   **60600**

1

Sex	Birth Date	Social Security No.	Telephone No.	Registration No.	Ethnic Group	U.S. Citizen	Report Date
F	3/15/70	123-45-6789	111-222-3333	7654321	White	Yes	12/15/87

High School Name and Code	First Language	Religion
JEFFERSON MEMORIAL HIGH SCHOOL 555555	English only	Lutheran Church in America

2

TEST SCORES		NOVEMBER 1987 SCHOLASTIC APTITUDE TEST	Percentiles	

Test	Score	Score Range	College-bound Seniors	
		200 300 400 500 600 700 800	National	State
SAT V	480	<<<>>>	66	54
SAT M	500	<<<<>>>>	58	43
TSWE	49		66	53

See the reverse side of this report for more information about these scores.

3

SUMMARY OF TEST SCORES							Achievement Tests				
Test Date	Grade Level	SAT Verbal	SAT Verbal Subscores		SAT Math	TSWE	Test Date	Grade Level	1	2	3
			Reading	Vocabulary							
Nov 87	12th	480	45	49	500	49	Jun 87	11th	EN 450	BY 500	M1 550
May 87	11th	460	44	47	480	46					

4

EDUCATIONAL BACKGROUND   (REPORTED ON STUDENT DESCRIPTIVE QUESTIONNAIRE 11/87)

Courses	Years	Honors	Average Grade	Coursework and Experience
ARTS AND MUSIC	4	Yes	A	Acting/Play Production,Dance,Drama App, Perform Music,Photography/Film,Studio Art
ENGLISH	4	Yes	B	Amer Lit,Comp,Grammar,Other Lit, Speaking/Listening
FOREIGN LANGUAGES	2		B	French
MATHEMATICS	4+	Yes	A	Algebra,Geometry,Trigonometry,Calculus, Computer Math
NATURAL SCIENCES	2		B	Biology,Chemistry
SOCIAL SCIENCES	4		A	U.S. Hist,U.S. Govt,European Hist,World Hist, Other
COMPUTER EXPERIENCE				Programming,Math,Word Processing

Grade Point Average	**A-**	Class Rank	**Second tenth**

5

PLANS FOR COLLEGE   (REPORTED ON STUDENT DESCRIPTIVE QUESTIONNAIRE 11/87)

Degree Goal	First Choice of Major	Certainty of First Choice
Bachelor's	**Arts: Visual and Performing**	**Very certain**

Other Majors Listed	Requested Services
Dramatic arts Art (painting, drawing, sculpture) Engineering/Engineering Technologies	Educational planning Part-time job

Preferred College Characteristics	College Programs and Activities
Type: 4 yr,Public,Private Size: Up to 1,000,10,000 to 20,000, Over 20,000 Setting: Large city,Suburban Distance from home: Undecided Other: Coed,On-campus housing	Art Dance Drama/Theater

Advanced Placement or Exemption Plans
Art,Math

72

A score report has been sent to the colleges and scholarship programs listed below. The information about the colleges is from *The College Handbook*. For more information about these and other schools, consult the *Handbook* or other materials available in your high school or library and talk with your counselor. Contact the colleges for application materials and additional information.

If you want to have your scores sent to other colleges and scholarship programs, complete an Additional Report Request Form. You received one of these forms with your Admission Ticket. Your high school counselor has additional forms.

1234
City College of Art
3030 West Street
Hill, California 90512
(213) 123-4567

BASIS FOR ADMISSION DECISION: School achievement record is very important. Interview, school and community activities and recommendations are considered.

ADMISSION APPLICATION DEADLINE: Closing date is August 27. Notification is on a continuous rolling basis.

FINANCIAL AID APPLICATION DEADLINE: No closing date; priority date is March 1. Notification is on a rolling basis starting on April 1.

1489
State University
89 Central Street
Center City, Texas 34567
(901) 678-9534

BASIS FOR ADMISSION DECISION: School achievement record, test scores and recommendations are important. Interview and school community activities are considered.

ADMISSION APPLICATION DEADLINE: Closing date is August 1. Applications received by April 1 are given priority. Notification is on a continual rolling basis.

FINANCIAL AID APPLICATION DEADLINE: Closing date is April 1. Notification is on a rolling basis beginning January 30.

7632
St. Michael's College
110 Hilford Street
Bankster, Ohio 06010
(101) 987-6734

BASIS FOR ADMISSION DECISION: School achievement record and test scores are very important. School and community activities and recommendations are important. Interview is considered. Achievement Tests are required of all applicants.

ADMISSION APPLICATION DEADLINE: Closing date is February 1. Notification begins on or about April 15.

FINANCIAL AID APPLICATION DEADLINE: Closing date is February 1. Notification date is April 1.

1920
Alma Mater
645 Southwest Street
Deerfield, New York 10310
(904) 272-6243

BASIS FOR ADMISSION DECISION: School achievement record and test scores are very important. School and community activities and recommendations are important. Interview and school community activities are considered.

ADMISSION APPLICATION DEADLINE: Closing date is January 15. Notification date is April 15.

FINANCIAL AID APPLICATION DEADLINE: Closing date is April 1. Notification date is April 10.

MARGARET   K WRIGHT
1234 TIGERLILY LANE
CHICAGO   IL 60600

TEST 2—FORM CODE 0Y

SECTION 1 Time—30 minutes 45 Questions

For each question in this section, choose the best answer and fill in the corresponding oval on the answer sheet.

Each question below consists of a word in capital letters, followed by five lettered words or phrases. Choose the word or phrase that is most nearly opposite in meaning to the word in capital letters. Since some of the questions require you to distinguish fine shades of meaning, consider all the choices before deciding which is best.

Example:

GOOD: (A) sour (B) bad (C) red
(D) hot (E) ugly

(A) ● (C) (D) (E)

1. PREMATURE: (A) presentable (B) robust
   (C) old (D) common (E) overdue

2. INTENSIFY: (A) weaken (B) darken
   (C) implant (D) appease (E) complicate

3. LUSCIOUS: (A) tiny (B) gloomy
   (C) unfamiliar (D) unpleasant to the taste
   (E) difficult to understand

4. DISCRIMINATING: (A) uncritical
   (B) infallible (C) inconsiderate
   (D) disrespectful (E) immoderate

5. OMISSION: (A) revival (B) decision
   (C) revision (D) inclusion (E) reversal

6. RATIFY: (A) accuse (B) doubt
   (C) reject (D) precede (E) transgress

7. DEMOTE: (A) attack (B) accuse
   (C) advance (D) invest (E) reveal

8. INERTIA: (A) disposition to action
   (B) sensitivity to pain (C) availability of funds
   (D) obstruction of justice (E) application of logic

9. STUPEFY: (A) purify (B) excite
   (C) reward (D) disown (E) endanger

10. GRATE: (A) grow (B) stretch
    (C) eliminate (D) repress (E) soothe

11. PERIPHERY: (A) flaw (B) core
    (C) noise (D) rapidity (E) shadow

12. GUILE: (A) candor (B) maturity
    (C) politeness (D) boredom (E) poise

13. CAPITULATE: (A) deprive (B) resist
    (C) entitle (D) concur (E) suspend

14. INDIGENOUS: (A) abundant (B) urban
    (C) vulgar (D) alien (E) effective

15. SURREPTITIOUSLY: (A) haphazardly
    (B) dispassionately (C) zealously
    (D) in an open manner (E) with reservations

Each sentence below has one or two blanks, each blank indicating that something has been omitted. Beneath the sentence are five lettered words or sets of words. Choose the word or set of words that, when inserted in the sentence, best fits the meaning of the sentence as a whole.

Example:

Although its publicity has been ----, the film itself is intelligent, well-acted, handsomely produced, and altogether ----.

(A) tasteless. .respectable (B) extensive. .moderate
(C) sophisticated. .amateur (D) risqué. .crude
(E) perfect. .spectacular

● (B) (C) (D) (E)

16. While a computer cannot ---- an instructor, it can take over many --- tasks, thus allowing the instructor to spend more time helping individual students.

    (A) obstruct. .arguable (B) contradict. .related
    (C) recommend. .creative (D) assist. .serious
    (E) replace. .routine

17. She was not really ----; it was just that she enjoyed ---- and withdrew from time to time to reflect on her life.

    (A) a recluse. .company (B) a scholar. .success
    (C) an introvert. .solitude (D) a reformer. .helping
    (E) a spectator. .entertainment

18. The viola has never commanded the popular appeal of the piano, and yet contemporary composers are ---- to write for such an outstanding violist as Karen Phillips.

    (A) afraid (B) unfit (C) eager
    (D) averse (E) powerless

19. The very ---- of sand in the area made it so ---- that even geologists did not stop to ask how it came to occupy its place in the landscape.

    (A) abundance. .familiar
    (B) appearance. .unusual
    (C) structure. .complex
    (D) composition. .unnatural
    (E) abrasiveness. .minute

20. When proposing long-range goals for science, Symes becomes uncharacteristically ----, a failure he shares with many who are more ---- as critics of existing undertakings than as visionaries of the future.

    (A) subtle. .devious (B) abstract. .appreciative
    (C) astute. .perceptive (D) explicit. .articulate
    (E) ambiguous. .lucid

GO ON TO THE NEXT PAGE

77

Each passage below is followed by questions based on its content. Answer the questions following each passage on the basis of what is stated or implied in that passage.

The voyagers scanned the shore.

On the distant dunes were set many little black cottages, and a tall white windmill reared above them. No man, nor dog, nor bicycle appeared on the beach. The cottages might have formed a deserted village.

A conference was held in the boat. "Well," said the captain, "if no help is coming, we might better try a run through the surf right away. If we stay out here much longer we will be too weak to do anything for ourselves at all." The others silently acquiesced in this reasoning. The boat was headed for the beach. The explorer wondered if people ever ascended the tall wind tower, and if then they ever looked seaward. This tower was a giant, standing with its back to the plight of the ants. It represented to a degree, to the explorer, the serenity of nature amid the struggles of the individual. Nature did not seem cruel to him then, nor beneficent, nor treacherous, nor wise. But she was indifferent, flatly indifferent. It is, perhaps, plausible that a man in this situation, impressed with the unconcern of the universe, should see the innumerable flaws of his life, and have them taste wickedly in his mind and wish for another chance. A distinction between right and wrong seems absurdly clear to him then, in his proximity to the grave edge, and he understands that if he were given another opportunity he would mend his conduct and his words, and be better and brighter during an introduction or at a tea.

"Now, boys," said the captain, "she is going to swamp, sure. All we can do is work her in as far as possible, and then when she swamps, pile out and scramble for the beach. Keep cool now, and don't jump until she swamps sure."

The stoker took the oars. "Captain," he said, "I think I'd better bring her about, and keep her head-on to the seas and back her in."

"All right, Willie," said the captain. "Back her in."

The monstrous inshore rollers heaved the boat high until the men were again enabled to see the white sheets of water scudding up the slanted beach. "We won't get in very close," said the captain. Each time a man could wrest his attention from the rollers, he turned his glance toward the shore, and in the expression of the eyes during this contemplation there was a singular quality. The explorer, observing the others, knew that they were not afraid, but the full meaning of their glances was shrouded.

21. The decision to try immediately for the land was made because the

(A) weather was worsening
(B) men were becoming increasingly fatigued
(C) men were becoming increasingly frightened
(D) boat would not last much longer
(E) men knew that the village was deserted

22. It was decided that the boat would ride best if it were

(A) parallel to the wave crests
(B) adjacent to the coral reef
(C) pointed into the wind
(D) pointed away from shore
(E) pointed into shore

23. The explorer in the passage shows himself to be

(A) more concerned with practical matters than the stoker
(B) resourceful in an emergency situation
(C) optimistic about his chances for survival
(D) frightened to the point of being helpless
(E) detached and pensive during the event related

24. In relation to the rest of the men, the captain is

(A) aloof and cynical
(B) worried and irritable
(C) modest and solicitous
(D) confused but jovial
(E) authoritative but informal

25. Which of the following contrasts represents an underlying theme in the passage?

(A) Action and contemplation
(B) Love and hate
(C) Skill and ineptitude
(D) Faithfulness and betrayal
(E) Loneliness and popularity

GO ON TO THE NEXT PAGE ▷

The classic difficulty felt with democracy arises from the fact that democracy can never express the will of the whole people because there never exists any such monolithic will (at least in any society that can call itself democratic). The concept of government of the whole people by the whole people must be looked on as being in the poetry rather than in the prose of democracy; the fact of prose is that real democracy means government by some kind of dominant majority.

And the ever-present danger, repeatedly realized in fact, is that this dominant majority may behave toward those who are not of the majority in such a manner as to undercut the moral basis of democracy itself—respect for human beings, for the right of people, because they are people, to have some important say in the setting of their own course and in the use of their own faculties. Other forms of government may similarly fail to respect human independence. But there is at least no contradiction in that; the underlying assumption of every kind of government by wisers and betters is that people on the whole are not fit to manage their own affairs, but must have someone else do it for them, and there is no paradox when such a government treats its subjects without respect, or deals with them on the basis of their having no rights that the government must take into account. But democracy affirms that people are fit to control themselves, and it cannot live in the same air with the theory that there is no limit to the extent to which public power—even the power of a majority—can interfere with the lives of people.

Rational limitation on power is therefore not a contradiction to democracy, but is of the very essence of democracy as such. Other sorts of government may impose such limitations on themselves as an act of grace, of noblesse oblige. Democracy is under the moral duty of limiting itself because such limitation is essential to the survival of that respect for humankind which is in the foundations of democracy. Respect for the freedom of all people cannot, of course, be the only guide, for there would then be no government. Delicate ongoing compromise is what must be looked for. But democracy, unless it is to deny its own moral basis, must accept the necessity for making this compromise and for giving real weight to the claims of those without the presently effective political power to make their claims prevail in elections.

26. By "the prose of democracy" (line 8) the author apparently means its
(A) theory (B) duties (C) compromises (D) actual operation (E) rational limitations

27. With respect to the failure of nondemocratic governments to respect human independence, the author says that this failure
(A) limits the political power of such governments
(B) is consistent with the basic premises of such governments
(C) interferes with the rights of the minority under such governments
(D) hampers the achievement of the ultimate objectives of such governments
(E) leads to consequences that cannot be anticipated by such governments

28. The respect for human liberty which the author advocates would, in its extreme form, lead to
(A) anarchy (B) tyranny (C) compromise (D) peace (E) nonconformity

29. According to the passage, which of the following does the author consider essential for the preservation of the moral basis of democracy?
I. Limitations on the power of the government
II. Consideration of the rights of the minority
III. Development of the abilities of the people
(A) I only (B) II only (C) I and II only (D) II and III only (E) I, II, and III

30. According to the passage, unlike other types of government, democratic governments believe that the
(A) minority must merge with the majority for effective government
(B) government must determine the course of its citizens' lives
(C) government cannot express the will of all the people
(D) individual is capable of directing his own affairs
(E) individual is subordinate to the state

GO ON TO THE NEXT PAGE

1

Select the word or set of words that best completes each of the following sentences.

31. A stone helmsman at the waterfront ---- the crew of a trawler that capsized in winter waters, the sailors helpless to clear masts ---- ice.

    (A) exonerates. .disguised by
    (B) chastises. .preserved with
    (C) isolates. .wasted by
    (D) commemorates. .encrusted with
    (E) immortalizes. .immune to

32. This is an essay invested with a mood of ----, even of bliss, without a single ---- note of repentance.

    (A) solemnity. .wistful   (B) remorse. .jarring
    (C) delight. .jubilant   (D) serenity. .discordant
    (E) apprehension. .melancholy

33. Modern scientists hold that truth is not something that we first ---- and then ---- in all its ramifications, but something found at the end of long investigations.

    (A) postulate. .explore   (B) prove. .discover
    (C) identify. .discredit   (D) predict. .attack
    (E) reveal. .impose

34. American courts have changed little in form over the years, but the role they perform has been far from ----.

    (A) simple   (B) static   (C) radical
    (D) dynamic   (E) unimportant

35. For all his familiarity with the peoples of every continent, Landers was the most ---- of historians; he looked out upon the whole world, but he looked through British spectacles.

    (A) shortsighted   (B) broad-minded
    (C) conservative   (D) parochial
    (E) introspective

Each question below consists of a related pair of words or phrases, followed by five lettered pairs of words or phrases. Select the lettered pair that best expresses a relationship similar to that expressed in the original pair.

Example:

    YAWN : BOREDOM ::   (A) dream : sleep
    (B) anger : madness   (C) smile : amusement
    (D) face : expression   (E) impatience : rebellion

    Ⓐ Ⓑ ● Ⓓ Ⓔ

36. EAT : GOBBLE ::   (A) read : summarize
    (B) hiss : giggle   (C) drink : guzzle
    (D) dance : leap   (E) bend : somersault

37. SCULPTOR : CHISEL ::   (A) potter : wheel
    (B) photographer : studio   (C) printer : mint
    (D) model : portrait   (E) engraver : design

38. VACCINATION : DISEASE ::
    (A) refrigeration : spoilage   (B) laceration : bruise
    (C) filtration : leakage   (D) dehydration : storage
    (E) pasteurization : health

39. RAMBLE : AIMLESSLY ::   (A) beckon : vocally
    (B) sprint : daintily   (C) totter : unsteadily
    (D) lunge : secretly   (E) doze : horizontally

40. MINISTER : CLERGY ::
    (A) philosopher : ethics   (B) layman : priesthood
    (C) principal : administration   (D) lawyer : jury
    (E) student : curriculum

41. STUBBLE : WHEATFIELD ::   (A) crops : furrow
    (B) cattle : meadow   (C) stumps : grove
    (D) footprints : trail   (E) bouquet : garden

42. RIDDLED : HOLES ::   (A) blighted : plants
    (B) wrinkled : creases   (C) erased : errors
    (D) patched : rips   (E) sheltered : enemies

43. BABBLE : MEANING ::   (A) argue : vehemence
    (B) shout : volume   (C) grumble : complaint
    (D) stammer : hesitation   (E) drone : emotion

44. PECCADILLO : CRIME ::   (A) speck : stain
    (B) chance : destiny   (C) larceny : perjury
    (D) asset : liability   (E) limerick : prose

45. OPAQUE : LIGHT ::   (A) speculative : reasoning
    (B) courageous : defeat   (C) intuitive : learning
    (D) inviolable : harm   (E) fanatical : spirit

IF YOU FINISH BEFORE TIME IS CALLED, YOU MAY CHECK YOUR WORK ON THIS SECTION ONLY. DO NOT TURN TO ANY OTHER SECTION IN THE TEST. **STOP**

80

SECTION **2** Time—30 minutes
25 Questions

In this section solve each problem, using any available space on the page for scratchwork. Then decide which is the best of the choices given and fill in the corresponding oval on the answer sheet.

The following information is for your reference in solving some of the problems.

Circle of radius r: Area = πr^2; Circumference = $2\pi r$
    The number of degrees of arc in a circle is 360.
The measure in degrees of a straight angle is 180.

Definition of symbols:
= is equal to $\leq$ is less than or equal to
$\neq$ is unequal to $\geq$ is greater than or equal to
< is less than $\parallel$ is parallel to
> is greater than $\perp$ is perpendicular to

Triangle: The sum of the measures in degrees of the angles of a triangle is 180.

If $\angle CDA$ is a right angle, then

(1) area of $\triangle ABC = \dfrac{AB \times CD}{2}$

(2) $AC^2 = AD^2 + DC^2$

Note: Figures that accompany problems in this test are intended to provide information useful in solving the problems. They are drawn as accurately as possible EXCEPT when it is stated in a specific problem that its figure is not drawn to scale. All figures lie in a plane unless otherwise indicated. All numbers used are real numbers.

1. Which of the following is equal to an odd number?

    (A) 8 X 7
    (B) 43 + 29
    (C) 37 – 13
    (D) 35 ÷ 5
    (E) 2^3

2. $\dfrac{x + y}{4} + \dfrac{z}{4} =$

    (A) $x + y + z$

    (B) $\dfrac{x + y + z}{2}$

    (C) $\dfrac{x + y + z}{4}$

    (D) $\dfrac{x + y + z}{8}$

    (E) $\dfrac{x + y + z}{16}$

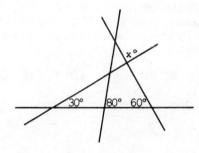

3. In the figure above, x =

    (A) 40   (B) 50   (C) 60   (D) 90   (E) 130

4. In a certain list of numbers, every odd-numbered term (beginning with the first) is $\dfrac{1}{2}$, and every even-numbered term (beginning with the second) is $-\dfrac{1}{2}$. What is the sum of the first 10 terms in this list?

    (A) –5   (B) $-\dfrac{1}{2}$ (C) 0   (D) $\dfrac{1}{2}$ (E) 5

GO ON TO THE NEXT PAGE

5. How many more boxes would be needed to package 1,200 magazines in boxes of 10 than in boxes of 12 ?

  (A) 2
  (B) 10
  (C) 20
  (D) 100
  (E) 200

6. If $\frac{4}{3} = \frac{12}{x}$, then x =

  (A) 1   (B) 9   (C) 11   (D) 12   (E) 16

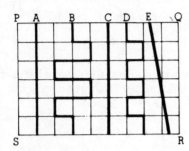

7. In the figure above, rectangle PQRS is divided into 54 squares of equal area. Which darkened path divides PQRS into two parts whose areas are in the ratio 1 to 2 ?

  (A) A   (B) B   (C) C   (D) D   (E) E

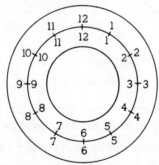

8. The outer dial in the figure above is to be turned clockwise four division marks, while the inner dial remains stationary. If each pair of adjacent numbers, one from the outer and one from the inner dial, is then added, what is the greatest such sum obtained?

  (A) 32   (B) 28   (C) 24   (D) 20   (E) 16

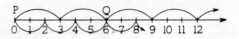

9. In the figure above, arcs are drawn above the number line every 3 units and below the number line every 2 units. If the arcs meet at P and at Q, at which of the following points on the number line will the arcs also meet?

  (A) 252
  (B) 253
  (C) 254
  (D) 255
  (E) 256

10. If $3x = \sqrt{25} - \sqrt{16}$, then x =

  (A) 9   (B) 3   (C) 1   (D) $\frac{1}{3}$ (E) $\frac{1}{9}$

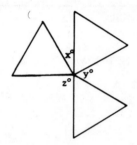

11. In the figure above, if the **three** equilateral triangles have a common vertex, then x + y + z =

  (A) 90   (B) 120   (C) 180   (D) 360

  (E) It cannot be determined from the information given.

GO ON TO THE NEXT PAGE

Student	First Test Score	Second Test Score
Amy	25	50
Biff	30	90
Chip	42	84
Dora	50	75

12. In the table above, which two students had the same per-cent of improvement in scores from the first to the second test?

(A) Biff and Chip
(B) Biff and Dora
(C) Amy and Dora
(D) Amy and Biff
(E) Amy and Chip

13. Which of the following figures could be folded along the dotted lines to form a closed rectangular box with no overlap?

(A)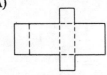
(B)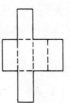

(C)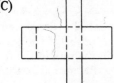
(D)

(E)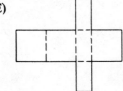

14. If $(5^3)(2^5) = 4(10^k)$, then $k =$

(A) 2
(B) 3
(C) 4
(D) 6
(E) 8

15. If x is subtracted from y and this difference is divided by the sum of x and y, the result is

(A) $\frac{y-x}{x+y}$ (B) $\frac{x-y}{x+y}$ (C) -1 (D) 1 (E) 0

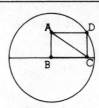

16. In the figure above, B is the center of the circle with radius r and ABCD is a rectangle. The length of diagonal AC is

(A) $\frac{r\sqrt{2}}{2}$

(B) $\frac{r\sqrt{3}}{2}$

(C) r

(D) $r\sqrt{2}$

(E) $r\sqrt{3}$

17. A number is given whose tens digit is t and whose units digit is u. If the digit 3 is placed between these two digits, the value of the new number is

(A) $t + u + 3$
(B) $10t + 30 + u$
(C) $10t + u + 3$
(D) $100t + 10u + 3$
(E) $100t + 30 + u$

18. The product of 3, 4, and y is equal to the sum of 4y and

(A) 3
(B) 8
(C) 12
(D) 3y
(E) 8y

GO ON TO THE NEXT PAGE

19. Some beads are arranged on a string as shown above. Starting with the bead at the arrow, how many beads must be moved from left to right in order for the fraction of beads on the left that are black to equal the fraction of beads on the right that are white?

   (A) None
   (B) One
   (C) Two
   (D) Three
   (E) Four

20. What is the least number of distinct lines in a plane that can be drawn so that the total number of points of intersection is 6 ?

   (A) 3   (B) 4   (C) 5   (D) 6   (E) 12

21. The cost C, in dollars, of producing X units of a product is given by the formula C = kX + b, where k and b are constants. If the cost of producing 100 units is $1,500 and the cost of producing 250 units is $2,250, then k =

   (A) 15
   (B) 12
   (C) 9
   (D) 7
   (E) 5

22. If $1 \leqq n < m \leqq 9$ and n and m are integers, what is the least possible value of $\dfrac{n+m}{nm}$?

   (A) $\dfrac{18}{81}$

   (B) $\dfrac{17}{72}$

   (C) $\dfrac{7}{10}$

   (D) $\dfrac{5}{6}$

   (E) $\dfrac{3}{2}$

EXPENDITURES IN FACTORY X FOR
RAW MATERIALS IN 1977

Material	Per Cent
Paper	28
Wood	32
Metal	40

23. In the table above, if the total amount spent on wood and paper by Factory X in 1977 was $277,200, how much was spent on paper?

   (A) $77,616
   (B) $129,360
   (C) $147,840
   (D) $184,800
   (E) It cannot be determined from the information given.

24. If a right triangle has two sides of lengths 1 and $\sqrt{2}$, which of the following could be the length of the third side?

   I.   1
   II. $\sqrt{2}$
   III. $\sqrt{3}$

   (A) I only   (B) II only   (C) III only

   (D) I and II only   (E) I and III only

25. Each face of a cube is marked with a different integer from 11 to 16 inclusive. If two such identical cubes are rolled, the sum of the faces up could be how many different numbers?

   (A) 11
   (B) 12
   (C) 18
   (D) 32
   (E) 34

IF YOU FINISH BEFORE TIME IS CALLED, YOU MAY CHECK YOUR WORK ON THIS SECTION ONLY. DO NOT TURN TO ANY OTHER SECTION IN THE TEST.   **STOP**

<table>
</table>

SECTION 4	Time—30 minutes 40 Questions	For each question in this section, choose the best answer and fill in the corresponding oval on the answer sheet.

Each question below consists of a word in capital letters, followed by five lettered words or phrases. Choose the word or phrase that is most nearly opposite in meaning to the word in capital letters. Since some of the questions require you to distinguish fine shades of meaning, consider all the choices before deciding which is best.

Example:

GOOD: (A) sour (B) bad (C) red (D) hot (E) ugly

Ⓐ ● Ⓒ Ⓓ Ⓔ

1. M___ ___E: (A) fade away
(B) ___ ___ (C) move quickly
(D) ch___ (E) defy description

2. POTENT: (A___ ___ B) determined
(C) tentative (___ (E) ineffectual

3. HEED:
(A) tamper with (B) sha___ ___ibility
(C) fall short of (D) pay n___ ___on to
(E) bear no resemblance to

4. DRAWL: (A) lift forcibly
(B) tilt dangerously (C) speak rapidly
(D) wave frantically (E) bypass deliberately

5. INCIDENTAL: (A) fundamental
(B) flagrant (C) unfounded
(D) unbiased (E) accomplished

6. SLUGGARD:
(A) fickle lover (B) impartial judge
(C) intelligent answer (D) energetic person
(E) immaculate attire

7. GERMINAL: (A) continually changing
(B) urgently requested (C) diligently studied
(D) actively pursued (E) fully developed

8. CAPRICIOUS: (A) quaint (B) stable
(C) effortless (D) formless (E) proud

9. JADED: (A) grim (B) mild
(C) even (D) fresh (E) formal

10. SALUBRIOUS: (A) cryptic (B) worldly
(C) pious (D) poisonous (E) intoxicating

Each sentence below has one or two blanks, each blank indicating that something has been omitted. Beneath the sentence are five lettered words or sets of words. Choose the word or set of words that, when inserted in the sentence, best fits the meaning of the sentence as a whole.

Example:

Although its publicity has been ----, the film itself is intelligent, well-acted, handsomely produced, and altogether ----.

(A) tasteless. .respectable (B) extensive. .moderate
(C) sophisticated. .amateur (D) risqué. .crude
(E) perfect. .spectacular

● Ⓑ Ⓒ Ⓓ Ⓔ

11. The loss of weight in fad dieting is invariably ----; weight returns as soon as one resumes --- eating habits.
(A) temporary. .normal (B) slight. .new
(C) injurious. .peculiar (D) slow. .regular
(E) costly. .expensive

12. Garrison was austere and ----, a man of immense reserve and dignity.
(A) lax (B) rowdy (C) aloof
(D) droll (E) abusive

13. There are so many ---- limitations to our ability to control the sun's bounty that using solar energy begins to seem hopelessly impractical.
(A) immutable (B) inconsequential
(___) irrelevant (D) innocuous (E) illusory

14. Rustin___ ___triolic attack was the climax of the ---- heaped on ___ ___ntings that today seem amazingly ----.
(A) criticism. .unp___ ___lar
(B) ridicule. .inoffens___
(C) praise. .amateurish
(D) indifference. .scandalous
(E) acclaim. .creditable

15. Although Ms. Martin's appraisal of the c___ council's work is the most perceptive I hav___ seen, it nonetheless contains some ---- features.
(A) candid (B) absorbing (C) dubious
(D) discerning (E) tangible

GO ON TO THE NEXT PAGE →

4

Each question below consists of a related pair of words or phrases, followed by five lettered pairs of words or phrases. Select the lettered pair that best expresses a relationship similar to that expressed in the original pair.

Example:

YAWN : BOREDOM ::   (A) dream : sleep
(B) anger : madness   (C) smile : amusement
(D) face : expression   (E) impatience : rebellion

Ⓐ Ⓑ ● Ⓓ Ⓔ

16. BOARDS : NAIL ::   (A) girders : rivet
(B) papers : pile   (C) stitches : thread
(D) whiskers : razor   (E) wheels : axle

17. SUITCASE : LUGGAGE ::   (A) basket : barrel
(B) chair : furniture   (C) passenger : vehicle
(D) vault : money   (E) menu : food

18. APPREHENSIVE : TERRIFIED ::
(A) somber : mellow   (B) stubborn : loyal
(C) emotional : hysterical   (D) sincere : popular
(E) affectionate : hostile

19. REMAIN : DEPART ::   (A) divide : add
(B) reform : continue   (C) sit : stand
(D) walk : run   (E) stagnate : flow

20. CLIENTELE : CUSTOMERS ::
(A) inventory : clerks
(B) repertoire : actors
(C) personnel : employees
(D) audience : participants
(E) protocol : diplomats

21. SONNET : POEM ::   (A) essay : fiction
(B) meter : rhyme   (C) proverb : myth
(D) carol : song   (E) stanza : ode

22. IMPROMPTU : REHEARSAL ::
(A) tragic : exertion
(B) dramatic : performance
(C) alone : accompaniment
(D) habitual : convenience
(E) controversial : debate

23. PILGRIMAGE : DEVOTION ::
(A) excursion : recreation
(B) crusade : ritual
(C) trek : business
(D) cruise : destination
(E) voyage : residence

24. CALDRON : SAUCEPAN ::   (A) harp : piano
(B) tome : pamphlet   (C) seed : blossom
(D) pillar : portal   (E) bust : pedestal

25. LYNCH : EXECUTE ::   (A) deface : destroy
(B) steal : impound   (C) abstain : vote
(D) subpoena : arrest   (E) incite : instigate

GO ON TO THE NEXT PAGE →

Each passage below is followed by questions based on its content. Answer the questions following each passage on the basis of what is stated or implied in that passage.

There is a heavy concentration of the poor in non-metropolitan areas and their poverty is severe. Over 12 million people living outside metropolitan centers were below the officially defined poverty level in 1968. Nearly one out of five nonmetropolitan residents were poor compared with about one in ten among metropolitan residents, despite the fact that the numbers of poor were about the same in each of the areas. The greater severity of poverty for the nonmetropolitan poor is reflected by their incomes. The metropolitan poor averaged $538 per family member in 1968 compared to $497 for the nonmetropolitan poor.

Services of many kinds are less often available to both the poor and the nonpoor in nonmetropolitan areas than in metropolitan areas. And where they are available, the services are often inadequate. Medical, clinical, and family planning services are relatively lacking in rural areas, and library, legal aid, and welfare counseling services are also needed. The picture of inadequate services is too huge, and perhaps known too well, for detailed description here.

Both facilities and personnel for providing services tend to concentrate in urban centers. The resulting discrepancies in services may be illustrated by visits to a doctor's office. In 1966-1967 people in metropolitan areas averaged 4.5 visits, whereas outside of metropolitan centers, nonfarm residents averaged 4.1 and farm residents only 3.3 visits.

The nonmetropolitan population as a whole differs in several important respects from the metropolitan population. Nonmetropolitan residents are older, more frequently widowed, more often in poverty, less well-educated, and have more children. In 1969, for example, over half of female family heads were widows in nonmetropolitan areas, and ten per cent of all nonmetropolitan residents were 65 or older.

Historically, barriers have impeded the government from providing the same services for people in less densely settled areas as for those living in urban centers. In part a sort of inertia has set in which still makes it difficult to extend programs to rural areas. The greater cost per person of extending services into sparsely settled areas is a perpetual rationale for not providing services. Often the sheer logistics of getting the needed service to rural people are exceedingly difficult. Distances and isolation continue to hamper the provision of services to all citizens despite the fact that we now have the technology and skills to solve such problems. What is needed is a strong national commitment to solve them.

26. Which of the following titles best summarizes the content of the passage?

(A) New Problems for the Poor of Rural America
(B) Americans Commit Their Energies to Aiding the Poor in Rural Areas
(C) Ways to Ease the Burdens of the Poor in Rural America
(D) Barriers that Keep the Poor in Poverty
(E) Needed: Improved Services for Rural Americans

27. According to the passage, in comparison to the nonmetropolitan population as a whole, metropolitan residents are

(A) poorer
(B) younger
(C) less well-educated
(D) more frequently widowed
(E) more likely to have large families

28. It can be inferred from the passage that in 1968 the average earnings for a nonmetropolitan poor family of four were approximately

(A) $497   (B) $538   (C) $994
 (D) $1,988   (E) $2,152

29. The author indicates that the need for improved services in rural America could be more adequately met if

(A) the public were made aware of the inadequacy of services in such areas
(B) new methods of dispensing services were devised
(C) local governments would assume full responsibility for provision of services
(D) present resources were mobilized according to a firm national resolve
(E) the individuals in rural America made greater efforts to have federal officials hear their grievances

30. The author's primary purpose in the passage is to

(A) compare various problems and indicate which is most urgent
(B) describe a continuing problem and urge its solution
(C) pinpoint the source of a problem and condemn those responsible for it
(D) propose answers to a problem and explain their application
(E) analyze popular attitudes to a problem and suggest ways of changing these attitudes

GO ON TO THE NEXT PAGE

Many Americans have been touched by Charles Drew's genius—either as blood donors, blood recipients, or as Red Cross and medical workers who have helped in the annual blood bank drives. Few of those who are familiar with the blood bank know the name of Charles Drew; fewer still know that he was black. And few, perhaps, know of Dr. Louis T. Wright, the brain surgeon and antibiotic expert who developed the smallpox vaccine that is used today. Few know of Dr. Daniel Hale Williams, the first surgeon to operate successfully on the human heart; or of Dr. Ernest E. Just, who pioneered cell study.

I have mentioned these blacks because they have made contributions to medicine and health that in other circumstances and times would have ranked them with Pasteur in the public mind. They achieved extraordinarily by any measure. That they did so while burdened with the senseless weight of racial discrimination is not only to their credit but to the everlasting shame and loss of America. The loss is incalculable, and indeed, we can be certain that many black youths of talent, and perhaps many hundreds of true genius, have been lost to the nation forever simply because prejudice stopped them from developing and exercising their intellectual powers.

31. The author indicates that few Americans know about Dr. Louis T. Wright because

   (A) others have taken credit for his contributions
   (B) his work has been overshadowed by recent developments in his field
   (C) racial discrimination prevented him from receiving widespread recognition
   (D) his work was in a highly specialized area of medicine
   (E) he was never allowed to reach his full potential as a scientific researcher

32. Which of the following does the author employ as his main tactic in indicating that America has wasted a valuable resource?

   (A) He emphasizes the failures people have made as a result of discrimination.
   (B) He cites examples of blacks who have succeeded in the scientific field.
   (C) He suggests methods of preventing discriminatory practices in the future.
   (D) He indicates that the loss of an individual is immeasurable and a price cannot be assigned to a person's life.
   (E) He supplies detailed biographies of black doctors.

33. At the conclusion of the passage, the author's tone is one of

   (A) indifference   (B) bitterness
   (C) bewilderment   (D) surprise
     (E) complacency

GO ON TO THE NEXT PAGE →

Dr. Austin Farrer once began a sermon with this statement:

"It is generally thought that preachers should be allowed to get away with vagueness. Preachers ought to bang about with resonant words, and to ask them what precisely they mean is to misunderstand the business. For preachers are either speaking of divine things, or moving us to virtue; and in neither case is it sensible to ask for precision."

Dr. Farrer goes on to point out that although this attitude may be commonly adopted, there are obviously problems that demand precise answers from the pulpit. The quotation, however, raises questions of fundamental importance to any discussion of the sermon as literature. It could be argued that there are no grounds for including preaching in the canon of accepted literature because the particular circumstances in which sermons are created preclude the possibility of comparison.

Certainly an interest in sermons is on the whole rarely to be found in literary critics, who may devote much time to a study of ephemeral pamphlets, but whose knowledge of pulpit oratory is confined to the better-known passages of a Taylor or a Donne. While it is true that many sermons originally have been given by gesture or by intonation, the fact remains that to ignore them as literature is to except too much. Milton's *Areopagitica* was certainly not written with the sole intention of leaving to posterity a lasting impression of literary resonance.

34. The passage is mainly concerned with

(A) whether sermons qualify as literature
(B) what accounts for the ephemeral nature of sermons
(C) why it is inevitable that sermons should be vague
(D) why preachers must depend upon gesture and intonation
(E) how we misunderstand the business of preaching

35. The author of the passage quotes the opening words of Dr. Farrer's sermon in order to

(A) explain why it is difficult for preachers to be precise
(B) show how Dr. Farrer differs from most other preachers
(C) illustrate the similarities between a Farrer and a Taylor or a Donne
(D) suggest why literary critics are inclined to give scant attention to sermons
(E) encourage the reader to be tolerant of the lack of precision in pulpit oratory

36. It can be inferred that Milton's *Areopagitica* is cited because it

(A) lacks precise reasoning
(B) is best remembered for its literary resonance
(C) has no intention of impressing us with its literary resonance
(D) needs the emphasis which only the speaking voice and gesture can provide
(E) has lasting literary merit

GO ON TO THE NEXT PAGE

Claude Bernard, the great nineteenth-century physiologist, hypothesized many years ago that veins lying next to arteries in the limbs take up heat from the arteries, thus intercepting some of the body heat before it reaches the extremities. Recent measurements have proved that there is in fact some artery-to-vein transfer of heat in the human body. But this heat exchange in humans is minor compared with that found in animals possessing special networks of blood vessels which act as heat traps. This type of network, called rete mirabile, is a bundle of small arteries and veins, all mixed together, with the counterflowing arteries and veins lying next to each other. The retia are generally situated at the places where the trunk of the animal deploys into extremities. There the retia trap most of the blood heat and return it to the trunk.

There is another finding, however, which at first sight is puzzling. Many animals that spend a great deal of time in cold water or live in Arctic snow seem to lack retia to sidetrack body heat from their limbs. The absence of retia in these animals is explained, though, when we consider that all the animals are heavily insulated over most of their bodies. Their principal problem lies in getting rid of body heat rather than in conserving it. Equally puzzling is the discovery of retia in many tropical animals. It may be that these animals are hypersensitive to the cool temperature of the night air.

37. If the human body possessed rete mirabile networks, one of the networks would most probably be located in which of the following areas?

(A) Chest cavity   (B) Knee joint   (C) Feet
(D) Finger tips   (E) Shoulder

38. Which of the following inferences can be made about animals with retia?

   I.   The blood circulating in their extremities is cooler than that in their trunk.
   II. They tend to live in cold climates.
   III. They have higher body temperatures than animals without retia.

(A) I only   (B) II only   (C) I and III only
(D) II and III only   (E) I, II, and III

39. It can be inferred that the primary function of the retia described in the passage is to

(A) control the flow of blood to animals' extremities
(B) facilitate the transmission of body heat to animals' extremities
(C) generate body heat for those animals exposed to severely cold temperatures
(D) preserve the body heat of animals lacking sufficient external insulation
(E) filter impurities from venous blood before they are transmitted to the arteries

40. The author credits Claude Bernard with having

(A) theorized that veins lie next to arteries in the limbs
(B) suggested that veins absorb heat from arteries
(C) proven that there is artery-to-vein heat transfer in humans
(D) discovered the rete mirabile networks in animals
(E) explained why many arctic animals lack retia

IF YOU FINISH BEFORE TIME IS CALLED, YOU MAY CHECK YOUR WORK ON THIS SECTION ONLY. DO NOT TURN TO ANY OTHER SECTION IN THE TEST.   **STOP**

SECTION **5** Time—30 minutes 35 Questions

In this section solve each problem, using any available space on the page for scratchwork. Then decide which is the best of the choices given and fill in the corresponding oval on the answer sheet.

The following information is for your reference in solving some of the problems.

Circle of radius r: Area = πr^2; Circumference = $2\pi r$
The number of degrees of arc in a circle is 360.
The measure in degrees of a straight angle is 180.

Definition of symbols:
= is equal to $\leqq$ is less than or equal to
$\neq$ is unequal to $\geqq$ is greater than or equal to
< is less than $\parallel$ is parallel to
> is greater than $\perp$ is perpendicular to

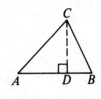

Triangle: The sum of the measures in degrees of the angles of a triangle is 180.
If $\angle CDA$ is a right angle, then

(1) area of $\triangle ABC = \dfrac{AB \times CD}{2}$

(2) $AC^2 = AD^2 + DC^2$

Note: Figures that accompany problems in this test are intended to provide information useful in solving the problems. They are drawn as accurately as possible EXCEPT when it is stated in a specific problem that its figure is not drawn to scale. All figures lie in a plane unless otherwise indicated. All numbers used are real numbers.

1. If burlap costs $0.48 per square meter, how many square meters of burlap can be bought for $6.00 ?

(A) $7\frac{2}{3}$ (B) 8   (C) 12   (D) $12\frac{1}{2}$ (E) 15

2. Which of the following is equal to 10 ?

(A) $2 \times [7 - (6 \div 3)]$
(B) $2 \times [(7 - 6) \div 3]$
(C) $[2 \times (7 - 6)] \div 3$
(D) $[(2 \times 7) - 6] \div 3$
(E) $(2 \times 7) - (6 \div 3)$

3. If $5 < x < 10$ and if x is one of the numbers 4, 6, 8, 10, or 12, what is the value of x ?

(A) 4   (B) 6   (C) 8   (D) 10
(E) It cannot be determined from the information given.

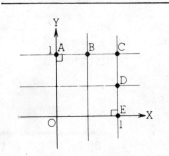

4. In the figure above, which of the lettered points is (are) the greatest distance from O ?

(A) C only
(B) B and D
(C) D and E
(D) A, B, and C
(E) All are equally distant from O.

5. If the average of 3 numbers is between 6 and 9, then the sum of the 3 numbers could be any one of the following EXCEPT

(A) 17   (B) $18\frac{1}{2}$ (C) 21   (D) 23   (E) $26\frac{1}{2}$

6. Sue is twice as old as Mary and Mary is one year older than Jim. If Jim is x years old, then an expression for Sue's age, in terms of x, is

(A) 2x + 1

(B) 2x + 2

(C) 2x - 2

(D) $\dfrac{x + 1}{2}$

(E) $\dfrac{x - 1}{2}$

7. If x is an odd integer and y is an even integer, which of the following could be an even integer?

(A) $x + y$ (B) $x - y$ (C) $\dfrac{x}{2} + y$

(D) $x + \dfrac{y}{2}$ (E) $\dfrac{x}{2} + \dfrac{y}{2}$

GO ON TO THE NEXT PAGE

5

Questions 8-27 each consist of two quantities, one in Column A and one in Column B. You are to compare the two quantities and on the answer sheet fill in oval

- A if the quantity in Column A is greater;
- B if the quantity in Column B is greater;
- C if the two quantities are equal;
- D if the relationship cannot be determined from the information given.

AN E RESPONSE WILL NOT BE SCORED.

Notes:

1. In certain questions, information concerning one or both of the quantities to be compared is centered above the two columns.
2. In a given question, a symbol that appears in both columns represents the same thing in Column A as it does in Column B.
3. Letters such as x, n, and k stand for real numbers.

	Column A	Column B
8.	x^2	$x^2 + 1$
9.	$3.9 \times 4{,}756$	$4 \times 4{,}756$

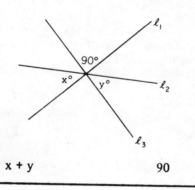

	Column A	Column B
10.	$x + y$	90
11.	$\dfrac{3}{5}$	60%
12.	The length of the hypotenuse of right $\triangle MNO$	The length of side PQ of equilateral $\triangle PQR$

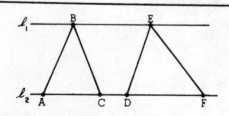

$$\ell_1 \parallel \ell_2$$

	Column A	Column B
13.	Length of the altitude of $\triangle ABC$ drawn to side AC	Length of the altitude of $\triangle DEF$ drawn to side DF

	Column A	Column B
	$x + 2 > 3$	
14.	$x + 1$	2
15.	$\dfrac{39 + 12}{13 - 6}$	$\dfrac{39}{13} - \dfrac{12}{6}$

Assume the clock above is accurate with the hour hand pointing to 10.

	Column A	Column B
16.	The number that the hour hand points to 6 hours after the time shown	The number that the hour hand points to 42 hours after the time shown

Tom bought x cans of tennis balls which come 3 to a can. He lost 1 unopened can of balls and 4 loose balls and then had 11 balls left.

	Column A	Column B
17.	x	6

GO ON TO THE NEXT PAGE ➡

SUMMARY DIRECTIONS FOR COMPARISON QUESTIONS

Answer: A if the quantity in Column A is greater;
          B if the quantity in Column B is greater;
          C if the two quantities are equal;
          D if the relationship cannot be determined from the information given.

AN E RESPONSE WILL NOT BE SCORED.

Column A	Column B

$$y = x + 3$$
$$z = x - 3$$

18. y z

The sides of a triangle are of lengths 6, 6, and x.

19.   6 x

---

x and $\dfrac{72}{x}$ are both integers greater than 1.

20.   Least possible value of $\dfrac{72}{x}$ 4

---

21. $\dfrac{21{,}951 - 27}{27}$ $\dfrac{21{,}951}{27} - 27$

$$x > 0$$

22. $x^2 + 1$ $x^3 - 1$

Column A	Column B

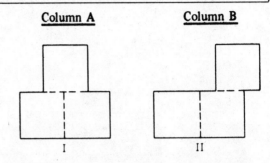

I   II

Six squares of equal size form the figures above.

23.   Perimeter of I   Perimeter of II

---

24. 0.1×0.1 $\dfrac{1}{200} + \dfrac{1}{200}$

Rectangle R and parallelogram P have equal bases and areas. P is not a rectangle.

25.   Perimeter of R   Perimeter of P

---

x and y are positive and $xy = 2$.

26. $x + y$ 3

The remainder is 1 when integer b is divided by 2.

27.   The remainder when b 1
     is divided by 4

GO ON TO THE NEXT PAGE ➡

5

Solve each of the remaining problems in this section using any available space for scratchwork. Then decide which is the best of the choices given and fill in the corresponding oval on the answer sheet.

28. Paul caught exactly 3 times as many fish as Eric and exactly 4 times as many as Steve. If they caught less than 100 fish altogether, what is the greatest number of fish that Paul could have caught?

    (A) 72
    (B) 66
    (C) 60
    (D) 50
    (E) 48

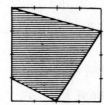

29. Each of the sides of the square above is divided into four equal segments. $\dfrac{\text{Area of shaded region}}{\text{Area of square}}$ =

    (A) $\dfrac{1}{4}$ (B) $\dfrac{3}{8}$ (C) $\dfrac{1}{2}$ (D) $\dfrac{5}{8}$ (E) $\dfrac{3}{4}$

30. If $\dfrac{5 + \dfrac{3}{8}}{3 + \dfrac{1}{4}} = \dfrac{10.75}{k}$, then k =

    (A) 3.25
    (B) 6.25
    (C) 6.50
    (D) 6.75
    (E) 9.75

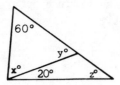

31. In the triangles above, what is the value of z in terms of x?

    (A) $\dfrac{x}{2}$ (B) x - 20   (C) x - 40

    (D) 80 - x   (E) 100 - x

32. If r and s are positive integers, how many integers are greater than rs and less than r(s + 1)?

    (A) 1
    (B) s + 1
    (C) s - 1
    (D) r + 1
    (E) r - 1

33. If $\textcircled{x}$ represents πx^4, then the area of a circle of radius 4 is represented by

    (A) $\textcircled{2}$ (B) $\textcircled{4}$ (C) $\textcircled{8}$

    (D) $\textcircled{16}$ (E) $\textcircled{16\pi}$

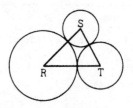

34. In the figure above, the circles with centers R, S, and T have three points of contact as shown. What is the ratio of the perimeter of $\triangle$RST to the sum of the circumferences of the three circles?

    (A) $\dfrac{1}{2}$ (B) $\dfrac{1}{3}$ (C) $\dfrac{1}{\pi}$ (D) $\dfrac{1}{2\pi}$ (E) $\dfrac{1}{3\pi}$

35. A group of 15 people starting a business planned to share equally the total expense of P dollars. If k people dropped out, by how many dollars did each remaining person's share of the expense increase?

    (A) $\dfrac{P}{15 - k}$

    (B) $\dfrac{P}{15 - kP}$

    (C) $\dfrac{P}{225 - 15k}$

    (D) $\dfrac{kP}{15k - 225}$

    (E) $\dfrac{kP}{225 - 15k}$

Correct Answers for Scholastic Aptitude Test
Form Code 0Y

VERBAL		MATHEMATICAL	
Section 1	Section 4	Section 2	Section 5
1. E	1. A	1. D	1. D
2. A	2. E	2. C	2. A
3. D	3. D	3. D	3. E
4. A	4. C	4. C	4. A
5. D	5. A	5. C	5. A
6. C	6. D	6. B	6. B
7. C	7. E	7. B	7. D
8. A	8. B	8. D	*8. B
9. B	9. D	9. A	*9. B
10. E	10. D	10. D	*10. C
11. B	11. A	11. C	*11. C
12. A	12. C	12. E	*12. D
13. B	13. A	13. C	*13. C
14. D	14. B	14. B	*14. A
15. D	15. C	15. A	*15. A
16. E	16. A	16. C	*16. C
17. C	17. B	17. E	*17. C
18. C	18. C	18. E	*18. A
19. A	19. E	19. C	*19. D
20. E	20. C	20. B	*20. B
21. B	21. D	21. E	*21. A
22. D	22. C	22. B	*22. D
23. E	23. A	23. B	*23. B
24. E	24. B	24. E	*24. C
25. A	25. B	25. A	*25. B
26. D	26. E		*26. D
27. B	27. B		*27. D
28. A	28. D		28. C
29. C	29. D		29. D
30. D	30. B		30. C
31. D	31. C		31. E
32. D	32. B		32. E
33. A	33. B		33. A
34. B	34. A		34. C
35. D	35. D		35. E
36. C	36. E		
37. A	37. E		
38. A	38. A		
39. C	39. D		
40. C	40. B		
41. C			
42. B			
43. E			
44. A			
45. D			

*Indicates four-choice questions. (All of the other questions are five-choice.)

The Scoring Process

Machine-scoring is done in three steps:

- *Scanning.* Your answer sheet is "read" by a scanning machine and the oval you filled in for each question is recorded on a computer tape.

- *Scoring.* The computer compares the oval filled in for each question with the correct response. Each correct answer receives one point; omitted questions do not count toward your score. For each wrong answer, a fraction of a point is subtracted to correct for random guessing. For questions with five answer choices, one-fourth of a point is subtracted for each wrong response; for questions with four answer choices, one-third of a point is subtracted for each wrong response. The SAT-verbal test has 85 questions with five answer choices each. If, for example, a student has 44 right, 32 wrong, and 9 omitted, the resulting raw score is determined as follows:

$$44 \text{ right} - \frac{32 \text{ wrong}}{4} = 44 - 8 = 36 \text{ raw score points}$$

Obtaining raw scores frequently involves the rounding of fractional numbers to the nearest whole number. For example, a raw score of 36.25 is rounded to 36, the nearest whole number. A raw score of 36.50 is rounded upward to 37.

- *Converting to reported scaled score.* Raw test scores are then placed on the College Board scale of 200 to 800 through a process that adjusts scores to account for minor differences in difficulty among different editions of the test. This process, known as equating, is performed so that a student's reported score is not affected by the edition of the test taken nor by the abilities of the group with whom the student takes the test. As a result of placing SAT scores on the College Board scale, scores earned by students at different times can be compared. For example, an SAT-verbal score of 400 on a test taken at one administration indicates the same level of developed verbal ability as a 400 score obtained on a different edition of the test taken at another time.

How to Score the Test

SAT-Verbal Sections 1 and 4

Step A: Count the number of correct answers for *section 1* and record the number in the space provided on the worksheet on the next page. Then do the same for the incorrect answers. (Do not count omitted answers.) To determine subtotal A, use the formula:

$$\text{number correct} - \frac{\text{number incorrect}}{4} = \text{subtotal A}$$

Step B: Count the number of correct answers and the number of incorrect answers for *section 4* and record the numbers in the spaces provided on the worksheet. To determine subtotal B, use the formula:

$$\text{number correct} - \frac{\text{number incorrect}}{4} = \text{subtotal B}$$

Step C: To obtain C, add subtotal A to subtotal B, keeping any decimals. Enter the resulting figure on the worksheet.

Step D: To obtain D, your raw verbal score, round C to the nearest whole number. (For example, any number from 44.50 to 45.49 rounds to 45.) Enter the resulting figure on the worksheet.

Step E: To find your reported SAT-verbal score, look up the total raw verbal score you obtained in step D in the conversion table on page 98. Enter this figure on the worksheet.

SAT-Mathematical Sections 2 and 5

Step A: Count the number of correct answers and the number of incorrect answers for *section 2* and record the numbers in the spaces provided on the worksheet. To determine subtotal A, use the formula:

$$\text{number correct} - \frac{\text{number incorrect}}{4} = \text{subtotal A}$$

Step B: Count the number of correct answers and the number of incorrect answers for the *five-choice questions (questions 1 through 7 and 28 through 35)* in section 5 and record the numbers in the spaces provided on the worksheet. To determine the subtotal B, use the formula:

$$\text{number correct} - \frac{\text{number incorrect}}{4} = \text{subtotal B}$$

Step C: Count the number of correct answers and the number of incorrect answers for the *four-choice questions (questions 8 through 27)* in section 5 and record the numbers in the spaces provided on the worksheet. To determine the subtotal C, use the formula:

$$\text{number correct} - \frac{\text{number incorrect}}{3} = \text{subtotal C}$$

Step D: To obtain D, add subtotal A, subtotal B, and subtotal C, keeping any decimals. Enter the resulting figure on the worksheet.

Step E: To obtain E, your raw mathematical score, round D to the nearest whole number. (For example, any number from 44.50 to 45.49 rounds to 45.) Enter the resulting figure on the worksheet.

Step F: To find your reported SAT-mathematical score, look up the total raw mathematical score you obtained in E in the conversion table on page 98. Enter this figure on the worksheet.

Test #2
VERBAL = 400
MATH = 400
8/13/90

SAT SCORING WORKSHEET

SAT-Verbal Sections

A. Section 1: _____ − ¼ (_____) = _____
    no. correct   no. incorrect   subtotal A

B. Section 4: _____ − ¼ (_____) = _____
    no. correct   no. incorrect   subtotal B

C. Total unrounded raw score
   (Total A + B)   _____
                                                              C

D. Total rounded raw score
   (Rounded to nearest whole number)   _____
                                                              D

E. SAT-verbal reported scaled score
   (See the conversion table on page 98.)   [   ]

                                                        SAT-verbal
                                                        score

SAT-Mathematical Sections

A. Section 2: _____ − ¼ (_____) = _____
    no. correct   no. incorrect   subtotal A

B. Section 5:
   Questions 1 through 7 and   _____ − ¼ (_____) = _____
   28 through 35 (5-choice)   no. correct   no. incorrect   subtotal B

C. Section 5:
   Questions 8 through 27   _____ − ⅓ (_____) = _____
   (4-choice)   no. correct   no. incorrect   subtotal C

D. Total unrounded raw score
   (Total A + B + C)   _____
                                                              D

E. Total rounded raw score
   (Rounded to nearest whole number)   _____
                                                              E

F. SAT-mathematical reported scaled score
   (See the conversion table on page 98.)   [   ]

                                                        SAT-math
                                                        score

Score Conversion Table
Scholastic Aptitude Test
Form Code 0Y

Raw Score	College Board Reported Score		Raw Score	College Board Reported Score	
	SAT-Verbal	SAT-Math		SAT-Verbal	SAT-Math
85	800		40	460	620
84	790		39	460	610
83	780		38	450	600
82	770		37	440	590
81	760		36	440	580
80	750		35	430	570
79	750		34	420	560
78	740		33	420	550
77	730		32	410	540
76	720		31	400	530
75	710		30	400	520
74	710		29	390	520
73	700		28	380	510
72	690		27	380	500
71	680		26	370	490
70	670		25	360	480
69	660		24	360	470
68	660		23	350	460
67	650		22	340	450
66	640		21	340	440
65	630		20	330	430
64	620		19	320	420
63	620		18	320	410
62	610		17	310	400
61	600		16	300	400
60	600	800	15	300	390
59	590	790	14	290	380
58	580	780	13	280	370
57	580	770	12	280	360
56	570	760	11	270	350
55	560	760	10	260	340
54	560	750	9	260	330
53	550	740	8	250	320
52	540	730	7	240	310
51	540	720	6	230	300
50	530	710	5	230	290
49	520	700	4	220	280
48	520	690	3	210	280
47	510	680	2	210	270
46	500	670	1	200	260
45	500	660	0	200	250
44	490	650	−1	200	240
43	480	640	−2	200	230
42	480	640	−3	200	220
41	470	630	−4	200	210
			−5 or below	200	200

COLLEGE BOARD — SCHOLASTIC APTITUDE TEST
and Test of Standard Written English   Side 1

Use a No. 2 pencil only. Be sure each mark is dark and completely fills the intended oval. Completely erase any errors or stray marks.

1.

YOUR NAME: _____
(Print)   Last   First   M.I.

SIGNATURE: _____ DATE: ___/___/___

HOME ADDRESS: _____
(Print)   Number and Street

_____
City   State   Zip Code

CENTER: _____
(Print)   City   State   Center Number

IMPORTANT: Please fill in these boxes exactly as shown on the back cover of your test book.

FOR ETS USE ONLY

2. TEST FORM

3. FORM CODE

4. REGISTRATION NUMBER
(Copy from your Admission Ticket.)

5. YOUR NAME

First 4 letters of last name | First Init. | Mid. Init.

(A–Z ovals grid)

6. DATE OF BIRTH

Month	Day	Year
Jan.		
Feb.		
Mar.		
Apr.		
May		
June		
July		
Aug.		
Sept.		
Oct.		
Nov.		
Dec.		

7. SEX
- Female
- Male

8. TEST BOOK SERIAL NUMBER

Start with number 1 for each new section. If a section has fewer than 50 questions, leave the extra answer spaces blank.

SECTION 1

1 (A) (B) (C) (D) (E)   26 (A) (B) (C) (D) (E)
2 (A) (B) (C) (D) (E)   27 (A) (B) (C) (D) (E)
3 (A) (B) (C) (D) (E)   28 (A) (B) (C) (D) (E)
4 (A) (B) (C) (D) (E)   29 (A) (B) (C) (D) (E)
5 (A) (B) (C) (D) (E)   30 (A) (B) (C) (D) (E)
6 (A) (B) (C) (D) (E)   31 (A) (B) (C) (D) (E)
7 (A) (B) (C) (D) (E)   32 (A) (B) (C) (D) (E)
8 (A) (B) (C) (D) (E)   33 (A) (B) (C) (D) (E)
9 (A) (B) (C) (D) (E)   34 (A) (B) (C) (D) (E)
10 (A) (B) (C) (D) (E)   35 (A) (B) (C) (D) (E)
11 (A) (B) (C) (D) (E)   36 (A) (B) (C) (D) (E)
12 (A) (B) (C) (D) (E)   37 (A) (B) (C) (D) (E)
13 (A) (B) (C) (D) (E)   38 (A) (B) (C) (D) (E)
14 (A) (B) (C) (D) (E)   39 (A) (B) (C) (D) (E)
15 (A) (B) (C) (D) (E)   40 (A) (B) (C) (D) (E)
16 (A) (B) (C) (D) (E)   41 (A) (B) (C) (D) (E)
17 (A) (B) (C) (D) (E)   42 (A) (B) (C) (D) (E)
18 (A) (B) (C) (D) (E)   43 (A) (B) (C) (D) (E)
19 (A) (B) (C) (D) (E)   44 (A) (B) (C) (D) (E)
20 (A) (B) (C) (D) (E)   45 (A) (B) (C) (D) (E)
21 (A) (B) (C) (D) (E)   46 (A) (B) (C) (D) (E)
22 (A) (B) (C) (D) (E)   47 (A) (B) (C) (D) (E)
23 (A) (B) (C) (D) (E)   48 (A) (B) (C) (D) (E)
24 (A) (B) (C) (D) (E)   49 (A) (B) (C) (D) (E)
25 (A) (B) (C) (D) (E)   50 (A) (B) (C) (D) (E)

SECTION 2

1 (A) (B) (C) (D) (E)   26 (A) (B) (C) (D) (E)
2 (A) (B) (C) (D) (E)   27 (A) (B) (C) (D) (E)
3 (A) (B) (C) (D) (E)   28 (A) (B) (C) (D) (E)
4 (A) (B) (C) (D) (E)   29 (A) (B) (C) (D) (E)
5 (A) (B) (C) (D) (E)   30 (A) (B) (C) (D) (E)
6 (A) (B) (C) (D) (E)   31 (A) (B) (C) (D) (E)
7 (A) (B) (C) (D) (E)   32 (A) (B) (C) (D) (E)
8 (A) (B) (C) (D) (E)   33 (A) (B) (C) (D) (E)
9 (A) (B) (C) (D) (E)   34 (A) (B) (C) (D) (E)
10 (A) (B) (C) (D) (E)   35 (A) (B) (C) (D) (E)
11 (A) (B) (C) (D) (E)   36 (A) (B) (C) (D) (E)
12 (A) (B) (C) (D) (E)   37 (A) (B) (C) (D) (E)
13 (A) (B) (C) (D) (E)   38 (A) (B) (C) (D) (E)
14 (A) (B) (C) (D) (E)   39 (A) (B) (C) (D) (E)
15 (A) (B) (C) (D) (E)   40 (A) (B) (C) (D) (E)
16 (A) (B) (C) (D) (E)   41 (A) (B) (C) (D) (E)
17 (A) (B) (C) (D) (E)   42 (A) (B) (C) (D) (E)
18 (A) (B) (C) (D) (E)   43 (A) (B) (C) (D) (E)
19 (A) (B) (C) (D) (E)   44 (A) (B) (C) (D) (E)
20 (A) (B) (C) (D) (E)   45 (A) (B) (C) (D) (E)
21 (A) (B) (C) (D) (E)   46 (A) (B) (C) (D) (E)
22 (A) (B) (C) (D) (E)   47 (A) (B) (C) (D) (E)
23 (A) (B) (C) (D) (E)   48 (A) (B) (C) (D) (E)
24 (A) (B) (C) (D) (E)   49 (A) (B) (C) (D) (E)
25 (A) (B) (C) (D) (E)   50 (A) (B) (C) (D) (E)

(Cut here to detach.)

Q1362-04

I.N. 574006—110VV25P3015

COLLEGE BOARD — SCHOLASTIC APTITUDE TEST
and Test of Standard Written English Side 2

Use a No. 2 pencil only. Be sure each mark is dark and completely fills the intended oval. Completely erase any errors or stray marks.

Start with number 1 for each new section. If a section has fewer than 50 questions, leave the extra answer spaces blank.

9. SIGNATURE:

SECTION 3	SECTION 4	SECTION 5	SECTION 6

(Answer grid: questions 1–50 for each section, with options Ⓐ Ⓑ Ⓒ Ⓓ Ⓔ)

FOR ETS USE ONLY

VTR	VTFS	VRR	VRFS	VVR	VVFS	WER	WEFS	M4R	M4FS	M5R	M5FS	MTFS
VTW	VTCS	VRW	VRCS	VVW	VVCS	WEW	WECS	M4W		M5W		MTCS

TEST 3—FORM CODE 0Z

SECTION 1 Time—30 minutes
45 Questions

For each question in this section, choose the best answer and fill in the corresponding oval on the answer sheet.

Each question below consists of a word in capital letters, followed by five lettered words or phrases. Choose the word or phrase that is most nearly opposite in meaning to the word in capital letters. Since some of the questions require you to distinguish fine shades of meaning, consider all the choices before deciding which is best.

Example:

GOOD: (A) sour (B) bad (C) red
(D) hot (E) ugly

Ⓐ ● Ⓒ Ⓓ Ⓔ

1. RECOLLECT: (A) disapprove (B) dispense
(C) forget (D) pardon (E) defer

2. EVACUATE: (A) invade (B) find
(C) strengthen (D) stabilize (E) delay

3. FALTER:
(A) ask (B) lie (C) become famous
(D) err repeatedly (E) move steadily

4. DEGENERATION: (A) suppression (B) isolation
(C) attention (D) similarity (E) progress

5. ZANY: (A) impious (B) friendly
(C) solemn (D) unyielding (E) uninformed

6. SCALE: (A) inflate (B) improve
(C) pull apart (D) climb down (E) leave behind

7. RETRACTION: (A) condolence
(B) reaffirmation (C) final decision
(D) obvious mistake (E) harsh judgment

8. DESTITUTION: (A) activity (B) curiosity
(C) maturity (D) prosperity (E) animosity

9. AFFABLE: (A) hardy (B) weary
(C) faulty (D) greedy (E) surly

10. OBLIQUE: (A) full (B) permanent
(C) direct (D) harmonious (E) unique

11. TENACIOUS: (A) fickle (B) bestial
(C) kindly (D) sober (E) ambitious

12. EXTOL: (A) defame (B) alienate
(C) conceal (D) refrain (E) reject

13. MERCURIAL: (A) servile (B) stolid
(C) prodigal (D) disgruntled (E) obese

14. TORPOR: (A) vivacity (B) coolness
(C) aloofness (D) partiality (E) antagonism

15. UPBRAID: (A) loosen (B) praise
(C) outwit (D) disguise (E) shorten

Each sentence below has one or two blanks, each blank indicating that something has been omitted. Beneath the sentence are five lettered words or sets of words. Choose the word or set of words that, when inserted in the sentence, best fits the meaning of the sentence as a whole.

Example:

Although its publicity has been ----, the film itself is intelligent, well-acted, handsomely produced, and altogether ----.

(A) tasteless. .respectable (B) extensive. .moderate
(C) sophisticated. .amateur (D) risqué. .crude
(E) perfect. .spectacular

● Ⓑ Ⓒ Ⓓ Ⓔ

16. Since we grow soy beans locally, we need not ---- them.

(A) feed (B) raise (C) breed
(D) import (E) coddle

17. Ironically, the protective law does not cover the type of worker who most obviously ---- the protection.

(A) dislikes (B) extends (C) needs
(D) opposes (E) exemplifies

18. Schultz cannot stand a situation that is ----, where there is no action.

(A) static (B) chaotic (C) imperfect
(D) stressful (E) brutal

19. The people were tired of reform crusades; they wanted no part of an idea that might turn into a ----.

(A) respite (B) reality (C) necessity
(D) mistake (E) cause

20. Curiously enough, the ---- of the outcome of the struggle in no way ---- its intensity.

(A) predictability. .condones
(B) uncertainty. .invalidates
(C) ambiguity. .confuses
(D) unimportance. .increases
(E) inevitability. .mitigates

GO ON TO THE NEXT PAGE

101

1

Each passage below is followed by questions based on its content. Answer the questions following each passage on the basis of what is stated or implied in that passage.

Americans profess a dedication to the cultural ideals of equality of opportunity and the brotherhood of man. The question facing us is whether, in James Baldwin's fine phrase, we shall achieve America.

The 1950's laid the foundation for drastic changes in American race relations. The 1960's were a decade characterized by alterations in the laws governing race relations, the role of race in politics, and even in economic relations between the races. By the mid-1960's the entire legal structure supporting racial segregation and discrimination had been altered. The beginnings of school desegregation had been made in every Southern state, and the federal government had exerted some pressure for more effective desegregation in both faculties and student bodies in Northern city schools. Increased black voter registration in the Southern states and effective political organization and participation of blacks helped to bring about the election of black mayors in Fayette, Mississippi, Gary, Indiana, and Cleveland, Ohio. By 1970 apprenticeships for blacks in the building-trades unions were being negotiated in several cities.

Many white Americans cherish the wistful hope that these gains achieved by black Americans will lessen the pressure for social change. Because the lives of blacks had improved over the last decade, the argument runs, it seems reasonable to expect less militancy, less friction, and reduced interracial conflict. From a social scientist's point of view, it makes better sense to predict increased pressure for equality, more widespread dissatisfaction with discrimination, and more insistent demands for access to the mainstream of American society. Revolutions, whether peaceful or violent, are made not by the most oppressed and downtrodden people in a society, but by those whose position has been improving and who find that access to further improvement is resisted or blocked. The United States became a nation when a revolution was organized by the thirteen best-governed colonies in the world. That revolution was followed by one in France made not by serfs or by an urban proletariat but by the bourgeoisie. The French bourgeoisie in the late eighteenth century had earned a position in some ways analogous to that of many Southern blacks in the 1950's: they had achieved a higher status than the social order was prepared to recognize. The civil rights protest movement of the 1950's and early 1960's was led not by sharecroppers or by unskilled laborers but by clergymen, lawyers, and college students—people who had achieved the occupational and educational levels of middle-class whites but whose new status was not recognized because of their color.

21. Which of the following pairs best describes the author's primary purpose in the passage?

    (A) To describe and condemn
    (B) To analyze and predict
    (C) To complain and criticize
    (D) To investigate and solve
    (E) To boast and encourage

22. The author attributes the election of black mayors in Gary, Indiana, Fayette, Mississippi, and Cleveland, Ohio to which of the following?

    I. Changing attitudes of white voters
    II. Increased registration of black voters
    III. Effective political organization of blacks

    (A) II only (B) III only (C) I and II only
    (D) II and III only (E) I, II, and III

23. According to the information in the passage, which of the following groups within a society would be most likely to start a revolution?

    (A) Those who had once held full privileges in the society but have renounced them
    (B) Unskilled laborers who are exploited and unable to enjoy the fruits of their labors
    (C) Those who have risen to the middle class but are denied its privileges
    (D) Those whose freedoms are severely and unjustly limited by a tyrannical government
    (E) Merchants who have earned profits from the exploitation of other groups

24. The author implies that many Americans' devotion to the ideal of the brotherhood of man is

    (A) somewhat superficial
    (B) unnecessarily optimistic
    (C) dangerously fanatical
    (D) hopelessly confused
    (E) becoming more sincere

25. Which of the following titles best summarizes the content of the passage?

    (A) Outlook for Increased Pressure for Equality from Black Americans
    (B) Americans Learn the Meaning of "Equal Opportunity"
    (C) New Hope for the Minorities of the World
    (D) A Summary of the Gains Made by the Civil Rights Movement
    (E) Black Americans Take a New Approach to Join the Mainstream of American Society

GO ON TO THE NEXT PAGE

Eighteenth-century physics had required about fifty years from the publication of the Principia to assume with ease the Newtonian posture. Biology has had to traverse even wider confusions before orienting itself cleanly around the Darwinian theory of evolution. Indeed, it has clarified its outlook through the instrumentality of modern genetics only since the 1930's. In 1929 Erik Nordenskjöld's History of Biology, still the foremost text, closed with a reference to "the dissolution of Darwinism." That natural selection "does not operate in the form imagined by Darwin must certainly be taken as proved," wrote Nordenskjöld. Exactly the contrary is now thought to be true. Since such shifts of scientific opinion were still to occur in the twentieth century, it is not surprising that the import of Darwin's theory for the whole science was not mastered at the time. Claude Bernard, perhaps the greatest of experimentalists in his skill and sobriety, saw the future of biology as existing in its reduction of physiology to laws of chemistry and physics. There was nothing for him in Darwin, whose work he did not distinguish from Naturphilosophie. "We must doubtless admire," he writes in his fine manifesto on Experimental Medicine, "those great horizons dimly seen by the genius of a Goethe, an Oken, a Carus, a Geoffroy Saint-Hilaire, a Darwin, in which a general conception shows us all living beings as the expression of types ceaselessly transformed in the evolution of organisms and species,—types in which every living being individually disappears like a reflection of a whole to which it belongs." But he did not admire them. He never thought this theory science. In the critical tradition of French learning, Darwin's mind and language seemed simply slack.

At the other extreme from Gallic indifference burgeoned the enthusiasm which made a religion of science, mistook nature for God, and adopted Darwin as the prophet. The German for this "ism," Darwinismus, best conveys its spirit and was always most at home in Germany. There Ernst Haeckel and his like, deploying all the rich capacity of their language for blurring distinctions, worked a syncretism between the Goethean sense of unity in nature and the Darwinian proof of organic evolution. All biology would be made over into evolution. Thus, to take only one example, embryology was henceforth to be ruled by the doctrine of recapitulation, by which every individual traverses in embryo the evolution of the race, from the single-celled through the invertebrate stage, the gill-breathing, the reptilean, and so on. Everyone, to adapt a saying of Huxley, climbs his own family tree out of the womb.

26. The author mentions Newton's Principia in order to

(A) distinguish between mathematics and biology
(B) demonstrate that new theories are not always valid
(C) compare the scientific attitudes of the eighteenth century with those of the nineteenth century
(D) show that valid original theories are not always immediately accepted by scientists
(E) point out the continuity of science from the eighteenth to the nineteenth century

27. According to the passage, biology did not fully adjust to Darwin's theory until

(A) Nordenskjöld published History of Biology
(B) modern genetics validated his concepts
(C) the doctrine of recapitulation was formulated
(D) the beginning of the twentieth century
(E) embryology was accepted as a valid science

28. The author suggests that in France and Germany scientists

(A) were largely indifferent to Darwin's theories
(B) deployed the capacities of their languages in order to blur distinctions
(C) misunderstood Darwin's theories in different ways
(D) divorced Goethe's theories from those of Darwin
(E) attempted to transform biology into evolution

29. Judging from the passage, one might assume that Ernst Haeckel would have agreed with all of the following statements EXCEPT:

(A) Darwin's theory should not be used to generalize about the nature of man.
(B) Evolution is a process that every organism must undergo.
(C) Goethe's view of nature may be harmonized with that of Darwin.
(D) Embryology obeys the laws of recapitulation.
(E) Biology and evolution are inseparably linked.

30. According to the passage, Haeckel seems to have used Darwin's theory to

(A) explain only human biology
(B) refute the claims that there is unity in nature
(C) reinforce the use of scientific method
(D) condemn those who confuse nature with God
(E) make very broad philosophical claims

GO ON TO THE NEXT PAGE

103

1

Select the word or set of words that best completes each of the following sentences.

31. Edwards had an ---- thirst for honor and glory, as though the balm of innumerable tributes could never quite ---- the wounds he suffered in those long years of failure and neglect.

    (A) unquenchable. .heal   (B) envious. .magnify
    (C) inconsequential. .avenge   (D) awesome. .shatter
    (E) insufficient. .soothe

32. In her description of the brain as an interpreter of messages from the nervous system, Henderson cautioned that interpreters, however proficient, are ---- and can ---- communications.

    (A) skillful. .disclose   (B) instructive. .convey
    (C) incompetent. .impart   (D) articulate. .garble
    (E) fallible. .distort

33. As most biographers have learned, the relationships between an artist's life and his or her work can be so --- and complicated that they ---- the most determined scrutiny.

    (A) tedious. .enliven   (B) momentous. .nullify
    (C) elusive. .resist   (D) conspicuous. .defy
    (E) fascinating. .discourage

34. The --- of governmental power makes it impossible for a potential ---- to know whom to flatter.

    (A) benignity. .statesman
    (B) ambiguity. .sycophant
    (C) changeability. .rebel
    (D) rigidity. .member
    (E) morality. .believer

35. Unless the special interests of a biological species demand --- of its members, it is obviously --- to spread the individuals as evenly as possible over the available habitat.

    (A) colonization. .demonstrative
    (B) decentralization. .convenient
    (C) minimization. .inefficient
    (D) aggregation. .expedient
    (E) concentration. .ineffective

Each question below consists of a related pair of words or phrases, followed by five lettered pairs of words or phrases. Select the lettered pair that best expresses a relationship similar to that expressed in the original pair.

Example:

YAWN : BOREDOM ::   (A) dream : sleep
(B) anger : madness   (C) smile : amusement
(D) face : expression   (E) impatience : rebellion

ⒶⒷ●ⒹⒺ

36. SANDPAPER : ABRASIVE ::
    (A) disinfectant : contagious   (B) ointment : painful
    (C) glue : sticky   (D) money : expensive
    (E) muffler : noisy

37. POLKA-DOTTED : SPOTS ::   (A) transparent : holes
    (B) speckled : threads   (C) knotted : fabrics
    (D) striped : lines   (E) plaid : triangles

38. PLANE : HANGAR ::   (A) coat : closet
    (B) house : garage   (C) food : store
    (D) submarine : water   (E) traffic : highway

39. ECHO : LISTENER ::   (A) microphone : speaker
    (B) leverage : lifter   (C) reflection : viewer
    (D) rehearsal : actor   (E) monotony : interrupter

40. REINDEER : TUNDRA ::   (A) bear : den
    (B) pony : stable   (C) sheep : sheepfold
    (D) mustang : corral   (E) camel : desert

41. EMACIATED : NOURISHMENT ::
    (A) rumpled : clothing   (B) neurotic : nerve
    (C) cured : medicine   (D) poisoned : hunger
    (E) flabby : exercise

42. BLUNDERBUSS : FIREARM ::   (A) galleon : vessel
    (B) lance : spear   (C) parachute : aircraft
    (D) khaki : uniform   (E) sword : dagger

43. COURAGEOUS : FOOLHARDY ::   (A) alert : severe
    (B) modest : slovenly   (C) generous : corrupt
    (D) innocent : liberal   (E) unpleasant : noxious

44. EXORCISM : DEMON ::   (A) divorce : infidelity
    (B) absolution : guilt   (C) convocation : angel
    (D) displacement : traveler   (E) revelation : spirit

45. PREVARICATION : LIAR ::   (A) banality : bore
    (B) blasphemy : idol   (C) idiom : imbecile
    (D) incantation : soloist   (E) compliment : egotist

IF YOU FINISH BEFORE TIME IS CALLED, YOU MAY CHECK YOUR WORK ON THIS SECTION ONLY. DO NOT TURN TO ANY OTHER SECTION IN THE TEST.   **S T O P**

SECTION **2**   Time—30 minutes
25 Questions

In this section solve each problem, using any available space on the page for scratchwork. Then decide which is the best of the choices given and fill in the corresponding oval on the answer sheet.

The following information is for your reference in solving some of the problems.

Circle of radius r: Area = πr^2; Circumference = $2\pi r$
   The number of degrees of arc in a circle is 360.
The measure in degrees of a straight angle is 180.

Definition of symbols:
= is equal to $\leq$ is less than or equal to
$\neq$ is unequal to $\geq$ is greater than or equal to
< is less than $\parallel$ is parallel to
> is greater than $\perp$ is perpendicular to

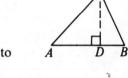

Triangle: The sum of the measures in degrees of the angles of a triangle is 180.

If $\angle CDA$ is a right angle, then

(1) area of $\triangle ABC = \dfrac{AB \times CD}{2}$

(2) $AC^2 = AD^2 + DC^2$

Note: Figures that accompany problems in this test are intended to provide information useful in solving the problems. They are drawn as accurately as possible EXCEPT when it is stated in a specific problem that its figure is not drawn to scale. All figures lie in a plane unless otherwise indicated. All numbers used are real numbers.

---

1. Which of the following must be even?

   I.   The sum of two odd numbers
   II. The sum of an odd and an even number
   III. The sum of two even numbers

   (A) I only   (B) II only   (C) I and II only
   (D) I and III only   (E) I, II, and III

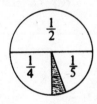

2. In the figure above, the shaded region is what fractional part of the area of the circle?

   (A) $\dfrac{1}{60}$ (B) $\dfrac{1}{40}$ (C) $\dfrac{1}{20}$ (D) $\dfrac{1}{10}$ (E) $\dfrac{1}{6}$

---

3. If $P_1 = 4 \times 0.095$ and $P_2 = 0.004 \times 0.095$, which of the following is true?

   (A) $P_1 = P_2$
   (B) $P_2 > P_1$
   (C) $P_1 + P_2 > 5$
   (D) $P_1 > 4$
   (E) $P_1 > P_2$

---

4. If $x + 3 = x - b$, then $b =$

   (A) −3   (B) 3   (C) −x   (D) x   (E) −2x + 3

---

5. In the figure above, $x + y =$

   (A) 30   (B) 45   (C) 60   (D) 90   (E) 120

---

6. How many numbers between 20 and 50 are each equal to 9 times an integer?

   (A) One
   (B) Two
   (C) Three
   (D) Four
   (E) Nine

---

7. If $(r + 1)\left(\dfrac{1}{r}\right) = 0$, what is r ?

   (A) 2   (B) 1   (C) −1
   (D) −2   (E) Any integer

GO ON TO THE NEXT PAGE

8. If x, y, and z are consecutive integers and x + y + z = 270, what is the value of the **LEAST** of the three integers?

    (A) 80   (B) 89   (C) 90   (D) 268

    (E) It cannot be determined from the information given.

9. If the average of 2 numbers is 7 and the product of the 2 numbers is 48, then the positive difference between the 2 numbers is

    (A) 1
    (B) 2
    (C) 3
    (D) 4
    (E) 6

10. If $3 \cdot 5 \cdot 7 = x$ and $3 \cdot 5 = y$, then $x - y$ is equal to the product of 15 and

    (A) 7   (B) 6   (C) 1   (D) -6   (E) -7

    _____

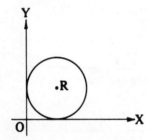

11. In the figure above, a circle with center R has an area of 36π square units and just touches the X- and Y-axes. What are the coordinates of R ?

    (A) (3, 12)   (B) (4, 9)   (C) (6, 6)
    (D) (18, 18)   (E) (36, 36)

    _____

12. If $\dfrac{1}{x + y} = 1$, then $x =$

    (A) $1 - y$ (B) $y - 1$ (C) $\dfrac{1}{1 + y}$

    (D) $1 + y$ (E) $-y$

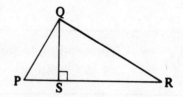

Note: Figure not drawn to scale.

13. In $\triangle PQR$ above, $QS \perp PR$. Which of the following conditions will insure that area $\triangle PQS <$ area $\triangle SQR$?

    (A) QS < PQ   (B) PQ < PR   (C) QR < PR
    (D) PQ < QR   (E) QS < PR

    _____

14. If 3 persons who work at the same rate can do a job together in 5 days, what fractional part of that job can one of these persons do in 1 day?

    (A) $\dfrac{1}{15}$ (B) $\dfrac{1}{12}$ (C) $\dfrac{1}{9}$ (D) $\dfrac{1}{5}$ (E) $\dfrac{1}{3}$

    _____

15. If the pattern of the first 5 arrows above continues to the right, the 107th arrow would be in which of the following directions?

    (A) ↓   (B) ↘   (C) ↗   (D) ↑   (E) →

    _____

Row A	7	2	5	4	6
Row B	3	8	6	9	7
Row C	5	4	3	8	2
Row D	9	5	7	3	6
Row E	5	6	3	7	4

16. Which row in the list above contains both the square of an integer and the cube of a <u>different</u> integer?

    (A) Row A   (B) Row B   (C) Row C
    (D) Row D   (E) Row E

    GO ON TO THE NEXT PAGE ➡

17. Jack begins reading at the top of page N and finishes at the bottom of page R. If the pages are numbered and read consecutively and if there are no blank pages, how many pages has he read?

    (A) R - N + 1
    (B) N - R + 1
    (C) N - R - 1
    (D) R - N
    (E) N - R

18. Out of a total of 154 games played, a ball team won 54 more games than it lost. If there were no ties, how many games did the team win?

    (A) 94
    (B) 98
    (C) 100
    (D) 102
    (E) 104

19. On a scale drawing, if 4 centimeters represent 16 meters, how many centimeters represent 2 meters 8 centimeters?
    (100 centimeters = 1 meter)

    (A) 0.52
    (B) 0.58
    (C) 0.70
    (D) 2.08
    (E) 2.50

20. If x is k per cent of y, what per cent of y is kx ?

    (A) $\frac{k}{100}$%

    (B) $\frac{100}{k}$%

    (C) k%

    (D) 100k%

    (E) k^2%

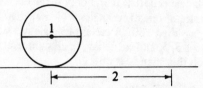

21. The figure above shows a circle with diameter 1. If $\frac{22}{7}$ is used as an approximation to π and if the circle rolls a distance 2, what part of a complete rotation does it make?

    (A) $\frac{7}{44}$

    (B) $\frac{7}{22}$

    (C) $\frac{7}{11}$

    (D) $\frac{11}{7}$

    (E) $\frac{22}{7}$

22. At a cost of 5 oranges for t cents, how many oranges can be bought for x dollars?

    (A) $\frac{500x}{t}$

    (B) $\frac{500t}{x}$

    (C) $\frac{20x}{t}$

    (D) $\frac{20t}{x}$

    (E) 20tx

GO ON TO THE NEXT PAGE

23. A triangle is obtuse if and only if the degree measure of one of its angles is greater than 90 and less than 180. A certain triangle has sides of lengths 5, 5, and x. What are all numbers x for which this triangle is obtuse?

(A) $5 \leqq x \leqq 5\sqrt{2}$

(B) $5 < x < 5\sqrt{2}$

(C) $5\sqrt{2} \leqq x \leqq 10$

(D) $5\sqrt{2} < x \leqq 10$

(E) $5\sqrt{2} < x < 10$

$$
\begin{array}{r}
A\,B \\
+\,C\,D \\
\hline
A\,A\,A
\end{array}
$$

24. In the correct addition problem shown above, A, B, C, and D represent nonzero digits. What is the value of C ?

(A) 9   (B) 8   (C) 7   (D) 1

(E) It cannot be determined from the information given.

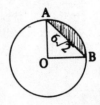

25. In the figure above, if O is the center of the circle and the length of side AB of right triangle AOB is $6\sqrt{2}$, what is the area of the shaded region?

(A) $27\pi + 18$

(B) $27\pi - 18$

(C) $9\pi + 18$

(D) $9\pi - 18$

(E) It cannot be determined from the information given.

IF YOU FINISH BEFORE TIME IS CALLED, YOU MAY CHECK YOUR WORK ON THIS SECTION ONLY. DO NOT TURN TO ANY OTHER SECTION IN THE TEST.   **STOP**

SECTION 3   Time—30 minutes
              40 Questions

For each question in this section, choose the best answer and fill in the corresponding oval on the answer sheet.

Each question below consists of a word in capital letters, followed by five lettered words or phrases. Choose the word or phrase that is most nearly opposite in meaning to the word in capital letters. Since some of the questions require you to distinguish fine shades of meaning, consider all the choices before deciding which is best.

Example:

GOOD: (A) sour   (B) bad   (C) red
(D) hot   (E) ugly

Ⓐ ● Ⓒ Ⓓ Ⓔ

1. CONFIDENTIAL: (A) baffling
   (B) amusing   (C) straightforward
   (D) widely known   (E) fully understood

2. ACCENT:
   (A) lack of emphasis   (B) loss of face
   (C) knack of writing   (D) difficulty in hearing
   (E) promptness in replying

3. EMERGE: (A) reduce   (B) disappear
   (C) float   (D) collide   (E) puncture

4. MANIPULATABLE: (A) creative
   (B) inflexible   (C) methodical
   (D) inconvenient   (E) exaggerated

5. DUBIOUS:
   (A) early   (B) lovely   (C) distinct
   (D) easily forgiven   (E) rapidly developing

6. EFFACE: (A) trust   (B) restore
   (C) embody   (D) contract   (E) appreciate

7. GLACIAL: (A) hot   (B) placid
   (C) smooth   (D) finite   (E) protected

8. DECOROUSNESS:
   (A) lack of propriety   (B) lack of respect
   (C) faulty perception   (D) extreme simplicity
   (E) uninspired performance

9. AMBULATORY: (A) irritable   (B) satisfactory
   (C) hospitalized   (D) self-propelled   (E) bedridden

10. TRACTABLE: (A) willful   (B) intact
    (C) delectable   (D) irksome   (E) obscure

Each sentence below has one or two blanks, each blank indicating that something has been omitted. Beneath the sentence are five lettered words or sets of words. Choose the word or set of words that, when inserted in the sentence, best fits the meaning of the sentence as a whole.

Example:

Although its publicity has been ----, the film itself is intelligent, well-acted, handsomely produced, and altogether ----.

(A) tasteless. .respectable (B) extensive. .moderate
(C) sophisticated. .amateur (D) risqué. .crude
(E) perfect. .spectacular

● Ⓑ Ⓒ Ⓓ Ⓔ

11. With modern equipment it is now possible to tell how far away from the observatory the earthquake ----; three observatories acting together can ---- the center of the quake.

(A) traveled. .reconstruct   (B) scattered. .calculate
(C) originated. .pinpoint   (D) ascended. .locate
(E) arose. .probe

12. Clichés abound not only in the writing style of this volume but also in its surpassingly ---- illustrations.

(A) subtle   (B) inventive   (C) moving
(D) trite   (E) uncertain

13. Food and sex are very basic requirements of animal life, but certain hermits eschewed sexual activity altogether and ---- food consumption to the lowest point ---- survival.

(A) limited. .injurious to
(B) cultivated. .vulnerable to
(C) reduced. .compatible with
(D) devoured. .recorded for
(E) expanded. .helpful for

GO ON TO THE NEXT PAGE

3

14. Even though this book has some ---- pages, even though it rarely breaks into eloquence or ----, the story it tells is nevertheless a deeply moving one.

    (A) insipid. .drivel
    (B) prosaic. .profundity
    (C) memorable. .credibility
    (D) tedious. .superficiality
    (E) insightful. .enlightenment

15. The ---- he exhibits in financial dealings is mirrored in his personal relationships; never have I seen a man so ---- kind words and considerate deeds.

    (A) extravagance. .oblivious to
    (B) haughtiness. .grateful for
    (C) parsimony. .chary of
    (D) rancor. .generous with
    (E) benevolence. .covetous of

Each question below consists of a related pair of words or phrases, followed by five lettered pairs of words or phrases. Select the lettered pair that best expresses a relationship similar to that expressed in the original pair.

Example:

YAWN : BOREDOM :: (A) dream : sleep
(B) anger : madness (C) smile : amusement
(D) face : expression (E) impatience : rebellion

Ⓐ Ⓑ ● Ⓓ Ⓔ

---

16. WORD : SENTENCE :: (A) signature : photograph
(B) question : response (C) paragraph : essay
(D) stamp : envelope (E) applause : performance

17. DUCK : DECOY :: (A) dog : bone
(B) bee : honey (C) horse : fodder
(D) insect : flyswatter (E) fish : bait

18. SLOUCH : POSTURE :: (A) scribble : penmanship
(B) hum : music (C) yawn : rest
(D) relax : formality (E) confuse : logic

19. LOOM : WEAVER :: (A) gallery : painter
(B) mobile : sculptor (C) nail : architect
(D) design : potter (E) anvil : blacksmith

20. STALE : BREAD :: (A) mellow : age
(B) skimmed : milk (C) sour : taste
(D) rancid : butter (E) fermented : yeast

21. RED TAPE : EFFICIENCY ::
(A) white gold : value
(B) bluestocking : poetry
(C) brownstone : building
(D) soft soap : flattery
(E) wet blanket : enthusiasm

22. APATHETIC : EMOTION ::
(A) bored : leisure
(B) hypothetical : imagination
(C) controversial : anger
(D) dramatic : quality
(E) neutral : bias

23. STOKE : FIRE :: (A) bake : oven
(B) laugh : joke (C) incite : crowd
(D) declaim : stage (E) hoard : money

24. GULLIBILITY : CHARLATAN ::
(A) bondage : slave (B) fear : bully
(C) courage : conspirator (D) desire : optimist
(E) submissiveness : follower

25. CORROSION : METAL :: (A) lethargy : action
(B) atrophy : body (C) illness : vision
(D) expansion : business (E) drought : land

GO ON TO THE NEXT PAGE →

Each passage below is followed by questions based on its content. Answer the questions following each passage on the basis of what is <u>stated</u> or <u>implied</u> in that passage.

The land has housed us, clothed us, and fed us, but again and again, out of indifference or sheer stupidity, we have squandered resources, defiled, destroyed, and moved on. The land was so rich,
Line
(5) so abundant, so very good, we believed, that there was just no end to its capacity to produce or to recover from our mistakes. "There is always more where that came from," we said.

Now, however, in the last third of the twentieth
(10) century, we are thinking differently. Our waste—our cutting down of entire forests, our poisoning of air and water, our mindless interference with the vital life cycles of plants and animals—is catching up with us. Although our productivity and our
(15) prosperity grow steadily, scientists keep warning of the terrible day of reckoning. As any thoughtful person realizes, we Americans and our land have reached a stage of crisis.

Future historians will no doubt point to this as
(20) the time when we first traveled far enough toward the stars to see with our own eyes our earth-home whole: a mere speck in space, but still our only home and the only source of life we know anything about.

26. All of the following are specifically mentioned in the passage as misuses of the Earth's resources EXCEPT

(A) interfering with the life cycle of plants and animals
(B) poisoning the water
(C) squandering our natural resources
(D) destroying our forests
(E) ruining the ecological balance of the oceans

27. In describing American attitudes about the land (lines 7-8), the author implies that

(A) people were shortsighted
(B) people's desires were limited
(C) America's resources were inexhaustible
(D) America has always been short on resources
(E) individuals must look out for their own best interests

28. According to the passage, for which of the following reasons did we exploit the land?

I. Carelessness
II. Insensitivity
III. A desire to conquer the land in order to move the frontier forward

(A) I only   (B) I and II only   (C) I and III only
(D) II and III only   (E) I, II, and III

GO ON TO THE NEXT PAGE

3

Animals are not moved by what they cannot react to. They live in a tiny world, a sliver of reality that keeps them walking behind their noses
Line and shuts out everything else. But look at humans.
(5) Here nature created an animal with no defense against full perception of the external world, an animal completely open to experience. Humans relate not only to others in their own species, but to animals in all other species. They can con-
(10) template not only what is edible for them, but everything that grows. They live not only in this moment, but they expand their inner selves to yesterday, their curiosity to years ago, their fears to five billion years from now when the sun will
(15) cool, their hopes to an eternity. They live not on a tiny territory, nor even on a planet, but in the universe. The burden is appalling. Humans cannot even take their bodies for granted as can other animals. Their limbs are not just "there," to be
(20) used and taken for granted. Not only is the body strange, but also its inner landscape, the memories and dreams. They do not know who they are or why they are born. Their existence is incomprehensible to them.

29. The main point of the passage is to

(A) show the development of human intelligence
(B) emphasize the problems that awareness brings to humans
(C) indicate the superiority of the human race over other animal species
(D) contrast the inner world of humans to the external world in which they live
(E) explain why animals react to stimuli the way they do

30. The author describes the world of animals as "a sliver of reality that keeps them walking behind their noses and shuts out everything else" (lines 2-4) in order to

(A) establish the difference between reality and the perception of reality
(B) demonstrate how much animals depend on their senses for survival
(C) show how animals react to members of their own species
(D) explain why strange stimuli are so frightening to animals
(E) exemplify the limitations of an animal's perception

31. The passage suggests that both animals and people are capable of

(A) dreaming
(B) curiosity
(C) living in a limited **sensory** environment
(D) reacting to others in their own species
(E) taking their bodies for granted

32. Which of the following most fully represents the "burden" referred to in line 17?

(A) "a sliver of reality" (lines 2-3)
(B) "full perception of the external world" (line 6)
(C) "five billion years from now when the sun will cool" (lines 14-15)
(D) "their bodies" (line 18)
(E) "memories and dreams" (lines 21-22)

GO ON TO THE NEXT PAGE ➡

A scientific theory is a step—in both senses of the word—toward understanding. A useful theory is in itself an advancement of our knowledge, and it is also a firm base for further advancement. Scientific theories are intellectual constructs that relate broad collections of experimentally observed facts. The advancement of knowledge inherent in a theory is in this relating or "explaining" of otherwise isolated and trivial sets of facts. The base for further advancement is in prediction, guidance of new experiments, and extension to new and broader theories. The basis, existence, and function of a scientific theory are pervaded by experimental observation.

Here, then, is why the atomic theory of the ancients cannot be considered a scientific theory in the modern sense. It was not based on observation, nor did it lead to experiments or further theories. Indeed, the notion of "ultimate particle" discouraged both experiment and speculation beyond this point. As long as the existence of atoms was postulated only because it seemed fitting, beautiful, moral, or God's will, no science had been created, and no understanding had been approached. But when John Dalton, in 1804, postulated an atomic structure because matter behaves in such a way that it must be particulate, our understanding took a long and bold step forward. The atomic theory became a scientific theory.

33. Which of the following best describes the content of the passage?

(A) A description of the first atomic theory
(B) An explanation of the characteristics of a scientific theory
(C) Advice to students concerning the application of scientific theory
(D) A summary of events leading to Dalton's theory of atomic structure
(E) A condemnation of present confusion about the nature of scientific theories

34. Which of the following pairs of words best represents what the author means by "both senses" of the word "step" (lines 1-2)?

(A) Space and size
(B) Challenge and rebuttal
(C) Imagination and success
(D) Foundation and progression
(E) Experiment and observation

35. It can be inferred that the ancients' atomic theory was based primarily on

(A) previous scientific theories
(B) primitive scientific experiments
(C) philosophical or theological judgments
(D) observations of isolated facts
(E) attempts to stimulate new experimentation

GO ON TO THE NEXT PAGE

"Well, if you wrote her about my illness, we are in a fix," the poor man said in a resigned tone. "Let's see if we can get out of it. Take a telegraph blank and a pencil, and let us compose a diplomatic dispatch." And slowly, with a quizzical smile playing about the corners of his mouth, he began to dictate: "Father better. Leaving as soon as possible for south of France with good nurse. I sail for home September first. Don't undertake voyage yourself. Utterly useless." He perused the telegram with caution. "We shall amplify one sentence," he observed judiciously. "We will say, 'Please don't undertake long voyage yourself.' That will sound more as if you had sent the telegram and not I."

Those two polite considerate words were not enough to deceive the practiced eye of Mrs. Alden. She saw that it was the Doctor's effort to keep her away. He was probably not better, except that he might have had worse moments. When the first of September came he would be worse again, and would keep Oliver from sailing. Her poor boy's feelings would be worked upon. He would be told not to abandon his dying father. And this dying father would live on, drag him to Marseilles, carry him away in that ill-fated yacht, cause him to miss his college year, and subject him to the evil influence of that wicked young Captain. Hadn't she employed a detective agency to look up the man's past and his present, and hadn't they discovered the most appalling facts, though nothing that she hadn't already known by instinct? It was a wicked plot to destroy whatever conscience and sense of decency might still remain in this weak, this sentimental boy. She would take the next steamer for Liverpool and defeat that conspiracy. She would sail from Boston, because the Boston boats would surely be safer; the Cunard line was of course the only right one—Letitia Lamb always traveled by it. Her reply to Oliver's cablegram was brief: "Sail Saturday Lucania." It was truer, she was happy to think, than the long one she had received, less expensive, and more expressive of a strong, upright, determined, unselfish character.

36. In this story, the most important aspect of the relationship between the Doctor and his wife is probably their

(A) underlying affection for one another
(B) rivalry for control of their son
(C) lack of concern for the welfare of the other
(D) refusal to disguise their deception of each other
(E) disagreement concerning the value of a college education

37. It can be inferred that Mrs. Alden's attitude toward Letitia Lamb is one of

(A) admiration   (B) curiosity   (C) distrust
(D) hypocrisy   (E) jealousy

38. Mrs. Alden thinks that the brevity of her telegram is most indicative of her

(A) need to economize
(B) fear of deception
(C) honest concern
(D) wrathful indignation
(E) forceful personality

39. The Doctor's primary purpose in changing the original draft of the telegram is to

(A) mislead Mrs. Alden into believing that he is concerned about her welfare
(B) mislead Mrs. Alden into believing that her son has written the message
(C) exaggerate the actual severity of his illness
(D) emphasize that he really wants Mrs. Alden to stay away
(E) disguise his real attitude toward Mrs. Alden

40. On the basis of the passage, the author's attitude toward Mrs. Alden can most accurately be termed one of

(A) scornful indifference
(B) sympathetic concern
(C) overt disapproval
(D) detached amusement
(E) sentimental involvement

IF YOU FINISH BEFORE TIME IS CALLED, YOU MAY CHECK YOUR WORK ON THIS SECTION ONLY. DO NOT TURN TO ANY OTHER SECTION IN THE TEST. **STOP**

SECTION **5** Time—30 minutes
35 Questions

In this section solve each problem, using any available space on the page for scratchwork. Then decide which is the best of the choices given and fill in the corresponding oval on the answer sheet.

The following information is for your reference in solving some of the problems.

Circle of radius r: Area $= \pi r^2$; Circumference $= 2\pi r$
   The number of degrees of arc in a circle is 360.
The measure in degrees of a straight angle is 180.

Definition of symbols:
= is equal to $\leq$ is less than or equal to
$\neq$ is unequal to $\geq$ is greater than or equal to
< is less than   ‖ is parallel to
> is greater than $\perp$ is perpendicular to

Triangle: The sum of the measures in degrees of the angles of a triangle is 180.
If $\angle CDA$ is a right angle, then

(1) area of $\triangle ABC = \dfrac{AB \times CD}{2}$

(2) $AC^2 = AD^2 + DC^2$

Note: Figures that accompany problems in this test are intended to provide information useful in solving the problems. They are drawn as accurately as possible EXCEPT when it is stated in a specific problem that its figure is not drawn to scale. All figures lie in a plane unless otherwise indicated. All numbers used are real numbers.

---

1. $(2^3 - 2^4)(2^2 - 2) =$

(A) 8   (B) 0   (C) −4   (D) −8   (E) −16

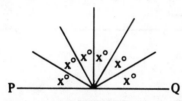

2. In the figure above, if PQ is a line segment, then $x =$

(A) 90
(B) 60
(C) 45
(D) 30
(E) 15

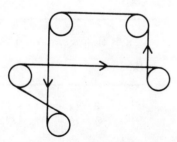

3. In the figure above, a belt which runs over five wheels moves in the direction of the arrows. How many of the wheels are turning clockwise?

(A) 1   (B) 2   (C) 3   (D) 4   (E) 5

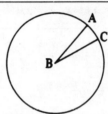

4. In the figure above, the length of the minor arc AC is $\dfrac{1}{18}$ of the circumference of the circle with center B. What is the measure of $\angle ABC$ in degrees?

(A) 30°   (B) 25°   (C) 20°   (D) 10°   (E) 5°

30, 31, 32, 33, 34, 35

5. If S is the sum of the remainders when each number in the list above is divided by 6, what is the remainder when S is divided by 6 ?

(A) 0   (B) 1   (C) 2   (D) 3   (E) 5

---

6. The average of positive numbers x, y, and z is what per cent of their sum?

(A) 25%   (B) $33\frac{1}{3}$%   (C) 50%   (D) $66\frac{2}{3}$%

(E) It cannot be determined from the information given.

---

7. If 70 tickets to a play were bought for a total of $50.00 and if tickets cost $1.00 for adults and $0.50 for children, how many children's tickets were bought?

(A) 20   (B) 25   (C) 30   (D) 35   (E) 40

GO ON TO THE NEXT PAGE

5

Questions 8-27 each consist of two quantities, one in Column A and one in Column B. You are to compare the two quantities and on the answer sheet fill in oval

  A if the quantity in Column A is greater;
  B if the quantity in Column B is greater;
  C if the two quantities are equal;
  D if the relationship cannot be determined from the information given.

AN E RESPONSE WILL NOT BE SCORED.

EXAMPLES			
	Column A	Column B	Answers
E1.	2×6	$2 + 6$	● Ⓑ Ⓒ Ⓓ Ⓔ
E2.	$180 - x$	y	Ⓐ Ⓑ ● Ⓓ Ⓔ
E3.	$p - q$	$q - p$	Ⓐ Ⓑ Ⓒ ● Ⓔ

For E2: $x°$ $y°$

Notes:

1. In certain questions, information concerning one or both of the quantities to be compared is centered above the two columns.
2. In a given question, a symbol that appears in both columns represents the same thing in Column A as it does in Column B.
3. Letters such as x, n, and k stand for real numbers.

	Column A	Column B
8.	$\frac{1}{2} + \frac{1}{3}$	$\frac{1}{4} + \frac{1}{5}$

PQRS is a square.

	Column A	Column B
9.	x^2	y^2

$$9 - 3x = 6$$
$$12 - 2y = 10$$

	Column A	Column B
10.	x	y
11.	$\sqrt{2} - 1$	$\sqrt{3} - 1$

In a certain class, every student studies either art or science or both; 12 study only art, 10 study only science, and x study both.

	Column A	Column B
12.	Number of students in the class who study art but not science	Number of students in the class who study science but not art

---

	Column A	Column B
13.	The perimeter of a triangle	The perimeter of a rectangle
14.	$1 + \dfrac{1}{1 + \frac{1}{2}}$	2
15.	The number of articles X can produce per hour if he produces at the rate of 25 articles in 15 minutes	The number of articles Y can produce per hour if he produces at the rate of 20 articles in 12 minutes

$$x > 0$$

	Column A	Column B
16.	$\sqrt{x + 1}$	$\sqrt{x} + 1$

k is an integer greater than 1.

	Column A	Column B
17.	$k^2(k - 1)^2$	36

$$P = (x - 2)(x + 3)$$
$$Q = (x - 3)(x + 2)$$

	Column A	Column B
18.	Value of P when $x = 2$	Value of Q when $x = 2$

GO ON TO THE NEXT PAGE →

Column A   Column B   Column A   Column B

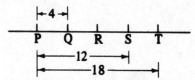

Rectangular Coordinates

19.   x   y

In a game, a fair coin is to be tossed 10 times and the score will be the number of heads obtained.

24. The chances of a score   The chances of a score
     of exactly 7   of exactly 3

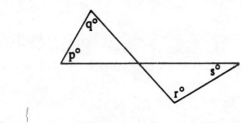

20.   p + q   r + s

Note: Figure not drawn to scale.

25.   ST   RS

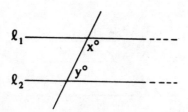

Lines ℓ₁ and ℓ₂ meet when extended to the right.

21.   x + y   180

BEEF PRICES

Brand	Price per Pound
X	$1.40
Y	$1.20

26. Average price per   Average price per
     pound of 2 pounds of   pound of 2 pounds of
     brand X beef and   brand X beef and
     3 pounds of brand Y   1 pound of brand Y
     beef   beef

A coat that was priced at $36.50 is sold at a 30 per cent discount.

22. Price of the coat after $25.55
     discount

$$x < 0$$

27. $(x + 2)(x + 3)$ $(x + 2)^2$

$$x < 0$$
$$y > 1$$

23.   xy $\frac{x}{y}$

GO ON TO THE NEXT PAGE

5

Solve each of the remaining problems in this section using any available space for scratchwork. Then decide which is the best of the choices given and fill in the corresponding oval on the answer sheet.

28. If $6t - p = 8$ and $4t - 3p = 7$, then $t + p =$

    (A) $\frac{1}{2}$ (B) 1   (C) $\frac{17}{14}$ (D) $\frac{27}{14}$ (E) 3

Questions 29–30 refer to the following definition.

For all real numbers p and q, where $q \neq 0$,

$$p \searrow_q = \frac{p^2}{q^2}$$

29. $\left(3 \searrow_5\right)\left(5 \searrow_6\right) =$

    (A) $\frac{1}{4}$ (B) $\frac{1}{2}$ (C) 2   (D) 4   (E) 8

30. If $pqrs \neq 0$, which of the following is (are) necessarily true?

    I. $p \searrow_q = q \searrow_p$

    II. $\left(p \searrow_q\right)\left(\frac{1}{p} \searrow_{\frac{1}{q}}\right) = 1$

    III. $\left(p \searrow_q\right)\left(r \searrow_s\right) = pr \searrow_{qs}$

    (A) I only
    (B) I and II only
    (C) I and III only
    (D) II and III only
    (E) I, II, and III

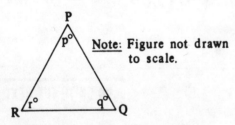

Note: Figure not drawn to scale.

31. In $\triangle PQR$ above, if $PQ < RQ < PR$, then

    (A) $q < r$ (B) $p < r$ (C) $q < p$
    (D) $p < 60$ (E) $r < 60$

32. A person is paid time and a half for all hours worked in excess of 7.5 hours per day. If the person works 10 hours in one day, by what per cent are his regular wages for the day increased?

    (A) 10%   (B) 20%   (C) 25%
    (D) $33\frac{1}{3}$%   (E) 50%

33. A closed rectangular tank 1 meter by 2 meters by 4 meters contains 4 cubic meters of water. When the tank is placed level on its various sides, the water depth changes. What is the greatest possible difference in water depths?

    (A) 0.5 m
    (B) 1 m
    (C) 1.5 m
    (D) 2 m
    (E) 3 m

34. If the average of the degree measures of two angles of an isosceles triangle is 50, which of the following could be the degree measure of one of the angles of the triangle?

    (A) 20   (B) 40   (C) 60   (D) 90
    (E) It cannot be any of the above.

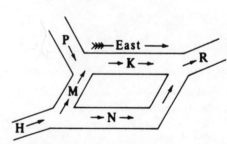

35. In the highway system illustrated above, one-tenth of the eastbound cars from highway H turn into M; the rest continue on N. One-fifth of the eastbound cars on K come from P; the rest, from M. If traffic on all highways is in the direction of the arrows, what is the ratio of the traffic on H to that on R ?

    (A) 1 to 2
    (B) 1 to 8
    (C) 5 to 7
    (D) 5 to 8
    (E) 40 to 41

IF YOU FINISH BEFORE TIME IS CALLED, YOU MAY CHECK YOUR WORK ON THIS SECTION ONLY. DO NOT TURN TO ANY OTHER SECTION IN THE TEST.   **STOP**

Correct Answers for Scholastic Aptitude Test
Form Code 0Z

VERBAL		MATHEMATICAL	
Section 1	Section 3	Section 2	Section 5
1. C	1. D	1. D	1. E
2. A	2. A	2. C	2. D
3. E	3. B	3. E	3. B
4. E	4. B	4. A	4. C
5. C	5. C	5. D	5. D
6. D	6. B	6. C	6. B
7. B	7. A	7. C	7. E
8. D	8. A	8. B	*8. A
9. E	9. E	9. B	*9. C
10. C	10. A	10. B	*10. C
11. A	11. C	11. C	*11. B
12. A	12. D	12. A	*12. A
13. B	13. C	13. D	*13. D
14. A	14. B	14. A	*14. B
15. B	15. C	15. B	*15. C
16. D	16. C	16. B or C	*16. B
17. C	17. E	17. A	*17. D
18. A	18. A	18. E	*18. A
19. E	19. E	19. A	*19. B
20. E	20. D	20. E	*20. C
21. B	21. E	21. C	*21. B
22. D	22. E	22. A	*22. C
23. C	23. C	23. E	*23. B
24. A	24. B	24. A	*24. C
25. A	25. B	25. D	*25. D
26. D	26. E		*26. B
27. B	27. A		*27. D
28. C	28. B		28. A
29. A	29. B		29. A
30. E	30. E		30. D
31. A	31. D		31. E
32. E	32. B		32. E
33. C	33. B		33. C
34. B	34. D		34. A
35. D	35. C		35. E
36. C	36. B		
37. D	37. A		
38. A	38. E		
39. C	39. B		
40. E	40. D		
41. E			
42. A			
43. E			
44. B			
45. A			

*Indicates four-choice questions. (All of the other questions are five-choice.)

The Scoring Process

Machine-scoring is done in three steps:

- *Scanning.* Your answer sheet is "read" by a scanning machine and the oval you filled in for each question is recorded on a computer tape.

- *Scoring.* The computer compares the oval filled in for each question with the correct response. Each correct answer receives one point; omitted questions do not count toward your score. For each wrong answer, a fraction of a point is subtracted to correct for random guessing. For questions with five answer choices, one-fourth of a point is subtracted for each wrong response; for questions with four answer choices, one-third of a point is subtracted for each wrong response. The SAT-verbal test has 85 questions with five answer choices each. If, for example, a student has 44 right, 32 wrong, and 9 omitted, the resulting raw score is determined as follows:

$$44 \text{ right} - \frac{32 \text{ wrong}}{4} = 44 - 8 = 36 \text{ raw score points}$$

Obtaining raw scores frequently involves the rounding of fractional numbers to the nearest whole number. For example, a raw score of 36.25 is rounded to 36, the nearest whole number. A raw score of 36.50 is rounded upward to 37.

- *Converting to reported scaled score.* Raw test scores are then placed on the College Board scale of 200 to 800 through a process that adjusts scores to account for minor differences in difficulty among different editions of the test. This process, known as equating, is performed so that a student's reported score is not affected by the edition of the test taken nor by the abilities of the group with whom the student takes the test. As a result of placing SAT scores on the College Board scale, scores earned by students at different times can be compared. For example, an SAT-verbal score of 400 on a test taken at one administration indicates the same level of developed verbal ability as a 400 score obtained on a different edition of the test taken at another time.

How to Score the Test

SAT-Verbal Sections 1 and 3

Step A: Count the number of correct answers for *section 1* and record the number in the space provided on the worksheet on the next page. Then do the same for the incorrect answers. (Do not count omitted answers.) To determine subtotal A, use the formula:

$$\text{number correct} - \frac{\text{number incorrect}}{4} = \text{subtotal A}$$

Step B: Count the number of correct answers and the number of incorrect answers for *section 3* and record the numbers in the spaces provided on the worksheet. To determine subtotal B, use the formula:

$$\text{number correct} - \frac{\text{number incorrect}}{4} = \text{subtotal B}$$

Step C: To obtain C, add subtotal A to subtotal B, keeping any decimals. Enter the resulting figure on the worksheet.

Step D: To obtain D, your raw verbal score, round C to the nearest whole number. (For example, any number from 44.50 to 45.49 rounds to 45.) Enter the resulting figure on the worksheet.

Step E: To find your reported SAT-verbal score, look up the total raw verbal score you obtained in step D in the conversion table on page 122. Enter this figure on the worksheet.

SAT-Mathematical Sections 2 and 5

Step A: Count the number of correct answers and the number of incorrect answers for *section 2* and record the numbers in the spaces provided on the worksheet. To determine the subtotal A, use the formula:

$$\text{number correct} - \frac{\text{number incorrect}}{4} = \text{subtotal A}$$

Step B: Count the number of correct answers and the number of incorrect answers for the *five-choice questions (questions 1 through 7 and 28 through 35)* in section 5 and record the numbers in the spaces provided on the worksheet. To determine the subtotal B, use the formula:

$$\text{number correct} - \frac{\text{number incorrect}}{4} = \text{subtotal B}$$

Step C: Count the number of correct answers and the number of incorrect answers for the *four-choice questions (questions 8 through 27)* in section 5 and record the numbers in the spaces provided on the worksheet. To determine the subtotal C, use the formula:

$$\text{number correct} - \frac{\text{number incorrect}}{3} = \text{subtotal C}$$

Step D: To obtain D, add subtotal A, subtotal B, and subtotal C, keeping any decimals. Enter the resulting figure on the worksheet.

Step E: To obtain E, your raw mathematical score, round D to the nearest whole number. (For example, any number from 44.50 to 45.49 rounds to 45.) Enter the resulting figure on the worksheet.

Step F: To find your reported SAT-mathematical score, look up the total raw mathematical score you obtained in E in the conversion table on page 122. Enter this figure on the worksheet.

SAT SCORING WORKSHEET

SAT-Verbal Sections

A. Section 1: _____ − ¼ (_____) = _____
                    no. correct   no. incorrect   subtotal A

B. Section 3: _____ − ¼ (_____) = _____
                    no. correct   no. incorrect   subtotal B

C. Total unrounded raw score
   (Total A + B)   _____
                                                       C

D. Total rounded raw score
   (Rounded to nearest whole number)   _____
                                                       D

E. SAT-verbal reported scaled score
   (See the conversion table on page 122.)

SAT-verbal
score

SAT-Mathematical Sections

A. Section 2: _____ − ¼ (_____) = _____
                    no. correct   no. incorrect   subtotal A

B. Section 5:
   Questions <u>1 through 7</u> and _____ − ¼ (_____) = _____
   <u>28 through 35</u> (5-choice)   no. correct   no. incorrect   subtotal B

C. Section 5:
   Questions <u>8 through 27</u> _____ − ⅓ (_____) = _____
   (4-choice)   no. correct   no. incorrect   subtotal C

D. Total unrounded raw score
   (Total A + B + C)   _____
                                                       D

E. Total rounded raw score
   (Rounded to nearest whole number)   _____
                                                       E

F. SAT-mathematical reported scaled score
   (See the conversion table on page 122.)

SAT-math
score

Score Conversion Table
Scholastic Aptitude Test
Form Code 0Z

Raw Score	College Board Reported Score		Raw Score	College Board Reported Score	
	SAT-Verbal	SAT-Math		SAT-Verbal	SAT-Math
85	800		40	470	600
84	790		39	460	590
83	780		38	460	590
82	770		37	450	580
81	760		36	440	570
80	750		35	440	560
79	740		34	430	550
78	730		33	420	540
77	730		32	420	530
76	720		31	410	530
75	710		30	400	520
74	700		29	400	510
73	690		28	390	500
72	680		27	380	490
71	680		26	380	480
70	670		25	370	470
69	660		24	360	470
68	660		23	360	460
67	650		22	350	450
66	640		21	340	440
65	640		20	340	430
64	630		19	330	420
63	620		18	320	410
62	620		17	320	410
61	610		16	310	400
60	600	800	15	310	390
59	600	790	14	300	380
58	590	780	13	290	370
57	580	770	12	290	360
56	580	760	11	280	350
55	570	750	10	270	350
54	560	740	9	270	340
53	560	730	8	260	330
52	550	720	7	250	320
51	540	710	6	250	310
50	540	700	5	240	300
49	530	690	4	230	290
48	520	680	3	230	290
47	520	670	2	220	280
46	510	660	1	210	270
45	500	650	0	210	260
44	500	640	− 1	200	250
43	490	630	− 2	200	240
42	480	620	− 3	200	230
41	480	610	− 4	200	230
			− 5	200	220
			− 6	200	210
			− 7 or below	200	200

COLLEGE BOARD — SCHOLASTIC APTITUDE TEST
and Test of Standard Written English Side 1

Use a No. 2 pencil only. Be sure each mark is dark and completely fills the intended oval. Completely erase any errors or stray marks.

1.

YOUR NAME: _____
(Print) Last First M.I.

SIGNATURE: _____ DATE: ___/___/___

HOME ADDRESS: _____
(Print) Number and Street

_____
City State Zip Code

CENTER: _____
(Print) City State Center Number

IMPORTANT: Please fill in these boxes exactly as shown on the back cover of your test book.

FOR ETS USE ONLY

5. YOUR NAME

First 4 letters of last name | First Init. | Mid Init.

(Lettered ovals A through Z in each column)

2. TEST FORM

3. FORM CODE

4. REGISTRATION NUMBER
(Copy from your Admission Ticket.)

6. DATE OF BIRTH

Month	Day	Year
Jan.		
Feb.		
Mar.	0 0	0 0
Apr.	1 1	1 1
May	2 2	2 2
June	3 3	3 3
July	4 4	4 4
Aug.	5 5	5 5
Sept.	6 6	6 6
Oct.	7 7	7 7
Nov.	8	8
Dec.	9	9

7. SEX

- Female
- Male

8. TEST BOOK SERIAL NUMBER

Start with number 1 for each new section. If a section has fewer than 50 questions, leave the extra answer spaces blank.

SECTION 1

1 A B C D E   26 A B C D E
2 A B C D E   27 A B C D E
3 A B C D E   28 A B C D E
4 A B C D E   29 A B C D E
5 A B C D E   30 A B C D E
6 A B C D E   31 A B C D E
7 A B C D E   32 A B C D E
8 A B C D E   33 A B C D E
9 A B C D E   34 A B C D E
10 A B C D E   35 A B C D E
11 A B C D E   36 A B C D E
12 A B C D E   37 A B C D E
13 A B C D E   38 A B C D E
14 A B C D E   39 A B C D E
15 A B C D E   40 A B C D E
16 A B C D E   41 A B C D E
17 A B C D E   42 A B C D E
18 A B C D E   43 A B C D E
19 A B C D E   44 A B C D E
20 A B C D E   45 A B C D E
21 A B C D E   46 A B C D E
22 A B C D E   47 A B C D E
23 A B C D E   48 A B C D E
24 A B C D E   49 A B C D E
25 A B C D E   50 A B C D E

SECTION 2

1 A B C D E   26 A B C D E
2 A B C D E   27 A B C D E
3 A B C D E   28 A B C D E
4 A B C D E   29 A B C D E
5 A B C D E   30 A B C D E
6 A B C D E   31 A B C D E
7 A B C D E   32 A B C D E
8 A B C D E   33 A B C D E
9 A B C D E   34 A B C D E
10 A B C D E   35 A B C D E
11 A B C D E   36 A B C D E
12 A B C D E   37 A B C D E
13 A B C D E   38 A B C D E
14 A B C D E   39 A B C D E
15 A B C D E   40 A B C D E
16 A B C D E   41 A B C D E
17 A B C D E   42 A B C D E
18 A B C D E   43 A B C D E
19 A B C D E   44 A B C D E
20 A B C D E   45 A B C D E
21 A B C D E   46 A B C D E
22 A B C D E   47 A B C D E
23 A B C D E   48 A B C D E
24 A B C D E   49 A B C D E
25 A B C D E   50 A B C D E

(Cut here to detach.)

COLLEGE BOARD — SCHOLASTIC APTITUDE TEST
and Test of Standard Written English   **Side 2**

Use a No. 2 pencil only. Be sure each mark is dark and completely fills the intended oval. Completely erase any errors or stray marks.

Start with number 1 for each new section. If a section has fewer than 50 questions, leave the extra answer spaces blank.

9. SIGNATURE:

SECTION 3

#					
1	Ⓐ	Ⓑ	Ⓒ	Ⓓ	Ⓔ
2	Ⓐ	Ⓑ	Ⓒ	Ⓓ	Ⓔ
3	Ⓐ	Ⓑ	Ⓒ	Ⓓ	Ⓔ
4	Ⓐ	Ⓑ	Ⓒ	Ⓓ	Ⓔ
5	Ⓐ	Ⓑ	Ⓒ	Ⓓ	Ⓔ
6	Ⓐ	Ⓑ	Ⓒ	Ⓓ	Ⓔ
7	Ⓐ	Ⓑ	Ⓒ	Ⓓ	Ⓔ
8	Ⓐ	Ⓑ	Ⓒ	Ⓓ	Ⓔ
9	Ⓐ	Ⓑ	Ⓒ	Ⓓ	Ⓔ
10	Ⓐ	Ⓑ	Ⓒ	Ⓓ	Ⓔ
11	Ⓐ	Ⓑ	Ⓒ	Ⓓ	Ⓔ
12	Ⓐ	Ⓑ	Ⓒ	Ⓓ	Ⓔ
13	Ⓐ	Ⓑ	Ⓒ	Ⓓ	Ⓔ
14	Ⓐ	Ⓑ	Ⓒ	Ⓓ	Ⓔ
15	Ⓐ	Ⓑ	Ⓒ	Ⓓ	Ⓔ
16	Ⓐ	Ⓑ	Ⓒ	Ⓓ	Ⓔ
17	Ⓐ	Ⓑ	Ⓒ	Ⓓ	Ⓔ
18	Ⓐ	Ⓑ	Ⓒ	Ⓓ	Ⓔ
19	Ⓐ	Ⓑ	Ⓒ	Ⓓ	Ⓔ
20	Ⓐ	Ⓑ	Ⓒ	Ⓓ	Ⓔ
21	Ⓐ	Ⓑ	Ⓒ	Ⓓ	Ⓔ
22	Ⓐ	Ⓑ	Ⓒ	Ⓓ	Ⓔ
23	Ⓐ	Ⓑ	Ⓒ	Ⓓ	Ⓔ
24	Ⓐ	Ⓑ	Ⓒ	Ⓓ	Ⓔ
25	Ⓐ	Ⓑ	Ⓒ	Ⓓ	Ⓔ
26	Ⓐ	Ⓑ	Ⓒ	Ⓓ	Ⓔ
27	Ⓐ	Ⓑ	Ⓒ	Ⓓ	Ⓔ
28	Ⓐ	Ⓑ	Ⓒ	Ⓓ	Ⓔ
29	Ⓐ	Ⓑ	Ⓒ	Ⓓ	Ⓔ
30	Ⓐ	Ⓑ	Ⓒ	Ⓓ	Ⓔ
31	Ⓐ	Ⓑ	Ⓒ	Ⓓ	Ⓔ
32	Ⓐ	Ⓑ	Ⓒ	Ⓓ	Ⓔ
33	Ⓐ	Ⓑ	Ⓒ	Ⓓ	Ⓔ
34	Ⓐ	Ⓑ	Ⓒ	Ⓓ	Ⓔ
35	Ⓐ	Ⓑ	Ⓒ	Ⓓ	Ⓔ
36	Ⓐ	Ⓑ	Ⓒ	Ⓓ	Ⓔ
37	Ⓐ	Ⓑ	Ⓒ	Ⓓ	Ⓔ
38	Ⓐ	Ⓑ	Ⓒ	Ⓓ	Ⓔ
39	Ⓐ	Ⓑ	Ⓒ	Ⓓ	Ⓔ
40	Ⓐ	Ⓑ	Ⓒ	Ⓓ	Ⓔ
41	Ⓐ	Ⓑ	Ⓒ	Ⓓ	Ⓔ
42	Ⓐ	Ⓑ	Ⓒ	Ⓓ	Ⓔ
43	Ⓐ	Ⓑ	Ⓒ	Ⓓ	Ⓔ
44	Ⓐ	Ⓑ	Ⓒ	Ⓓ	Ⓔ
45	Ⓐ	Ⓑ	Ⓒ	Ⓓ	Ⓔ
46	Ⓐ	Ⓑ	Ⓒ	Ⓓ	Ⓔ
47	Ⓐ	Ⓑ	Ⓒ	Ⓓ	Ⓔ
48	Ⓐ	Ⓑ	Ⓒ	Ⓓ	Ⓔ
49	Ⓐ	Ⓑ	Ⓒ	Ⓓ	Ⓔ
50	Ⓐ	Ⓑ	Ⓒ	Ⓓ	Ⓔ

SECTION 4

(entire section shaded/hatched over, marks obscured)

SECTION 5

#					
1	Ⓐ	Ⓑ	Ⓒ	Ⓓ	Ⓔ
2	Ⓐ	Ⓑ	Ⓒ	Ⓓ	Ⓔ
3	Ⓐ	Ⓑ	Ⓒ	Ⓓ	Ⓔ
4	Ⓐ	Ⓑ	Ⓒ	Ⓓ	Ⓔ
5	Ⓐ	Ⓑ	Ⓒ	Ⓓ	Ⓔ
6	Ⓐ	Ⓑ	Ⓒ	Ⓓ	Ⓔ
7	Ⓐ	Ⓑ	Ⓒ	Ⓓ	Ⓔ
8	Ⓐ	Ⓑ	Ⓒ	Ⓓ	Ⓔ
9	Ⓐ	Ⓑ	Ⓒ	Ⓓ	Ⓔ
10	Ⓐ	Ⓑ	Ⓒ	Ⓓ	Ⓔ
11	Ⓐ	Ⓑ	Ⓒ	Ⓓ	Ⓔ
12	Ⓐ	Ⓑ	Ⓒ	Ⓓ	Ⓔ
13	Ⓐ	Ⓑ	Ⓒ	Ⓓ	Ⓔ
14	Ⓐ	Ⓑ	Ⓒ	Ⓓ	Ⓔ
15	Ⓐ	Ⓑ	Ⓒ	Ⓓ	Ⓔ
16	Ⓐ	Ⓑ	Ⓒ	Ⓓ	Ⓔ
17	Ⓐ	Ⓑ	Ⓒ	Ⓓ	Ⓔ
18	Ⓐ	Ⓑ	Ⓒ	Ⓓ	Ⓔ
19	Ⓐ	Ⓑ	Ⓒ	Ⓓ	Ⓔ
20	Ⓐ	Ⓑ	Ⓒ	Ⓓ	Ⓔ
21	Ⓐ	Ⓑ	Ⓒ	Ⓓ	Ⓔ
22	Ⓐ	Ⓑ	Ⓒ	Ⓓ	Ⓔ
23	Ⓐ	Ⓑ	Ⓒ	Ⓓ	Ⓔ
24	Ⓐ	Ⓑ	Ⓒ	Ⓓ	Ⓔ
25	Ⓐ	Ⓑ	Ⓒ	Ⓓ	Ⓔ
26	Ⓐ	Ⓑ	Ⓒ	Ⓓ	Ⓔ
27	Ⓐ	Ⓑ	Ⓒ	Ⓓ	Ⓔ
28	Ⓐ	Ⓑ	Ⓒ	Ⓓ	Ⓔ
29	Ⓐ	Ⓑ	Ⓒ	Ⓓ	Ⓔ
30	Ⓐ	Ⓑ	Ⓒ	Ⓓ	Ⓔ
31	Ⓐ	Ⓑ	Ⓒ	Ⓓ	Ⓔ
32	Ⓐ	Ⓑ	Ⓒ	Ⓓ	Ⓔ
33	Ⓐ	Ⓑ	Ⓒ	Ⓓ	Ⓔ
34	Ⓐ	Ⓑ	Ⓒ	Ⓓ	Ⓔ
35	Ⓐ	Ⓑ	Ⓒ	Ⓓ	Ⓔ
36	Ⓐ	Ⓑ	Ⓒ	Ⓓ	Ⓔ
37	Ⓐ	Ⓑ	Ⓒ	Ⓓ	Ⓔ
38	Ⓐ	Ⓑ	Ⓒ	Ⓓ	Ⓔ
39	Ⓐ	Ⓑ	Ⓒ	Ⓓ	Ⓔ
40	Ⓐ	Ⓑ	Ⓒ	Ⓓ	Ⓔ
41	Ⓐ	Ⓑ	Ⓒ	Ⓓ	Ⓔ
42	Ⓐ	Ⓑ	Ⓒ	Ⓓ	Ⓔ
43	Ⓐ	Ⓑ	Ⓒ	Ⓓ	Ⓔ
44	Ⓐ	Ⓑ	Ⓒ	Ⓓ	Ⓔ
45	Ⓐ	Ⓑ	Ⓒ	Ⓓ	Ⓔ
46	Ⓐ	Ⓑ	Ⓒ	Ⓓ	Ⓔ
47	Ⓐ	Ⓑ	Ⓒ	Ⓓ	Ⓔ
48	Ⓐ	Ⓑ	Ⓒ	Ⓓ	Ⓔ
49	Ⓐ	Ⓑ	Ⓒ	Ⓓ	Ⓔ
50	Ⓐ	Ⓑ	Ⓒ	Ⓓ	Ⓔ

SECTION 6

#					
1	Ⓐ	Ⓑ	Ⓒ	Ⓓ	Ⓔ
2	Ⓐ	Ⓑ	Ⓒ	Ⓓ	Ⓔ
3	Ⓐ	Ⓑ	Ⓒ	Ⓓ	Ⓔ
4	Ⓐ	Ⓑ	Ⓒ	Ⓓ	Ⓔ
5	Ⓐ	Ⓑ	Ⓒ	Ⓓ	Ⓔ
6	Ⓐ	Ⓑ	Ⓒ	Ⓓ	Ⓔ
7	Ⓐ	Ⓑ	Ⓒ	Ⓓ	Ⓔ
8	Ⓐ	Ⓑ	Ⓒ	Ⓓ	Ⓔ
9	Ⓐ	Ⓑ	Ⓒ	Ⓓ	Ⓔ
10	Ⓐ	Ⓑ	Ⓒ	Ⓓ	Ⓔ
11	Ⓐ	Ⓑ	Ⓒ	Ⓓ	Ⓔ
12	Ⓐ	Ⓑ	Ⓒ	Ⓓ	Ⓔ
13	Ⓐ	Ⓑ	Ⓒ	Ⓓ	Ⓔ
14	Ⓐ	Ⓑ	Ⓒ	Ⓓ	Ⓔ
15	Ⓐ	Ⓑ	Ⓒ	Ⓓ	Ⓔ
16	Ⓐ	Ⓑ	Ⓒ	Ⓓ	Ⓔ
17	Ⓐ	Ⓑ	Ⓒ	Ⓓ	Ⓔ
18	Ⓐ	Ⓑ	Ⓒ	Ⓓ	Ⓔ
19	Ⓐ	Ⓑ	Ⓒ	Ⓓ	Ⓔ
20	Ⓐ	Ⓑ	Ⓒ	Ⓓ	Ⓔ
21	Ⓐ	Ⓑ	Ⓒ	Ⓓ	Ⓔ
22	Ⓐ	Ⓑ	Ⓒ	Ⓓ	Ⓔ
23	Ⓐ	Ⓑ	Ⓒ	Ⓓ	Ⓔ
24	Ⓐ	Ⓑ	Ⓒ	Ⓓ	Ⓔ
25	Ⓐ	Ⓑ	Ⓒ	Ⓓ	Ⓔ
26	Ⓐ	Ⓑ	Ⓒ	Ⓓ	Ⓔ
27	Ⓐ	Ⓑ	Ⓒ	Ⓓ	Ⓔ
28	Ⓐ	Ⓑ	Ⓒ	Ⓓ	Ⓔ
29	Ⓐ	Ⓑ	Ⓒ	Ⓓ	Ⓔ
30	Ⓐ	Ⓑ	Ⓒ	Ⓓ	Ⓔ
31	Ⓐ	Ⓑ	Ⓒ	Ⓓ	Ⓔ
32	Ⓐ	Ⓑ	Ⓒ	Ⓓ	Ⓔ
33	Ⓐ	Ⓑ	Ⓒ	Ⓓ	Ⓔ
34	Ⓐ	Ⓑ	Ⓒ	Ⓓ	Ⓔ
35	Ⓐ	Ⓑ	Ⓒ	Ⓓ	Ⓔ
36	Ⓐ	Ⓑ	Ⓒ	Ⓓ	Ⓔ
37	Ⓐ	Ⓑ	Ⓒ	Ⓓ	Ⓔ
38	Ⓐ	Ⓑ	Ⓒ	Ⓓ	Ⓔ
39	Ⓐ	Ⓑ	Ⓒ	Ⓓ	Ⓔ
40	Ⓐ	Ⓑ	Ⓒ	Ⓓ	Ⓔ
41	Ⓐ	Ⓑ	Ⓒ	Ⓓ	Ⓔ
42	Ⓐ	Ⓑ	Ⓒ	Ⓓ	Ⓔ
43	Ⓐ	Ⓑ	Ⓒ	Ⓓ	Ⓔ
44	Ⓐ	Ⓑ	Ⓒ	Ⓓ	Ⓔ
45	Ⓐ	Ⓑ	Ⓒ	Ⓓ	Ⓔ
46	Ⓐ	Ⓑ	Ⓒ	Ⓓ	Ⓔ
47	Ⓐ	Ⓑ	Ⓒ	Ⓓ	Ⓔ
48	Ⓐ	Ⓑ	Ⓒ	Ⓓ	Ⓔ
49	Ⓐ	Ⓑ	Ⓒ	Ⓓ	Ⓔ
50	Ⓐ	Ⓑ	Ⓒ	Ⓓ	Ⓔ

TEST 4—FORM CODE 1Z

For each question in this section, choose the best answer and fill in the corresponding oval on the answer sheet.

Each question below consists of a word in capital letters, followed by five lettered words or phrases. Choose the word or phrase that is most nearly opposite in meaning to the word in capital letters. Since some of the questions require you to distinguish fine shades of meaning, consider all the choices before deciding which is best.

Example:

GOOD: (A) sour   (B) bad   (C) red
(D) hot   (E) ugly

Ⓐ ● Ⓒ Ⓓ Ⓔ

1. RECUPERATE: (A) concentrate   (B) limit
(C) sicken   (D) seek help   (E) change hands

2. FRUITLESS: (A) sour   (B) adult
(C) responsive   (D) malodorous
(E) productive

3. REBELLION:
(A) ability to lead
(B) desire for wealth
(C) expectation of success
(D) acquiescence to authority
(E) conservation of resources

4. GIDDY: (A) well-meaning   (B) undemanding
(C) unpretentious   (D) levelheaded
(E) knowledgeable

5. ESTEEM: (A) modesty   (B) curiosity
(C) disrespect   (D) feigned unconcern
(E) restless uncertainty

6. UNFLAPPABLE: (A) talented
(B) prosperous   (C) sympathetic
(D) easily upset   (E) humbly grateful

7. REFUGE: (A) misrepresentation
(B) ornamentation   (C) offensive statement
(D) optimistic attitude   (E) dangerous place

8. PROSTRATION: (A) vitality   (B) brevity
(C) priority   (D) fixity   (E) unity

9. TERSE:
(A) open-minded
(B) long-winded
(C) overpermissive
(D) easily amused
(E) tactlessly honest

10. VIABLE: (A) necessary
(B) infamous   (C) mesmerized
(D) calculable   (E) moribund

Each sentence below has one or two blanks, each blank indicating that something has been omitted. Beneath the sentence are five lettered words or sets of words. Choose the word or set of words that, when inserted in the sentence, best fits the meaning of the sentence as a whole.

Example:

Although its publicity has been ----, the film itself is intelligent, well-acted, handsomely produced, and altogether ----.

(A) tasteless. .respectable (B) extensive. .moderate
(C) sophisticated. .amateur (D) risqué. .crude
(E) perfect. .spectacular

● Ⓑ Ⓒ Ⓓ Ⓔ

11. The women remained convinced that the adverse ruling was only a temporary setback—that their progress had merely been ----, not halted.

(A) enhanced   (B) negated   (C) interrupted
(D) perpetuated   (E) terminated

12. Science has conquered the forces of nature and compelled them to serve humanity; inhospitable forests have been ---- fertile fields.

(A) incorporated into
(B) transformed into
(C) developed from
(D) combined into
(E) produced by

13. It is unnecessary to say that their philosophy is ---- to his; for, since they knew little else besides his work, how could their philosophy be very ----.

(A) hostile..creative   (B) identical..imitative
(C) similar..different   (D) indebted..parallel
(E) akin..uniform

GO ON TO THE NEXT PAGE →

125

14. By labeling their opponents' views a ---- doctrine, they persuaded themselves that it would fail to ---- through the years.

    (A) reliable..survive
    (B) foolish..succumb
    (C) rigid..adapt
    (D) sound..flourish
    (E) hateful..regress

15. I find it hard to ---- such a ---- translation since it has much the same effect on Tourneau's lucid and vibrant prose that a steamroller would have on a flower bed.

    (A) overrate..fluent
    (B) praise..sublime
    (C) excuse..pedestrian
    (D) censure..ludicrous
    (E) condone..deft

Each question below consists of a related pair of words or phrases, followed by five lettered pairs of words or phrases. Select the lettered pair that best expresses a relationship similar to that expressed in the original pair.

Example:

    YAWN : BOREDOM :: (A) dream : sleep
    (B) anger : madness (C) smile : amusement
    (D) face : expression (E) impatience : rebellion

    Ⓐ Ⓑ ● Ⓓ Ⓔ

---

16. FANG:SNAKE :: (A) pit:viper (B) tusk:elephant
    (C) hoof:horse (D) spot:leopard
    (E) wing:robin

17. COLOR : DULLED ::
    (A) vision : scrutinized
    (B) ore : mined
    (C) tone : muted
    (D) alcohol : preserved
    (E) experiment : verified

18. THREAD : BUTTON :: (A) nail : hammer
    (B) alphabet : language (C) paste : wallpaper
    (D) handle : pitcher (E) frame : picture

19. EXPEL : PUPIL :: (A) acquit : defendant
    (B) deter : criminal (C) deport : alien
    (D) rebuke : child (E) exploit : friend

20. NAVIGABLE : WATERWAY ::
    (A) inflatable : balloon
    (B) inhabitable : home
    (C) accessible : voyage
    (D) invulnerable : fort
    (E) passable : trail

21. GNAT : INSECT :: (A) bird : mammal
    (B) minnow : fish (C) peacock : eagle
    (D) python : venom (E) butterfly : moth

22. BEQUEST : HEIR :: (A) blood : donor
    (B) meal : waiter (C) thrift : miser
    (D) gift : recipient (E) cause : protester

23. DWINDLE : SIZE :: (A) melt : warmth
    (B) wither : vigor (C) gamble : luck
    (D) petrify : age (E) multiply : number

24. MURAL : VIGNETTE ::
    (A) epic : ballad
    (B) drama : script
    (C) portrait : statue
    (D) symphony : orchestra
    (E) rhythm : syncopation

25. OMNIPOTENT : POWER :: (A) universal : deity
    (B) tyrannical : actions (C) eternal : duration
    (D) total : application (E) law : government

GO ON TO THE NEXT PAGE ➡

Each passage below is followed by questions based on its content. Answer the questions following each passage on the basis of what is stated or implied in that passage.

For a long time, African religions were written off as only animism. We know now that they represent more, actually a very complicated system of philosophy. Like peoples everywhere, the Africans have wrestled with the big questions. What is the nature of existence? What happens after death? Is life a gigantic hoax or has it purpose and meaning?

The answers Africans have given to these questions have determined the form of their religions. There is, to begin with, a supreme God who created the earth. There is also a pantheon of lesser gods identified sometimes with terrestrial objects. Intertwined with these concepts are the cults of fate and ancestor worship. Undergirding all is the basic concept of "life forces." The life force of a creator is thought to be present in all things, animate and inanimate. This force, "a kind of individualized fragment of the Supreme Being itself," continues to exist, even after the death of the individual. It continues, the Africans say, in a pure and perfect state which could influence the lives of living things.

Some scholars have found parallels between African philosophy and modern physics. "African thought," they say, "is conditioned by African ontology, that is, their theory of the nature of being. For them being is a process and not a mere state, and the nature of things is thought of in terms of force or energy rather than matter; the forces of the spirit, human, animal, vegetable, and mineral worlds are all constantly influencing each other, and by a proper knowledge and use of them, human beings may influence their own lives and those of others."

Religion, to many Africans, is important in all aspects of life. Every event is suffused with religious significance, and the climax of life is death. The African attitude that death is a transition from one state to another, anthropologists say, survived the Atlantic crossing and took root in the soil of black existence in America.

26. It can be inferred from the passage that the form of African religions has been determined by

(A) a belief in the principle of individualism
(B) customs handed down from ancient civilizations
(C) a philosophy concerning life and death
(D) practices transmitted by spiritual leaders
(E) a desire for peace and tranquility

27. The author's attitude toward African religion is best described as

(A) facetious
(B) dubious
(C) censorious
(D) sympathetic
(E) indifferent

28. In terms of African philosophy, the word "god" could be applied to which of the following?

I. A creator
II. A force that animates living creatures
III. Energy within inanimate objects

(A) I only
(B) I and II only
(C) I and III only
(D) II and III only
(E) I, II, and III

29. The author is primarily concerned with discussing the

(A) basic philosophy underlying African religions
(B) efforts of scholars to understand African religions
(C) relationship of African religion to Western philosophy
(D) significance of African ritualism
(E) African's attitude toward a life after death

30. Which of the following statements is in accord with the principles of African ontology as presented in the passage?

(A) The spirit of humanity has no influence upon its destiny.
(B) The interaction of all spirits, animate and inanimate, influences humanity.
(C) Humanity is controlled by capricious gods.
(D) The spirit of humanity controls the spirit of the inanimate.
(E) The spirit of humanity should be removed from worldly considerations.

GO ON TO THE NEXT PAGE

The differences in relative growth of various areas of scientific research have several causes. Some of these causes are completely legitimate results of social needs.
Others are a legitimate consequence of particular ad-
Line
(5) vances in science being to some extent self-accelerating. Some, however, are less legitimate processes of differential growth in which preconceptions of the form scientific theory ought to take, by persons in authority, act to alter the growth pattern of different areas. This is a
(10) new problem which is probably not yet ineradicable; but it is a frightening trend.

This trend began during the Second World War, when several governments came to the conclusion that the specific demands that a government may want to make of
(15) its scientific establishment cannot generally be foreseen in detail. It can be predicted, however, that from time to time questions will arise which will require specific scientific answers. It is therefore generally valuable to treat the scientific establishment as a resource or machine
(20) to be kept in functional order. This seems to be most effectively done by supporting a certain amount of research not related to immediate goals but of possible consequence in the future. This kind of support, like all government support, requires decisions about the appropriate
(25) recipients of funds. Decisions based on utility as opposed to lack of utility are straightforward. But a decision among projects none of which has immediate utility is more difficult. The goal of the supporting agencies is the laudable one of supporting "good" as opposed to "bad" science,
(30) but a valid determination is difficult to make. Generally, the idea of good science tends to become confounded with the capacity of the field in question to generate an elegant theory. However, the world is so made that elegant systems are in principle unable to deal with some of
(35) the world's more fascinating and delightful aspects. New forms of thought as well as new subjects for thought must arise in the future as they have in the past, giving rise to new standards of elegance.

The fact that science has become an adjunct of national
(40) policy does not, in itself, necessarily eliminate the possibility of new and radical concepts arising from science. This possibility will be eliminated, however, as soon as the government no longer feels reluctant to close whole areas of research as "unimportant." Any system of in-
(45) tellectual constructs which is espoused by the agents of secular power seems to generate its own metaphysical orthodoxy. Science fought its way free of government-sponsored religion only to threaten now to become a new government-sponsored orthodoxy.

31. According to the passage, the research trend that began during the Second World War was characterized by governmental

(A) recognition of the importance of science to national security
(B) support of projects that were currently non-utilitarian
(C) inquiry into specific scientific questions
(D) decision that certain scientific theories were dangerous
(E) support of scientific projects that had become self-accelerating

32. The author does all of the following in his discussion EXCEPT

(A) suggest new ways of deciding which projects should be sponsored
(B) point out problems with present ways of deciding between projects
(C) explain the possible consequences of present methods of evaluating specific projects
(D) explain why governments sponsor scientific projects
(E) explain why some projects are currently supported while others are neglected

33. It can be inferred that "Decisions based on utility" (line 25) are most probably decisions concerning projects that

(A) attempt to answer specific questions that a government wants solved
(B) may yield results applicable to the development of new research models
(C) are considered laudable by the scientific community
(D) promise to generate an elegant theory in a particular area
(E) tend to develop a new theory to explain an aspect of the universe

34. The main purpose of the passage is to

(A) describe the ways in which areas of scientific research have deteriorated since the Second World War
(B) explore ways of inhibiting the growth of certain areas of scientific research
(C) point out the areas in which new scientific theories need to be developed
(D) examine the motives of scientists who accept government support for their research
(E) discuss the role of supporting agencies in the differential advancement of scientific research

35. The author specifically suggests that "good" science (line 29) is equated at times with areas of research that

(A) are financially profitable to the supporting agencies
(B) are in a field considered crucial to immediate national interest
(C) seem metaphysically unorthodox to those in power
(D) may generate theories which seem elegant to those who support research
(E) show promise of having practical applicability in the near future

GO ON TO THE NEXT PAGE

1

If the field of history is enormous today, that of philosophy is diffuse. In approaching the subject one must keep carefully in mind the distinction between general wisdom and the technical work of trained philosophers going about professional tasks paralleling those of economists or mathematicians. Our present interest is in philosophers in this professional sense. The century opened in the Golden Age of American philosophy when Josiah Royce, William James, George Santayana, and John Dewey were each propounding systematic thought in his own way. In this brilliant quartet, philosophy in America reached a height it has not yet regained. Despite admirable thinkers now living, it seems fair to say that no systematic philosophy propounded by any American since the death of Dewey seems likely to exercise the influence of the thinkers of the Golden Age.

But philosophers have not been idle. Stunning advances in mathematical and physical theories leading to the Einsteinian intellectual revolution of our time have given philosophy so much to analyze that it is not surprising that no general system now dominates the field. Under the merciless knife of intellectual analysis, every system of philosophy has been found inconsistent or somewhere fallacious. Because the present temper of American philosophy is extremely analytical, that sort of synthesis out of which systems develop is not at the moment much in evidence.

The matter is of more than passing importance for the humanities. In contrast to the scientist with his or her opportunity for a place in industry, and to the social scientist with his or her chance at jobs in government or business, the humanistic scholar is in the main confined to the academic world. But there are grades of opportunity even among humanists, scholars in history and literature, for example, having occasional job opportunities in libraries and special institutes. The occupational area of philosophers, however, is in the academic world, since government does not employ metaphysicians, and business and industry do not hire logicians as they hire chemists.

If the partnership of philosophy at the moment is with science in the philosophic endeavor to ascertain the basis of the dependability both of knowledge and of the intellectual process, the partnership is not irrevocable, and there is some reason to suppose there will be a slow swing back to the Platonic goal of the philosopher as citizen and magistrate.

36. The author states in the third paragraph that philosophers can be distinguished from other humanists in America in which of the following respects?

    I. Their point of view
    II. The areas in which they are employed
    III. Their partnership with science

    (A) I only
    (B) II only
    (C) III only
    (D) I and II only
    (E) II and III only

37. The author indicates that the field of philosophy in America is currently diffuse for which of the following reasons?

    (A) Each person has his or her own personal philosophy.
    (B) American philosophy is dominated by a single system of thought.
    (C) American philosophy has never had sufficient time to formulate an identifiable system of thought.
    (D) The Golden Age in America initiated four different systems of thought.
    (E) American philosophy is analytical in nature.

38. Which of the following are mentioned in the passage as defects of philosophical systems?

    I. Contradictions
    II. Fragmented ideas
    III. False ideas

    (A) I only
    (B) II only
    (C) III only
    (D) I and II only
    (E) I and III only

39. According to the passage, which of the following is at present an impediment to the development of a systematic philosophy?

    (A) Philosophers are currently concentrating on dissection and examination.
    (B) Today's generation cannot produce professional philosophers as talented as the thinkers produced in the Golden Age.
    (C) It has finally been realized that no philosophical system can be perfect.
    (D) Scientific advances have relegated philosophy to a less relevant position in today's world.
    (E) The tools of other disciplines, like history, are being used by philosophers.

40. The author's attitude toward philosophy's role in the future can best be described as

    (A) cautiously optimistic that philosophy will become more involved in society
    (B) deliberately noncommittal as to the function philosophy should perform
    (C) concerned that philosophy will become merely an academic exercise
    (D) regretfully resigned to the fact that the scientific disciplines must control thinking in the modern world
    (E) skeptical that philosophy will attain a position equal to that held by science

IF YOU FINISH BEFORE TIME IS CALLED, YOU MAY CHECK YOUR WORK ON THIS SECTION ONLY. DO NOT TURN TO ANY OTHER SECTION IN THE TEST. **STOP**

SECTION **3**   Time—30 minutes   In this section solve each problem, using any available space on the
25 Questions   page for scratchwork. Then decide which is the best of the choices
given and fill in the corresponding oval on the answer sheet.

The following information is for your reference in solving some of the problems.

Circle of radius r: Area = πr^2; Circumference = $2\pi r$
   The number of degrees of arc in a circle is 360.
The measure in degrees of a straight angle is 180.

Definition of symbols:
= is equal to   ≦ is less than or equal to
≠ is unequal to   ≧ is greater than or equal to
< is less than   ‖ is parallel to
> is greater than   ⊥ is perpendicular to

Triangle: The sum of the measures in
degrees of the angles of a
triangle is 180.
If ∠CDA is a right angle, then

(1) area of $\triangle ABC = \dfrac{AB \times CD}{2}$

(2) $AC^2 = AD^2 + DC^2$

Note: Figures that accompany problems in this test are intended to provide information useful in solving the problems.
They are drawn as accurately as possible EXCEPT when it is stated in a specific problem that its figure is not drawn
to scale. All figures lie in a plane unless otherwise indicated. All numbers used are real numbers.

1. If $x + 1 = 7$, then $(x + 2)^2 =$

   (A) 25   (B) 36   (C) 49   (D) 64   (E) 81

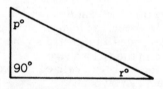

2. In the triangle above, $p + r =$

   (A) 30
   (B) 45
   (C) 60
   (D) 90
   (E) 180

3. A farmer has completed fencing all but one side of
   a square field. If he has already used $3x$ meters of
   fencing, how many meters will he need for the last
   side?

   (A) $\dfrac{3x}{4}$ (B) x (C) $\dfrac{4x}{3}$ (D) $3x$ (E) $4x$

4. If $0 < x < \dfrac{1}{2}$, which of the following could NOT
   be x?

   (A) $\dfrac{1}{4}$ (B) $\dfrac{3}{10}$ (C) $\dfrac{5}{8}$ (D) $\dfrac{7}{16}$ (E) $\dfrac{9}{32}$

5. There are 3 roads from Town A to Town B and
   4 other roads from Town B to Town C. Mrs. Smith
   must drive from Town A to Town C through Town B
   every day to her job. How many times could
   Mrs. Smith make the trip from A to B to C without
   taking exactly the same route twice?

   (A) 15   (B) 12   (C) 7   (D) 4   (E) 3

6. In a mythical country, 1 tong equals 5 sooks and
   10 sooks equal 1 kant. How many tongs equal
   6 kants?

   (A) $1\dfrac{1}{5}$ (B) $8\dfrac{1}{3}$ (C) 12   (D) 60   (E) $83\dfrac{1}{3}$

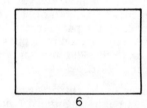

6

7. If the rectangle above has perimeter 20 and
   length 6, what is its area?

   (A) 24   (B) 42   (C) 48   (D) 120

   (E) It cannot be determined from the information
       given.

GO ON TO THE NEXT PAGE ⟩

8. In the figure above, each dot represents a missing number. The product of numbers in any row or column inside the square must be equal to the number in the corresponding position outside the square. If the table is completed, which number would go below 12 ?

(A) 3   (B) 6   (C) 9   (D) 18   (E) 27

Expression 1: 6 + 2 + 1 + 3 + 4 + y
Expression 2: 5 + 7 + 8 + y

9. A positive number x is added to one of the two expressions above and subtracted from the other. If the resulting expressions are equal, then x =

(A) 2
(B) 3
(C) 4
(D) 5
(E) 6

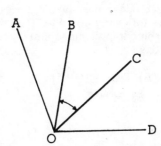

10. In the figure above, ∠AOC = 70°, ∠BOD = 80°, and ∠AOD = 110°. What is the degree measure of ∠BOC ?

(A) 10   (B) 20   (C) 30   (D) 40   (E) 50

---

11. If $x^2 - 5x + 6 > x^2 + 5x + 6$, which of the following describes x ?

(A) x < 0
(B) x = 0
(C) x = 2
(D) x = 3
(E) x > 3

12. In a certain school system a child must be at least five years old on March 1 to start school on September 1 of that year. The youngest possible age, in months, on September 1, of a child starting school in this school system would be

(A) 55   (B) 56   (C) 57   (D) 65   (E) 66

13. If $\frac{4}{N}$ is an odd integer, which of the following could be a value of N ?

(A) $\frac{4}{3}$

(B) $\frac{5}{4}$

(C) $\frac{3}{4}$

(D) $\frac{2}{3}$

(E) $\frac{1}{3}$

TRI-SCHOOL MEET

	Event I	Event II	Event III
First Place (5 points)	C	A	
Second Place (3 points)	A		
Third Place (1 point)	B		

14. In a three-school meet, schools A, B, and C each entered one team for each of 3 events. If the score card above is completed and shows no ties in any event, what is the greatest possible number of points by which B's total score could exceed A's total score?

(A) 0
(B) 2
(C) 4
(D) 8
(E) 9

GO ON TO THE NEXT PAGE

15. If $2a + 3b = 17$ and $a + 2b = 7$, then $\dfrac{3a + 5b}{2} =$

   (A) 10
   (B) 12
   (C) 18
   (D) 20
   (E) 24

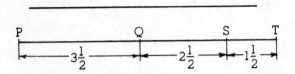

16. On the straight line in the figure above, if M, not shown, is the midpoint of QS and if N, not shown, is the midpoint of PT, what is the length of MN ?

   (A) 1   (B) $1\frac{1}{2}$ (C) 2   (D) $2\frac{1}{2}$ (E) $3\frac{3}{4}$

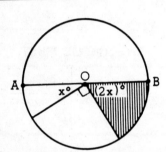

17. In the figure above, if the radius of the circle with diameter AB and center O is 1, then the area of the shaded region is

   (A) $\dfrac{\pi}{12}$ (B) $\dfrac{\pi}{8}$ (C) $\dfrac{\pi}{6}$ (D) $\dfrac{\pi}{4}$ (E) $\dfrac{\pi}{3}$

18. If the average of p, q, and r equals the average of p and q, what is r in terms of p and q ?

   (A) $\dfrac{p+q}{3}$ (B) $\dfrac{p+q}{2}$ (C) $p + q$

   (D) $2(p + q)$ (E) $3(p + q)$

19. If $\dfrac{x + 100}{y + 200} = 1$, then y is what per cent of x ?

   (A) 50%   (B) 100%   (C) 150%   (D) 200%

   (E) It cannot be determined from the information given.

20. Containers P, Q, and R have capacities in the ratio 2 to 1 to 3, respectively; P is $\frac{3}{4}$ full and Q and R are both empty. If Q is filled to capacity by pouring from P and if the remaining contents of P are poured into R, what part of R is filled?

   (A) $\dfrac{1}{8}$

   (B) $\dfrac{1}{6}$

   (C) $\dfrac{1}{4}$

   (D) $\dfrac{1}{3}$

   (E) $\dfrac{1}{2}$

21. Five contestants competed for two days in a sports event in which there were no ties in standings. At the end of each day, the standings were recorded. Which of the following could NOT be the total number of contestants whose standings changed on the second day?

   (A) One   (B) Two   (C) Three
   (D) Four   (E) Five

GO ON TO THE NEXT PAGE

22. The dimensions of two boxes are p, q, and r and s, t, and u, respectively. If s < q, t < p, u < t, t < r, and q < u, what is the diameter of the largest ball that will fit into both boxes?

(A) q
(B) r
(C) u
(D) t
(E) s

23. If X, Y, and Z are the hundreds', tens', and units' digits, respectively, of a number, how many hundreds are equal to that number?

(A) $X + \dfrac{Y + Z}{100}$

(B) $X + \dfrac{10Y + Z}{100}$

(C) $\dfrac{X}{100} + 10Y + Z$

(D) $\dfrac{ZYX}{100}$

(E) $100X + 10Y + Z$

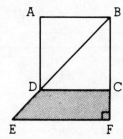

24. In the figure above, isosceles right triangle BEF overlaps square ABCD as shown. If AB = 1 and EB = 2, what is the area of the shaded region CDEF ?

(A) 2

(B) $\sqrt{2}$

(C) 1

(D) $\dfrac{\sqrt{2}}{2}$

(E) $\dfrac{1}{2}$

25. A watch loses x minutes every y hours. At this rate, how many <u>hours</u> will the watch lose in 1 week

(A) 7xy   (B) $\dfrac{7y}{x}$ (C) $\dfrac{x}{7y}$ (D) $\dfrac{14y}{5x}$ (E) $\dfrac{14x}{5y}$

IF YOU FINISH BEFORE TIME IS CALLED, YOU MAY CHECK YOUR WORK ON THIS SECTION ONLY. DO NOT TURN TO ANY OTHER SECTION IN THE TEST.   **S T O P**

5

SECTION 5   Time—30 minutes
35 Questions

In this section solve each problem, using any available space on the page for scratchwork. Then decide which is the best of the choices given and fill in the corresponding oval on the answer sheet.

The following information is for your reference in solving some of the problems.

Circle of radius r: Area = πr^2; Circumference = $2\pi r$
The number of degrees of arc in a circle is 360.
The measure in degrees of a straight angle is 180.

Definition of symbols:
$=$ is equal to
$\neq$ is unequal to
$<$ is less than
$>$ is greater than
$\leq$ is less than or equal to
$\geq$ is greater than or equal to
$\parallel$ is parallel to
$\perp$ is perpendicular to

Triangle: The sum of the measures in degrees of the angles of a triangle is 180.

If $\angle CDA$ is a right angle, then

(1) area of $\triangle ABC = \dfrac{AB \times CD}{2}$

(2) $AC^2 = AD^2 + DC^2$

Note: Figures that accompany problems in this test are intended to provide information useful in solving the problems. They are drawn as accurately as possible EXCEPT when it is stated in a specific problem that its figure is not drawn to scale. All figures lie in a plane unless otherwise indicated. All numbers used are real numbers.

1. $10^3 + 10^2 + 10^1 + 1 =$

(A) 1,001
(B) 1,010
(C) 1,011
(D) 1,110
(E) 1,111

2. The list price of a certain book is $3.95. If it is sold at a 20 per cent discount, how much does the buyer save?

(A) $0.20   (B) $0.79   (C) $0.95
(D) $1.98   (E) $3.16

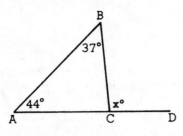

Note: Figure not drawn to scale.

3. In the figure above, if AD is a line, then $x =$

(A) 81   (B) 90   (C) 99   (D) 136   (E) 143

4. If sugar costs m cents a kilogram, how many kilograms of sugar can be bought for $2.00 ?

(A) 2m   (B) 200m   (C) $\dfrac{2}{m}$ (D) $\dfrac{200}{m}$ (E) $\dfrac{m}{200}$

5. If   7!   means $7 \cdot 6 \cdot 5 \cdot 4 \cdot 3 \cdot 2 \cdot 1$,

$7!_e$ means $6 \cdot 4 \cdot 2$,

and $7!_o$ means $7 \cdot 5 \cdot 3 \cdot 1$,

which of the following is true?

(A) $\dfrac{7!_e}{7!_o} = 1$

(B) $7!_e \times 7!_o = 7!$

(C) $7!_e - 7!_o = 0$

(D) $7!_e + 7!_o = 7!$

(E) $7!_o < 7!_e$

6. If x, y, and z are consecutive integers and $x < y < z$, then, in terms of z, $x =$

(A) $z - 2$ (B) $z - 1$ (C) $z + 1$

(D) $z + 2$ (E) $\dfrac{z}{2}$

7. If $x = \dfrac{-2}{4}$, then x is equivalent to all of the following EXCEPT

(A) $\dfrac{-1}{2}$

(B) $-\dfrac{1}{-2}$

(C) $-\dfrac{1}{2}$

(D) $\dfrac{1}{-2}$

(E) $-\dfrac{-1}{-2}$

GO ON TO THE NEXT PAGE

Questions 8-27 each consist of two quantities, one in Column A and one in Column B. You are to compare the two quantities and on the answer sheet fill in oval

- A if the quantity in Column A is greater;
- B if the quantity in Column B is greater;
- C if the two quantities are equal;
- D if the relationship cannot be determined from the information given.

AN E RESPONSE WILL NOT BE SCORED.

EXAMPLES

	Column A	Column B	Answers
E1.	2×6	$2 + 6$	● Ⓑ Ⓒ Ⓓ Ⓔ

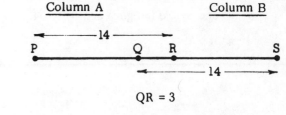

E2.	$180 - x$	y	Ⓐ Ⓑ ● Ⓓ Ⓔ
E3.	$p - q$	$q - p$	Ⓐ Ⓑ Ⓒ ● Ⓔ

Notes:

1. In certain questions, information concerning one or both of the quantities to be compared is centered above the two columns.
2. In a given question, a symbol that appears in both columns represents the same thing in Column A as it does in Column B.
3. Letters such as x, n, and k stand for real numbers.

Column A	Column B

8. $\dfrac{1,058}{23}$ $\dfrac{1,058}{46}$

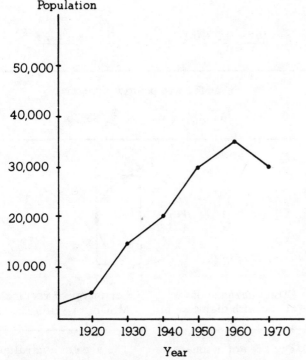

Population

9. Average rate of increase in population from 1930 to 1960   Average rate of increase in population from 1940 to 1970

10. $\dfrac{1}{\frac{1}{5}}$ $\dfrac{1}{0.2}$

Column A	Column B

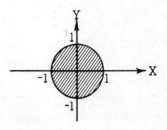

$QR = 3$

11. PS   28

$x > y + 1$

12. x y

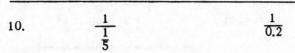

13. x if (x, y) is a point in the shaded region   0

14. x if $2x < 25$ y if $2y > 25$

15. Time: 12 minutes less than 3 hours   Time: $2\frac{5}{6}$ hours

GO ON TO THE NEXT PAGE ➡

5

Column A	Column B

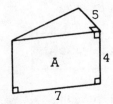 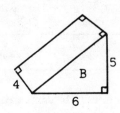

Solids A and B are halves of different rectangular boxes.

16. Volume of solid A   Volume of solid B

---

k and x are integers and $k^x = 64$.

17. k x

---

18. This question was not counted in computing scores.

---

y is the least possible value of $x^2 + 1$.

19. y 0

$\langle n \rangle = (n - 4)^2$ for all positive integers n.

20. $\langle 3 \rangle$ $\langle 5 \rangle$

Column A	Column B

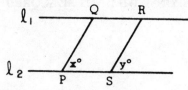

Note: Figure not drawn to scale.

Lines ℓ_1 and ℓ_2 are parallel and $x < y < 90$.

21.   PQ   RS

Pat bought x items and paid 5 cents each for 3 of them and 10 cents each for the others.

22. The cost, in cents, of the x items $15 + 10(x - 3)$

$x \neq 0$

23. $\dfrac{0.1 + 0.1 + 0.1}{0.1}$ $\dfrac{x + x + x}{x}$

---

x and y are positive integers.

24. 90% of x plus 80% of y 85% of $(x + y)$

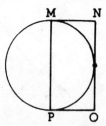

25. Circumference of the circle with diameter MP   Perimeter of rectangle MNOP

---

26. The area of a square with perimeter 16   The area of a parallelogram with perimeter 20

---

x is an even integer.

27. The number of distinct prime factors of x The number of distinct prime factors of $2x$

GO ON TO THE NEXT PAGE

Solve each of the remaining problems in this section using any available space for scratchwork. Then decide which is the best of the choices given and fill in the corresponding oval on the answer sheet.

28. A kindergarten class wants to buy a $77 tropical tree for the school. If the teacher agrees to pay twice as much as the class and the administration promises to pay 4 times as much as the class, how much should the teacher pay?

    (A) $11.00   (B) $15.40   (C) $22.00
    (D) $25.70   (E) $38.50

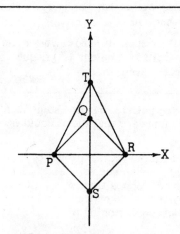

29. In square PQRS shown above, the coordinates of P and R are $(-5, 0)$ and $(5, 0)$ respectively. If the area of $\triangle$PTR equals the area of square PQRS, what are the coordinates of T ?

    (A) $(0, 5\sqrt{2})$ (B) $(0, 10)$ (C) $(0, 10\sqrt{2})$
    (D) $(10, 0)$ (E) $(10\sqrt{2}, 0)$

30. If $m\left(\dfrac{1}{n}\right) = 1$, which of the following is NOT necessarily true?

    (A) $m - n = 0$ (B) $m + n = 2n$ (C) $mn = m^2$
    (D) $m^2 + n^2 = 2m^2$ (E) $m = \dfrac{1}{n}$

31. The average grade x of a class of 24 students was below the passing grade of 70. If 6 of the students had raised their grades by 12 points each, the average for the class would have been passing or above. Which of the following describes all possible values of x ?

    (A) $58 \leqq x < 70$ (B) $67 < x < 70$ (C) $67 < x \leqq 70$
    (D) $67 \leqq x < 70$ (E) $58 < x < 70$

32. Starting at A, Julia traveled $\dfrac{z}{5}$ of the distance from A to B by bus, then traveled 15 miles by car, and then walked 3 miles to reach B. For what fractional part of her trip from A to B was Julia traveling by bus or by car?

    (A) $\dfrac{1}{5}$ (B) $\dfrac{3}{5}$ (C) $\dfrac{7}{10}$ (D) $\dfrac{4}{5}$ (E) $\dfrac{9}{10}$

33. A number is divisible by 9 if the sum of its digits is divisible by 9. Which of the following numbers is divisible by 45 ?

    (A) 63,345
    (B) 72,365
    (C) 99,999
    (D) 72,144
    (E) 98,145

34. If the area of each circle in the figure above is $\dfrac{\pi}{4}$ and the distance between the centers of circles P and Q is $\sqrt{3}$, what is the area of rectangle ABCD ?

    (A) $3 + 3\sqrt{3}$
    (B) $3 + 4\sqrt{2}$
    (C) 16
    (D) $16 + 16\sqrt{3}$
    (E) 64

35. If x, y, and z are three positive whole numbers and $x > y > z$, then, of the following, which is closest to the product xyz ?

    (A) $(x - 1)yz$ (B) $x(y - 1)z$ (C) $xy(z - 1)$
    (D) $x(y + 1)z$ (E) $xy(z + 1)$

IF YOU FINISH BEFORE TIME IS CALLED, YOU MAY CHECK YOUR WORK ON THIS SECTION ONLY. DO NOT TURN TO ANY OTHER SECTION IN THE TEST.   **STOP**

6

Each question below consists of a word in capital letters, followed by five lettered words or phrases. Choose the word or phrase that is most nearly opposite in meaning to the word in capital letters. Since some of the questions require you to distinguish fine shades of meaning, consider all the choices before deciding which is best.

Example:

GOOD: (A) sour (B) bad (C) red
(D) hot (E) ugly

Ⓐ ● Ⓒ Ⓓ Ⓔ

1. MERGE: (A) brighten (B) separate
(C) irritate (D) harden (E) ignore

2. BEFUDDLED: (A) brawny (B) famous
(C) clearheaded (D) charitable (E) energetic

3. RESIDE: (A) solicit (B) gratify
(C) limit (D) measure (E) migrate

4. UNACCOUNTABLE: (A) freely given
(B) widely rumored (C) slavishly obeyed
(D) easily explained (E) quickly remembered

5. INCESSANT: (A) malicious (B) external
(C) voluptuous (D) intermittent (E) distinctive

6. CORRUPT: (A) prove (B) punish
(C) heed (D) divide (E) regenerate

7. ABRIDGE: (A) engulf (B) expand
(C) tunnel (D) avoid (E) circumvent

8. TEEMING: (A) competent (B) deserted
(C) watchful (D) objective (E) petulant

9. INCARCERATE: (A) purify (B) extinguish
(C) disqualify (D) set free (E) speed up

10. TENACITY: (A) laxness (B) gaiety
(C) graceful walk (D) happy expression
(E) logical argument

11. AUSTERE: (A) indulgent (B) forthright
(C) modest (D) progressive (E) mundane

12. EUPHONIOUS: (A) inappropriate (B) devious
(C) raucous (D) unfriendly (E) impotent

13. GRATIS: (A) earned (B) outcast
(C) broken (D) static (E) praised

14. SECULAR: (A) hypocritical (B) theoretical
(C) autonomous (D) religious (E) pure

15. ENSCONCE: (A) uproot (B) measure
(C) perceive (D) expedite action
(E) assume authority

Each sentence below has one or two blanks, each blank indicating that something has been omitted. Beneath the sentence are five lettered words or sets of words. Choose the word or set of words that, when inserted in the sentence, best fits the meaning of the sentence as a whole.

Example:

Although its publicity has been ----, the film itself is intelligent, well-acted, handsomely produced, and altogether ----.

(A) tasteless. .respectable (B) extensive. .moderate
(C) sophisticated. .amateur (D) risqué. .crude
(E) perfect. .spectacular

● Ⓑ Ⓒ Ⓓ Ⓔ

16. Truisms are beliefs that are so generally ---- that people are unaware that there could be any ---- the beliefs.

(A) contradictory..disapproval of
(B) upheld..substance to
(C) accepted..opposition to
(D) supported..reason for
(E) suspect..questioning of

17. Although a few contemporaries ---- the book, most either ignored or mocked it.

(A) degraded (B) disregarded (C) ridiculed
(D) slighted (E) appreciated

18. Lacking direct ---- racketeering, the average American citizen fails to see any reason for ----.

(A) information on. .apathy
(B) confrontation with. .alarm
(C) control of. .curiosity
(D) evidence of. .allegiance
(E) compliance with. .regulation

19. He claims that life on this planet was the result of a combination of circumstances so ---- that they could never occur again.

(A) intense (B) impressive (C) confined
(D) improbable (E) unimaginable

20. Sheila Rowbotham sees her book not as an ---- work but as the initial exploration of an unmapped field.

(A) introductory (B) investigative
(C) innovative (D) exhaustive (E) enlightening

GO ON TO THE NEXT PAGE

Each passage below is followed by questions based on its content. Answer the questions following each passage on the basis of what is stated or implied in that passage.

Geronimo was not the only grandchild of the Great Chief who confronted the Mexicans in hostile times. His cousin Nah-thle-tla, my mother, also encountered them during this period.

Nah-thle-tla was twelve years old when Halley's Comet appeared. She remembered "the night the stars fell." When she died at the age of one hundred and twelve, she was honored as the oldest woman in the United States. I inherited this quality from her. She also taught me all my earliest lore as my father, Nah-thle-tla's second husband, was killed in a buffalo stampede in my infancy.

Nah-thle-tla fell in love first with Shnowin, an Apache. Though his affection was intense, he was too bashful to show it and Nah-thle-tla, because of tradition, could not reveal her own feelings. Finally, Shnowin's parents visited Nah-thle-tla's family secretly to arrange the marriage price, two horses, but the young people were kept apart and the arrangements private.

After the ceremony, Shnowin went on the warpath against the Mexicans. The Apaches won a victory, but unfortunately Shnowin was killed. During his absence Nah-thle-tla had been living with her parents near the border. Apaches felt safe there since the treaty between the United States and Mexico prevented troops from crossing the border for any reason. When the Apaches saw men approaching, they believed they were the returning warriors.

Nah-thle-tla was captured by the raiders and marched south toward Chihuahua. The Mexican commander was harsh with her because of her boasted kinship with Geronimo who had, as I described, fought against the Mexicans. He made her walk to Casas Grandes, over one hundred miles, instead of riding like the other captives. He didn't realize that this was nothing unusual for an Apache woman. Nah-thle-tla never wept during this journey as did the other women. Even after they were sold into slavery she said, "We are still close to our homeland and will one day find our people again. Cheer up."

Nah-thle-tla worked for a wealthy Mexican family in Albuquerque for two years, grinding corn, making tortillas, and cooking. The señor always saw that Nah-thle-tla was supplied with the expensive fresh fruit she loved. But one night during a fiesta Nah-thle-tla escaped. She was a wiry girl, and though she was equipped with only a butcher knife, she managed to gather food, ward off animals, and walk the mountainous terrain for ten days until she reached the Magdalena Mountains. There she cried for the first time, for she saw the smoke of campfires and knew from the bands around the hair of the women that the people were Apaches.

21. The author mentions that Nah-thle-tla had fresh fruit while she lived in Albuquerque in order to give an indication of the

(A) kindness of the wealthy Mexican family
(B) sort of vegetation to be found in the region
(C) freedom Nah-thle-tla enjoyed there
(D) diet of wealthy people in the old Southwest
(E) taste for rare foods which Nah-thle-tla retained

22. What quality does the author say he inherited from his mother?

(A) Wisdom (B) Loyalty (C) Longevity
(D) Patience (E) Wiriness

23. It can be inferred that Nah-thle-tla and her parents did not flee from the Mexicans because they

(A) believed the United States Army would protect them from harm
(B) thought the Mexicans were Apache warriors
(C) realized flight was useless in their defenseless position
(D) did not see the men approaching until it was too late to flee
(E) felt sure the Mexicans would not attack women and old people

24. It can be inferred that in the paragraphs immediately preceding the passage, the author discussed

(A) Nah-thle-tla's early life with the Apaches
(B) Geronimo's battles with the Mexicans
(C) his reasons for revering Geronimo
(D) his relationship to the Great Chief
(E) Nah-thle-tla's memory of "the night the stars fell"

25. Which of the following titles best summarizes the content of the passage?

(A) Geronimo's and Nah-thle-tla's Stories
(B) An Apache Confrontation
(C) An Apache Woman in Mexico
(D) The Closeness of an Apache Family
(E) Episodes from My Mother's Past

GO ON TO THE NEXT PAGE

The general features of the low-level jet stream are now fairly well known. On the days that it occurs, it begins to build up in the late afternoon; it reaches its maximum in the middle of the night and decays in the early morning. At the peak of the jet, the winds in its core, between 800 and 2,000 feet up, can attain between 50 and 80 miles per hour, decreasing to 10 to 20 miles per hour between 3,000 and 4,000 feet and to zero at the ground.

Meteorologists generally agree that the diurnal cycle of heating and cooling of the earth plays a major part in the development of low-level jets. On a clear day, as the ground soaks up solar energy and grows warmer, it heats the layer of air immediately above it. If this layer gets hot enough, it begins to push its way up through the cooler air above it and a convection pattern is set up, with warm air rising over some parts of the surface and cooler air descending over others. This convective turbulence, as it is called, mixes the air at different levels. Also contributing to the mixing is mechanical turbulence, which depends on the strength of the wind and the roughness of the terrain. The interchange makes the pattern of wind speeds through the first few thousand feet more nearly uniform than it would otherwise be. Air moving closest to the surface is subject to the maximum frictional drag from the ground. As a result the wind in the lowest levels is slower than in the layers above it. Mixing partly offsets this effect: the ascending parcels of air carry up with them their lower speeds, while the descending cells bring down the higher speeds.

If the day has been calm as well as clear, with little mechanical turbulence, mixing falls off sharply as the sun goes down and the heating of the lower air decreases. The lowest air layers, still affected by surface drag but cut off now from the momentum supplied from above during the day, move more and more slowly. At the same time the upper layers are no longer sapped by contributions of momentum to the surface layers or slowed by injections of slower surface air. The winds aloft therefore speed up, and the jet begins to form.

The build-up of the jet is assisted by another nighttime weather phenomenon: temperature inversion. During the day the temperature of the first few thousand feet of atmosphere generally decreases with height. After the sun goes down, the ground begins to lose heat by radiation. If there is no blanket of clouds, the surface and the adjacent layers of air soon become cooler than the air above them. Here the temperature increases with height through the first thousand feet or so, and each succeeding parcel of air through the layer is warmer and lighter than the one below it. This is a stable arrangement, which further damps out vertical mixing. On nights when the jet develops, the depth of the inversion layer increases during the hours just after sunset, and the fastest winds are just above the top of the deepening inversion.

26. The primary purpose of the author apparently is to

(A) explain meteorological terminology
(B) illustrate what is meant by "convective turbulence"
(C) explain the effects of the diurnal cycle
(D) describe the formation of low-altitude jet streams
(E) relate temperature inversion to jet stream formation

27. According to the passage, temperature inversion is important in the formation of the low-level jet stream because it

(A) reduces mixing
(B) occurs at night
(C) cools the surface air
(D) creates layers of air
(E) reduces heat loss by radiation

28. On the basis of the passage, when does a low-level jet stream seem most likely to be at maximum intensity?

(A) Morning   (B) Noon   (C) Midafternoon
(D) Evening   (E) Midnight

29. By mixing the air from different levels, mechanical turbulence and convective turbulence tend to

(A) create winds particularly at the higher levels
(B) slow the lower-level air
(C) speed up the upper-level air
(D) produce temperature inversion
(E) equalize the momentum at the two levels

30. It can be inferred from the passage that the condition most essential for the formation of a low-level jet stream is

(A) a rise in the temperature of the higher levels of air
(B) a minimum of vertical mixing of air
(C) surface drag on the lowest air layers
(D) mechanical turbulence during the day
(E) a maximum of momentum transfer between air layers

GO ON TO THE NEXT PAGE

Select the word or set of words that best completes each of the following sentences.

31. ---- for its own sake is so admired that we find ourselves paying respectful attention not only to Channel swimmers but also to flagpole sitters or people who can dance without stopping for the longest period of time.

    (A) Skill (B) Fame (C) Levity
    (D) Endurance (E) Bravery

32. Accounts of scientific experiments are generally ---- because those writing about science are careful in checking the ---- of their reports.

    (A) routine..reviews
    (B) tentative..sources
    (C) correct..accuracy
    (D) misunderstood..wording
    (E) misleading..validity

33. Nearly all the cultivated plants utilized by the Chinese have been of ---- origin; even rice, though known in China since Neolithic times, came from India.

    (A) foreign (B) ancient (C) wild
    (D) obscure (E) common

34. Loud people sometimes imply that a subdued tone is inconsistent with ----, but, unless it can be shown that the seat of candor is in the lungs, there seems to be no reason why a loud person should not be given to ----.

    (A) openness..deception
    (B) effectiveness..competence
    (C) falsehood..hypocrisy
    (D) intelligence..wisdom
    (E) subtlety..straightforwardness

35. We jokingly described our doctor as a ----, for it seemed he habitually called all sorts of ---- by the same name and was thus able to prescribe the same treatment for each one.

    (A) prophet..symptoms
    (B) therapist..remedies
    (C) specialist..maladies
    (D) philanthropist..patients
    (E) hypochondriac..ailments

Each question below consists of a related pair of words or phrases, followed by five lettered pairs of words or phrases. Select the lettered pair that best expresses a relationship similar to that expressed in the original pair.

Example:

YAWN : BOREDOM :: (A) dream : sleep
(B) anger : madness (C) smile : amusement
(D) face : expression (E) impatience : rebellion

Ⓐ Ⓑ ● Ⓓ Ⓔ

36. CHOP : AX :: (A) knit : sweater
(B) cut : scissors (C) unwind : spool
(D) deflate : balloon (E) aim : rifle

37. ORCHESTRA : CONDUCTOR :: (A) class : student
(B) baton : majorette (C) chorus : vocalist
(D) jury : witness (E) troupe : director

38. DOODLE : DRAW :: (A) stroke : swim
(B) battle : fight (C) meander : walk
(D) flatter : praise (E) bemoan : complain

39. REDUCE : LESS :: (A) dismantle : equal
(B) conceal : valuable (C) illuminate : pale
(D) pinpoint : obvious (E) restrain : active

40. SKEPTICAL : DOUBT :: (A) shrewd : resent
(B) emotional : love (C) critical : pity
(D) credulous : trust (E) zealous : suffer

41. DESECRATION : SHRINE :: (A) deference : royalty
(B) vandalism : prisoner (C) slander : reputation
(D) pillage : war (E) blasphemy : heretic

42. OSSIFY : BONE :: (A) congeal : metal
(B) freeze : ice (C) excise : tumor
(D) stimulate : nerve (E) anoint : oil

43. DEPLORE : REGRETFULNESS :: (A) deride : contempt
(B) defy : enemy (C) differ : condescension
(D) dominate : inferiority (E) deprive : misery

44. PARRY : BLOW :: (A) kindle : fire
(B) ban : book (C) repudiate : friend
(D) denounce : traitor (E) evade : question

45. OVERWROUGHT : EXCITED ::
(A) amplified : intense (B) diversified : interesting
(C) vain : irritating (D) baffled : angry
(E) surfeited : full

IF YOU FINISH BEFORE TIME IS CALLED, YOU MAY CHECK YOUR WORK ON THIS SECTION ONLY. DO NOT TURN TO ANY OTHER SECTION IN THE TEST. **STOP**

Correct Answers for Scholastic Aptitude Test
Form Code 1Z

VERBAL		MATHEMATICAL	
Section 1	Section 6	Section 3	Section 5
1. C	1. B	1. D	1. E
2. E	2. C	2. D	2. B
3. D	3. E	3. B	3. A
4. D	4. D	4. C	4. D
5. C	5. D	5. B	5. B
6. D	6. E	6. C	6. A
7. E	7. B	7. A	7. B
8. A	8. B	8. C	*8. A
9. B	9. D	9. A	*9. A
10. E	10. A	10. D	*10. C
11. C	11. A	11. A	*11. B
12. B	12. C	12. E	*12. A
13. C	13. A	13. A	*13. D
14. C	14. D	14. A	*14. B
15. C	15. A	15. B	*15. B
16. B	16. C	16. A	*16. A
17. C	17. E	17. C	*17. D
18. C	18. B	18. B	*18. †
19. C	19. D	19. E	*19. A
20. E	20. D	20. B	*20. C
21. B	21. A	21. A	*21. A
22. D	22. C	22. E	*22. C
23. B	23. B	23. B	*23. C
24. A	24. B	24. E	*24. D
25. C	25. E	25. E	*25. A
26. C	26. D		*26. D
27. D	27. A		*27. C
28. E	28. E		28. C
29. A	29. E		29. B
30. B	30. B		30. E
31. B	31. D		31. D
32. A	32. C		32. E
33. A	33. A		33. E
34. E	34. A		34. A
35. D	35. C		35. A
36. B	36. B		
37. E	37. E		
38. E	38. C		
39. A	39. D		
40. A	40. D		
	41. C		
	42. B		
	43. A		
	44. E		
	45. E		

*Indicates four-choice questions. (All of the other questions are five-choice.)
†Not scored

The Scoring Process

Machine-scoring is done in three steps:

- *Scanning.* Your answer sheet is "read" by a scanning machine and the oval you filled in for each question is recorded on a computer tape.

- *Scoring.* The computer compares the oval filled in for each question with the correct response. Each correct answer receives one point; omitted questions do not count toward your score. For each wrong answer, a fraction of a point is subtracted to correct for random guessing. For questions with five answer choices, one-fourth of a point is subtracted for each wrong response; for questions with four answer choices, one-third of a point is subtracted for each wrong response. The SAT-verbal test has 85 questions with five answer choices each. If, for example, a student has 44 right, 32 wrong, and 9 omitted, the resulting raw score is determined as follows:

$$44 \text{ right} - \frac{32 \text{ wrong}}{4} = 44 - 8 = 36 \text{ raw score points}$$

Obtaining raw scores frequently involves the rounding of fractional numbers to the nearest whole number. For example, a raw score of 36.25 is rounded to 36, the nearest whole number. A raw score of 36.50 is rounded upward to 37.

- *Converting to reported scaled score.* Raw test scores are then placed on the College Board scale of 200 to 800 through a process that adjusts scores to account for minor differences in difficulty among different editions of the test. This process, known as equating, is performed so that a student's reported score is not affected by the edition of the test taken nor by the abilities of the group with whom the student takes the test. As a result of placing SAT scores on the College Board scale, scores earned by students at different times can be compared. For example, an SAT-verbal score of 400 on a test taken at one administration indicates the same level of developed verbal ability as a 400 score obtained on a different edition of the test taken at another time.

How to Score the Test

SAT-Verbal Sections 1 and 6

Step A: Count the number of correct answers for *section 1* and record the number in the space provided on the worksheet on the next page. Then do the same for the incorrect answers. (Do not count omitted answers.) To determine subtotal A, use the formula:

$$\text{number correct} - \frac{\text{number incorrect}}{4} = \text{subtotal A}$$

Step B: Count the number of correct answers and the number of incorrect answers for *section 6* and record the numbers in the spaces provided on the worksheet. To determine subtotal B, use the formula:

$$\text{number correct} - \frac{\text{number incorrect}}{4} = \text{subtotal B}$$

Step C: To obtain C, add subtotal A to subtotal B, keeping any decimals. Enter the resulting figure on the worksheet.

Step D: To obtain D, your raw verbal score, round C to the nearest whole number. (For example, any number from 44.50 to 45.49 rounds to 45.) Enter the resulting figure on the worksheet.

Step E: To find your reported SAT-verbal score, look up the total raw verbal score you obtained in step D in the conversion table on page 146. Enter this figure on the worksheet.

SAT-Mathematical Sections 3 and 5

Step A: Count the number of correct answers and the number of incorrect answers for *section 3* and record the numbers in the spaces provided on the worksheet. To determine the subtotal A, use the formula:

$$\text{number correct} - \frac{\text{number incorrect}}{4} = \text{subtotal A}$$

Step B: Count the number of correct answers and the number of incorrect answers for the *five-choice questions (questions 1 through 7 and 28 through 35)* in section 5 and record the numbers in the spaces provided on the worksheet. To determine the subtotal B, use the formula:

$$\text{number correct} - \frac{\text{number incorrect}}{4} = \text{subtotal B}$$

Step C: Count the number of correct answers and the number of incorrect answers for the *four-choice questions (questions 8 through 27)* in section 5 and record the numbers in the spaces provided on the worksheet. To determine the subtotal C, use the formula:

$$\text{number correct} - \frac{\text{number incorrect}}{3} = \text{subtotal C}$$

Step D: To obtain D, add subtotal A, subtotal B, and subtotal C, keeping any decimals. Enter the resulting figure on the worksheet.

Step E: To obtain E, your raw mathematical score, round D to the nearest whole number. (For example, any number from 44.50 to 45.49 rounds to 45.) Enter the resulting figure on the worksheet.

Step F: To find your reported SAT-mathematical score, look up the total raw mathematical score you obtained in E in the conversion table on page 146. Enter this figure on the worksheet.

SAT SCORING WORKSHEET

SAT-Verbal Sections

A. Section 1:

_____ − ¼ (_____) = _____
no. correct   no. incorrect   subtotal A

B. Section 6:

_____ − ¼ (_____) = _____
no. correct   no. incorrect   subtotal B

C. Total unrounded raw score
(Total A + B)

_____
C

D. Total rounded raw score
(Rounded to nearest whole number)

_____
D

E. SAT-verbal reported scaled score
(See the conversion table on page 146.)

SAT-verbal
score

SAT-Mathematical Sections

A. Section 3:

_____ − ¼ (_____) = _____
no. correct   no. incorrect   subtotal A

B. Section 5:
Questions 1 through 7 and
28 through 35 (5-choice)

_____ − ¼ (_____) = _____
no. correct   no. incorrect   subtotal B

C. Section 5:
Questions 8 through 27
(4-choice)

_____ − ⅓ (_____) = _____
no. correct   no. incorrect   subtotal C

D. Total unrounded raw score
(Total A + B + C)

_____
D

E. Total rounded raw score
(Rounded to nearest whole number)

_____
E

F. SAT-mathematical reported scaled score
(See the conversion table on page 146.)

SAT-math
score

Score Conversion Table
Scholastic Aptitude Test
Form Code 1Z

Raw Score	College Board Reported Score		Raw Score	College Board Reported Score	
	SAT-Verbal	SAT-Math		SAT-Verbal	SAT-Math
85	800		40	470	630
84	790		39	460	620
83	780		38	460	610
82	770		37	450	600
81	760		36	440	590
80	750		35	430	580
79	740		34	430	570
78	740		33	420	560
77	730		32	410	560
76	720		31	410	550
75	710		30	400	540
74	710		29	390	530
73	700		28	390	520
72	690		27	380	510
71	690		26	370	500
70	680		25	360	490
69	670		24	360	480
68	670		23	350	470
67	660		22	340	470
66	650		21	340	460
65	640		20	330	450
64	640		19	320	440
63	630		18	320	430
62	620		17	310	420
61	620		16	300	410
60	610		15	290	400
59	600	800	14	290	390
58	600	790	13	280	390
57	590	780	12	270	380
56	580	770	11	270	370
55	570	760	10	260	360
54	570	750	9	250	350
53	560	740	8	240	340
52	550	730	7	240	330
51	550	730	6	230	320
50	540	720	5	220	310
49	530	710	4	220	300
48	530	700	3	210	300
47	520	690	2	200	290
46	510	680	1	200	280
45	500	670	0	200	270
44	500	660	−1	200	260
43	490	650	−2	200	250
42	480	650	−3	200	240
41	480	640	−4	200	230
			−5	200	220
			−6	200	210
			−7	200	210
			−8 or below	200	200

COLLEGE BOARD — SCHOLASTIC APTITUDE TEST
and Test of Standard Written English   Side 1

Use a No. 2 pencil only. Be sure each mark is dark and completely fills the intended oval. Completely erase any errors or stray marks.

1.
YOUR NAME: _____
(Print)   Last   First   M.I.

SIGNATURE: _____ DATE: ____ / ____ / ____

HOME ADDRESS: _____
(Print)   Number and Street

_____
City   State   Zip Code

CENTER: _____
(Print)   City   State   Center Number

IMPORTANT: Please fill in these boxes exactly as shown on the back cover of your test book.

FOR ETS USE ONLY

5. YOUR NAME

First 4 letters of last name | First Init. | Mid. Init.

(Grid of ovals A–Z for each of the 6 columns)

2. TEST FORM

3. FORM CODE

4. REGISTRATION NUMBER
(Copy from your Admission Ticket.)

6. DATE OF BIRTH

Month	Day	Year
Jan.		
Feb.		
Mar.		
Apr.		
May		
June		
July		
Aug.		
Sept.		
Oct.		
Nov.		
Dec.		

Form Code ovals:
Row 0: 0 A J S 0 0 0 0 0 0 0 0 0 0 0
Row 1: 1 B K T 1 1 1 1 1 1 1 1 1 1 1
Row 2: 2 C L U 2 2 2 2 2 2 2 2 2 2 2
Row 3: 3 D M V 3 3 3 3 3 3 3 3 3 3 3
Row 4: 4 E N W 4 4 4 4 4 4 4 4 4 4 4
Row 5: 5 F O X 5 5 5 5 5 5 5 5 5 5 5
Row 6: 6 G P Y 6 6 6 6 6 6 6 6 6 6 6
Row 7: 7 H Q Z 7 7 7 7 7 7 7 7 7 7 7
Row 8: 8 I R 8 8 8 8 8 8 8 8 8 8
Row 9: 9 9 9 9 9 9 9 9 9 9 9

7. SEX
○ Female
○ Male

8. TEST BOOK SERIAL NUMBER

Start with number 1 for each new section. If a section has fewer than 50 questions, leave the extra answer spaces blank.

SECTION 1

1 A B C D E   26 A B C D E
2 A B C D E   27 A B C D E
3 A B C D E   28 A B C D E
4 A B C D E   29 A B C D E
5 A B C D E   30 A B C D E
6 A B C D E   31 A B C D E
7 A B C D E   32 A B C D E
8 A B C D E   33 A B C D E
9 A B C D E   34 A B C D E
10 A B C D E   35 A B C D E
11 A B C D E   36 A B C D E
12 A B C D E   37 A B C D E
13 A B C D E   38 A B C D E
14 A B C D E   39 A B C D E
15 A B C D E   40 A B C D E
16 A B C D E   41 A B C D E
17 A B C D E   42 A B C D E
18 A B C D E   43 A B C D E
19 A B C D E   44 A B C D E
20 A B C D E   45 A B C D E
21 A B C D E   46 A B C D E
22 A B C D E   47 A B C D E
23 A B C D E   48 A B C D E
24 A B C D E   49 A B C D E
25 A B C D E   50 A B C D E

SECTION 2

1 A B C D E   26 A B C D E
2 A B C D E   27 A B C D E
3 A B C D E   28 A B C D E
4 A B C D E   29 A B C D E
5 A B C D E   30 A B C D E
6 A B C D E   31 A B C D E
7 A B C D E   32 A B C D E
8 A B C D E   33 A B C D E
9 A B C D E   34 A B C D E
10 A B C D E   35 A B C D E
11 A B C D E   36 A B C D E
12 A B C D E   37 A B C D E
13 A B C D E   38 A B C D E
14 A B C D E   39 A B C D E
15 A B C D E   40 A B C D E
16 A B C D E   41 A B C D E
17 A B C D E   42 A B C D E
18 A B C D E   43 A B C D E
19 A B C D E   44 A B C D E
20 A B C D E   45 A B C D E
21 A B C D E   46 A B C D E
22 A B C D E   47 A B C D E
23 A B C D E   48 A B C D E
24 A B C D E   49 A B C D E
25 A B C D E   50 A B C D E

(Cut here to detach.)

Q1362-04

I.N. 574006—110VV25P3015

COLLEGE BOARD — SCHOLASTIC APTITUDE TEST
and Test of Standard Written English — Side 2

Use a No. 2 pencil only. Be sure each mark is dark and completely fills the intended oval. Completely erase any errors or stray marks.

Start with number 1 for each new section. If a section has fewer than 50 questions, leave the extra answer spaces blank.

9. SIGNATURE:

SECTION 3

1 (A) (B) (C) (D) (E)
2 (A) (B) (C) (D) (E)
3 (A) (B) (C) (D) (E)
4 (A) (B) (C) (D) (E)
5 (A) (B) (C) (D) (E)
6 (A) (B) (C) (D) (E)
7 (A) (B) (C) (D) (E)
8 (A) (B) (C) (D) (E)
9 (A) (B) (C) (D) (E)
10 (A) (B) (C) (D) (E)
11 (A) (B) (C) (D) (E)
12 (A) (B) (C) (D) (E)
13 (A) (B) (C) (D) (E)
14 (A) (B) (C) (D) (E)
15 (A) (B) (C) (D) (E)
16 (A) (B) (C) (D) (E)
17 (A) (B) (C) (D) (E)
18 (A) (B) (C) (D) (E)
19 (A) (B) (C) (D) (E)
20 (A) (B) (C) (D) (E)
21 (A) (B) (C) (D) (E)
22 (A) (B) (C) (D) (E)
23 (A) (B) (C) (D) (E)
24 (A) (B) (C) (D) (E)
25 (A) (B) (C) (D) (E)
26 (A) (B) (C) (D) (E)
27 (A) (B) (C) (D) (E)
28 (A) (B) (C) (D) (E)
29 (A) (B) (C) (D) (E)
30 (A) (B) (C) (D) (E)
31 (A) (B) (C) (D) (E)
32 (A) (B) (C) (D) (E)
33 (A) (B) (C) (D) (E)
34 (A) (B) (C) (D) (E)
35 (A) (B) (C) (D) (E)
36 (A) (B) (C) (D) (E)
37 (A) (B) (C) (D) (E)
38 (A) (B) (C) (D) (E)
39 (A) (B) (C) (D) (E)
40 (A) (B) (C) (D) (E)
41 (A) (B) (C) (D) (E)
42 (A) (B) (C) (D) (E)
43 (A) (B) (C) (D) (E)
44 (A) (B) (C) (D) (E)
45 (A) (B) (C) (D) (E)
46 (A) (B) (C) (D) (E)
47 (A) (B) (C) (D) (E)
48 (A) (B) (C) (D) (E)
49 (A) (B) (C) (D) (E)
50 (A) (B) (C) (D) (E)

SECTION 4

(answer spaces 1–50, filled/marked)

SECTION 5

1 (A) (B) (C) (D) (E)
2 (A) (B) (C) (D) (E)
3 (A) (B) (C) (D) (E)
4 (A) (B) (C) (D) (E)
5 (A) (B) (C) (D) (E)
6 (A) (B) (C) (D) (E)
7 (A) (B) (C) (D) (E)
8 (A) (B) (C) (D) (E)
9 (A) (B) (C) (D) (E)
10 (A) (B) (C) (D) (E)
11 (A) (B) (C) (D) (E)
12 (A) (B) (C) (D) (E)
13 (A) (B) (C) (D) (E)
14 (A) (B) (C) (D) (E)
15 (A) (B) (C) (D) (E)
16 (A) (B) (C) (D) (E)
17 (A) (B) (C) (D) (E)
18 (A) (B) (C) (D) (E)
19 (A) (B) (C) (D) (E)
20 (A) (B) (C) (D) (E)
21 (A) (B) (C) (D) (E)
22 (A) (B) (C) (D) (E)
23 (A) (B) (C) (D) (E)
24 (A) (B) (C) (D) (E)
25 (A) (B) (C) (D) (E)
26 (A) (B) (C) (D) (E)
27 (A) (B) (C) (D) (E)
28 (A) (B) (C) (D) (E)
29 (A) (B) (C) (D) (E)
30 (A) (B) (C) (D) (E)
31 (A) (B) (C) (D) (E)
32 (A) (B) (C) (D) (E)
33 (A) (B) (C) (D) (E)
34 (A) (B) (C) (D) (E)
35 (A) (B) (C) (D) (E)
36 (A) (B) (C) (D) (E)
37 (A) (B) (C) (D) (E)
38 (A) (B) (C) (D) (E)
39 (A) (B) (C) (D) (E)
40 (A) (B) (C) (D) (E)
41 (A) (B) (C) (D) (E)
42 (A) (B) (C) (D) (E)
43 (A) (B) (C) (D) (E)
44 (A) (B) (C) (D) (E)
45 (A) (B) (C) (D) (E)
46 (A) (B) (C) (D) (E)
47 (A) (B) (C) (D) (E)
48 (A) (B) (C) (D) (E)
49 (A) (B) (C) (D) (E)
50 (A) (B) (C) (D) (E)

SECTION 6

(answer spaces 1–50, filled/marked)

TEST 5—FORM CODE 1S

Each question below consists of a word in capital letters, followed by five lettered words or phrases. Choose the word or phrase that is most nearly opposite in meaning to the word in capital letters. Since some of the questions require you to distinguish fine shades of meaning, consider all the choices before deciding which is best.

Example:

GOOD: (A) sour (B) bad (C) red
(D) hot (E) ugly

Ⓐ ● Ⓒ Ⓓ Ⓔ

1. BAN: (A) borrow (B) regret
(C) permit (D) conquer (E) exaggerate

2. COMPRESSION: (A) equality (B) expansion
(C) exposure (D) endurance (E) excitement

3. FRAUDULENT: (A) dynamic (B) masterly
(C) possible (D) genuine (E) abundant

4. PARASITE: (A) expert (B) imposter
(C) instigator (D) self-assured snob
(E) self-sufficient individual

5. SPARSE: (A) thick (B) tidy
(C) wealthy (D) round (E) sticky

6. DENOUNCE: (A) overstate (B) acclaim
(C) destroy (D) refuse (E) hasten

7. FLY-BY-NIGHT: (A) unbalanced (B) moderate
(C) permanent (D) incredible (E) modern

8. STERILE: (A) venal (B) productive
(C) generous (D) variegated (E) unalloyed

9. REJOICE: (A) defend against (B) shrug off
(C) criticize (D) bemoan (E) discriminate

10. FANATICISM: (A) optimism (B) hedonism
(C) penitence (D) didacticism (E) apathy

11. VESTIGIAL: (A) fully developed
(B) publicly announced (C) offensive
(D) provincial (E) miraculous

12. DIVERT: (A) bore (B) rescue (C) espouse
(D) judge fairly (E) question relentlessly

13. HACKNEYED: (A) integrated (B) appealing
(C) inventive (D) acceptable (E) improper

14. ALACRITY: (A) indolence (B) bravery
(C) wisdom (D) pungency (E) retention

15. BURGEON: (A) fail to prove
(B) shrivel and die (C) pursue and capture
(D) disobey regulations (E) speak incoherently

Each sentence below has one or two blanks, each blank indicating that something has been omitted. Beneath the sentence are five lettered words or sets of words. Choose the word or set of words that, when inserted in the sentence, best fits the meaning of the sentence as a whole.

Example:

Although its publicity has been ----, the film itself is intelligent, well-acted, handsomely produced, and altogether ----.

(A) tasteless. .respectable (B) extensive. .moderate
(C) sophisticated. .amateur (D) risqué. .crude
(E) perfect. .spectacular

● Ⓑ Ⓒ Ⓓ Ⓔ

16. Rather than ---- wagon trains and ---- the pioneer's movement westward, many American Indians acted as guides and companions.

(A) encountering. .helping
(B) seeking. .encouraging
(C) attacking. .hindering
(D) welcoming. .allowing
(E) repulsing. .following

17. Although Ricardo looked tired, he was enormously ---- by Maria's election, a victory they had both labored so hard for.

(A) elated (B) baffled (C) fatigued
(D) surprised (E) exasperated

18. The earth's atmosphere ---- surface temperatures by distributing heat absorbed on the sunlit side to the side in shadow.

(A) warms (B) resists (C) generates
(D) moderates (E) amasses

19. Professor Greene's ----, detailed, and lucid lectures match the gravity of her subject.

(A) blithe (B) studious (C) jaundiced
(D) obscure (E) uproarious

20. It would seem that the ---- of science, the building and making of things, have stirred the American imagination, but that the ---- roots of such activities have not.

(A) applications. .theoretical
(B) hypotheses. .practical
(C) formulas. .actual
(D) offshoots. .extrinsic
(E) products. .future

GO ON TO THE NEXT PAGE →

1

Each passage below is followed by questions based on its content. Answer the questions following each passage on the basis of what is <u>stated</u> or <u>implied</u> in that passage.

(This passage was written in 1961.)

The classics are the great works of human intelligence that, whether produced in Israel, Greece, Rome, or England, have demonstrated the capacity for being understood over a long period of time and in a variety of places. They introduce the student to the significant ideas common to Western civilization. But most students are so busy learning the language of the classics that they never become acquainted with the ideas in them.

I know not how many Gauls Caesar slaughtered. But I know that learning Latin from the *Gallic Wars* has killed the interest of generations of Americans in the classics. More than sixty years ago, a committee of educational consultants affirmed that the *Gallic Wars* did not belong in the classroom. According to the committee, "The book is altogether too difficult for beginners; it is too military in content to be generally interesting. Its vocabulary is too restricted to marches, sieges, and battles to afford the best introduction to subsequent reading." Yet, of the glory that was Greece and Rome, this is what high school students first encounter. And since they are forced to further waste time by reading it in the original, this is often their only encounter.

The stubborn attachment to Caesar springs from an underlying insistence that the ultimate purpose of teaching the classics is to teach Latin and that therefore the simple style of Caesar is appropriate. For the same reason, *Beowulf* has been set as an impenetrable barrier to a love of English literature by those who believe that the study of English literature must begin with the knowledge of the Anglo-Saxon language.

However, if we use the classics to offer a glimpse of the seminal ideas of Western culture, quite different texts can be held forth. All students can read some Aristophanes or Thucydides or Chaucer with interest. Inclusive lists are of no importance, for these texts should be the beginning, rather than the sum, of their reading. And they should begin by reading the good English translations that are available. No translation is, of course, the equivalent of the original. But the question is not whether *The Clouds* should be read in Greek or in English; the question is whether it should be read in English or not read at all. It is more likely that a few students will be drawn to study the language through knowledge of its literature than that any will be drawn to the literature through drill in the language.

21. Which of the following best expresses the main idea of the passage?

   (A) The *Gallic Wars* is more appropriate today than it was many years ago.
   (B) Most students are more interested in learning languages than in learning history.
   (C) The place of the classics in high school has been greatly overrated.
   (D) Good English translations of the classics are usually stylistically superior to the originals.
   (E) The classics should be used in the high school to present meaningful ideas.

22. It can be inferred that the committee of educational consultants mentioned in the passage recommended that

   (A) Latin be studied in the high schools, but from a text other than Caesar's *Gallic Wars*
   (B) Caesar's *Gallic Wars* continue to be studied in American schools, but from a good English translation
   (C) the study of the classics be dropped from American school curricula
   (D) Latin be studied from Caesar's *Gallic Wars* because the style, if not the content, is appropriate for beginners
   (E) an abridged version of the *Gallic Wars*, omitting much of the military content, be published

23. Which of the following would the author probably recommend as the best approach to the study of classics in American high schools?

   (A) The classics should not be studied in any form.
   (B) The classics should be studied in the original language, but a restricted vocabulary should be used.
   (C) An appreciation of the classics should grow out of a thorough knowledge of them in their original languages.
   (D) The classics should be read in English translations.
   (E) The classics should be studied in relation to the literary theories of the time in which each work was written.

24. The author refers to Aristophanes and Thucydides as examples of classical authors who are

   (A) included in most high school courses
   (B) of intrinsic interest to young people
   (C) destroyed by awkward translations
   (D) of no interest because of their difficulty
   (E) difficult to relate to the rest of the literature curriculum

25. According to the author, the use of the classics in high schools was primarily based on the instructor's desire to

   (A) stimulate students' interest in languages
   (B) teach students self-discipline and promote a methodical approach to learning
   (C) develop in students a familiarity with a particular language
   (D) give young people an appreciation of contemporary achievements
   (E) familiarize students with the important names in Western literature

GO ON TO THE NEXT PAGE

150

The renewed interest in ragtime is one of the most curious cases of changing musical taste in recent years. The resurgence began in 1970 when a recording of eight rags by the inimitable Scott Joplin appeared.

Line
(5)

This recording was not a rediscovery of forgotten material, for ragtime had remained popular with jazz and Dixieland audiences. Jazz musicians had altered the steady beat of the

(10) music, adding syncopations and, in the process, eliminating the contrasts that highlighted the melodies; Dixieland musicians had done the pieces very fast, damaging the lyrical qualities. But in the 1970 recording, the music was played

(15) exactly as Joplin had written it. What emerged was a delicate music, with graceful melodies and compelling rhythms, that captivated a large new audience. Since then, modified ragtime recordings have inundated the market.

(20) Ragtime was created during the last years of the nineteenth century by itinerant black musicians of the Midwest out of previously disparate elements. From the minstrel song they took the melodic style characteristic of banjo accompani-

(25) ment; from the march they took the bass figures and rhythms; from the cakewalk they took a mock-serious combination of stately procession and energetic improvisation.

Present-day ragtime enthusiasts seem to delight

(30) in emphasizing the difficulties that faced ragtime composers. However, to cast a man such as Joplin as an "all-but-forgotten black American genius" not only ignores important elements of Joplin's life, but also misrepresents the develop-

(35) ment of popular music in the twentieth century. Within months of the publication of "Maple Leaf Rag," Joplin became a rich and famous man and remained so until his death. Also, the relative decline of ragtime cannot be blamed on hostility

(40) to black culture, since another form of black music, jazz, became the new rage when the original ragtime boom receded.

The attempt to assimilate ragtime into the romantic myth of the artist neglected by society

(45) can be seen as part of an effort to recast ragtime as "serious" or "classical" music. Admittedly, of all the forms of popular music, ragtime is the most amenable to "classical" treatment. Unlike jazz and folk music, ragtime is not improvisatory.

(50) It is fully written out, with no reliance on aural tradition. And unlike the work of the popular songwriters, ragtime is written for the solo piano— the preeminent classical instrument. Nevertheless, it is also true that the rag is a modest form, with

(55) an elementary structure and technique. Burdening ragtime with an unnecessary load of musical pre- tension and political meaning may sink this music into a deeper oblivion than the relative neglect from which it has been rescued.

26. According to the passage, Dixieland musicians altered the original style of ragtime music by

(A) highlighting the melodies
(B) adding syncopations
(C) playing the music very fast
(D) giving the music a steady beat
(E) omitting the lyrics of the music

27. By the statement "previously disparate elements" (lines 22-23), the author is referring to the fact that

(A) blacks had never before organized to develop an authentic style of music
(B) the source of a particular style of music had never before been attributed to a particular region of the country
(C) ragtime was the first black music to attract a large and varied audience
(D) ragtime was the first black music in which the piano rather than the banjo was the dominant instrument
(E) ragtime was created by mixing various aspects of other types of music

28. It can be inferred from the passage that, when it was written, Scott Joplin's music was

(A) overrated by critics
(B) dismissed as unprofitable
(C) ignored by audiences
(D) acknowledged as unique and praiseworthy
(E) considered classical rather than popular

29. With which of the following statements regarding ragtime would the author probably agree?

I. What is best in ragtime may be lost in the effort to make it something it is not.
II. Joplin's ragtime did more than any other style of music to revolutionize American music.
III. Ragtime differs in some important ways from most other popular music.

(A) I only   (B) I and II only   (C) I and III only
(D) II and III only   (E) I, II, and III

30. In developing the passage, the author does all of the following EXCEPT

(A) present evidence from other people to support the views expressed
(B) give historical information regarding the origins of ragtime music
(C) attempt to convey a feeling of the nature of ragtime music
(D) offer statements to refute certain aspects of the opposing point of view
(E) describe a potential consequence of the opposing point of view

GO ON TO THE NEXT PAGE

1

Select the word or set of words that best completes each of the following sentences.

31. Many of the officers were unsympathetic, even ----, to their new and inexperienced commander.

    (A) lukewarm   (B) indulgent
    (C) servile   (D) hostile   (E) impartial

32. The rural Republican and the urban Democrat were immensely different, and the ---- that separated them was not ---- successfully during the postwar era.

    (A) bulwark. .built
    (B) goal. .achieved
    (C) gulf. .bridged
    (D) economy. .widened
    (E) electorate. .enfranchised

33. Whereas his predecessors were careful to stay within the boundaries of factual evidence, Dr. Artman delivered an address that was ---- by pretentious and ---- theorizing.

    (A) marred. .irresponsible
    (B) undermined. .unassuming
    (C) supported. .flawless
    (D) refuted. .unverifiable
    (E) represented. .unquestionable

34. Because of their extremely simple structures, viruses have proved invaluable to those scientists who are interested in constructing ---- for the larger, more complex molecules.

    (A) a cure   (B) a response   (C) an edifice
    (D) a universe   (E) a paradigm

35. Many early Americans, for all their dislike of monarchy, firmly believed in ---- society.

    (A) a democratic   (B) an idealistic
    (C) a stratified   (D) a historic   (E) a flexible

Each question below consists of a related pair of words or phrases, followed by five lettered pairs of words or phrases. Select the lettered pair that best expresses a relationship similar to that expressed in the original pair.

Example:

YAWN : BOREDOM ::   (A) dream : sleep
(B) anger : madness   (C) smile : amusement
(D) face : expression   (E) impatience : rebellion

Ⓐ Ⓑ ● Ⓓ Ⓔ

36. FOOD : STARVATION ::   (A) liquor : inebriation
    (B) water : saturation   (C) heat : inflammation
    (D) privacy : isolation   (E) air : suffocation

37. TAPE RECORDER : EAR ::   (A) radio : antenna
    (B) camera : eye   (C) phonograph : volume
    (D) journal : hand   (E) telephone : speech

38. SUMMONS : ATTENDANCE ::
    (A) allowance : money   (B) bill : payment
    (C) purchase : article   (D) question : examination
    (E) continuation : action

39. HOPE : DESPAIRING ::   (A) confidence : friendly
    (B) respect : governing   (C) wittiness : humorous
    (D) jollity : gloomy   (E) unconcern : poised

40. ACT : TRAGEDY ::   (A) stanza : poem
    (B) palette : artist   (C) inventor : machine
    (D) gate : fence   (E) cover : book

41. ENIGMA : MYSTERIOUS ::
    (A) beginning : vague
    (B) decision : cautious
    (C) memory : forgotten
    (D) meeting place : random
    (E) turning point : significant

42. WHELP : DOG ::   (A) mule : horse
    (B) kitten : pet   (C) child : human being
    (D) criminal : community   (E) school : fish

43. ANNOY : ABUSE ::   (A) alter : change
    (B) encourage : prod   (C) clamor : silence
    (D) violate : revolt   (E) consider : discover

44. PARTICLE : AGGREGATE ::   (A) athlete : rivalry
    (B) molecule : surface   (C) asteroid : planet
    (D) animal : herd   (E) motor : power

45. UNWITTING : INTENTION ::
    (A) inconspicuous : strategy
    (B) alone : assistance
    (C) lavish : expense
    (D) impractical : explanation
    (E) futile : disappointment

IF YOU FINISH BEFORE TIME IS CALLED, YOU MAY CHECK YOUR WORK ON THIS SECTION ONLY. DO NOT TURN TO ANY OTHER SECTION IN THE TEST.   **STOP**

SECTION **2**   Time—30 minutes   In this section solve each problem, using any available space on the
25 Questions   page for scratchwork. Then decide which is the best of the choices given and fill in the corresponding oval on the answer sheet.

The following information is for your reference in solving some of the problems.

Circle of radius r: Area = πr^2; Circumference = $2\pi r$
   The number of degrees of arc in a circle is 360.
The measure in degrees of a straight angle is 180.

Definition of symbols:
= is equal to $\leqq$ is less than or equal to
$\neq$ is unequal to $\geqq$ is greater than or equal to
< is less than $\parallel$ is parallel to
> is greater than $\perp$ is perpendicular to

Triangle: The sum of the measures in degrees of the angles of a triangle is 180.
If $\angle CDA$ is a right angle, then

(1) area of $\triangle ABC = \dfrac{AB \times CD}{2}$

(2) $AC^2 = AD^2 + DC^2$

Note: Figures that accompany problems in this test are intended to provide information useful in solving the problems. They are drawn as accurately as possible EXCEPT when it is stated in a specific problem that its figure is not drawn to scale. All figures lie in a plane unless otherwise indicated. All numbers used are real numbers.

---

1. If $x^2 - 1 = y$ and $x = 3$, then $y^2 =$

   (A) 81   (B) 64   (C) 9   (D) 8   (E) 4

Red + Blue : Purple
Red + Yellow : Orange
Blue + Yellow : Green

2. The figure above shows strips of colored glass that overlap to form other colors as shown by the color chart. Which two labeled triangular regions would be green?

   (A) I and III
   (B) I and IV
   (C) II and V
   (D) III and VI
   (E) IV and VI

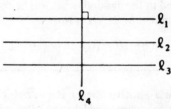

3. In the figure above, if $\ell_1 \parallel \ell_2$, $\ell_2 \parallel \ell_3$, and $\ell_1 \perp \ell_4$, which of the following statements must be true?

   I. $\ell_1 \parallel \ell_3$
   II. $\ell_2 \perp \ell_4$
   III. $\ell_3 \perp \ell_4$

   (A) None   (B) I only   (C) I and II only

   (D) II and III only   (E) I, II, and III

---

4. If $100 \leqq k \leqq 400$ and k is a multiple of 5, 6, 7, and 10, then $k =$

   (A) 105
   (B) 150
   (C) 210
   (D) 300
   (E) 350

GO ON TO THE NEXT PAGE

5. In a restaurant where the sales tax on a $4.00 lunch is $0.24, what will be the sales tax due on a $15.00 dinner?

(A) $0.60
(B) $0.75
(C) $0.90
(D) $1.20
(E) $1.74

1st Row				0	1	0				
2nd Row			0	1	1	0				
3rd Row			0	1	2	1	0			
4th Row		0	1	3	3	1	0			
5th Row	0	1	4	6	4	1	0			
6th Row →										

6. The nonzero numbers above form a triangular array. Beginning with the second row, each nonzero number in a row is the sum of the two numbers nearest to it in the row immediately above. If a sixth row is added in this fashion, what will be the sum of all the numbers in the sixth row?

(A) 8   (B) 10   (C) 16   (D) 32   (E) 64

---

7. If x is a positive integer and $x^2 + x = n$, which of the following could be the value of n?

(A) 14
(B) 15
(C) 18
(D) 23
(E) 30

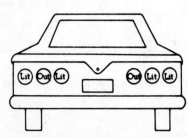

8. If one more of the lit signals on the rear of the car above were out, what per cent of all the rear signals would then be lit?

(A) 25%   (B) $33\frac{1}{3}$%   (C) 50%

(D) $66\frac{2}{3}$%   (E) 75%

9. If $111{,}111 + N = 181{,}111$, then $N =$

(A) 7×10^3
(B) 7×10^4
(C) 7×10^5
(D) 8×10^4
(E) 9×10^4

10. In the United States in a certain year, food production per person was 15 per cent greater than food consumption per person. If the average daily consumption per person in the United States in that year was 3,000 calories, what was the average daily production (in calories) per person in that year?

(A) 3,200   (B) 3,450   (C) 3,600
(D) 3,850   (E) 4,500

11. 0.06 is the ratio of 6 to

(A) 1,000   (B) 100   (C) 10
(D) $\frac{1}{10}$ (E) $\frac{1}{100}$

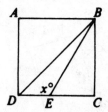

12. In the figure above, $ABCD$ is a square. If $BE = 2EC$, then $x =$

(A) 100   (B) 110   (C) 120
(D) 150   (E) 160

GO ON TO THE NEXT PAGE

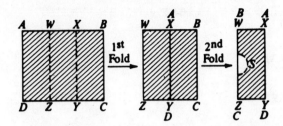

13. In the figure above, a rectangular piece of paper *ABCD* is folded along dotted line *WZ* so that *A* is on top of *X* and *D* is on top of *Y* and then folded along *XY* so that *B* is on top of *W* and *C* is on top of *Z*. A small semicircle *S* with diameter on *BC* is cut out of the folded paper. If the paper is unfolded, which of the following could be the result?

(A)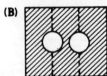

(B)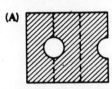

(C)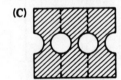

(D)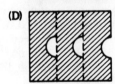

(E)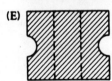

14. If $5x - 3y = 8$ and $x = \frac{7y}{5}$, then $y =$

(A) $\frac{5}{4}$

(B) $\frac{8}{5}$

(C) 2

(D) $\frac{8}{3}$

(E) 4

15. Amy is twice as old as Bill. Five years ago she was 3 times as old as Bill was then. How old is Bill now?

(A) 20
(B) 15
(C) 10
(D) 5
(E) It cannot be determined from the information given.

16. $(3x^2 - 4x + 7) - (2x + 1)(x - 5) =$

(A) $x^2 + 5x + 12$

(B) $x^2 - 5x + 12$

(C) $x^2 - 5x + 2$

(D) $5x^2 - 13x + 2$

(E) $5x^2 + 13x + 12$

17. In $\triangle ABC$, the ratio of the length of side *AB* to the perimeter is 1 to 3. What is the ratio of the length of side *BC* to the perimeter?

(A) $\frac{1}{4}$

(B) $\frac{1}{3}$

(C) $\frac{5}{12}$

(D) $\frac{1}{2}$

(E) It cannot be determined from the information given.

18. $\dfrac{(N-2)(N-4)(N-6)(N-8) - 1}{2}$ is an integer if *N* is equal to

(A) 1 only
(B) 2 only
(C) 9 only
(D) any odd integer
(E) any even integer

GO ON TO THE NEXT PAGE ⟩

2

19. Three equal semicircles are drawn on a diameter of the circle with center O as shown above. If the area of circle O is 9π, then the area of the shaded region is

    (A) $\dfrac{7\pi}{2}$ (B) 4π (C) $\dfrac{9\pi}{2}$ (D) 5π (E) $\dfrac{11\pi}{2}$

20. If each angle of quadrilateral $ABCD$ measures less than $180°$ and if 3 of its angles each measure $x°$, which of the following must be true?

    (A) $x > 60$

    (B) $x = 60$

    (C) $x < 60$

    (D) $ABCD$ is a parallelogram but not a square.

    (E) $ABCD$ is a square.

21. The set P consists of all numbers which are the sum of 3 consecutive prime numbers. For example, the number 109 is in P, since $31 + 37 + 41 = 109$. The least prime number in P is

    (A) 13
    (B) 17
    (C) 19
    (D) 23
    (E) 31

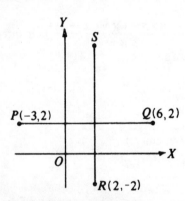

22. The coordinates of points P, Q, and R are shown in the figure above. If $PQ = RS$ and $PQ \perp RS$, what are the coordinates of S ?

    (A) $(2, 6)$ (B) $(2, 7)$ (C) $(2, 8)$

    (D) $(2, 9)$ (E) $(7, 2)$

23. How many <u>minutes</u> will it take a rocket to travel 4,000 miles if its average rate is 100 miles every t seconds?

    (A) $\dfrac{2t}{3}$

    (B) $\dfrac{3t}{2}$

    (C) $\dfrac{2}{3t}$

    (D) $40t$

    (E) $2,400t$

24. If the average of x, y, and 80 is 6 more than the average of y, z, and 80, what is the value of $x - z$?

    (A) 2
    (B) 3
    (C) 6
    (D) 18
    (E) It cannot be determined from the information given.

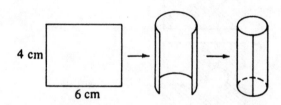

25. The figure above shows how a rectangular piece of paper is rolled to form a cylindrical tube. If it is assumed that the 4-centimeter sides of the rectangle meet with no overlap, what is the area, in square centimeters, of the circular base region enclosed?

    (A) 16π

    (B) 9π

    (C) 4π

    (D) $\dfrac{9}{\pi}$

    (E) $\dfrac{4}{\pi}$

SECTION 3   Time—30 minutes
40 Questions

For each question in this section, choose the best answer and fill in the corresponding oval on the answer sheet.

Each question below consists of a word in capital letters, followed by five lettered words or phrases. Choose the word or phrase that is most nearly opposite in meaning to the word in capital letters. Since some of the questions require you to distinguish fine shades of meaning, consider all the choices before deciding which is best.

Example:

GOOD: (A) sour (B) bad (C) red
(D) hot (E) ugly

Ⓐ ● Ⓒ Ⓓ Ⓔ

1. ORDINARY: (A) numerical (B) rational
(C) impolite (D) staunch (E) abnormal

2. ATHEIST: (A) believer (B) scholar
(C) recluse (D) expatriate (E) pauper

3. FLICKER: (A) rise slowly (B) burn steadily
(C) warm completely (D) fume (E) collide

4. SERRATED: (A) undervalued (B) aggressive
(C) smooth and even (D) loose and flexible
(E) supremely confident

5. COSMOPOLITAN: (A) indecisive (B) ineffectual
(C) antagonistic (D) parochial (E) deferential

6. HYPOCRITICAL: (A) guileless (B) eccentric
(C) perspicacious (D) untrustworthy
(E) sagacious

7. ACCOLADE: (A) appetizer (B) censure
(C) recoil (D) seizure (E) referendum

8. PROPOUND:

(A) remove from consideration
(B) defend without evidence
(C) avoid without reason
(D) view with humility
(E) rescue from imprisonment

9. EBULLIENT: (A) staid (B) anxious
(C) feminine (D) unique (E) respectful

10. EXCULPATE: (A) require (B) yield
(C) reinstate (D) vivify (E) convict

Each sentence below has one or two blanks, each blank indicating that something has been omitted. Beneath the sentence are five lettered words or sets of words. Choose the word or set of words that, when inserted in the sentence, best fits the meaning of the sentence as a whole.

Example:

Although its publicity has been ----, the film itself is intelligent, well-acted, handsomely produced, and altogether ----.

(A) tasteless. .respectable (B) extensive. .moderate
(C) sophisticated. .amateur (D) risqué. .crude
(E) perfect. .spectacular

● Ⓑ Ⓒ Ⓓ Ⓔ

11. As tourism and industry develop along the shores of the Gulf of California, it is possible that the increased human ---- may drive the gray whales from their ---- calving sites.

(A) access. .forsaken
(B) knowledge. .impending
(C) activity. .preferred
(D) indifference. .destined
(E) concern. .despoiled

12. Because of its immense scope, critics have rightly referred to the book as the most ---- examination of minority concerns in the United States ever written.

(A) deficient (B) intuitive (C) obscure
(D) unaspiring (E) comprehensive

13. The ---- of personality that strikes us in Julia Cameron's best pictures gives her work a coherence that is ---- in the work of less accomplished personal photographers.

(A) idea. .compounded (B) image. .implied
(C) theory. .evolving (D) force. .lacking
(E) feeling. .restrained

GO ON TO THE NEXT PAGE

14. In addition to the traditional functions of collecting and displaying, a museum establishes the official ---- of an artist's works, ---- them a prestige unattainable in a commercial showcase.

    (A) utility. .proposing for
    (B) subjectivity. .sharing with
    (C) style. .conceding to
    (D) importance. .conferring on
    (E) destiny. .diverting from

15. Although Spalding ---- the importance of the physical necessities of life, her most successful endeavor was the ---- of the condition of the impoverished.

    (A) deprecated. .alleviation
    (B) emphasized. .investigation
    (C) accentuated. .amelioration
    (D) epitomized. .delineation
    (E) disregarded. .desecration

Each question below consists of a related pair of words or phrases, followed by five lettered pairs of words or phrases. Select the lettered pair that <u>best</u> expresses a relationship similar to that expressed in the original pair.

Example:

YAWN : BOREDOM :: (A) dream : sleep
(B) anger : madness (C) smile : amusement
(D) face : expression (E) impatience : rebellion

 Ⓐ Ⓑ ● Ⓓ Ⓔ

---

16. SANDBOX : PLAY ::
    (A) picture : see (B) office : work
    (C) library : publish (D) restaurant : guide
    (E) kindergarten : manipulate

17. TENANT : RENT :: (A) salesperson : commission
    (B) performer : ticket (C) investor : interest
    (D) client : fee (E) professor : tuition

18. DAWN : DAY :: (A) moon : night (B) star : sun
    (C) week : year (D) birth : life (E) beginning : end

19. MALLET : POLO :: (A) putter : club
    (B) bat : baseball (C) field : football
    (D) puck : hockey (E) lane : bowling

20. TERRESTRIAL : LUNG :: (A) marsupial : pouch
    (B) floral : root (C) aquatic : gill
    (D) perennial : seed (E) canine : mouth

21. DEFAME : REPUTATION ::
    (A) demoralize : misery (B) challenge : opinion
    (C) promote : talent (D) disfigure : appearance
    (E) jeopardize : peril

22. NEUTER : GENDER :: (A) sincere : truth
    (B) uniform : errors (C) futile : hindrance
    (D) nimble : energy (E) destitute : possessions

23. HONE : BLADE :: (A) cut : scissors
    (B) strike : bell (C) reduce : fat
    (D) focus : image (E) flatten : hill

24. DEBATE : FORENSIC ::

    (A) decathlon : athletic
    (B) applause : dramatic
    (C) controversy : scientific
    (D) anthology : descriptive
    (E) diagnosis : experimental

25. ANNEX : BUILDING :: (A) tenure : office
    (B) rider : document (C) lease : apartment
    (D) chapter : text (E) limb : extremity

GO ON TO THE NEXT PAGE →

Each passage below is followed by questions based on its content. Answer the questions following each passage on the basis of what is <u>stated</u> or <u>implied</u> in that passage.

One of the favorite operations of the alchemists was a process they called "calcining." It consisted of placing a mineral or a metal into a crucible and heating it until it was completely converted into a powdery solid. Since this powdery solid evidently resisted prolonged heating better than anything else, it was believed to have special "virtues" and was called "calx," as for example, the calx of arsenic. Calcining, incidentally, provided further proof of the superiority of gold because gold did not have a calx.

In 1489 a German alchemist, Eck von Sulzbach, made the startling discovery that the calx of a metal weighed more than the metal before calcining. The only explanation he could think of was that a "ghost" had come from somewhere and moved into the calx, thereby increasing its weight.

We now know that Eck von Sulzbach had come close to the truth. Calcining a metal means, in present-day terminology, to oxidize it with the oxygen in the atmosphere, and naturally the compound of metal plus oxygen will weigh more than the metal itself. But the fifteenth-century alchemist could not arrive at this conclusion because Aristotle, whose word was still undisputed, had said that air was an element that did not combine with metals. However, the time was not far off when this statement was to be questioned.

26. The passage primarily answers which of the following questions?

(A) Why was calcining a favorite process of the alchemists?
(B) Who was Eck von Sulzbach and how has he influenced the progress of science?
(C) To what extent were alchemists influenced by the teachings of Aristotle?
(D) What is calcining and how did the alchemists interpret it?
(E) How did other alchemists react to Eck von Sulzbach's discovery of a "ghost"?

27. According to the passage, the calx of two ounces of arsenic will weigh

(A) less than one ounce
(B) one ounce
(C) one and one-half ounces
(D) two ounces
(E) more than two ounces

28. The last sentence of the passage suggests that, after the fifteenth century, some alchemists began to wonder whether

(A) the calx of a metal had any special "virtues"
(B) air or some part of it could combine with metals
(C) Aristotle's description of gold was accurate
(D) calcining increased or decreased the value of a metal
(E) the calx of metal really weighed more than the metal did before calcining

GO ON TO THE NEXT PAGE

"That's right. My suitcases were on the gangplank and there was Annie on the quay. That was the first time I thought of her at all. Annie is my wife, but she wasn't then. I looked at her in the pouring rain with tears in her eyes and the porters hitting up against her. I got to thinking of the things I'd said to her one time or another. You know the things you're apt to say to a girl?"

"I do," said the young man.

"I tried to get back for a few last words with her but I had to keep standing aside to let people pass.

"'Come on up, Manny,' shouted the lads from the deck.

"'Goodbye, Manny,' Annie called in a little voice."

"You didn't go down!"

"Down I went. The boys called me to come back but the wind blew their words away.

"'I knew you'd come to your senses,' Annie said. 'Where's your fiddle?'

"By God, if I hadn't left the fiddle on deck! I shouted at Timmy Coyne—that's the fellow next to me in the photo. He played the piano in our band, by the way.

"'The fiddle!' I shouted against the noise and confusion of the boat pulling away. Timmy right away ducks down then ups and rests the fiddle case on the rails. 'Catch!' he shouts.

"A fellow in the crowd next to me leaps to catch it but you know how slippery them wooden boards can be? Well, down slips the fellow and fiddle and case and even the little bow were smashed to smithereens. You should have heard the crowd laughing."

"What did Annie say?"

"'It's the hand of God,' she said."

29. In the context of the passage, the phrase "That's right" (line 1) suggests primarily that

(A) Manny and the person he is addressing are in complete agreement
(B) the conversation we are about to read is already in progress
(C) Manny is eager to recount his experience to whomever will listen
(D) one story has been told and another is about to begin
(E) Manny wants his listener to believe what he has told him

30. It can be inferred that all of the following contributed to Manny's decision to rejoin Annie on the dock EXCEPT

(A) Annie's tears
(B) the sight of Annie in the rain
(C) the sight of Annie jostled by porters
(D) the weakness of Annie's voice saying goodbye
(E) the attitude of the men on the deck toward Annie

31. In the context of the passage, the fiddle is representative of all of the following EXCEPT

(A) freedom
(B) youth
(C) religious faith
(D) creative imagination
(E) unexplored possibility

GO ON TO THE NEXT PAGE

Those who think of evolution as merely a process of adaptation to particular environments regard the emergence of life from the water as having been made possible by its adaptation to the dry environment outside. Though this hypothesis is not false in itself, it represents too short a view. In the long view, evolution has been toward an ever-increasing independence of the natural external environment, whatever it may be.

Let me give an example. To this day, the development of a fertilized animal cell through the embryonic stage can take place only in a liquid environment. Therefore, the first organisms to emerge on land, represented today by frogs, had to return to the water to lay their eggs. What finally brought about complete independence from the water was the development of the amniotic egg, which packaged the watery environment required by the embryo inside a membrane or shell (i.e., an amnion). So the liquid environment that a human embryo requires is provided inside an amnion inside the mother's womb. A human embryo, unlike that of a fish, is independent of the environment external to its mother, indifferent to changes of temperature—indifferent, even, to whether the environment is wet or dry.

The first human beings to emerge from the earth's atmospheric envelope, in the 1960's, were able to do so because they packaged that atmosphere in their amniotic spacesuits and spaceships. Thus, human beings are now able to visit the moon in spite of a lunar environment that would kill them on contact. What these astronauts represent is not adaptation to the natural environment but independence of it.

32. The author's primary purpose in the passage is to

(A) reveal the miracle of human reproduction
(B) offer a wider interpretation of evolution
(C) explain the larger meaning of the word "amnion"
(D) illustrate the difference between a frog embryo and a human embryo
(E) compare the space age with the emergence of life from the water

33. From the tone and content of the passage it can be inferred that the author is addressing which of the following audiences?

(A) Highly specialized scientists
(B) Marine biologists
(C) Educated nonprofessionals
(D) Aspiring astronauts
(E) Environmental conservationists

34. The author uses the development of the amniotic egg to illustrate which of the following?

(A) The freeing of the reproductive process from its earlier dependence on the external environment
(B) The continual dependence of life on a liquid, external environment, despite the emergence of creatures on land
(C) The adaptation of organic life to the external environment
(D) The independence of the first organisms to emerge on land
(E) The adaptive nature of the evolutionary process

35. We can infer from the passage that the author sees spacesuits and spaceships as examples of

(A) atmospheric adaptation
(B) artificial progress
(C) futuristic apparel
(D) a technological variation of evolutionary progress
(E) an innovative packaging in modern technology

GO ON TO THE NEXT PAGE

Among economists, John Maynard Keynes ranks with Adam Smith and Karl Marx in the influence that his views have exerted on the general public.

Line
(5) He had the vision to see that economics lacked a general theory of demand, and he proceeded with boldness and brilliance to construct one.

His theory produced the startling conclusion that highly developed industrial countries suffer from a chronic deficiency of demand and that this deficien-
(10) cy is bound to grow worse as countries become richer. Hence, Keynes called on government to assume a new responsibility and a new function: to close the growing gap between the power of progressive economies to produce and the size of effective
(15) private demand. Keynes suggested two general lines of action—that of controlling the size of the gap through changes in the distribution of income and that of offsetting the gap through greater government spending.

(20) Keynes's theory contributed invaluable tools of analysis to economics and started hundreds of able economists in many lands studying the important problems that the theory opened up. No one in the history of economics has done as much as Keynes
(25) to stimulate good work. But Keynes's theory has turned out to be wrong in all its essentials. Although intended to be a "general" theory, applicable to all conditions, it was unduly molded by the depressed Thirties, the period during which Keynes composed
(30) it. Since then, economists have determined that advanced economies do not suffer from a chronic deficiency of demand—they suffer from a chronic excess of demand. It would be hard today to find an advanced economy that is not struggling to con-
(35) trol demand, and most of them are having only partial success.

It is among the undeveloped economies, precisely where Keynes did not expect to find a chronic shortage of demand, that unemployment is endemic and
(40) most severe. Keynes's theory that unemployment is caused by an excessive disposition to save obviously does not explain the high unemployment in countries that are too poor to have any savings at all. The high unemployment in undeveloped countries is best ex-
(45) plained by Marx's theory of unemployment—that people lack work because savings are insufficient to provide the growing labor force with the tools of production.

Why has Keynes turned out to have been so
(50) completely wrong? He made two basic mistakes. In the first place, he assigned to consumers a relatively passive role in determining the demand for goods. In the second place, he overlooked the fact that the development of investment opportunities is itself an
(55) expanding industry, able to supply the community with a rapidly growing number of investment outlets.

36. The author is primarily concerned with which of the following?

(A) Rebutting Keynes's theory of demand
(B) Presenting a theoretical approach to the problem of unemployment
(C) Extending the range of influence of Keynesian theory
(D) Contrasting Keynesian economics with Marxist theories
(E) Establishing the economic responsibilities of modern governments

37. It can be inferred that the author attributes the unsoundness of Keynes's theory chiefly to the fact that it

(A) lacks conclusive proof and is untried
(B) rejects a positive course of action
(C) considers as universal some rules that pertain to a specific economic era
(D) allows too many exceptions to its basic concepts
(E) does not concur with theories of contemporary economists

38. Which of the following does the author particularly emphasize as a Keynesian contribution to the field of economics?

(A) Formulation of a new attitude toward government
(B) Analysis of the theory of unemployment
(C) Development of a theory of income distribution
(D) Stimulation of the thought and work of other economists
(E) Expansion of the theories of Smith and Marx

39. The author notes that one of the causes of unemployment that Keynes overlooked is

(A) excessive private demand
(B) insufficient savings
(C) governmental intervention
(D) lack of initiative
(E) mechanization

40. As used in line 39, the word "endemic" can best be interpreted to mean

(A) contagious and increasing
(B) exclusive and persistent
(C) unlikely to be found
(D) difficult to explain
(E) native to the locality

IF YOU FINISH BEFORE TIME IS CALLED, YOU MAY CHECK YOUR WORK ON THIS SECTION ONLY. DO NOT TURN TO ANY OTHER SECTION IN THE TEST.

S T O P

SECTION 5 Time—30 minutes 35 Questions

In this section solve each problem, using any available space on the page for scratchwork. Then decide which is the best of the choices given and fill in the corresponding oval on the answer sheet.

The following information is for your reference in solving some of the problems.

Circle of radius r: Area = πr^2; Circumference = $2\pi r$
  The number of degrees of arc in a circle is 360.
The measure in degrees of a straight angle is 180.

Definition of symbols:
= is equal to $\leq$ is less than or equal to
$\neq$ is unequal to $\geq$ is greater than or equal to
< is less than $\parallel$ is parallel to
> is greater than $\perp$ is perpendicular to

Triangle: The sum of the measures in degrees of the angles of a triangle is 180.
If $\angle CDA$ is a right angle, then

(1) area of $\triangle ABC = \dfrac{AB \times CD}{2}$

(2) $AC^2 = AD^2 + DC^2$

Note: Figures that accompany problems in this test are intended to provide information useful in solving the problems. They are drawn as accurately as possible EXCEPT when it is stated in a specific problem that its figure is not drawn to scale. All figures lie in a plane unless otherwise indicated. All numbers used are real numbers.

1. If $2x + 4 = 9$, then $x - \dfrac{1}{2} =$

(A) 2 (B) 3 (C) 6 (D) 12 (E) 14

2. $(8\sqrt{4})(2\sqrt{9}) =$

(A) 48 (B) 72 (C) 96 (D) 298 (E) 576

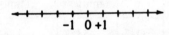
$-1\ \ 0\ +1$

3. On the number line above, a particle starts at 0 and moves a distance of 2 to the right, then from there moves 4 to the left, then 6 to the right, and so on, alternating directions and lengthening each move by 2. At the end of the fifth move, where on the number line will the particle be located?

(A) −8 (B) −4 (C) +1 (D) +6 (E) +10

4. In the figure above, $x =$

(A) 120 (B) 90 (C) 60 (D) 45 (E) 30

5. If x and y are positive integers and if $\dfrac{x}{y} = 1$ and $(x + y)^2 = z$, which of the following CANNOT equal z?

(A) 4
(B) 9
(C) 16
(D) 36
(E) 64

6. If a $27,000 prize was divided among three people in the ratio of $2:3:5$, what was the value of the largest share?

(A) $18,900
(B) $13,500
(C) $8,100
(D) $5,400
(E) $2,700

7. If y is some number between 4 and 10, which of the following could be the average of the numbers $2, 5, 6, 8, 9,$ and y?

(A) 4.3
(B) 6.2
(C) 7.8
(D) 9.1
(E) 10.0

GO ON TO THE NEXT PAGE

5

Questions 8-27 each consist of two quantities, one in Column A and one in Column B. You are to compare the two quantities and on the answer sheet fill in oval

A if the quantity in Column A is greater;
B if the quantity in Column B is greater;
C if the two quantities are equal;
D if the relationship cannot be determined from the information given.

AN E RESPONSE WILL NOT BE SCORED.

Notes:

1. In certain questions, information concerning one or both of the quantities to be compared is centered above the two columns.
2. In a given question, a symbol that appears in both columns represents the same thing in Column A as it does in Column B.
3. Letters such as x, n, and k stand for real numbers.

	Column A	Column B
8.	$6 + 4^2$	20

$$x + 5 = 19$$
$$y + 5 = 14$$

	Column A	Column B
9.	x	y

$$a = b = c = d = e$$

	Column A	Column B
10.	$a + 2b$	$c + d + e$

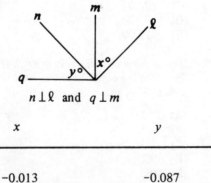

$n \perp \ell$ and $q \perp m$

	Column A	Column B
11.	x	y
12.	-0.013	-0.087

$$x \neq 0$$

	Column A	Column B
13.	$3x^2$	$(3x)^2$

	Column A	Column B
		$p > q > r > 0$
14.	$p^2 + q^2$	$pq + qr$

TELEPHONE RATES

From P to	First 3 Minutes	Each Additional Minute
Q	45¢	10¢
S	15¢	5¢

	Column A	Column B
15.	The cost of a 20-minute call from P to S	$1.00

$$xyz > 0$$
$$x < 0$$

	Column A	Column B
16.	y	z

$$16\% \text{ of } 2x = 96.$$

	Column A	Column B
17.	16% of x	48

GO ON TO THE NEXT PAGE ➡

164

SUMMARY DIRECTIONS FOR COMPARISON QUESTIONS

Answer: A if the quantity in Column A is greater;
B if the quantity in Column B is greater;
C if the two quantities are equal;
D if the relationship cannot be determined from the information given.

AN E RESPONSE WILL NOT BE SCORED.

Column A	Column B

$-7 < n < -3$

18.   8 n^2

19. Volume of a cylinder with radius 2   Volume of a cylinder with radius 4

$x + y = 8$
$x - y = 12$

20. y 0

A car travels d kilometers in t minutes at a constant rate of 60 kilometers per hour.

21. t d

LIST I: 1, 2, 3
LIST II: 2, 3, 4

x is a number chosen at random from List I and y is a number chosen at random from List II.

22. The most likely value of $x + y$ 5

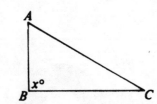

Note: Figure not drawn to scale.

$x \neq 90$

23. $AB^2 + BC^2$ AC^2

Column A	Column B

x is an integer greater than 1. $\boxed{x}$ denotes the smallest positive integer factor of x not equal to 1.

24. $\boxed{x}$ $\boxed{x^2}$

n is a positive integer.

25. $(-1)^n$ $[1 + (-1)]^n$

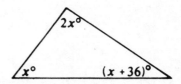

Note: Figure not drawn to scale.

26. $2x$ $x + 36$

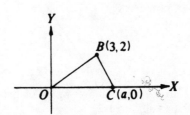

Note: Figure not drawn to scale.

$\triangle OBC$ has an area of 12.

27. a 8

GO ON TO THE NEXT PAGE →

5

Solve each of the remaining problems in this section using any available space for scratchwork. Then decide which is the best of the choices given and fill in the corresponding oval on the answer sheet.

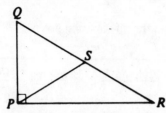

28. In the figure above, if $\triangle PQS$ is equilateral, what is the ratio $\dfrac{PS}{SR}$?

(A) $\dfrac{1}{2}$ (B) $\dfrac{1}{\sqrt{3}}$ (C) $\dfrac{\sqrt{3}}{2}$ (D) 1   (E) 2

29. The difference between $6\dfrac{2}{3}$ hours and $7\dfrac{3}{5}$ hours is how many <u>minutes</u>?

(A) 40   (B) 45   (C) 50   (D) 56   (E) 64

30. For $a \neq 0$, $\dfrac{a^{x+y}}{a^x} =$

(A) a^y (B) $\dfrac{1}{a^y}$ (C) $-a^y$

(D) a^{1+y} (E) $1 + a^y$

31. In the figure above, which of the following must be equal to 1 ?

   I. $\dfrac{a+b}{c+d}$

   II. $\dfrac{ab}{cd}$

   III. $\dfrac{c+d-a}{b}$

(A) None   (B) I only   (C) II only

(D) I and II only   (E) I, II, and III

32. The possible scores on a weekly math quiz range from 0 to 100. If Pat receives scores of 65 and 75 on the first two quizzes, what is the lowest possible score Pat can receive on the third in order to average 75 on the first 4 quizzes?

(A) 50
(B) 55
(C) 60
(D) 65
(E) 70

33. In the figure above, the area of the semicircle is

(A) 36π (B) 18π (C) 12π (D) 9π (E) $\dfrac{9}{2}\pi$

34. There are fewer than 40 students enrolled in a certain class. If, at a certain time, $\dfrac{2}{9}$ of the students are absent from school and $\dfrac{1}{4}$ of those in school have gone to the library, what is the total class enrollment?

(A) 18
(B) 27
(C) 28
(D) 32
(E) 36

35. In the figure above, what is the greatest number of nonoverlapping regions into which the shaded region can be divided with exactly two straight lines?

(A) 6   (B) 5   (C) 4   (D) 3   (E) 2

IF YOU FINISH BEFORE TIME IS CALLED, YOU MAY CHECK YOUR WORK ON THIS SECTION ONLY. DO NOT TURN TO ANY OTHER SECTION IN THE TEST.   **STOP**

Correct Answers for Scholastic Aptitude Test
Form Code 1S

VERBAL		MATHEMATICAL	
Section 1	Section 3	Section 2	Section 5
1. C	1. E	1. B	1. A
2. B	2. A	2. B	2. C
3. D	3. B	3. E	3. D
4. E	4. C	4. C	4. E
5. A	5. D	5. C	5. B
6. B	6. A	6. D	6. B
7. C	7. B	7. E	7. B
8. B	8. A	8. C	*8. A
9. D	9. A	9. B	*9. A
10. E	10. E	10. B	*10. C
11. A	11. C	11. B	*11. C
12. A	12. E	12. C	*12. A
13. C	13. D	13. A	*13. B
14. A	14. D	14. C	*14. A
15. B	15. A	15. C	*15. C
16. C	16. B	16. A	*16. D
17. A	17. D	17. E	*17. C
18. D	18. D	18. D	*18. B
19. B	19. B	19. B	*19. D
20. A	20. C	20. A	*20. B
21. E	21. D	21. D	*21. C
22. A	22. E	22. B	*22. C
23. D	23. D	23. A	*23. D
24. B	24. A	24. D	*24. C
25. C	25. B	25. D	*25. D
26. C	26. D		*26. C
27. E	27. E		*27. A
28. D	28. B		28. D
29. C	29. B		29. D
30. A	30. E		30. A
31. D	31. C		31. E
32. C	32. B		32. C
33. A	33. C		33. D
34. E	34. A		34. E
35. C	35. D		35. B
36. E	36. A		
37. B	37. C		
38. B	38. D		
39. D	39. B		
40. A	40. E		
41. E			
42. C			
43. B			
44. D			
45. B			

*Indicates four-choice questions. (All of the other questions are five-choice.)

The Scoring Process

Machine-scoring is done in three steps:

- *Scanning.* Your answer sheet is "read" by a scanning machine and the oval you filled in for each question is recorded on a computer tape.

- *Scoring.* The computer compares the oval filled in for each question with the correct response. Each correct answer receives one point; omitted questions do not count toward your score. For each wrong answer, a fraction of a point is subtracted to correct for random guessing. For questions with five answer choices, one-fourth of a point is subtracted for each wrong response; for questions with four answer choices, one-third of a point is subtracted for each wrong response. The SAT-verbal test has 85 questions with five answer choices each. If, for example, a student has 44 right, 32 wrong, and 9 omitted, the resulting raw score is determined as follows:

$$44 \text{ right} - \frac{32 \text{ wrong}}{4} = 44 - 8 = 36 \text{ raw score points}$$

Obtaining raw scores frequently involves the rounding of fractional numbers to the nearest whole number. For example, a raw score of 36.25 is rounded to 36, the nearest whole number. A raw score of 36.50 is rounded upward to 37.

- *Converting to reported scaled score.* Raw test scores are then placed on the College Board scale of 200 to 800 through a process that adjusts scores to account for minor differences in difficulty among different editions of the test. This process, known as equating, is performed so that a student's reported score is not affected by the edition of the test taken nor by the abilities of the group with whom the student takes the test. As a result of placing SAT scores on the College Board scale, scores earned by students at different times can be compared. For example, an SAT-verbal score of 400 on a test taken at one administration indicates the same level of developed verbal ability as a 400 score obtained on a different edition of the test taken at another time.

How to Score the Test

SAT-Verbal Sections 1 and 3

Step A: Count the number of correct answers for *section 1* and record the number in the space provided on the worksheet on the next page. Then do the same for the incorrect answers. (Do not count omitted answers.) To determine subtotal A, use the formula:

$$\text{number correct} - \frac{\text{number incorrect}}{4} = \text{subtotal A}$$

Step B: Count the number of correct answers and the number of incorrect answers for *section 3* and record the numbers in the spaces provided on the worksheet. To determine subtotal B, use the formula:

$$\text{number correct} - \frac{\text{number incorrect}}{4} = \text{subtotal B}$$

Step C: To obtain C, add subtotal A to subtotal B, keeping any decimals. Enter the resulting figure on the worksheet.

Step D: To obtain D, your raw verbal score, round C to the nearest whole number. (For example, any number from 44.50 to 45.49 rounds to 45.) Enter the resulting figure on the worksheet.

Step E: To find your reported SAT-verbal score, look up the total raw verbal score you obtained in step D in the conversion table on page 170. Enter this figure on the worksheet.

SAT-Mathematical Sections 2 and 5

Step A: Count the number of correct answers and the number of incorrect answers for *section 2* and record the numbers in the spaces provided on the worksheet. To determine the subtotal A, use the formula:

$$\text{number correct} - \frac{\text{number incorrect}}{4} = \text{subtotal A}$$

Step B: Count the number of correct answers and the number of incorrect answers for the *five-choice questions (questions 1 through 7 and 28 through 35) in section 5* and record the numbers in the spaces provided on the worksheet. To determine the subtotal B, use the formula:

$$\text{number correct} - \frac{\text{number incorrect}}{4} = \text{subtotal B}$$

Step C: Count the number of correct answers and the number of incorrect answers for the *four-choice questions (questions 8 through 27) in section 5* and record the numbers in the spaces provided on the worksheet. To determine the subtotal C, use the formula:

$$\text{number correct} - \frac{\text{number incorrect}}{3} = \text{subtotal C}$$

Step D: To obtain D, add subtotal A, subtotal B, and subtotal C, keeping any decimals. Enter the resulting figure on the worksheet.

Step E: To obtain E, your raw mathematical score, round D to the nearest whole number. (For example, any number from 44.50 to 45.49 rounds to 45.) Enter the resulting figure on the worksheet.

Step F: To find your reported SAT-mathematical score, look up the total raw mathematical score you obtained in E in the conversion table on page 170. Enter this figure on the worksheet.

SAT SCORING WORKSHEET

SAT-Verbal Sections

A. Section 1: _____ − ¼ (_____) = _____
   no. correct   no. incorrect   subtotal A

B. Section 3: _____ − ¼ (_____) = _____
   no. correct   no. incorrect   subtotal B

C. Total unrounded raw score
   (Total A + B)   _____
                                                        C

D. Total rounded raw score
   (Rounded to nearest whole number)   _____
                                                        D

E. SAT-verbal reported scaled score
   (See the conversion table on page 170.)   [   ]

                                                    SAT-verbal
                                                      score

SAT-Mathematical Sections

A. Section 2: _____ − ¼ (_____) = _____
   no. correct   no. incorrect   subtotal A

B. Section 5:
   Questions 1 through 7 and _____ − ¼ (_____) = _____
   28 through 35 (5-choice)   no. correct   no. incorrect   subtotal B

C. Section 5:
   Questions 8 through 27 _____ − ⅓ (_____) = _____
   (4-choice)   no. correct   no. incorrect   subtotal C

D. Total unrounded raw score
   (Total A + B + C)   _____
                                                        D

E. Total rounded raw score
   (Rounded to nearest whole number)   _____
                                                        E

F. SAT-mathematical reported scaled score
   (See the conversion table on page 170.)   [   ]

                                                    SAT-math
                                                      score

Score Conversion Table
Scholastic Aptitude Test
Form Code 1S

Raw Score	College Board Reported Score		Raw Score	College Board Reported Score	
	SAT-Verbal	SAT-Math		SAT-Verbal	SAT-Math
85	800		40	460	620
84	790		39	460	610
83	780		38	450	610
82	770		37	440	600
81	760		36	440	590
80	760		35	430	580
79	750		34	420	570
78	740		33	410	560
77	730		32	410	550
76	720		31	400	540
75	720		30	390	530
74	710		29	390	520
73	700		28	380	510
72	690		27	370	500
71	690		26	360	490
70	680		25	360	480
69	670		24	350	470
68	670		23	340	460
67	660		22	340	450
66	650		21	330	440
65	640		20	320	430
64	640		19	310	420
63	630		18	310	410
62	620		17	300	400
61	620		16	290	400
60	610	800	15	290	390
59	600	790	14	280	380
58	590	780	13	270	370
57	590	770	12	260	360
56	580	760	11	260	350
55	570	750	10	250	340
54	560	750	9	240	330
53	560	740	8	230	320
52	550	730	7	230	310
51	540	720	6	220	300
50	540	710	5	210	290
49	530	700	4	210	280
48	520	700	3	200	280
47	510	690	2	200	270
46	510	680	1	200	260
45	500	670	0	200	250
44	490	660	−1	200	240
43	490	650	−2	200	240
42	480	640	−3	200	230
41	470	630	−4	200	220
			−5	200	210
			−6 or below	200	200

COLLEGE BOARD — SCHOLASTIC APTITUDE TEST
and Test of Standard Written English   Side 1

Use a No. 2 pencil only. Be sure each mark is dark and completely fills the intended oval. Completely erase any errors or stray marks.

1.

YOUR NAME: _____
(Print)   Last   First   M.I.

SIGNATURE: _____   DATE: ___/___/___

HOME ADDRESS: _____
(Print)   Number and Street

_____
City   State   Zip Code

CENTER: _____
(Print)   City   State   Center Number

IMPORTANT: Please fill in these boxes exactly as shown on the back cover of your test book.

FOR ETS USE ONLY

5. YOUR NAME

First 4 letters of last name				First Init.	Mid. Init.

(A B C D E F G H I J K L M N O P Q R S T U V W X Y Z ovals for each column)

3. FORM CODE

(O A J S / 1 B K T / 2 C L U / 3 D M V / 4 E N W / 5 F O X / 6 G P Y / 7 H Q Z / 8 I R / 9)

4. REGISTRATION NUMBER
(Copy from your Admission Ticket.)

(0–9 ovals for each column)

6. DATE OF BIRTH

Month	Day	Year
○ Jan.		
○ Feb.		
○ Mar.	0 0	0 0
○ Apr.	1 1	1 1
○ May	2 2	2 2
○ June	3 3	3 3
○ July	4 4	4 4
○ Aug.	5 5	5 5
○ Sept.	6 6	6 6
○ Oct.	7 7	7 7
○ Nov.	8	8
○ Dec.	9	9

7. SEX
○ Female
○ Male

8. TEST BOOK SERIAL NUMBER
_____

Start with number 1 for each new section. If a section has fewer than 50 questions, leave the extra answer spaces blank.

SECTION 1

1 (A B C D E)   26 (A B C D E)
2 (A B C D E)   27 (A B C D E)
3 (A B C D E)   28 (A B C D E)
4 (A B C D E)   29 (A B C D E)
5 (A B C D E)   30 (A B C D E)
6 (A B C D E)   31 (A B C D E)
7 (A B C D E)   32 (A B C D E)
8 (A B C D E)   33 (A B C D E)
9 (A B C D E)   34 (A B C D E)
10 (A B C D E)   35 (A B C D E)
11 (A B C D E)   36 (A B C D E)
12 (A B C D E)   37 (A B C D E)
13 (A B C D E)   38 (A B C D E)
14 (A B C D E)   39 (A B C D E)
15 (A B C D E)   40 (A B C D E)
16 (A B C D E)   41 (A B C D E)
17 (A B C D E)   42 (A B C D E)
18 (A B C D E)   43 (A B C D E)
19 (A B C D E)   44 (A B C D E)
20 (A B C D E)   45 (A B C D E)
21 (A B C D E)   46 (A B C D E)
22 (A B C D E)   47 (A B C D E)
23 (A B C D E)   48 (A B C D E)
24 (A B C D E)   49 (A B C D E)
25 (A B C D E)   50 (A B C D E)

SECTION 2

1 (A B C D E)   26 (A B C D E)
2 (A B C D E)   27 (A B C D E)
3 (A B C D E)   28 (A B C D E)
4 (A B C D E)   29 (A B C D E)
5 (A B C D E)   30 (A B C D E)
6 (A B C D E)   31 (A B C D E)
7 (A B C D E)   32 (A B C D E)
8 (A B C D E)   33 (A B C D E)
9 (A B C D E)   34 (A B C D E)
10 (A B C D E)   35 (A B C D E)
11 (A B C D E)   36 (A B C D E)
12 (A B C D E)   37 (A B C D E)
13 (A B C D E)   38 (A B C D E)
14 (A B C D E)   39 (A B C D E)
15 (A B C D E)   40 (A B C D E)
16 (A B C D E)   41 (A B C D E)
17 (A B C D E)   42 (A B C D E)
18 (A B C D E)   43 (A B C D E)
19 (A B C D E)   44 (A B C D E)
20 (A B C D E)   45 (A B C D E)
21 (A B C D E)   46 (A B C D E)
22 (A B C D E)   47 (A B C D E)
23 (A B C D E)   48 (A B C D E)
24 (A B C D E)   49 (A B C D E)
25 (A B C D E)   50 (A B C D E)

(Cut here to detach.)

Q1362-04

I.N. 574006—110VV25P3015

COLLEGE BOARD — SCHOLASTIC APTITUDE TEST
and Test of Standard Written English   Side 2

Use a No. 2 pencil only. Be sure each mark is dark and completely fills the intended oval. Completely erase any errors or stray marks.

Start with number 1 for each new section. If a section has fewer than 50 questions, leave the extra answer spaces blank.

SECTION 3 **SECTION 4** **SECTION 5** **SECTION 6**

9. SIGNATURE:

FOR ETS USE ONLY	VTR	VTFS	VRR	VRFS	VVR	VVFS	WER	WEFS	M4R	M4FS	M5R	M5FS	MTFS	
	VTW	VTCS	VRW	VRCS	VVW	VVCS	WEW	WECS	M4W		M5W		MTCS	

TEST 6—FORM CODE 3I

Each question below consists of a word in capital letters, followed by five lettered words or phrases. Choose the word or phrase that is most nearly opposite in meaning to the word in capital letters. Since some of the questions require you to distinguish fine shades of meaning, consider all the choices before deciding which is best.

Example:

GOOD: (A) sour   (B) bad   (C) red
(D) hot   (E) ugly

Ⓐ ● Ⓒ Ⓓ Ⓔ

1. FERTILE: (A) eccentric   (B) inept
(C) unproductive   (D) weary   (E) unimportant

2. RECLINE: (A) improve   (B) sit up
(C) worry   (D) slow down   (E) desist

3. MODERATE: (A) moralist   (B) extremist
(C) clairvoyant   (D) winner   (E) civilian

4. RUTHLESS: (A) willing   (B) talented
(C) hopeful   (D) deliberate   (E) merciful

5. CHAOS: (A) validity   (B) chance
(C) authority   (D) order   (E) insight

6. TAPERING: (A) failing   (B) focusing
(C) cracking   (D) broadening   (E) revealing

7. VIVID: (A) tardy   (B) harmless   (C) similar
(D) lackluster   (E) inaccurate

8. COALESCE: (A) revitalize   (B) surround
(C) enumerate   (D) deny access   (E) break up

9. INNATE: (A) tested   (B) active   (C) learned
(D) parallel   (E) approved

10. RAZE: (A) construct   (B) gather   (C) harass
(D) provide food   (E) make beautiful

11. SAVANT: (A) performer   (B) plaintiff
(C) dunce   (D) provocative remark
(E) confused opinion

12. GARNER: (A) ignite   (B) obstruct
(C) disperse   (D) disprove   (E) precede

13. METTLE: (A) inflexibility   (B) ingenuity
(C) dishonesty   (D) lack of courage
(E) lack of planning

14. PERDITION: (A) anxiety   (B) celebration
(C) salvation   (D) seclusion   (E) solemnity

15. MUNIFICENT: (A) parsimonious
(B) malicious   (C) bourgeois
(D) contemptible   (E) blasphemous

Each sentence below has one or two blanks, each blank indicating that something has been omitted. Beneath the sentence are five lettered words or sets of words. Choose the word or set of words that, when inserted in the sentence, best fits the meaning of the sentence as a whole.

Example:

Although its publicity has been ----, the film itself is intelligent, well-acted, handsomely produced, and altogether ----.

(A) tasteless. .respectable (B) extensive. .moderate
(C) sophisticated. .amateur (D) risqué. .crude
(E) perfect. .spectacular

● Ⓑ Ⓒ Ⓓ Ⓔ

16. The dramatist was ---- over his lack of funds and his inability to sell any of his plays, and his letters to his wife reflected his unhappiness.

(A) despondent   (B) supercilious   (C) prudent
(D) encouraged   (E) fortified

17. The history of commissions indicates that they are most effective when dealing with ---- problem and least effective when the scope of the problem is broad.

(A) an obvious   (B) a limited   (C) a difficult
(D) a persistent   (E) an immaterial

18. Mobility has scattered families and ---- the continuities that once cemented local loyalties.

(A) fused   (B) eroded   (C) cradled
(D) perpetuated   (E) consolidated

19. Until Florence Nightingale made nursing ----, it was considered a ---- profession.

(A) scientific. .painstaking
(B) essential. .dangerous
(C) noble. .lofty
(D) patriotic. .worthy
(E) respectable. .degrading

20. There is ---- material in these books, but unfortunately it is ---- by the author's rambling style and buried in excessive detail.

(A) trivial. .marred
(B) insipid. .diluted
(C) imaginative. .highlighted
(D) fascinating. .obscured
(E) unforgettable. .exaggerated

GO ON TO THE NEXT PAGE

1

Each passage below is followed by questions based on its content. Answer the questions following each passage on the basis of what is <u>stated</u> or <u>implied</u> in that passage.

(This passage was written in 1929.)

In the history of education, the most striking phenomenon is that schools of learning, which in one era are alive with a ferment of genius, in a
Line succeeding generation exhibit mere pedantry and
(5) routine. The reason is that these schools are over-laden with inert ideas—that is to say, ideas that are merely received into the mind without being used, or tested, or thrown into fresh combinations. Education with inert ideas is not only useless; it is,
(10) above all things, harmful. Except at rare intervals of intellectual ferment, education in the past has been radically infected with inert ideas. That is the reason why, in an age when only men received formal higher education, intelligent women who
(15) had seen much of the world made up the most cultured part of the community. They had escaped the enormous disadvantage of inert ideas. Every intellectual revolution that has ever stirred humanity into greatness has been a passionate protest against
(20) inert ideas. Then, alas, with pathetic ignorance of human psychology, each revolution has proceeded by some educational scheme to bind humanity afresh with inert ideas of its own fashioning.

Let us now ask how in our system of education
(25) we are to guard against this mental dry rot. We enunciate two educational commandments: "Do not teach too many subjects," and again, "What you teach, teach thoroughly."

The result of teaching small parts of a large
(30) number of subjects is the passive reception of disconnected ideas, not illumined with any spark of vitality. Let the main ideas that are introduced into a child's education be few and important, and let them be thrown into every combination possible.
(35) All children should make them their own possessions and should understand their application in the cir-cumstances of daily life. From the very beginning of an education, the child should experience the joy of discovering that general ideas give an under-
(40) standing of that stream of events that pours through one's life, that *is* one's life. By understanding I mean more than a mere logical analysis, though that is included. I mean "understanding" in the sense in which it is used in the French proverb, "To
(45) understand all is to forgive all." Pedants sneer at an education that is useful. But if education is not use-ful, what is it? Is it a talent, to be hidden away in a napkin? Of course, education should be useful, whatever your aim in life. It was useful to Saint
(50) Augustine, a philosopher, and it was useful to Napoleon, a general. It is useful because under-standing is useful.

21. A primary concern of the author is to suggest the

(A) unreliability of education based on ideas
(B) most beneficial type of education
(C) theoretical justifications of modern teaching methods
(D) importance of exposing children to a wide range of concepts
(E) strength of earlier educational methods and ideas

22. The author's attitude toward those whose teaching is hampered by "inert ideas" (line 6) is best described as

(A) respect for the success of their work
(B) tolerance for the difficulty of their task
(C) nostalgia for concepts of an earlier era
(D) disapproval of their negative influence
(E) hostility toward their revolutionary concepts

23. According to the passage, the author believes that certain women of an earlier time had an intellectual advantage because

(A) they were committed to revolutionary ideas
(B) travel was considered an optional part of higher education
(C) their minds were not hampered by useless ideas
(D) they concentrated on developing skill in the fine arts
(E) they were able to meet people who had received formal education

24. The author implies that which of the following would be the result of teaching students a little bit about many subjects?

(A) Attentiveness to detail
(B) Respect for creative thinking
(C) Apathy and incomplete understanding
(D) Curiosity and tolerance for diversity
(E) Rejection of modern ideas

25. In the author's opinion, education is "useful" (line 48) if it is taught by which of the following methods?

(A) Showing children famous people to be imitated
(B) Encouraging the student to learn to do only one thing very well
(C) Presenting many ideas that provide mental stimulation
(D) Giving each person the means to make sense of life
(E) Urging students to pursue their special interests

GO ON TO THE NEXT PAGE

Valley glaciers are powerful agents of erosion, which they bring about primarily by plucking and abrasion. Plucking takes place mainly near the "head" (the back wall) of the glacier where the ice

Line
(5) freezes to the rock wall and pulls off slabs as the glacier moves forward. Usually a large crack or crevasse, called a bergschrund, develops between the ice and the wall of rock as a result of the tension at the head of the glacier. The bergschrund rarely

(10) becomes much wider than 10-15 feet, though, because each winter it is filled with snow that in turn becomes part of the glacier, freezes to the rock wall, and continues to pluck rock as the glacier slowly moves downhill. The continuous plucking

(15) action of the glacier results in the formation of a deep amphitheater called a cirque.

Abrasion is caused by rock fragments that are frozen into the bottom and sides of the glacier. These fragments act as a huge file or rasp as the ice
(20) moves down its course. Valleys eroded by streams are V-shaped, but glaciers scour and grind the sides and bottoms to form the characteristic U-shaped cross section found in practically all the valleys in glacial areas. Since the main glaciers are usually at
(25) least a half-mile thick, the results of glaciation can be seen far up the sides of the large valleys.

The tributaries of glacial valleys are also peculiar in that they usually enter high above the floor of the main valley and thus are known as hanging valleys.
(30) The thicker the stream of ice, the more erosion it is capable of causing; consequently the main valley becomes greatly deepened, whereas the smaller glacier in the tributary valley does not cut so rapidly, leaving its valley "hanging" high above the floor of the
(35) major valley. Fortunately, the ice has melted from innumerable glacial valleys, exposing many hanging valleys to view. Among the most spectacular sights in countless glacial valleys are the tumultuous waterfalls that leap from hanging valleys and drop their
(40) thundering ribbons of white to the placid waters in the valleys far below.

Even more conspicious than the large U-shaped valleys and their hanging tributaries are the sharp-crested ridges that form the background of glacial
(45) mountain ranges. These features, known as arêtes, owe their origin to glaciers. As long valley glaciers enlarge their cirques and cut farther in toward the center of the range, this area is finally reduced to a very narrow steep-sided ridge, the arête. In certain
(50) places three or more glaciers on the same ridge pluck their way back toward a common point, leaving at their heads a conspicuous, sharp, pointed peak known as a horn.

26. Which of the following titles would be most appropriate for this passage?

   (A) Glaciers and Their Effects on the Land
   (B) The Glacier as an Agent of Destruction
   (C) How and Why Glaciers Advance and Recede
   (D) The Last Remnants of the Ice Age
   (E) The Surprising Beauty of Glaciers

27. According to the passage, hanging valleys are formed by

   (A) glaciers that develop before main glaciers do
   (B) the plucking action of main glaciers high on mountain sides
   (C) the slower action of glaciers smaller than the main glacier
   (D) the rapid melting of tributary glaciers before main glaciers melt
   (E) glaciers that cause erosion by plucking rather than by abrasion

28. As it is used in the passage, the phrase "thundering ribbons of white" (line 40) emphasizes which of the following?

   (A) The erosive power of waterfalls
   (B) The ever-changing landscape in glacial regions
   (C) The danger of waterfalls at high elevations
   (D) The various forms of water in glacial regions
   (E) The majestic beauty brought about by glaciers

29. It can be inferred from the passage that the most extensive erosion in glacial regions results from the

   (A) alternate freezing and thawing as seasons change
   (B) cracking that occurs during the formation of a bergschrund
   (C) cutting action of melting ice
   (D) plucking action of a tributary glacier
   (E) abrasive action of a main glacier

30. The author develops the passage by doing all of the following EXCEPT

   (A) analyzing the process that causes glacial movement
   (B) defining terminology relating to glacial action
   (C) including a simile to explain glacial erosion
   (D) describing the results of glacial erosion on the landscape
   (E) comparing glacial erosion to another type of erosion

GO ON TO THE NEXT PAGE

1

Select the word or set of words that best completes each of the following sentences.

31. Considering Edwin's tendency to ---- those whom he encountered as he journeyed through hostile lands, it was a miracle that he survived at all.

    (A) idolize (B) enchant (C) placate
    (D) provoke (E) appease

32. Ethnic groups usually respond to sociocultural changes either by rapidly losing their cultural ---- or by ---- and emphasizing their cultural identity and uniqueness.

    (A) heritage. .forgetting
    (B) distinctiveness. .retaining
    (C) vitality. .misdirecting
    (D) selectivity. .rejecting
    (E) awareness. .misplacing

33. The ---- of drug-resistant strains of bacteria and viruses has ---- researchers' hopes that permanent victories against many diseases have been achieved.

    (A) vigor. .corroborated
    (B) feebleness. .dashed
    (C) proliferation. .blighted
    (D) destruction. .disputed
    (E) disappearance. .frustrated

34. There has been little ---- criticism written about de la Mare; indeed, that which has been written is at the two extremes, either appallingly ---- or bitterly antagonistic.

    (A) hostile. .ambiguous
    (B) recent. .illogical
    (C) fervent. .complimentary
    (D) objective. .sycophantic
    (E) temperate. .censorious

35. If it is to satisfy its supporters, an administration that claims to have received a popular mandate to make sweeping changes should not leave ---- the most ---- features of the old order.

    (A) unauthorized. .neglected
    (B) unscathed. .exceptionable
    (C) uncounted. .idealistic
    (D) unstated. .prestigious
    (E) unbalanced. .irrevocable

Each question below consists of a related pair of words or phrases, followed by five lettered pairs of words or phrases. Select the lettered pair that best expresses a relationship similar to that expressed in the original pair.

Example:

YAWN : BOREDOM :: (A) dream : sleep
(B) anger : madness   (C) smile : amusement
(D) face : expression   (E) impatience : rebellion

Ⓐ Ⓑ ● Ⓓ Ⓔ

36. FLEA : DOG :: (A) tusk : elephant
(B) spot : leopard   (C) parasite : host
(D) receptacle : jar   (E) insect : pest

37. WHITTLE : STICK :: (A) lick : hand
(B) shatter : glass   (C) hammer : nail
(D) chisel : stone   (E) nuzzle : nose

38. MONARCH : SUBJECTS :: (A) victim : defenders
(B) tenant : employers   (C) truant : pupils
(D) witness : jurors   (E) general : soldiers

39. REFINE : PETROLEUM :: (A) consume : fuel
(B) smelt : ore   (C) prospect : uranium
(D) blend : alloy   (E) import : rubber

40. MINUET : DANCE :: (A) beret : bowler
(B) clarinet : symphony   (C) chariot : wheel
(D) sonnet : poem   (E) gown : petticoat

41. TIDINGS : MESSENGER :: (A) clue : detective
(B) gossip : telltale   (C) verdict : convict
(D) inauguration : voter   (E) exposure : spy

42. COMPLEX : BUILDING :: (A) tapestry : fabric
(B) apple : tree   (C) classroom : campus
(D) federation : state   (E) highway : truck

43. HELPFUL : OFFICIOUS ::
(A) distraught : villainous
(B) compliant : slavish
(C) congenial : complacent
(D) passionate : faithful
(E) inscrutable : curious

44. WAYLAY : PROGRESS ::
(A) view : vista
(B) hesitate : indecision
(C) check : movement
(D) enhance : reputation
(E) advocate : advancement

45. SURREPTITIOUS : STEALTH ::
(A) clandestine : secrecy
(B) subversive : unity
(C) omnipresent : generosity
(D) verbose : enunciation
(E) opulent : simplicity

IF YOU FINISH BEFORE TIME IS CALLED, YOU MAY CHECK YOUR WORK ON THIS SECTION ONLY. DO NOT TURN TO ANY OTHER SECTION IN THE TEST.   S T O P

SECTION 2   Time—30 minutes   25 Questions

In this section solve each problem, using any available space on the page for scratchwork. Then decide which is the best of the choices given and fill in the corresponding oval on the answer sheet.

The following information is for your reference in solving some of the problems.

Circle of radius r: Area $= \pi r^2$; Circumference $= 2\pi r$
The number of degrees of arc in a circle is 360.
The measure in degrees of a straight angle is 180.

Definition of symbols:
$=$ is equal to $\leq$ is less than or equal to
$\neq$ is unequal to $\geq$ is greater than or equal to
$<$ is less than $\parallel$ is parallel to
$>$ is greater than $\perp$ is perpendicular to

Triangle: The sum of the measures in degrees of the angles of a triangle is 180.
If $\angle CDA$ is a right angle, then

(1) area of $\triangle ABC = \dfrac{AB \times CD}{2}$

(2) $AC^2 = AD^2 + DC^2$

Note: Figures that accompany problems in this test are intended to provide information useful in solving the problems. They are drawn as accurately as possible EXCEPT when it is stated in a specific problem that its figure is not drawn to scale. All figures lie in a plane unless otherwise indicated. All numbers used are real numbers.

---

1. All of the following are equal to $\dfrac{3}{7}$ EXCEPT

    (A) $\dfrac{6}{14}$ (B) $\dfrac{9}{21}$ (C) $\dfrac{12}{27}$ (D) $\dfrac{15}{35}$ (E) $\dfrac{18}{42}$

2. If $2y + 9 = 5y$, then $y =$

    (A) -3

    (B) $\dfrac{7}{9}$

    (C) $\dfrac{9}{7}$

    (D) 3

    (E) 27

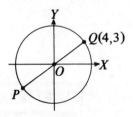

3. In the figure above, POQ is a diameter of circle O with center at the origin. If the coordinates of Q are $(4, 3)$, then the coordinates of P are

    (A) $(-4, -3)$ (B) $(-3, -4)$ (C) $(-4, 3)$
    (D) $(4, -3)$ (E) $(3, 4)$

4. If $5x\left(\dfrac{1}{5}y\right) = 1$, then $xy =$

    (A) 0   (B) $\dfrac{1}{25}$ (C) 1   (D) 5   (E) 25

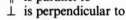

5. The diagram above shows the values of some of the coins used in the United States. How many combinations of complete regions shown could be shaded to indicate 75 cents?

    (A) One   (B) Two   (C) Three
    (D) Four   (E) Five

GO ON TO THE NEXT PAGE

6. If $\frac{1}{3}$ of a certain number is $\frac{1}{2}$, then $\frac{2}{3}$ of this number is

(A) $\frac{1}{6}$

(B) $\frac{2}{9}$

(C) $\frac{1}{3}$

(D) $\frac{2}{3}$

(E) 1

7. Carlos bought gasoline at a price of \$1.299 per gallon. Of the following, which is closest to the number of gallons Carlos bought if he paid \$26 for the gasoline?

(A) 21   (B) 20   (C) 19   (D) 18   (E) 13

8. In the figure above, the hand pointing to 5 moves clockwise to the next numeral every hour. At the end of 24 hours, to which numeral will it point?

(A) 7   (B) 5   (C) 3   (D) 2   (E) 1

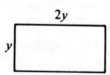

9. If the area of the rectangle above is 32, what is the value of y ?

(A) 2   (B) 4   (C) 6   (D) 8   (E) 16

10. The first of four identical bottles is $\frac{1}{2}$ full of water, the second is $\frac{3}{4}$ full, the third is $\frac{7}{8}$ full, and the fourth is $\frac{15}{16}$ full. After water is poured from the fourth bottle to fill each of the first three bottles, what fraction of the fourth bottle will be full?

(A) $\frac{1}{32}$ (B) $\frac{1}{16}$ (C) $\frac{1}{12}$ (D) $\frac{1}{9}$ (E) $\frac{1}{8}$

11. If n is an integer, which of the following will NEVER represent an even number?

(A) $2n$ (B) $2n + 1$ (C) $3n + 2$

(D) $2(n - 1)$ (E) $2(n + 1)^2$

12. If $x + y = 7$, $3x - y = 5$, and $2x - y = r - 1$, what is the value of r ?

(A) −3
(B) −1
(C) 1
(D) 2
(E) 3

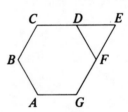

13. Eight toothpicks of equal length form the figure shown above. If the perimeter of $\triangle DEF$ is 4 inches, what is the perimeter, in inches, of hexagon $ABCDFG$?

(A) 6   (B) 8   (C) 12   (D) 18   (E) 24

GO ON TO THE NEXT PAGE

14. If n faces of a cube are painted, the area of the <u>unpainted</u> faces is what fraction of the total surface area of the cube?

    (A) $\frac{n}{6}$ (B) $\frac{n}{8}$ (C) $\frac{n-6}{6}$

    (D) $\frac{6-n}{6}$ (E) $\frac{6-n}{8}$

15. Alan is twice as old as Sue and half as old as Joseph. If the average (arithmetic mean) of all three ages is 14, how old is Sue?

    (A) 6
    (B) 7
    (C) 14
    (D) 16
    (E) 21

<u>Questions 16-17</u> refer to the following definition.

    For all real numbers p and q,
    $$\overline{p\lfloor q} = 2pq - (p+q).$$

16. $\overline{5\lfloor 4} =$

    (A) 2   (B) 11   (C) 31   (D) 39   (E) 49

17. Which of the following must be true for all real numbers p and q ?

    I. $\overline{p\lfloor q} = \overline{q\lfloor p}$

    II. $\overline{0\lfloor q} = 0$

    III. $\overline{p\lfloor p} = 2p(p-1)$

    (A) I only
    (B) II only
    (C) III only
    (D) I and III only
    (E) I, II, and III

18. In a restaurant Patty's share of the expenses for lunch was $2 more than Karen's. Karen did not have enough money to pay her share, so Patty paid $8 of the expenses and Karen paid the remaining $4. How much did Karen owe Patty to settle the lunch expenses?

    (A) $1
    (B) $3
    (C) $5
    (D) $6
    (E) $9

19. The degree measures of the angles of a triangle are x, y, and z. If x, y, and z are integers and $x < y < z$, what is the least possible value of z ?

    (A) 58°
    (B) 59°
    (C) 60°
    (D) 61°
    (E) 62°

20. A team has won 60 percent of the 20 games it has played so far this season. If the team plays a total of 50 games all season and wins 80 percent of the remaining games, then the percent of games it won for the entire season will be

    (A) 66%
    (B) 68%
    (C) 70%
    (D) 72%
    (E) 74%

GO ON TO THE NEXT PAGE

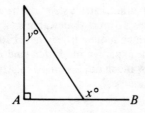

Note: Figure not drawn to scale.

21. In the figure above, if AB is a line segment and $x = 6y$, what is the value of y ?

    (A) 18 (B) 24 (C) 30 (D) 45 (E) 60

22. There are 10 children in a room. The ratio of boys to girls increased when another boy and another girl entered the room. What is the greatest number of boys that could originally have been in the room?

    (A) 1
    (B) 4
    (C) 5
    (D) 9
    (E) 10

$$\overset{\text{0 remainder 3}}{A\,\overline{)B}}$$

23. In the division problem above, if $A > 0$, which of the following must be true?

    (A) $A = 3$ (B) $A = 3B$ (C) $B = 0$
    (D) $B = 3$ (E) $B = 3A$

24. If the area of an isosceles right triangle is 36, what is its perimeter?

    (A) $12 + 12\sqrt{2}$
    (B) $12 + 6\sqrt{2}$
    (C) $6 + 12\sqrt{2}$
    (D) $18\sqrt{2}$
    (E) $12\sqrt{2}$

25. If the population of a town doubles every 10 years, the population in year $X + 100$ will be how many times the population in year X ?

    (A)   20
    (B)   100
    (C)   200
    (D)   512
    (E) 1,024

IF YOU FINISH BEFORE TIME IS CALLED, YOU MAY CHECK YOUR WORK ON THIS SECTION ONLY. DO NOT TURN TO ANY OTHER SECTION IN THE TEST. **S T O P**

SECTION 4   Time—30 minutes   For each question in this section, choose the best answer and fill in
             40 Questions   the corresponding oval on the answer sheet.

Each question below consists of a word in capital letters, followed by five lettered words or phrases. Choose the word or phrase that is most nearly opposite in meaning to the word in capital letters. Since some of the questions require you to distinguish fine shades of meaning, consider all the choices before deciding which is best.

Example:

GOOD: (A) sour (B) bad (C) red
       (D) hot   (E) ugly

Ⓐ ● Ⓒ Ⓓ Ⓔ

Each sentence below has one or two blanks, each blank indicating that something has been omitted. Beneath the sentence are five lettered words or sets of words. Choose the word or set of words that, when inserted in the sentence, best fits the meaning of the sentence as a whole.

Example:

Although its publicity has been ----, the film itself is intelligent, well-acted, handsomely produced, and altogether ----.

(A) tasteless. .respectable (B) extensive. .moderate
 (C) sophisticated. .amateur (D) risqué. .crude
   (E) perfect. .spectacular

● Ⓑ Ⓒ Ⓓ Ⓔ

1. ADJACENT: (A) frequently noticed
   (B) widely separated (C) sparse
   (D) harmonious (E) expanded

2. RECREATION: (A) labor (B) growth
   (C) generous reward (D) economical purchase
   (E) exchange of information

3. QUAKE: (A) examine (B) favor
   (C) diminish (D) become bright
   (E) remain motionless

4. ABOLISH: (A) release (B) betray
   (C) recuperate (D) initiate (E) surpass

5. METAPHORICALLY: (A) positively
   (B) rationally (C) partially
   (D) literally (E) hurriedly

6. ENGAGING: (A) honest (B) dissimilar
   (C) liberal (D) offensive (E) indecisive

7. GUILE: (A) willingness (B) tolerance
   (C) openness (D) influence (E) consciousness

8. LANGUISH: (A) accept (B) misuse
   (C) desire (D) become strong
   (E) speak correctly

9. ANTEDILUVIAN: (A) brawny (B) truthful
   (C) cooperative (D) posthumous
   (E) ultramodern

10. GAMBOL: (A) oppose (B) escape
    (C) avoid (D) trudge (E) bore

11. Since energy costs rise as fuel supplies diminish, we will not be able to maintain price ---- unless we are able to develop a renewable energy source.

    (A) differentiation (B) identity
     (C) augmentation (D) consideration
       (E) stability

12. The essence of the scientific attitude is the abandonment of personal ----: one must, that is, ---- private likes and dislikes.

    (A) interests. .divulge
    (B) experimentation. .pursue
    (C) inquisitiveness. .promote
    (D) inhibitions. .integrate
    (E) prejudices. .overcome

GO ON TO THE NEXT PAGE →

13. Professor Chen believes that the universal character of art refutes the prevalent notion that art is a ---- of civilization, a cultural frill, a social veneer.

    (A) guarantee   (B) hallmark   (C) record
    (D) luxury   (E) depiction

14. Paradoxically, while the country's government officially operated with the ---- usual in any communist regime, factions within that government carried on shrieking debates with each other.

    (A) incompetence   (B) unanimity
    (C) opposition   (D) illegality
    (E) discordancy

15. Even though she was then callow and unabashedly eager for ---- reviews, the young actress found the drama critic's ---- flattery revoltingly unrestrained.

    (A) banal. .perspicacious   (B) affirmative. .laconic
    (C) laudatory. .fulsome   (D) intelligible. .suave
    (E) antagonistic. .torpid

Each question below consists of a related pair of words or phrases, followed by five lettered pairs of words or phrases. Select the lettered pair that best expresses a relationship similar to that expressed in the original pair.

Example:

YAWN : BOREDOM ::   (A) dream : sleep
(B) anger : madness   (C) smile : amusement
(D) face : expression   (E) impatience : rebellion

Ⓐ Ⓑ ● Ⓓ Ⓔ

---

16. LUNG : WHALE ::   (A) shell : clam
    (B) claw : crab   (C) gill : fish
    (D) fin : shark   (E) pearl : oyster

17. PULPIT : MINISTER ::   (A) chair : dentist
    (B) sink : plumber   (C) podium : conductor
    (D) ship : sailor   (E) pedestal : sculptor

18. DASHIKI : GARMENT ::   (A) spoon : utensil
    (B) hat : coat   (C) cotton : summer
    (D) foot : shoe   (E) plate : table

19. ACROPHOBIA : HEIGHT ::
    (A) hydrophobia : water   (B) pyromania : fire
    (C) claustrophobia : fear   (D) hemophilia : heredity
    (E) psychology : behavior

20. SPOUSE : WIFE ::   (A) husband : uncle
    (B) son : mother   (C) child : daughter
    (D) brother : sister   (E) grandparent : parent

21. BARRIER : ACCESS ::
    (A) tonic : vigor   (B) barge : commerce
    (C) gag : speech   (D) cot : relaxation
    (E) refrigerator : storage

22. DEFOLIATE : LEAVES ::   (A) domesticate : pets
    (B) unwrap : presents   (C) germinate : seeds
    (D) undress : clothes   (E) harvest : fields

23. ABSTRUSE : COMPREHEND ::
    (A) antique : renovate
    (B) valid : authenticate
    (C) indistinct : discern
    (D) unethical : expurgate
    (E) practical : utilize

24. GRATIS : COST ::   (A) threateningly : menace
    (B) immediately : past   (C) freely : hindrance
    (D) wisely : choice   (E) gratefully : comment

25. MUTINOUS : TRACTABLE ::
    (A) fractious : competent   (B) morose : grave
    (C) precious : stilted   (D) fervent : disinterested
    (E) perverse : witty

GO ON TO THE NEXT PAGE

Each passage below is followed by questions based on its content. Answer the questions following each passage on the basis of what is <u>stated</u> or <u>implied</u> in that passage.

It was cool in the shade of the trees and high up in them Nick could hear the breeze that was rising. No sun came through as they walked and Nick knew
Line there would be no sun through the high top branches
(5) until nearly noon. His sister put her hand in his and walked close to him.

"I'm not scared, Nickie. But it makes me feel very strange."

"Me too. I always feel strange. Like the way I
(10) ought to feel in church."

"Nickie, where we're going to live isn't as solemn as this, is it?"

"No. Don't you worry. There it is cheerful. You just enjoy this, Littless. This is good for you.
(15) This is the way forests were in the olden days. This is about the last good country there is left. Nobody's going to chase us through here."

"I love the olden days. But I wouldn't want it all this solemn. It's wonderful walking though. I
(20) thought behind our house was wonderful, but this is better. This kind of woods makes me feel awfully religious."

"That's why they build cathedrals to be like this."

(25) "You've never seen a cathedral, have you?"

"No, but I've read about them and I can imagine them. This is the best one we have around here."

"Do you think we can go to Europe sometime and see cathedrals?"

(30) "Sure we will. But first I have to get out of this trouble and learn how to make some money."

"Let's be cheerful, Nickie," his sister said. "These woods make us too solemn."

"We'll be out of them pretty soon," Nick told her. "Then you'll see where we're going to live."

26. Nick's attitude toward his sister can best be characterized as

(A) domineering (B) protective (C) romantic
(D) uncaring (E) submissive

27. How does Nick's sister respond to Nick's references to being in trouble (lines 16-17 and lines 30-31) ?

(A) She avoids discussion of the subject.
(B) She tries to convince Nick that things will work out.
(C) She analyzes the problem and tries to solve it.
(D) She worries about the consequences for herself.
(E) She gets angry at Nick's brooding.

28. Nick and his sister both find the forest to be chiefly

(A) relaxing (B) exciting (C) cheerful
(D) awe-inspiring (E) frightening

GO ON TO THE NEXT PAGE

If a complicated social organization is a valid measure of the success of a species, then bumblebees have somehow failed. They have much simpler
Line colonies than honeybees: less distinct castes, for
(5) example, and no comparable information dissemination system. But whatever its virtues may be, an elaborate social order also seems to entail a perpetual energy crisis. A large society in a fixed location tends to deplete the neighborhood of those resources
(10) the society needs. One way of dealing with this is to stockpile resources when they become available. The resulting huge reserves attract predators, however, which makes an elaborate defense establishment necessary, and this in turn further drains available
(15) resources.

From this perspective, the bumblebees are a great success. They have achieved a modest social order without committing themselves to the costly business of supporting a large standing army. They can man-
(20) age this because they have learned how to forage successfully in weather that keeps most other species of bees in the hive. Bumblebees, which some biologists believe evolved in the Arctic, have the remarkable ability to control their body heat. They have
(25) also developed a talent for foraging among widely scattered and minute food sources. Thus they are not obliged to accumulate surpluses as protection against future shortages. Honeybees, on the other hand, evolved in tropical Asia and adapted to capital-
(30) izing quickly on the discovery of major food sources, such as large flowering trees. They have developed in such a way that they are committed to a corporate, garrison existence.

29. It can be inferred that, in line 19, "a large standing army" refers to those bees whose primary function is to

   (A) scout for new food sources
   (B) attack the hives of other bees
   (C) compete with other bees for major food sources
   (D) act as sentries outside the hive in bad weather
   (E) protect the food stockpiled in the hive

30. According to the passage, the success of the bumblebees' social organization derives from bumblebees' ability to do which of the following?

   I.   Range widely to find food
   II.   Find food in cold weather
   III.   Defend themselves against predators

   (A) I only
   (B) II only
   (C) I and II only
   (D) II and III only
   (E) I, II, and III

31. It can be inferred that a honeybee hive is most similar to which of the following?

   (A) A wealthy city-state always prepared to fend off attacks
   (B) A palace in which treasures are stored and never used
   (C) A completely self-sufficient nation on a remote island
   (D) A community of resourceful but eccentric pioneers
   (E) A highly civilized society whose greatest fear is internal revolt

GO ON TO THE NEXT PAGE ▶

(This passage was written in 1963.)

In any nonviolent campaign there are four basic steps: (1) collection of the facts to determine whether injustices are alive; (2) negotiation; (3) self-purification; and (4) direct action. We have gone
(5) through all these steps.

As in so many experiences of the past we were confronted with blasted hopes, and the dark shadow of a deep disappointment settled upon us. So we had no alternative except that of preparing for direct
(10) action, whereby we would present our very bodies as a means of laying our case before the conscience of the local and national community. We were not unmindful of the difficulties involved. So we decided to go through a process of self-purification.
(15) We started having workshops on nonviolence and repeatedly asked ourselves the questions, "Are you able to accept blows without retaliating? Are you able to endure the ordeals of jail?" This reveals that we did not move irresponsibly into direct action.
(20) You may well ask, "Why direct action? Why sit-ins, marches, etc.? Isn't negotiation a better path?" You are exactly right in your call for negotiation. Indeed, this is the purpose of direct action. Nonviolent direct action seeks to create such a crisis and
(25) such a creative tension that a community that has constantly refused to negotiate is forced to confront the issue. It seeks to so dramatize the issue that it can no longer be ignored. Just as Socrates felt that it was necessary to create a tension in the
(30) mind so that individuals could rise from the bondage of myths and half-truths to the unfettered realm of creative analysis and objective appraisal, we must see the need of having nonviolent gadflies to create the kind of tension in society that will help men
(35) rise from the dark depths of prejudice and racism to the majestic heights of understanding and brotherhood. So the purpose of direct action is to create a situation so crisis-packed that it will inevitably open the door to negotiation.
(40) History is the long and tragic story of the fact that privileged groups seldom give up their privileges voluntarily. Individuals may see the moral light and voluntarily give up their unjust posture; but as Reinhold Niebuhr has reminded us, groups are more
(45) immoral than individuals. We know from painful experience that freedom is never voluntarily given by the oppressor; it must be demanded by the oppressed. For years now I have heard the word "Wait!" This "wait" has almost always meant
(50) "never." We must come to see with the distinguished jurist of yesterday that "justice too long delayed is justice denied."

32. The content and tone of the passage suggest that the primary purpose of the author is to
   (A) define the difficulties of correcting social injustice
   (B) summarize the effects of civil disobedience in a specific community
   (C) establish the relationship between the oppressors and the oppressed
   (D) apply Socrates' ideas on nonviolence to modern social conditions
   (E) describe and justify a nonviolent campaign for social justice

33. The passage indicates that without the preparatory step of self-purification, the practitioners of nonviolent action would be
   (A) prone to respond to violence with violence
   (B) deserving of the ordeals of imprisonment
   (C) uncertain whether injustices in fact existed
   (D) unclear about what result they were seeking
   (E) guilty of the same motivations as their oppressors

34. Which of the following serves as the best example of the kind of direct action discussed in lines 20-28 ?
   (A) Harrassing members of the opposition by slandering them in newspaper editorials
   (B) Preventing an establishment from doing business by peacefully blocking the entrances to the building
   (C) Conducting a series of workshops and discussions for those who are interested in bringing about social changes
   (D) Recruiting students from local schools to distribute pamphlets and information door-to-door in the community
   (E) Holding a member of the opposition hostage until negotiations are opened and made public

35. It can be inferred from the context of the passage that the "nonviolent gadflies" mentioned in line 33 are
   (A) leaders who are remarkable primarily for their patience
   (B) strategists who concentrate on planning diversionary tactics
   (C) activists who advocate the effectiveness of civil disobedience
   (D) individuals who are able to serve as objective mediators
   (E) idealists who are inspired by the violent actions of others

GO ON TO THE NEXT PAGE

36. According to the author, a lesson to be learned from history is that

(A) persistent and direct confrontation is usually necessary to bring about significant social change
(B) a delay in the eventual gratification of a desire will lessen the degree of satisfaction
(C) any efforts to implement reforms in order to benefit society are doomed to failure
(D) it is as impossible to change individuals as it is to change history
(E) it is time to reverse the social positions of the oppressors and the oppressed

An unusual view of the *Conquista* is presented in a picture by Jan Mostaert, probably dating from the 1540's. This remarkable work depicts an imaginary scene of the conquest rather than any specific incident. The pastoral landscape, similar to that which Mostaert provided for Adam and Eve in another painting, is one that the artist and other European readers of Columbus might well have imagined to exist in the West Indies. And the nude figures with the lithe, athletic, well-proportioned bodies of Greek and Roman warriors drawn by Mantegna, Pollaiuolo, and others accord perfectly with the Indians as seen through the spectacles of a Renaissance humanist. Only the strange straw huts and a monkey squatting on a tree stump are manifestly exotic. It is a vision of the Golden Age of the Indies glimpsed at the moment when it is shattered by Spanish steel. While sheep and cows browse impassively on this fresh green breast of the New World, the inhabitants, clutching rudimentary weapons, streak across the panel to encounter a posse of Europeans, armed with pikes and halberds and cannon, remorselessly advancing from the shore where they have beached their boats. Mostaert no doubt had personal experience of the behavior of Spanish soldiers and the picture may well allude, if only obliquely, to their activities in his native Low Countries. But more generally, it is a visual parable on the peace of unspoilt nature and the destructive urge of all peoples—a parallel to his painting of Eve banished from the pastoral dream of Eden, with Cain killing Abel nearby. It is a theme that was to echo down the ages in the Americas.

37. The central purpose of the passage is to

(A) announce the discovery of a great artist
(B) describe and analyze a work of art
(C) point out the historical inaccuracies of a painting
(D) provide an example of the pastoral school of landscape painting
(E) criticize the behavior of the Spanish in the New World

38. The author uses all of the following in discussing Mostaert's painting of the conquest EXCEPT

(A) comparison with other paintings
(B) analysis of the techniques of painting
(C) reference to classical imagery
(D) direct description of the pictorial content
(E) reference to Mostaert's life

39. It can be inferred from the passage that the author's interest in Mostaert's painting centers chiefly on its

(A) ideological content
(B) geographical accuracy
(C) elements of exoticism
(D) drawing of the figures
(E) treatment of the landscape

40. The passage indicates that all of the following exerted an influence on Mostaert's painting of the *Conquista* EXCEPT

(A) paintings of classical figures
(B) biblical mythology
(C) personal experience and preconceptions
(D) readings of Columbus
(E) other paintings of the conquest of the Indies

IF YOU FINISH BEFORE TIME IS CALLED, YOU MAY CHECK YOUR WORK ON THIS SECTION ONLY. DO NOT TURN TO ANY OTHER SECTION IN THE TEST.   **STOP**

SECTION **5**   Time—30 minutes   35 Questions   In this section solve each problem, using any available space on the page for scratchwork. Then decide which is the best of the choices given and fill in the corresponding oval on the answer sheet.

The following information is for your reference in solving some of the problems.

Circle of radius r: Area $= \pi r^2$; Circumference $= 2\pi r$
The number of degrees of arc in a circle is 360.
The measure in degrees of a straight angle is 180.

Definition of symbols:
$=$ is equal to $\leq$ is less than or equal to
$\neq$ is unequal to $\geq$ is greater than or equal to
$<$ is less than $\parallel$ is parallel to
$>$ is greater than $\perp$ is perpendicular to

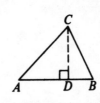

Triangle: The sum of the measures in degrees of the angles of a triangle is 180.
If $\angle CDA$ is a right angle, then

(1) area of $\triangle ABC = \dfrac{AB \times CD}{2}$

(2) $AC^2 = AD^2 + DC^2$

Note: Figures that accompany problems in this test are intended to provide information useful in solving the problems. They are drawn as accurately as possible EXCEPT when it is stated in a specific problem that its figure is not drawn to scale. All figures lie in a plane unless otherwise indicated. All numbers used are real numbers.

1. If $10x - 4 = 8$, then $10x - 5 =$

(A) -17 (B) -1 (C) 3 (D) 7 (E) 12

2. If $x = 1$, which of the following is greatest?

(A) $1 + x$

(B) $1 - x$

(C) $\dfrac{1}{x}$

(D) x^2

(E) x^3

3. If X is the midpoint of the segment AB, which of the following is NOT true?

(A) $AX + XB = AB$
(B) $XB < AB$
(C) $XB < AX$
(D) $AX < AB$
(E) $AX = XB$

4. $(5 - 1)(4 - 1)(3 - 1)(2 - 1) - (4 - 1)(3 - 1)(2 - 1) =$

(A) 4 (B) 5 (C) 12 (D) 18 (E) 24

5. If $a = 2$ and $b = 4$, which of the following is NOT equal to any of the others?

(A) $(a - b)^2$
(B) $2a$
(C) $(b - a)^2$
(D) $8a - 3b$
(E) $4a - 2b$

6. How many hours are equal to 264 minutes?

(A) $4\dfrac{1}{4}$ (B) $4\dfrac{2}{5}$ (C) $4\dfrac{1}{2}$

(D) $4\dfrac{2}{3}$ (E) $4\dfrac{4}{5}$

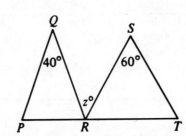

7. In the figure above, if $PQ = QR$, $RS = ST$, and PRT is a line segment, then $z =$

(A) 40 (B) 50 (C) 60 (D) 80 (E) 100

GO ON TO THE NEXT PAGE

5

Questions 8-27 each consist of two quantities, one in Column A and one in Column B. You are to compare the two quantities and on the answer sheet fill in oval

- A if the quantity in Column A is greater;
- B if the quantity in Column B is greater;
- C if the two quantities are equal;
- D if the relationship cannot be determined from the information given.

AN E RESPONSE WILL NOT BE SCORED.

	EXAMPLES		
	Column A	Column B	Answers
E1.	2×6	$2 + 6$	● Ⓑ Ⓒ Ⓓ Ⓔ
E2.	$180 - x$	y	Ⓐ Ⓑ ● Ⓓ Ⓔ
E3.	$p - q$	$q - p$	Ⓐ Ⓑ Ⓒ ● Ⓔ

For E2 the diagram shows angles $x°$ and $y°$.

Notes:

1. In certain questions, information concerning one or both of the quantities to be compared is centered above the two columns.
2. In a given question, a symbol that appears in both columns represents the same thing in Column A as it does in Column B.
3. Letters such as x, n, and k stand for real numbers.

	Column A	Column B
8.	$\dfrac{5 \times 10 \times 15}{5 \times 5 \times 5}$	6

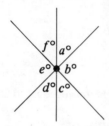

Three lines intersect in a point.

	Column A	Column B
9.	$a + c + e$	$b + d + f$

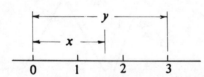

10.	Total length of 300 non-overlapping x-lengths	Total length of 200 non-overlapping y-lengths

If Bill weighed 40 pounds less, his weight would be half as much as it actually is.

11.	Bill's weight	40 pounds

The measures of the angles of a certain triangle are $x°$, $30°$, and $50°$.

12.	x	90

$$a + b = 0$$

13.	a	b

14.	$\sqrt{3^4}$	9

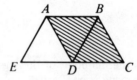

$\triangle ADE$, $\triangle ABD$, and $\triangle BCD$ are equilateral.

15.	Perimeter of quadrilateral $ABCE$	Perimeter of shaded parallelogram $ABCD$

16.	The circumference of a circle having radius $\dfrac{1}{\pi}$	π

17.	$(a + b)^2$	$a(a + b) + b(a + b)$

GO ON TO THE NEXT PAGE →

	Column A	Column B		Column A	Column B

18. $\frac{1}{4}x$ $\frac{1}{2}x$

S is the set of integers on the number line from 1 to 100 inclusive.

19. The number of integers in S that are closer to 35 than to 45   The number of integers in S that are closer to 45 than to 35

20. 3% of (2% of 30)   6% of 30

A box contains a single layer of 30 randomly arranged pieces of candy of which 15 are caramels, 10 are coconut creams, and 5 are chocolates. Jane took a piece of candy without looking.

21. The chance that Jane took a caramel   The chance that Jane did not take a caramel

$$17 + x = 10 + y$$

22. x y

$$x \neq -2$$

23. $\dfrac{x^2 - x - 6}{x + 2}$ $x - 3$

$$p > q > r > 0$$

24. $q - p$ $r - q$

25.

This question was not counted in computing scores.

26. $\dfrac{1}{\sqrt{2} - 1}$ $\sqrt{2} - 1$

27. Perimeter of a rectangle with area 20   Perimeter of a triangle with area 20

GO ON TO THE NEXT PAGE ➡

5

Solve each of the remaining problems in this section using any available space for scratchwork. Then decide which is the best of the choices given and fill in the corresponding oval on the answer sheet.

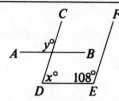

28. In the figure above, $AB \parallel DE$ and $CD \parallel EF$. What is the value of $x + y$?

    (A) 72   (B) 108   (C) 144

    (D) 180   (E) 216

29. If the ratio of x to y is 3 to 4 and the ratio of y to z is 2 to 1, then the ratio of x to z is

    (A) 3 to 2
    (B) 3 to 1
    (C) 2 to 4
    (D) 2 to 3
    (E) 2 to 1

30. Which of the following equations is (are) true for all positive integers a, b, and c?

    I. $(a - b) - c = a - (b + c)$
    II. $(a \div b) \div c = a \div (b \div c)$
    III. $(a \div b) + c = a \div (b + c)$

    (A) None   (B) I only   (C) II only

    (D) II and III only   (E) I, II, and III

31. For any positive integer x, define $\textcircled{x}$ by the following equation.

    $$\textcircled{x} = x + (x - 1) + (x - 2) + \ldots + 2 + 1$$

    For example, $\textcircled{4} = 4 + 3 + 2 + 1$. What is the value of $\textcircled{42} - \textcircled{40}$?

    (A) 2
    (B) 41
    (C) 42
    (D) 82
    (E) 83

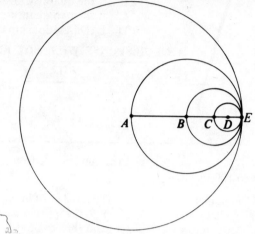

32. In the figure above, A, B, C, and D are centers of the four circles that meet at point E. If these five points lie on the same line and the area of the circle with center D is π, then the radius of the circle with center A is

    (A) 4   (B) 6   (C) 8   (D) 12   (E) 16

33. A car travels 180 kilometers from A to B at 60 kilometers per hour and returns from B to A along the same route at 90 kilometers per hour. The average speed in kilometers per hour for the round trip is

    (A) 72   (B) 75   (C) 78   (D) 81   (E) 84

34. If $w = 2x = 3y$, then $5w$ is equal to which of the following?

    I. $15y$
    II. $2x + 12y$
    III. $4x + 8y$

    (A) I only   (B) II only   (C) III only

    (D) I and II   (E) I and III

$$\begin{array}{r} 6RS \\ + \ RR4 \\ \hline P,QPQ \end{array}$$

35. In the addition problem above, $P, Q, R,$ and S represent four different digits. What digit does S represent?

    (A) 1   (B) 2   (C) 5   (D) 6   (E) 8

IF YOU FINISH BEFORE TIME IS CALLED, YOU MAY CHECK YOUR WORK ON THIS SECTION ONLY. DO NOT TURN TO ANY OTHER SECTION IN THE TEST. **STOP**

Correct Answers for Scholastic Aptitude Test
Form Code 3l

VERBAL		MATHEMATICAL	
Section 1	Section 4	Section 2	Section 5
1. C	1. B	1. C	1. D
2. B	2. A	2. D	2. A
3. B	3. E	3. A	3. C
4. E	4. D	4. C	4. D
5. D	5. D	5. B	5. E
6. D	6. D	6. E	6. B
7. D	7. C	7. B	7. B
8. E	8. D	8. E	*8. C
9. C	9. E	9. B	*9. C
10. A	10. D	10. B	*10. B
11. C	11. E	11. B	*11. A
12. C	12. E	12. E	*12. A
13. D	13. D	13. B	*13. D
14. C	14. B	14. D	*14. C
15. A	15. C	15. A	*15. A
16. A	16. C	16. C	*16. B
17. B	17. C	17. D	*17. C
18. B	18. A	18. A	*18. D
19. E	19. A	19. D	*19. B
20. D	20. C	20. D	*20. B
21. B	21. C	21. A	*21. C
22. D	22. D	22. B	*22. B
23. C	23. C	23. D	*23. C
24. C	24. C	24. A	*24. D
25. D	25. D	25. E	*25. †
26. A	26. B		*26. A
27. C	27. A		*27. D
28. E	28. D		28. D
29. E	29. E		29. A
30. A	30. C		30. B
31. D	31. A		31. E
32. B	32. E		32. C
33. C	33. A		33. A
34. D	34. B		34. D
35. B	35. C		35. E
36. C	36. A		
37. D	37. B		
38. E	38. B		
39. B	39. A		
40. D	40. E		
41. B			
42. D			
43. B			
44. C			
45. A			

*Indicates four-choice questions. (All of the other questions are five-choice.)
†Not scored

The Scoring Process

Machine-scoring is done in three steps:

- *Scanning.* Your answer sheet is "read" by a scanning machine and the oval you filled in for each question is recorded on a computer tape.

- *Scoring.* The computer compares the oval filled in for each question with the correct response. Each correct answer receives one point; omitted questions do not count toward your score. For each wrong answer, a fraction of a point is subtracted to correct for random guessing. For questions with five answer choices, one-fourth of a point is subtracted for each wrong response; for questions with four answer choices, one-third of a point is subtracted for each wrong response. The SAT-verbal test has 85 questions with five answer choices each. If, for example, a student has 44 right, 32 wrong, and 9 omitted, the resulting raw score is determined as follows:

$$44 \text{ right} - \frac{32 \text{ wrong}}{4} = 44 - 8 = 36 \text{ raw score points}$$

Obtaining raw scores frequently involves the rounding of fractional numbers to the nearest whole number. For example, a raw score of 36.25 is rounded to 36, the nearest whole number. A raw score of 36.50 is rounded upward to 37.

- *Converting to reported scaled score.* Raw test scores are then placed on the College Board scale of 200 to 800 through a process that adjusts scores to account for minor differences in difficulty among different editions of the test. This process, known as equating, is performed so that a student's reported score is not affected by the edition of the test taken nor by the abilities of the group with whom the student takes the test. As a result of placing SAT scores on the College Board scale, scores earned by students at different times can be compared. For example, an SAT-verbal score of 400 on a test taken at one administration indicates the same level of developed verbal ability as a 400 score obtained on a different edition of the test taken at another time.

How to Score the Test

SAT-Verbal Sections 1 and 4

Step A: Count the number of correct answers for *section 1* and record the number in the space provided on the worksheet on the next page. Then do the same for the incorrect answers. (Do not count omitted answers.) To determine subtotal A, use the formula:

$$\text{number correct} - \frac{\text{number incorrect}}{4} = \text{subtotal A}$$

Step B: Count the number of correct answers and the number of incorrect answers for *section 4* and record the numbers in the spaces provided on the worksheet. To determine subtotal B, use the formula:

$$\text{number correct} - \frac{\text{number incorrect}}{4} = \text{subtotal B}$$

Step C: To obtain C, add subtotal A to subtotal B, keeping any decimals. Enter the resulting figure on the worksheet.

Step D: To obtain D, your raw verbal score, round C to the nearest whole number. (For example, any number from 44.50 to 45.49 rounds to 45.) Enter the resulting figure on the worksheet.

Step E: To find your reported SAT-verbal score, look up the total raw verbal score you obtained in step D in the conversion table on page 194. Enter this figure on the worksheet.

SAT-Mathematical Sections 2 and 5

Step A: Count the number of correct answers and the number of incorrect answers for *section 2* and record the numbers in the spaces provided on the worksheet. To determine the subtotal A, use the formula:

$$\text{number correct} - \frac{\text{number incorrect}}{4} = \text{subtotal A}$$

Step B: Count the number of correct answers and the number of incorrect answers for the *five-choice questions (questions 1 through 7 and 28 through 35) in section 5* and record the numbers in the spaces provided on the worksheet. To determine the subtotal B, use the formula:

$$\text{number correct} - \frac{\text{number incorrect}}{4} = \text{subtotal B}$$

Step C: Count the number of correct answers and the number of incorrect answers for the *four-choice questions (questions 8 through 27) in section 5* and record the numbers in the spaces provided on the worksheet. To determine the subtotal C, use the formula:

$$\text{number correct} - \frac{\text{number incorrect}}{3} = \text{subtotal C}$$

Step D: To obtain D, add subtotal A, subtotal B, and subtotal C, keeping any decimals. Enter the resulting figure on the worksheet.

Step E: To obtain E, your raw mathematical score, round D to the nearest whole number. (For example, any number from 44.50 to 45.49 rounds to 45.) Enter the resulting figure on the worksheet.

Step F: To find your reported SAT-mathematical score, look up the total raw mathematical score you obtained in E in the conversion table on page 194. Enter this figure on the worksheet.

SAT SCORING WORKSHEET

SAT-Verbal Sections

A. Section 1: _____ − ¼ (_____) = _____
      no. correct   no. incorrect   subtotal A

B. Section 4: _____ − ¼ (_____) = _____
      no. correct   no. incorrect   subtotal B

C. Total unrounded raw score
   (Total A + B)
      _____
           C

D. Total rounded raw score
   (Rounded to nearest whole number)
      _____
           D

E. SAT-verbal reported scaled score
   (See the conversion table on page 194.)

      SAT-verbal
        score

SAT-Mathematical Sections

A. Section 2: _____ − ¼ (_____) = _____
      no. correct   no. incorrect   subtotal A

B. Section 5:
   Questions 1 through 7 and   _____ − ¼ (_____) = _____
   28 through 35 (5-choice)   no. correct   no. incorrect   subtotal B

C. Section 5:
   Questions 8 through 27   _____ − ⅓ (_____) = _____
   (4-choice)   no. correct   no. incorrect   subtotal C

D. Total unrounded raw score
   (Total A + B + C)
      _____
           D

E. Total rounded raw score
   (Rounded to nearest whole number)
      _____
           E

F. SAT-mathematical reported scaled score
   (See the conversion table on page 194.)

      SAT-math
        score

Score Conversion Table
Scholastic Aptitude Test
Form Code 3I

Raw Score	College Board Reported Score		Raw Score	College Board Reported Score	
	SAT-Verbal	SAT-Math		SAT-Verbal	SAT-Math
85	800		40	450	600
84	780		39	440	590
83	760		38	440	580
82	750		37	430	570
81	740		36	420	570
80	730		35	420	560
79	720		34	410	550
78	710		33	400	540
77	700		32	400	530
76	690		31	390	520
75	690		30	380	510
74	680		29	380	500
73	670		28	370	490
72	660		27	370	480
71	660		26	360	470
70	650		25	350	470
69	640		24	350	460
68	630		23	340	450
67	630		22	330	440
66	620		21	330	430
65	610		20	320	420
64	610		19	320	410
63	600		18	310	400
62	590		17	300	390
61	590		16	300	390
60	580		15	290	380
59	570	800	14	280	370
58	570	780	13	280	360
57	560	760	12	270	350
56	550	750	11	270	350
55	550	730	10	260	340
54	540	720	9	250	330
53	530	710	8	250	320
52	530	700	7	240	320
51	520	690	6	240	310
50	510	690	5	230	300
49	510	680	4	220	300
48	500	670	3	220	290
47	500	660	2	210	280
46	490	650	1	200	270
45	480	640	0	200	270
44	480	630	−1	200	260
43	470	630	−2	200	250
42	460	620	−3	200	250
41	460	610	−4	200	240
			−5	200	230
			−6	200	220
			−7	200	220
			−8	200	210
			−9 or below	200	200

COLLEGE BOARD — SCHOLASTIC APTITUDE TEST
and Test of Standard Written English   Side 1

Use a No. 2 pencil only. Be sure each mark is dark and completely fills the intended oval. Completely erase any errors or stray marks.

1.

YOUR NAME: _____
(Print)   Last   First   M.I.

SIGNATURE: _____   DATE: ___ / ___ / ___

HOME ADDRESS: _____
(Print)   Number and Street

_____
City   State   Zip Code

CENTER: _____
(Print)   City   State   Center Number

IMPORTANT: Please fill in these boxes exactly as shown on the back cover of your test book.

FOR ETS USE ONLY

2. TEST FORM

3. FORM CODE

4. REGISTRATION NUMBER
(Copy from your Admission Ticket.)

5. YOUR NAME

First 4 letters of last name				First Init.	Mid. Init.

6. DATE OF BIRTH

Month	Day	Year
○ Jan.		
○ Feb.		
○ Mar.		
○ Apr.		
○ May		
○ June		
○ July		
○ Aug.		
○ Sept.		
○ Oct.		
○ Nov.		
○ Dec.		

7. SEX
○ Female
○ Male

8. TEST BOOK SERIAL NUMBER

Start with number 1 for each new section. If a section has fewer than 50 questions, leave the extra answer spaces blank.

SECTION 1

(Answer grid: questions 1–50, each with options A B C D E)

SECTION 2

(Answer grid: questions 1–50, each with options A B C D E)

(Cut here to detach.)

COLLEGE BOARD — SCHOLASTIC APTITUDE TEST and Test of Standard Written English **Side 2**

Use a No. 2 pencil only. Be sure each mark is dark and completely fills the intended oval. Completely erase any errors or stray marks.

Start with number 1 for each new section. If a section has fewer than 50 questions, leave the extra answer spaces blank.

SECTION 3	SECTION 4	SECTION 5	SECTION 6
1 A B C D E	1 A B C D E	1 A B C D E	1 A B C D E
2 A B C D E	2 A B C D E	2 A B C D E	2 A B C D E
3 A B C D E	3 A B C D E	3 A B C D E	3 A B C D E
4 A B C D E	4 A B C D E	4 A B C D E	4 A B C D E
5 A B C D E	5 A B C D E	5 A B C D E	5 A B C D E
6 A B C D E	6 A B C D E	6 A B C D E	6 A B C D E
7 A B C D E	7 A B C D E	7 A B C D E	7 A B C D E
8 A B C D E	8 A B C D E	8 A B C D E	8 A B C D E
9 A B C D E	9 A B C D E	9 A B C D E	9 A B C D E
10 A B C D E	10 A B C D E	10 A B C D E	10 A B C D E
11 A B C D E	11 A B C D E	11 A B C D E	11 A B C D E
12 A B C D E	12 A B C D E	12 A B C D E	12 A B C D E
13 A B C D E	13 A B C D E	13 A B C D E	13 A B C D E
14 A B C D E	14 A B C D E	14 A B C D E	14 A B C D E
15 A B C D E	15 A B C D E	15 A B C D E	15 A B C D E
16 A B C D E	16 A B C D E	16 A B C D E	16 A B C D E
17 A B C D E	17 A B C D E	17 A B C D E	17 A B C D E
18 A B C D E	18 A B C D E	18 A B C D E	18 A B C D E
19 A B C D E	19 A B C D E	19 A B C D E	19 A B C D E
20 A B C D E	20 A B C D E	20 A B C D E	20 A B C D E
21 A B C D E	21 A B C D E	21 A B C D E	21 A B C D E
22 A B C D E	22 A B C D E	22 A B C D E	22 A B C D E
23 A B C D E	23 A B C D E	23 A B C D E	23 A B C D E
24 A B C D E	24 A B C D E	24 A B C D E	24 A B C D E
25 A B C D E	25 A B C D E	25 A B C D E	25 A B C D E
26 A B C D E	26 A B C D E	26 A B C D E	26 A B C D E
27 A B C D E	27 A B C D E	27 A B C D E	27 A B C D E
28 A B C D E	28 A B C D E	28 A B C D E	28 A B C D E
29 A B C D E	29 A B C D E	29 A B C D E	29 A B C D E
30 A B C D E	30 A B C D E	30 A B C D E	30 A B C D E
31 A B C D E	31 A B C D E	31 A B C D E	31 A B C D E
32 A B C D E	32 A B C D E	32 A B C D E	32 A B C D E
33 A B C D E	33 A B C D E	33 A B C D E	33 A B C D E
34 A B C D E	34 A B C D E	34 A B C D E	34 A B C D E
35 A B C D E	35 A B C D E	35 A B C D E	35 A B C D E
36 A B C D E	36 A B C D E	36 A B C D E	36 A B C D E
37 A B C D E	37 A B C D E	37 A B C D E	37 A B C D E
38 A B C D E	38 A B C D E	38 A B C D E	38 A B C D E
39 A B C D E	39 A B C D E	39 A B C D E	39 A B C D E
40 A B C D E	40 A B C D E	40 A B C D E	40 A B C D E
41 A B C D E	41 A B C D E	41 A B C D E	41 A B C D E
42 A B C D E	42 A B C D E	42 A B C D E	42 A B C D E
43 A B C D E	43 A B C D E	43 A B C D E	43 A B C D E
44 A B C D E	44 A B C D E	44 A B C D E	44 A B C D E
45 A B C D E	45 A B C D E	45 A B C D E	45 A B C D E
46 A B C D E	46 A B C D E	46 A B C D E	46 A B C D E
47 A B C D E	47 A B C D E	47 A B C D E	47 A B C D E
48 A B C D E	48 A B C D E	48 A B C D E	48 A B C D E
49 A B C D E	49 A B C D E	49 A B C D E	49 A B C D E
50 A B C D E	50 A B C D E	50 A B C D E	50 A B C D E

9. SIGNATURE: ____________________

FOR ETS USE ONLY	VTR	VTFS	VRR	VRFS	VVR	VVFS	WER	WEFS	M4R	M4FS	M5R	M5FS	MTFS	
	VTW	VTCS	VRW	VRCS	VVW	VVCS	WEW	WECS	M4W		M5W		MTCS	

TEST 7—FORM CODE 4W

Each question below consists of a word in capital letters, followed by five lettered words or phrases. Choose the word or phrase that is most nearly opposite in meaning to the word in capital letters. Since some of the questions require you to distinguish fine shades of meaning, consider all the choices before deciding which is best.

Example:

GOOD: (A) sour   (B) bad   (C) red
(D) hot   (E) ugly

Ⓐ ● Ⓒ Ⓓ Ⓔ

1. NUTRITIOUS: (A) bland   (B) dietetic
   (C) crude   (D) unusual   (E) unwholesome

2. WARP: (A) remove   (B) straighten
   (C) lengthen   (D) choke   (E) pierce

3. CLEAR-CUT: (A) unique   (B) useless
   (C) undefined   (D) disagreeable
   (E) permanent

4. VENTURESOME: (A) delinquent   (B) busy
   (C) cautious   (D) fictitious   (E) profitable

5. SEVER: (A) choose   (B) distribute
   (C) simplify   (D) connect   (E) report

6. WAVER: (A) fail to acknowledge
   (B) speak quietly   (C) seem indifferent
   (D) pretend to believe   (E) stand firm

7. HERALDED: (A) unaccompanied
   (B) unannounced   (C) uncommitted
   (D) forestalled   (E) foregone

8. PERPETUAL: (A) inconstant   (B) sluggish
   (C) improbable   (D) illogical   (E) miniature

9. SUBMISSIVE: (A) misguided   (B) suspect
   (C) rebellious   (D) happy   (E) talkative

10. PROFUSION: (A) impurity   (B) division
    (C) originality   (D) brittleness   (E) scarcity

11. EUPHEMISM: (A) tasteful design
    (B) angry argument   (C) difficult decision
    (D) coarse expression   (E) deceptive appearance

12. BELEAGUER: (A) shield from
    (B) impress upon   (C) reject   (D) convert
    (E) discriminate

13. ABROGATE: (A) indicate   (B) respond
    (C) review   (D) violate   (E) establish

14. DISCURSIVE: (A) concise   (B) printed
    (C) profound   (D) polite   (E) laudatory

15. ENGENDER: (A) pervade   (B) preoccupy
    (C) revise   (D) acclimate   (E) squelch

Each sentence below has one or two blanks, each blank indicating that something has been omitted. Beneath the sentence are five lettered words or sets of words. Choose the word or set of words that, when inserted in the sentence, best fits the meaning of the sentence as a whole.

Example:

Although its publicity has been ----, the film itself is intelligent, well-acted, handsomely produced, and altogether ----.

(A) tasteless. .respectable (B) extensive. .moderate
(C) sophisticated. .amateur (D) risqué. .crude
(E) perfect. .spectacular

● Ⓑ Ⓒ Ⓓ Ⓔ

16. Until the nature of the aging process is better understood, the possibility of discovering a medicine that can block the fundamental process of aging seems very ----.

(A) urgent   (B) remote   (C) practical
(D) substantial   (E) desirable

17. Among the mysteries of the Mayan civilization are its hieroglyphics, which can only be partially ----.

(A) amended   (B) obscured   (C) dismantled
(D) deciphered   (E) improved

18. Queen Margrethe II is in fact the first formally ---- Queen of Denmark named Margrethe; her ----, who ruled in the fourteenth century, was never actually crowned.

(A) contending. .antecedent
(B) ordering. .ancestor
(C) reigning. .predecessor
(D) challenging. .forerunner
(E) delegating. .introduction

19. Bees and other social insects have extremely precise mechanisms of communication, but this precision probably ---- their ability to change their behavior in order to meet new situations.

(A) enhances   (B) increases
(C) explains   (D) limits   (E) interrupts

20. A stroke of humor toward the end is not sufficient to balance the ---- of the piece.

(A) harmony   (B) irony
(C) subtlety   (D) gravity   (E) flippancy

GO ON TO THE NEXT PAGE ➡

197

In that year when the moon ate the sun, Nah-goey persuaded twenty Kogui warriors to separate temporarily from their main tribe, the Kiowas, and move southward. Two Comanches also accepted Nah-goey's pipe—An-zah-te and Tau-kan-ta-le, or Antelope Boy, who was a medicine man. It would be a difficult expedition. The men would have to cover much territory during the short hours of daylight. It was essential that the leader be resourceful and acquainted with the water holes.

The group first swam their horses across the Red River, ferrying their equipment on pontoons made of rawhide and brush. One of the ten sacred medicines of the Kiowas became waterlogged and everyone except Nah-goey, an atheist, considered this a bad sign. They hastened to build a sweat lodge in which to offer prayers of propitiation to the gods. During the ceremony, a robe thrown over the frame of the lodge caught fire. This was a warning to abandon the expedition, but Nah-goey expressed scorn for his companions' fears.

Their misgivings increased later when they frightened a hibernating bear. It stood on its hind legs, appearing to wave the warriors back. This should have been enough for anyone, but as usual the person who took a positive stand prevailed, and Nah-goey convinced the men to continue. He further discounted such omens as a flight of crows and a swarm of flies (unexplainable in this arid land).

Finally, Nah-goey said, "Who will go ahead to build an altar?" By this he was calling for an advance scout. An-zah-te offered his services. Antelope Boy acted as rear scout. It was Kiowa custom that unrecognized members of the party take the most arduous assignments. The scouts had a hard time since they had to travel farther and faster than the main body. When the two scouts returned, An-zah-te told Nah-goey of a few riders ahead, but Nah-goey remarked, "People are often fooled by herds of elk which look like men on horseback." An-zah-te was indignant at this criticism, especially as it made him a laughingstock among the men. Then Antelope Boy reported sighting a Wichita war party to the rear. He said, "Perhaps elks wear feathers in their hair and carry shields too."

But like others of various times and peoples, Nah-goey was a leader who encouraged his followers by a show of optimism, allowing it to neutralize a caution that might have saved them all. My grandfather was An-zah-te, who told me how the Kiowas mourned for Nah-goey and all his men, for they were brave Kiowa warriors.

The reading passages in this test are brief excerpts or adaptations of excerpts from published material. The ideas contained in them do not necessarily represent the opinions of the College Board or Educational Testing Service. To make the text suitable for testing purposes, we may in some cases have altered the style, contents, or point of view of the original.

21. According to the author, the position of scout was a difficult one because scouts

(A) usually bore the brunt of enemy attack
(B) had to cover more territory than the other warriors
(C) were often blamed for the failure of an expedition
(D) had to travel light, doing without certain provisions
(E) got very little gratitude or reward for their services

22. It can be inferred that, by saying the warriors "accepted Nah-goey's pipe," the author means that they

(A) drove a hard bargain
(B) planned an expedition
(C) made peace with the Kiowas
(D) agreed to follow Nah-goey
(E) offered a prayer

23. It can be inferred that the events of the story most likely took place during

(A) the dry season in the mountains
(B) the autumn after the annual flood of the Red River
(C) an unusually mild winter on the plains
(D) a season of hot days and cold, starless nights
(E) the winter of an eclipse of the sun

24. According to the author, An-zah-te, who acted as advance scout for the party, was

(A) not a Kiowa
(B) eager for glory
(C) afraid of Nah-goey
(D) familiar with the terrain
(E) the most experienced warrior

25. Which of the following would the author most likely consider to be Nah-goey's chief virtue and chief vice?

(A) Strength, opportunism
(B) Generosity, gullibility
(C) Bravery, rashness
(D) Ambition, cruelty
(E) Resourcefulness, envy

GO ON TO THE NEXT PAGE →

In the eighteenth and nineteenth centuries, Newton's mechanics not only came to be thought of as compatible with common sense but had even been identified with common-sense judgment. As a result, in twentieth-century physics, the theory of relativity and the quantum theory were regarded by many as incompatible with common sense. These theories were regarded as "absurd" or, at least, "unnatural" and were rejected as Francis Bacon had rejected the Copernican system. Looking at the historical record, we notice that the requirement of compatibility with common sense and the rejection of "unnatural theories" have been advocated with a highly emotional undertone, and it is reasonable to raise the question: What was the source of heat in those fights against new and "absurd" theories? Surveying these battles, we easily find one common feature: the apprehension that a disagreement with common sense may deprive scientific theories of their value as incentives for desirable human behavior. In other words, by becoming incompatible with common sense, scientific theories lose their fitness to support desirable attitudes in the domain of ethics, politics, and religion.

Examples are abundant from all periods of theory-building. According to an old theory that was prevalent in ancient Greece and was accepted by such thinkers as Plato and Aristotle, the sun, planets, and other celestial bodies were made of a material that was completely different from the materials of which our earth consists. There were those (for example, the followers of Epicurus) who rejected this view and assumed that all bodies in the universe—earth and stars—consist of the same material. Nevertheless, many educators and political leaders were afraid that denial of the exceptional status of the celestial bodies in physical science would make it more difficult to teach the belief in the existence of spiritual beings as distinct from material things; and since it was their general conviction that the belief in spiritual beings is a powerful instrument to bring about a desirable conduct among citizens, a physical theory that supported this belief seemed to be highly desirable.

Plato, in his philosophical treatise *Laws*, suggested that people in his ideal state who taught the "materialistic" doctrine about the constitution of sun and stars would be jailed. We learn from this ancient example how scientific theories have served as instruments of indoctrination. Obviously, fitness to support the desirable conduct of citizens, or, briefly, to support moral behavior, has served through the ages as a reason for acceptance of a theory. When the "scientific criteria" did not uniquely determine a theory, its fitness to support moral or political indoctrination became an important factor for its acceptance.

26. According to the passage, heated scientific debates frequently began because

(A) a truly absurd theory had been proposed
(B) a new theory jeopardized existing moral attitudes
(C) scientists were unconcerned with politics and ethics
(D) scientific theories had been adopted too hastily
(E) a prevailing theory was incorrect but popular

27. Which of the following statements about Plato is supported by the passage?

(A) He was the originator of the theory that the material of the celestial bodies differs from that of the earth.
(B) He was a proponent of the "materialistic" theory regarding the composition of the earth and stars.
(C) He was a lawmaker who punished offenders against society.
(D) He was an advocate of the censorship of ideas and theories.
(E) He was a political leader who founded and directed an ideal state.

28. The main point of the passage is that scientific theories

(A) are sometimes misinterpreted
(B) ought not to be related to morality
(C) have to be compatible with common sense
(D) have changed through the ages
(E) have often been used to support moral rules

29. Which of the following would be the most appropriate title for the passage?

(A) The Case for Common Sense in Theory-Building
(B) A Survey of "Unnatural" Scientific Theories
(C) Factors in the Acceptance of Scientific Theories
(D) The Moral Responsibility of Scientific Investigation
(E) The Legacy of Greek Scientific Thought

30. The author's assertion that "We learn from this ancient example how scientific theories have served as instruments of indoctrination" (lines 48-50) is most weakened by the counterargument that

(A) Plato was not describing a real event and his ideal state did not exist
(B) ancient Greek ideas about matter were not really scientific theories
(C) Plato believed that the "materialistic" doctrine would lead to immorality
(D) the passage implies that scientific theories ought to be subordinate to the political needs of society
(E) the passage implies that without indoctrination there would be no stable government

GO ON TO THE NEXT PAGE

31. Chronic criticism may be ---- habit rather than a malicious weapon, but its effects on the ---- are destructive and embittering.

    (A) a thoughtless. .victim
    (B) a harmless. .bystander
    (C) a useless. .enemy
    (D) an uncouth. .indifferent
    (E) an unforgivable. .onlooker

32. Some extremist factions ---- the democratic process by denying the open competition of ---- views.

    (A) repudiate. .diverse
    (B) explain. .conflicting
    (C) exemplify. .opposing
    (D) expand. .informed
    (E) subvert. .synonymous

33. What people believe about life, though it is seldom ---- their material circumstances, is by no means necessarily ---- these circumstances.

    (A) reflected in. .responsive to
    (B) unaffected by. .determined by
    (C) applied to. .contained in
    (D) dependent upon. .subordinate to
    (E) implicit in. .excluded by

34. The fact that some consumer advocate committees are funded directly by the very agencies whose policies they might oppose seems to ---- the ---- of the committees.

    (A) nullify. .bias
    (B) preclude. .impartiality
    (C) bolster. .versatility
    (D) compromise. .futility
    (E) assure. .objectivity

35. After the initial shock of its ----, the counterculture movement had, in the end, a rejuvenating influence on American culture in general.

    (A) authoritarianism   (B) iconoclasm
    (C) diversion   (D) speculation
    (E) inspiration

Each question below consists of a related pair of words or phrases, followed by five lettered pairs of words or phrases. Select the lettered pair that best expresses a relationship similar to that expressed in the original pair.

Example:

YAWN : BOREDOM ::   (A) dream : sleep
(B) anger : madness   (C) smile : amusement
(D) face : expression   (E) impatience : rebellion
Ⓐ Ⓑ ● Ⓓ Ⓔ

36. TISSUE : HANDKERCHIEF ::
    (A) cream : milk
    (B) story : magazine illustration
    (C) warranty : guarantee
    (D) nostril : nose
    (E) paper plate : dish

37. ATMOSPHERE : METEOROLOGIST ::
    (A) book : botanist   (B) muscle : physicist
    (C) rock : geologist   (D) rain : astrologist
    (E) patient : pharmacist

38. ALCOVE : ROOM ::   (A) niche : statue
    (B) cranny : nook   (C) blister : skin
    (D) inlet : ocean   (E) mainland : peninsula

39. AFTERTHOUGHT : IDEA ::   (A) postscript : letter
    (B) reflection : mirror   (C) departure : journey
    (D) crescendo : music   (E) ingredient : recipe

40. BEQUEATH : LEGACY ::   (A) achieve : goal
    (B) worship : idol   (C) enforce : law
    (D) endow : gift   (E) endure : pain

41. LABORED : SPEECH ::   (A) censored : letter
    (B) undisciplined : behavior   (C) completed : task
    (D) retraced : step   (E) tortured : thought

42. SATURATE : SPRINKLE ::   (A) release : free
    (B) stagnate : run   (C) stand : dance
    (D) separate : chasten   (E) vilify : admonish

43. GLUTTON : RESTRAINT ::
    (A) pariah : popularity
    (B) coquette : attractiveness
    (C) skeptic : sarcasm
    (D) perfectionist : morals
    (E) enthusiast : vigor

44. PRODIGAL : SPEND ::   (A) ostentatious : buy
    (B) innocent : protest   (C) prolific : produce
    (D) dangerous : risk   (E) meticulous : choose

45. BRIDLE : HORSE ::   (A) bone : dog
    (B) olive branch : dove   (C) valor : soldier
    (D) precept : conduct   (E) devotion : duty

IF YOU FINISH BEFORE TIME IS CALLED, YOU MAY CHECK YOUR WORK ON THIS SECTION ONLY. DO NOT TURN TO ANY OTHER SECTION IN THE TEST.   **STOP**

The following information is for your reference in solving some of the problems.

Circle of radius r: Area = πr^2; Circumference = $2\pi r$
   The number of degrees of arc in a circle is 360.
The measure in degrees of a straight angle is 180.

Definition of symbols:
= is equal to	≤ is less than or equal to
≠ is unequal to	≥ is greater than or equal to
< is less than	∥ is parallel to
> is greater than	⊥ is perpendicular to

Triangle: The sum of the measures in degrees of the angles of a triangle is 180.
If $\angle CDA$ is a right angle, then

(1) area of $\triangle ABC = \dfrac{AB \times CD}{2}$

(2) $AC^2 = AD^2 + DC^2$

Note: Figures that accompany problems in this test are intended to provide information useful in solving the problems. They are drawn as accurately as possible EXCEPT when it is stated in a specific problem that its figure is not drawn to scale. All figures lie in a plane unless otherwise indicated. All numbers used are real numbers.

1. If $x + 2x + 3x = 1 + 2 + 3$, then $x =$

   (A) -1   (B) 0   (C) $\dfrac{1}{6}$ (D) 1   (E) 6

2. On a mathematics test, Anita solved correctly 36 of the 40 problems. What per cent of the problems did she solve correctly?

   (A) 9%   (B) 10%   (C) 76%
   (D) 90%   (E) 96%

3. If $4^a = 16$, then $2 \times 2^a =$

   (A) 4   (B) 8   (C) 16   (D) 32   (E) 64

$$\begin{array}{r} RS \\ \times V7 \\ \hline 245 \\ 245 \\ \hline 2{,}695 \end{array}$$

4. If, in the correctly computed multiplication problem above, R, S, and V each represents one of the digits 0 through 9, then $R =$

   (A) 2
   (B) 3
   (C) 4
   (D) 5
   (E) 7

5. If Mr. Smith deposits $50 in his savings account, the total in the account will amount to twice his original deposit of $120. What is the amount in his savings account just before this $50 deposit?

   (A) $10
   (B) $70
   (C) $170
   (D) $190
   (E) $290

6. If a and b are negative numbers, which of the following must be negative?

   (A) ab

   (B) $(ab)^2$

   (C) $a + b$

   (D) $a - b$

   (E) $\dfrac{a}{b}$

7. The gross (loaded) allowable weight of an airplane is 2,400 pounds. Its empty weight is 1,230 pounds. If the average weight per passenger of its four passengers is 150 pounds, how many additional pounds are allowable?

   (A)   570
   (B)   600
   (C)   1,020
   (D)   1,800
   (E)   2,250

8. If $x \neq 0$, $x = y$, and $\dfrac{3a}{x} = \dfrac{9b}{y}$, what is the value of a in terms of b?

   (A) $\dfrac{b}{3}$ (B) b (C) $3b$ (D) $6b$ (E) $9b$

GO ON TO THE NEXT PAGE

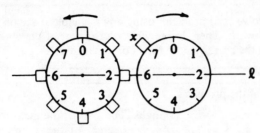

Wheel A   Wheel B

9. In the figure above, wheel B moves in a clockwise direction. Whenever cog x meets wheel A along line ℓ, it causes wheel A to move from one cog to the next in a counterclockwise direction. How many complete revolutions of wheel B are necessary to move wheel A 2 complete revolutions?

(A) 2   (B) 4   (C) 8   (D) 12   (E) 16

_____

10. The product of 3, 4, and 5 is equal to twice the sum of 10 and

(A)   3
(B)   20
(C)   30
(D)   50
(E)   110

11. If the area of each of the following rectangles is 1, which has a length of $\frac{3}{2}$?

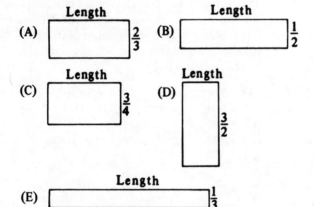

(A) Length $\frac{2}{3}$
(B) Length $\frac{1}{2}$
(C) Length $\frac{3}{4}$
(D) Length $\frac{3}{2}$
(E) Length $\frac{1}{3}$

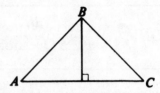

12. In $\triangle ABC$ above, if $AB = BC$ and if $\angle ABC$ is a right angle, exactly how many 45-degree angles are formed by pairs of the line segments?

(A) None   (B) Two   (C) Three
(D) Four   (E) Five

_____

TRISCHOOL TRACK MEET

	Event I	Event II	Event III
First Place (5 Points)			
Second Place (3 Points)			
Third Place (1 Point)	A		A

13. The figure above is a partially completed score card for a trischool track meet. Schools A, B, and C each entered one person in each of the three events. Each school ran in every event and there were no ties. What is the LEAST possible score for School B at this meet?

(A)   1
(B)   7
(C)   9
(D)   10
(E)   It cannot be determined from the information given.

GO ON TO THE NEXT PAGE

14. To make fruit punch for 8 people, $\frac{1}{2}$ liter of concentrate is mixed with $3\frac{1}{2}$ liters of water. How many liters of this concentrate are needed to make fruit punch of this strength for 28 people?

(A) 1

(B) $1\frac{3}{4}$

(C) 2

(D) $3\frac{1}{2}$

(E) 7

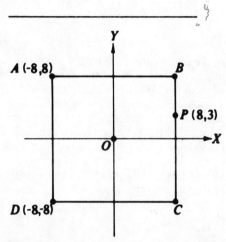

15. In the figure above, if Q is a point (not shown) such that segment PQ bisects the area of the square region $ABCD$, what are the coordinates of Q?

(A) (−8, −3) (B) (−8, 3) (C) (3, −8)
(D) (8, −3) (E) (3, 8)

16. In the land of Rad, the Holiday of the Harvest Moon is always celebrated on the third Monday in September. The earliest day in September that the holiday could occur is

(A) Sept. 14 (B) Sept. 15 (C) Sept. 20
(D) Sept. 21 (E) Sept. 22

17. If $\frac{x}{2} = y$ and $2y = y$, what is the value of x?

(A) 0 (B) 1 (C) 2 (D) 4
(E) It cannot be determined from the information given.

18. Of the following, which is closest to 5 ?

(A) $\dfrac{5.17 \times 4.91}{0.51}$

(B) $\dfrac{51.7 \times 4.91}{0.51}$

(C) $\dfrac{51.7 \times 4.91}{5.1}$

(D) $\dfrac{0.517 \times 49.1}{5.1}$

(E) $\dfrac{51.7 \times 49.1}{51}$

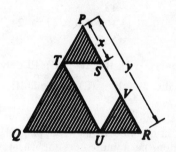

19. In the figure above, $\triangle PQR$ and the three shaded triangles are equilateral. If $PR = y$ and $PS = x$, what is the perimeter of quadrilateral $STUV$ in terms of x and y?

(A) $2y$ (B) $3y - 2x$ (C) $2y - x$
(D) $2y + x$ (E) $2y - 2x$

20. This question was not counted in computing scores.

GO ON TO THE NEXT PAGE

21. Points P, Q, and R lie on a straight line. P is 3 kilometers from R, which is 2 kilometers from Q. What is the distance, in kilometers, between P and Q?

(A) 1
(B) 3
(C) $\sqrt{13}$
(D) 5
(E) It cannot be determined from the information given.

22. For all integers x and y, let $x \star y = 3x + 2y$. Which of the following must be true?

I. $3 \star 2 = 13$
II. $(0 \star 1) \star 2 = 0 \star (1 \star 2)$
III. $x \star y = y \star x$

(A) I only   (B) II only   (C) III only

(D) II and III only   (E) I, II, and III

23. A wheel with radius 0.75 meters covers 1,000 meters in one hour without slipping. How many revolutions per <u>minute</u> does the wheel make?

(A) $\dfrac{4,000\pi}{3}$

(B) $\dfrac{4,000}{3\pi}$

(C) $\dfrac{2,000}{3\pi}$

(D) $\dfrac{200\pi}{9}$

(E) $\dfrac{100}{9\pi}$

24. Which of the following indicates the set of all numbers x such that there is a triangle with sides of lengths $x, x - 2$, and $7 - x$?

(A) $2 < x$
(B) $x < 7$
(C) $0 < x < 9$
(D) $2 < x < 5$
(E) $3 < x < 5$

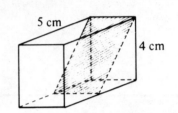

25. In the figure above, the empty box has a flap lid of area 15 cm². One of the three unattached edges of the lid rests on the bottom of the box as shown and separates the box into two compartments. If it is assumed that the lid is rigid and fits tightly, the larger, open compartment has volume

(A) 18 cm³   (B) 24 cm³   (C) 36 cm³

(D) 42 cm³   (E) 60 cm³

IF YOU FINISH BEFORE TIME IS CALLED, YOU MAY CHECK YOUR WORK ON THIS SECTION ONLY. DO NOT TURN TO ANY OTHER SECTION IN THE TEST.   **STOP**

204

Each question below consists of a word in capital letters, followed by five lettered words or phrases. Choose the word or phrase that is most nearly opposite in meaning to the word in capital letters. Since some of the questions require you to distinguish fine shades of meaning, consider all the choices before deciding which is best.

Example:

GOOD: (A) sour (B) bad (C) red
(D) hot (E) ugly

Ⓐ ● Ⓒ Ⓓ Ⓔ

1. UNCOMMON: (A) small and unimportant
(B) frequent and usual (C) monotonous
(D) predictable (E) exclusive

2. DISSOCIATE: (A) reveal (B) cleanse
(C) join together (D) increase rapidly
(E) approve of

3. VULGARITY: (A) honesty
(B) strong conviction (C) marked similarity
(D) refinement (E) binding declaration

4. CONTEMPT: (A) respect (B) ability
(C) confusion (D) discretion (E) revelation

5. COMPATIBILITY: (A) lack of freedom
(B) lack of accord (C) need for expansion
(D) need for training (E) need for change

6. EFFERVESCE: (A) display boredom
(B) suffer injury (C) endure hardship
(D) become definite (E) speak frankly

7. URBANE: (A) greedy (B) blameworthy
(C) powerful (D) delightful (E) boorish

8. LARGESS: (A) solemnity (B) discontent
(C) inferiority (D) imperfection
(E) miserliness

9. DIURNAL: (A) occurring on land
(B) occurring frequently (C) occurring at night
(D) occurring suddenly (E) occurring in secret

10. APOCRYPHAL: (A) irrevocable
(B) immeasurable (C) distinguishable
(D) of significant value (E) of known origin

Each sentence below has one or two blanks, each blank indicating that something has been omitted. Beneath the sentence are five lettered words or sets of words. Choose the word or set of words that, when inserted in the sentence, best fits the meaning of the sentence as a whole.

Example:

Although its publicity has been ----, the film itself is intelligent, well-acted, handsomely produced, and altogether ----.

(A) tasteless. .respectable (B) extensive. .moderate
(C) sophisticated. .amateur (D) risqué. .crude
(E) perfect. .spectacular

● Ⓑ Ⓒ Ⓓ Ⓔ

11. Although she enjoys her fame, Andrienne is a woman who craves ---, who needs quiet and repose.

(A) suspense (B) ceremony
(C) solitude (D) ferment (E) prosperity

12. Much of ancient Africa became progressively ----, with forest giving way to savanna, savanna to prairie, and prairie to ----.

(A) populated. .jungle
(B) domesticated. .wildlife
(C) savage. .farmland
(D) desiccated. .desert
(E) polluted. .cultivation

13. The ---- of the instrument proved the --- care with which it had been constructed.

(A) precision. .meticulous
(B) usefulness. .scanty
(C) defects. .painstaking
(D) inefficiency. .artistic
(E) expensiveness. .scientific

14. Lakes tend to become ---- with time because their waves ---- promontories that jut out into them.

(A) round. .wear away (B) dangerous. .avoid
(C) longer. .wash over (D) irregular. .demolish
(E) shallow. .break against

15. An allusion is highly ---; like a richly connotative word or symbol, it suggests far more than it says.

(A) simplistic (B) evocative (C) descriptive
(D) imaginary (E) persuasive

205

Each question below consists of a related pair of words or phrases, followed by five lettered pairs of words or phrases. Select the lettered pair that best expresses a relationship similar to that expressed in the original pair.

Example:

YAWN : BOREDOM ::   (A) dream : sleep
(B) anger : madness   (C) smile : amusement
(D) face : expression   (E) impatience : rebellion

Ⓐ Ⓑ ● Ⓓ Ⓔ

16. CRUMB : BREAD ::   (A) ounce : unit
(B) splinter : wood   (C) water : bucket
(D) twine : rope   (E) bit : fraction

17. TELESCOPE : MAGNIFICATION ::
(A) architecture : acoustics
(B) treaty : ratification
(C) umbrella : rain
(D) megaphone : amplification
(E) microscope : microorganism

18. UNMASK : DISGUISE ::   (A) introduce : speaker
(B) inscribe : message   (C) dissolve : water
(D) ruffle : hair   (E) disrobe : garment

19. DRAFT : NOVELIST ::   (A) stanza : poet
(B) diagram : grammarian   (C) fabric : seamstress
(D) sketch : painter   (E) lens : photographer

20. EMBARK : JOURNEY ::   (A) capture : prey
(B) copy : invention   (C) commence : activity
(D) interrupt : procedure   (E) extinguish : fire

21. DROWSY : SLEEP ::   (A) weary : strive
(B) curious : hide   (C) sluggish : fidget
(D) cunning : blunder   (E) edgy : fret

22. ACCELERATE : VELOCITY ::
(A) deplete : supply   (B) surround : width
(C) enlarge : size   (D) hurry : distance
(E) evaluate : worth

23. ANARCHIC : GOVERNMENT ::
(A) freethinking : dogma
(B) malfunctioning : eclipse
(C) tyrannical : monarchy
(D) plagiarized : scholarship
(E) stern : discipline

24. CELEBRITY : ACCLAIM ::
(A) hero : battle   (B) leader : deference
(C) outcast : flattery   (D) admirer : limelight
(E) pioneer : immigration

25. TURPITUDE : SCOUNDREL ::
(A) impassivity : scholar
(B) initiative : conformist
(C) insignificance : nonentity
(D) incompetence : expert
(E) impotence : follower

GO ON TO THE NEXT PAGE

206

By 1746, England had, once and for all, turned civilian. Afterward the English fought many wars, but they took place a long way off, and the contestants were regular soldiers fighting for pay. People
Line
(5) seem to have felt about the sword in those days as Dr. Johnson said he thought about the pen when he declared that no one but a blockhead ever wrote except for money. The age of economists and calculators had come. Whether it was Napoleon or
(10) Adam Smith who called the English a nation of shopkeepers, it was someone speaking in the eighteenth century, the age of Jeremy Bentham and his gospel of utility. In his *Fragment on Government* in 1776, that economist and philosopher begged his
(15) readers not to blame him if he wrote "a mercenary language"; if we are not to say that happiness or pleasure can be measured in terms of money, is there anything meaningful that the legislator can say about it, he wondered. Quantity, not quality, alone
(20) is measurable, and law and the legislator can be, and should be, interested in nothing else.

This is one of the things that repelled, and continues to repel, many people about eighteenth-century England. "Soul dead, stomach well-alive"
(25) was how Thomas Carlyle was to summarize a century that ended with Bentham's "Felicific Calculus," a calculus of pleasures and pains.

26. The passage as a whole is concerned with

(A) the financial status of people in eighteenth-century England
(B) a marked change in attitude of the common people toward the intrinsic value of work
(C) the search for tangible rewards for what was once voluntary labor
(D) the development of a society that emphasized business and measured worth in terms of economic gain
(E) economic development that no longer emphasized class distinctions but found that each person contributed to financial growth

27. In the context of the passage, the phrase "a nation of shopkeepers" (lines 10-11) is probably meant as

(A) a compliment, because it recognizes the business skill of the enemy
(B) a denunciation, because it suggests the abusive treatment of the impoverished in that age
(C) a call to arms, for it suggests the prejudices that the English needed to overcome
(D) a warning, for it analyzes the intelligence and even the craftiness that brought English business such huge profits
(E) an insult, for it suggests the narrow interests and profit-centered motives of the English of that time

28. According to the passage, Bentham's philosophy is basically an attempt to

(A) suggest the inadequacy of then current life-styles because they relied to a great extent on finance
(B) emphasize the value of happiness, which is not easily measured
(C) reject pleasure as a possibility in the human sphere of activity because it cannot be measured
(D) suggest that what is valuable in life can be quantified
(E) invalidate the assumed quality of eighteenth-century life

GO ON TO THE NEXT PAGE

Bacteria stick, often with exquisite specificity, to surfaces ranging from the human tooth or lung to a rock submerged in a stream. They do so by means of a mass of tangled fibers of polysaccharides, or branching sugar molecules, that extend from the bacterial surface and form a feltlike glycocalyx surrounding an individual cell or a colony of cells. The adhesion mediated by the glycocalyx explains particular locations of bacteria in most natural environments; more specifically, it is a major determinant in the initiation of bacterial diseases ranging from dental caries to pneumonia.

These major—and with the benefit of hindsight, obvious—facts about the bacterial cell surface have become known only within the past decade. Ironically, the main reason for the late discovery of the bacterial glycocalyx was the long reliance of microbiologists on an otherwise eminently effective investigative system: the pure laboratory culture of an individual bacterial strain. To generate and maintain a glycocalyx, a bacterial cell must expend energy, and in the protected environment of a pure culture, the glycocalyx is a metabolically expensive luxury conferring no selective advantage. Cells that fabricate these elaborate coatings are usually eliminated from pure cultures by uncoated mutants that can devote more of their energy budget to proliferation. It is these uncoated mutants that microbiologists have usually studied.

29. Which of the following can be inferred from the passage about bacteria that expend energy to produce adhesive capacity in a laboratory culture?

    (A) They have a limited advantage over those that do not.
    (B) They are likely to proliferate more rapidly than uncoated bacteria.
    (C) They waste resources that would enhance their chances for survival.
    (D) They draw energy away from neighboring uncoated bacteria.
    (E) They are more resistant to disease than are uncoated bacteria.

30. The passage indicates that the failure of microbiologists to recognize bacterial adhesive properties is best described as

    (A) an inevitable result of studying laboratory cultures
    (B) a result of careless laboratory techniques
    (C) an astounding lack of scientific judgment
    (D) a confused reaction to previous overemphasis on bacterial mutations
    (E) a result of an inability to identify all the surfaces adhered to by bacteria

31. Which of the following statements concerning the specificity of bacterial adhesion is (are) supported by the passage?

    I. It is indispensable in bacterial proliferation.
    II. It is less evident in laboratory cultures.
    III. It is unimportant in most natural environments.

    (A) I only   (B) II only   (C) III only
    (D) I and II only   (E) II and III only

32. The primary purpose of the passage is to

    (A) explain a previous gap in the knowledge of bacterial surface function
    (B) describe the various surfaces to which bacteria can adhere
    (C) call for reevaluation of current microbiological beliefs
    (D) demonstrate how bacterial disease can be initiated by adhesion
    (E) explore the possibility of making environmental bacteria nonadhesive

GO ON TO THE NEXT PAGE

Many social anthropologists and other scientific observers of human communities have emphasized the similarities in the sex roles in various communities. One very distinguished anthropologist, Margaret Mead, in her book *Male and Female*, gives this summary description of the sex roles: "The home shared by a man or men and female partners, into which men bring the food and women prepare it, is the basic common picture the world over. But this picture can be modified, and the modifications provide proof that the pattern itself is not something deeply biological."

It is surprising that Margaret Mead, with her extensive and intensive personal experience of diverse communities throughout the world, should venture upon such a dubious generalization. She is right in describing the preparation of food as a monopoly for women in nearly all communities, but the surmise that the provision of food is a man's prerogative is unwarranted. In fact, an important distinction can be made between two kinds or patterns of subsistence agriculture: one in which food production is taken care of by women, with little help from men, and one in which food is produced by the men with relatively little help from women. As a convenient terminology I propose to denote these two systems as the female and male systems of farming.

33. Which of the following best explains what the author means by "the similarities in the sex roles" (lines 2-3)?

(A) The equality of men's and women's traditional tasks
(B) The likenesses in patterns of division of labor between men and women
(C) The universal acceptance of the need for co-operation between men and women within a community
(D) The overlapping of tasks performed by men and women in various communities
(E) The correspondence between a community's attitude toward women and the traditional tasks they perform

34. The author's attitude toward the statement by Margaret Mead is one of

(A) reluctant consent
(B) intrigued curiosity
(C) respectful disagreement
(D) apologetic defensiveness
(E) mild endorsement

35. Which of the following best describes the relation between the two paragraphs in the passage?

(A) The second disputes aspects of the opinions presented in the first.
(B) The second explains the logic behind the arguments summarized in the first.
(C) The second provides specific examples of the general statements presented in the first.
(D) The second questions the social importance of the issues raised in the first.
(E) The second analyzes the implications for the future of the theories described in the first.

GO ON TO THE NEXT PAGE

Areopagitica, written in 1643 and published in 1644, is one of Milton's important prose works. The ordinance of Parliament that occasioned it—an act requiring that all books be licensed by an official censor before publication—had been passed in June 1643. Milton addressed the work to Parliament in the hope of influencing its members to repeal a decree inconsistent, in his view, with their own history and purposes as the restorers of English liberties. After complimenting this body on its past achievements and excusing himself for venturing this criticism of their recent act, Milton reviews the history of licensing from ancient times, showing that it has always been a concomitant of tyranny. Secondly, he enters upon a noble defense of the benefit of books freely used, showing how necessary reading of every sort is to the attainment of knowledge and experience in a world where good and evil grow up indiscriminately together. Next, he deals with the impossibility of the attempt to make people virtuous by external restraint. Corrupting influences are present everywhere and can be met only by building up inner discipline and the power of rational choosing. This is the fundamental tenet of Milton's ethical philosophy. He goes on to argue that the present law will be ineffective even as applied to publication. *Areopagitica* itself was published in defiance of the law. Finally, Milton attacks the order as a discouragement to intellectual activity and a hindrance to the cause of truth. The plea here is one of resolute faith in the competence of human nature, and particularly of English nature, to work out its own intellectual salvation, and in the divine property of Truth itself, which is sure to prevail ultimately over error if the two are allowed to grapple. Milton expresses with extraordinary forcefulness the resentment of the mature mind at being kept under watch and ward, and vividly displays the results of such policy in spiritual stagnation and a "starched conformity of opinion." The spirit of English protest speaks through him; his principles are as vital and his warnings as necessary today as they ever were.

Milton's plea for liberty failed in its immediate purpose, but it was employed when the issue was raised again in 1679 and 1693; it furnished Mirabeau with the substance of a pamphlet on the freedom of the press in 1788; and it has armed the minds of individuals in all times against the ever-recurring attempt to silence thought.

36. The primary emphasis of the passage is on

   (A) presenting the historical background of the publication of *Areopagitica*
   (B) detailing the influence of Milton's ethical philosophy
   (C) arguing against Parliament's system of censorship
   (D) sketching an overview of the arguments contained in *Areopagitica*
   (E) debating the validity of Milton's ethical philosophy in *Areopagitica*

37. According to the passage, Milton believed that the licensing of books would result in which of the following?

   I. The spread of corruption
   II. The hindrance of truth
   III. Spiritual stagnation

   (A) II only   (B) III only   (C) I and II only
   (D) I and III only   (E) I, II, and III

38. The author's tone in the second paragraph can best be described as

   (A) carefully impartial   (B) frankly approving
   (C) faintly critical   (D) notably ambivalent
   (E) thoroughly disapproving

39. It can be inferred from the passage that Milton believed that Parliament's moral responsibility to the English public was to

   (A) lead by its good example
   (B) control major corrupting influences
   (C) dictate public morality through noncoercive means
   (D) punish only individuals who defied the law
   (E) allow the public full freedom in moral matters

40. It can be argued that the ideas contained in *Areopagitica* are most applicable today in defense of

   (A) judicious censorship
   (B) copyright legislation
   (C) freedom of religion
   (D) freedom of the press
   (E) democratic elections

IF YOU FINISH BEFORE TIME IS CALLED, YOU MAY CHECK YOUR WORK ON THIS SECTION ONLY. DO NOT TURN TO ANY OTHER SECTION IN THE TEST.   **STOP**

SECTION 5   Time—30 minutes
35 Questions

In this section solve each problem, using any available space on the page for scratchwork. Then decide which is the best of the choices given and fill in the corresponding oval on the answer sheet.

The following information is for your reference in solving some of the problems.

Circle of radius r: Area $= \pi r^2$; Circumference $= 2\pi r$
The number of degrees of arc in a circle is 360.
The measure in degrees of a straight angle is 180.

Definition of symbols:
= is equal to $\leq$ is less than or equal to
$\neq$ is unequal to $\geq$ is greater than or equal to
< is less than $\|$ is parallel to
> is greater than $\perp$ is perpendicular to

Triangle: The sum of the measures in degrees of the angles of a triangle is 180.

If $\angle CDA$ is a right angle, then

(1) area of $\triangle ABC = \dfrac{AB \times CD}{2}$

(2) $AC^2 = AD^2 + DC^2$

Note: Figures that accompany problems in this test are intended to provide information useful in solving the problems. They are drawn as accurately as possible EXCEPT when it is stated in a specific problem that its figure is not drawn to scale. All figures lie in a plane unless otherwise indicated. All numbers used are real numbers.

1. $\dfrac{3^2 + 3^2 + 3^2}{2^3 + 2^3 + 2^3} =$

(A) $\dfrac{9}{8}$ (B) 1   (C) $\dfrac{8}{9}$ (D) $\dfrac{3}{4}$ (E) $\dfrac{729}{1{,}028}$

2. Which of the following products is (are) equal to 1 ?

I. $\dfrac{2}{3} \times \dfrac{3}{2} \times \dfrac{2}{3} \times \dfrac{3}{2}$

II. $\dfrac{2}{3} \times \dfrac{3}{2} \times \dfrac{2}{3} \times \dfrac{3}{2} \times \dfrac{2}{3}$

III. $\dfrac{2}{3} \times \dfrac{3}{2} \times \dfrac{2}{3} \times \dfrac{3}{2} \times \dfrac{2}{3} \times \dfrac{3}{2}$

(A) I only
(B) II only
(C) I and III only
(D) II and III only
(E) I, II, and III

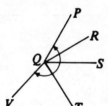

Note: Figure not drawn to scale.

3. In the figure above, if $\angle PQS = 60°$, $\angle RQT = 70°$, $\angle TQV = 50°$, and $\angle RQS = 30°$, then the marked $\angle PQV =$

(A) $80°$ (B) $120°$ (C) $150°$

(D) $210°$ (E) $220°$

4. If $S = 1 + \dfrac{1}{2} + \dfrac{1}{3} + \dfrac{1}{4} + \dfrac{1}{5}$ and

$T = 1 + \dfrac{1}{2} + \dfrac{1}{3} + \dfrac{1}{4}$, then $S - T =$

(A) $-\dfrac{1}{30}$ (B) $-\dfrac{1}{5}$ (C) $\dfrac{1}{30}$ (D) $\dfrac{1}{5}$ (E) $\dfrac{131}{30}$

5. If the average of $-12, -5, -3, -6,$ and y is -6, then $y =$

(A) -56
(B) -4
(C) 2
(D) 4
(E) 14

6. If $\boxed{x,y}$ is defined as $\dfrac{x-1}{y+1}$ where x and y are positive integers, which of the following is least?

(A) $\boxed{2,2}$ (B) $\boxed{3,3}$ (C) $\boxed{5,3}$

(D) $\boxed{3,5}$ (E) $\boxed{2,4}$

7. The length of a certain rectangle is 3 times its width. If x represents the width of the rectangle, which of the following represents the perimeter of the rectangle?

(A) $4x$

(B) $\dfrac{8}{3}x$

(C) $8x$

(D) $3x + 2$

(E) $3x^2$

GO ON TO THE NEXT PAGE

Questions 8-27 each consist of two quantities, one in Column A and one in Column B. You are to compare the two quantities and on the answer sheet fill in oval

A if the quantity in Column A is greater;
B if the quantity in Column B is greater;
C if the two quantities are equal;
D if the relationship cannot be determined from the information given.

AN E RESPONSE WILL NOT BE SCORED.

	EXAMPLES		
	Column A	Column B	Answers
E1.	2×6	$2 + 6$	● Ⓑ Ⓒ Ⓓ Ⓔ
E2.	$180 - x$	y	Ⓐ Ⓑ ● Ⓓ Ⓔ
E3.	$p - q$	$q - p$	Ⓐ Ⓑ Ⓒ ● Ⓔ

For E2 there is a figure showing an angle $x°$ and $y°$ on a straight line.

Notes:

1. In certain questions, information concerning one or both of the quantities to be compared is centered above the two columns.
2. In a given question, a symbol that appears in both columns represents the same thing in Column A as it does in Column B.
3. Letters such as x, n, and k stand for real numbers.

	Column A	Column B
8.	0.21	0.0392

Scott is taller than Kathy and
Maria is taller than Kathy.

	Column A	Column B
9.	Scott's height	Maria's height

$$\sqrt{25} + \sqrt{144} = x$$

	Column A	Column B
10.	13	x
11.	$3\left(\dfrac{1}{2} + \dfrac{1}{8}\right)$	$\dfrac{3}{2} + \dfrac{3}{8}$

$$\frac{3}{5} = \frac{x}{20}$$

$$\frac{4}{8} = \frac{y}{24}$$

	Column A	Column B
12.	x	y

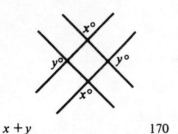

	Column A	Column B
13.	$x + y$	170

	Column A	Column B
14.	$10 \cdot 9 \cdot 8 \cdot 7$	$70 \cdot 72$

m is an even integer and
n is an odd integer.

	Column A	Column B
15.	The probability that $m + n$ is even	The probability that mn is even
16.	$1^{10} + 2^{10}$	3^{10}
17.	The number of positive integer factors of 7	The number of positive integer factors of 19
18.	$\dfrac{10}{11}$	$\dfrac{11}{12}$

$x + y + z = 8$ and $y = z$

	Column A	Column B
19.	z	4

GO ON TO THE NEXT PAGE

SUMMARY DIRECTIONS FOR COMPARISON QUESTIONS

Answer: A if the quantity in Column A is greater;
         B if the quantity in Column B is greater;
         C if the two quantities are equal;
         D if the relationship cannot be determined from the information given.

AN E RESPONSE WILL NOT BE SCORED.

Column A | Column B

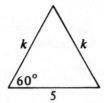

20. $2k$ 10

---

21. The total surface area   2
     of a cube having edge
     0.5

$$y = (x - 1)(x + 2)$$

22. The least value of x -1
     for which $y = 0$

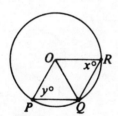

O is the center of the circle and
segment $PQ >$ segment QR.

23. x y

Column A | Column B

24. Area of a square with a   Area of a parallelogram
     diagonal of length 4   with a diagonal of
                                length 4

On a certain blueprint, 1 centimeter represents
2 meters.

25. The area represented by   116 square meters
     29 square centimeters
     on this blueprint

---

26. $\sqrt{x^4 + 4x^2 + 4}$ $x^2 + 2x + 2$

Let ⧉ be defined by the equation a ⧉ $b = a^3$.

27. x ⧉ 4 x ⧉ 5

GO ON TO THE NEXT PAGE

28. If P is the greatest positive 4-digit integer with nonzero digits, none of which is repeated, and Q is the least of such positive integers, then $P - Q =$

   (A) 2,468
   (B) 5,555
   (C) 8,642
   (D) 8,646
   (E) 8,999

29. Which of the following designs can be formed by combining rectangles with size and shading the same as that shown above if overlap is not permitted?

   I.   II.   III.

   (A) I only   (B) II only   (C) I and II only
   (D) II and III only   (E) I, II, and III

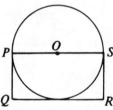

30. In the figure above, $PQRS$ is a rectangle with sides PQ, QR, and RS touching the circle with center O. If the diameter of the circle is x, what is the perimeter of $PQRS$ in terms of x?

   (A) $2x^2$ (B) $\frac{x^2}{2}$ (C) $6x$ (D) $5x$ (E) $3x$

31. A man willed $\frac{2}{5}$ of his estate to his daughter and $\frac{1}{20}$ to each of his three sons. Another $\frac{1}{10}$ was divided equally among his five grandchildren. If the remainder of the man's estate was left to his wife, what part of his estate did his wife receive?

   (A) $\frac{1}{5}$ (B) $\frac{3}{10}$ (C) $\frac{7}{20}$ (D) $\frac{2}{5}$ (E) $\frac{9}{20}$

32. If car X starts from point P and travels at an average rate of 50 kilometers per hour and car Y starts from point P 6 hours later and travels on the same route at an average rate of 60 kilometers per hour, exactly how many hours after car Y leaves P will it overtake car X?

   (A) 36   (B) 30   (C) 24   (D) 11   (E) 5

33. If $x \neq 0$ and $x = 3y = 5t$, what is the value of $x - y$ in terms of t?

   (A) $\frac{1}{5}t$

   (B) $\frac{5}{3}t$

   (C) $2t$

   (D) $\frac{10}{3}t$

   (E) $10t$

34. On a biology quiz, the average score for a class was 80. If 20 per cent of the class scored 90 and 30 per cent scored 70, what was the average score for the remainder of the class?

   (A) 76   (B) 78   (C) 80   (D) 82   (E) 84

35. If the shaded region above is bounded by three nonoverlapping semicircles each with a radius of 1, what is the area of the region?

   (A) $\frac{\sqrt{3}}{4} + \frac{3\pi}{8}$

   (B) $\sqrt{3} + \frac{3}{2}\pi$

   (C) $2 + \frac{3}{2}\pi$

   (D) 3π

   (E) $\frac{\sqrt{2}}{2} + 3\pi$

IF YOU FINISH BEFORE TIME IS CALLED, YOU MAY CHECK YOUR WORK ON THIS SECTION ONLY. DO NOT TURN TO ANY OTHER SECTION IN THE TEST.   STOP

Correct Answers for Scholastic Aptitude Test
Form Code 4W

VERBAL		MATHEMATICAL	
Section 1	Section 4	Section 2	Section 5
1. E	1. B	1. D	1. A
2. B	2. C	2. D	2. C
3. C	3. D	3. B	3. C
4. C	4. A	4. B	4. D
5. D	5. B	5. D	5. B
6. E	6. A	6. C	6. E
7. B	7. E	7. A	7. C
8. A	8. E	8. C	*8. A
9. C	9. C	9. E	*9. D
10. E	10. E	10. B	*10. B
11. D	11. C	11. A	*11. C
12. A	12. D	12. D	*12. C
13. E	13. A	13. B	*13. A
14. A	14. A	14. B	*14. C
15. E	15. B	15. A	*15. B
16. B	16. B	16. B	*16. B
17. D	17. D	17. A	*17. C
18. C	18. E	18. D	*18. B
19. D	19. D	19. C	*19. D
20. D	20. C	20. †	*20. C
21. B	21. E	21. E	*21. B
22. D	22. C	22. A	*22. B
23. E	23. A	23. E	*23. A
24. A	24. B	24. E	*24. D
25. C	25. C	25. D	*25. C
26. B	26. D		*26. D
27. D	27. E		*27. C
28. E	28. D		28. C
29. C	29. C		29. D
30. A	30. A		30. E
31. A	31. B		31. C
32. A	32. A		32. B
33. B	33. B		33. D
34. B	34. C		34. D
35. B	35. A		35. B
36. E	36. D		
37. C	37. E		
38. D	38. B		
39. A	39. E		
40. D	40. D		
41. E			
42. E			
43. A			
44. C			
45. D			

*Indicates four-choice questions. (All of the other questions are five-choice.)
†Not scored

215

The Scoring Process

Machine-scoring is done in three steps:

- *Scanning.* Your answer sheet is "read" by a scanning machine and the oval you filled in for each question is recorded on a computer tape.

- *Scoring.* The computer compares the oval filled in for each question with the correct response. Each correct answer receives one point; omitted questions do not count toward your score. For each wrong answer, a fraction of a point is subtracted to correct for random guessing. For questions with five answer choices, one-fourth of a point is subtracted for each wrong response; for questions with four answer choices, one-third of a point is subtracted for each wrong response. The SAT-verbal test has 85 questions with five answer choices each. If, for example, a student has 44 right, 32 wrong, and 9 omitted, the resulting raw score is determined as follows:

$$44 \text{ right} - \frac{32 \text{ wrong}}{4} = 44 - 8 = 36 \text{ raw score points}$$

Obtaining raw scores frequently involves the rounding of fractional numbers to the nearest whole number. For example, a raw score of 36.25 is rounded to 36, the nearest whole number. A raw score of 36.50 is rounded upward to 37.

- *Converting to reported scaled score.* Raw test scores are then placed on the College Board scale of 200 to 800 through a process that adjusts scores to account for minor differences in difficulty among different editions of the test. This process, known as equating, is performed so that a student's reported score is not affected by the edition of the test taken nor by the abilities of the group with whom the student takes the test. As a result of placing SAT scores on the College Board scale, scores earned by students at different times can be compared. For example, an SAT-verbal score of 400 on a test taken at one administration indicates the same level of developed verbal ability as a 400 score obtained on a different edition of the test taken at another time.

How to Score the Test

SAT-Verbal Sections 1 and 4

Step A: Count the number of correct answers for *section 1* and record the number in the space provided on the worksheet on the next page. Then do the same for the incorrect answers. (Do not count omitted answers.) To determine subtotal A, use the formula:

$$\text{number correct} - \frac{\text{number incorrect}}{4} = \text{subtotal A}$$

Step B: Count the number of correct answers and the number of incorrect answers for *section 4* and record the numbers in the spaces provided on the worksheet. To determine subtotal B, use the formula:

$$\text{number correct} - \frac{\text{number incorrect}}{4} = \text{subtotal B}$$

Step C: To obtain C, add subtotal A to subtotal B, keeping any decimals. Enter the resulting figure on the worksheet.

Step D: To obtain D, your raw verbal score, round C to the nearest whole number. (For example, any number from 44.50 to 45.49 rounds to 45.) Enter the resulting figure on the worksheet.

Step E: To find your reported SAT-verbal score, look up the total raw verbal score you obtained in step D in the conversion table on page 218. Enter this figure on the worksheet.

SAT-Mathematical Sections 2 and 5

Step A: Count the number of correct answers and the number of incorrect answers for *section 2* and record the numbers in the spaces provided on the worksheet. To determine the subtotal A, use the formula:

$$\text{number correct} - \frac{\text{number incorrect}}{4} = \text{subtotal A}$$

Step B: Count the number of correct answers and the number of incorrect answers for the *five-choice questions (questions 1 through 7 and 28 through 35) in section 5* and record the numbers in the spaces provided on the worksheet. To determine the subtotal B, use the formula:

$$\text{number correct} - \frac{\text{number incorrect}}{4} = \text{subtotal B}$$

Step C: Count the number of correct answers and the number of incorrect answers for the *four-choice questions (questions 8 through 27) in section 5* and record the numbers in the spaces provided on the worksheet. To determine the subtotal C, use the formula:

$$\text{number correct} - \frac{\text{number incorrect}}{3} = \text{subtotal C}$$

Step D: To obtain D, add subtotal A, subtotal B, and subtotal C, keeping any decimals. Enter the resulting figure on the worksheet.

Step E: To obtain E, your raw mathematical score, round D to the nearest whole number. (For example, any number from 44.50 to 45.49 rounds to 45.) Enter the resulting figure on the worksheet.

Step F: To find your reported SAT-mathematical score, look up the total raw mathematical score you obtained in E in the conversion table on page 218. Enter this figure on the worksheet.

SAT SCORING WORKSHEET
SAT-Verbal Sections

A. Section 1: _____ − ¼ (_____) = _____
                     no. correct   no. incorrect   subtotal A

B. Section 4: _____ − ¼ (_____) = _____
                     no. correct   no. incorrect   subtotal B

C. Total unrounded raw score
(Total A + B)   _____
                                                 C

D. Total rounded raw score
(Rounded to nearest whole number)   _____
                                                 D

E. SAT-verbal reported scaled score
(See the conversion table on page 218.)

                                               SAT-verbal
                                                score

SAT-Mathematical Sections

A. Section 2: _____ − ¼ (_____) = _____
                     no. correct   no. incorrect   subtotal A

B. Section 5:
Questions 1 through 7 and _____ − ¼ (_____) = _____
28 through 35 (5-choice)   no. correct   no. incorrect   subtotal B

C. Section 5:
Questions 8 through 27 _____ − ⅓ (_____) = _____
(4-choice)   no. correct   no. incorrect   subtotal C

D. Total unrounded raw score
(Total A + B + C)   _____
                                                 D

E. Total rounded raw score
(Rounded to nearest whole number)   _____
                                                 E

F. SAT-mathematical reported scaled score
(See the conversion table on page 218.)

                                               SAT-math
                                               score

Score Conversion Table
Scholastic Aptitude Test
Form Code 4W

Raw Score	College Board Reported Score		Raw Score	College Board Reported Score	
	SAT-Verbal	SAT-Math		SAT-Verbal	SAT-Math
85	800		40	470	610
84	790		39	460	600
83	780		38	450	600
82	770		37	450	590
81	760		36	440	580
80	750		35	430	570
79	740		34	430	560
78	730		33	420	550
77	720		32	410	540
76	710		31	410	530
75	700		30	400	520
74	700		29	390	510
73	690		28	390	510
72	680		27	380	500
71	670		26	370	490
70	670		25	370	480
69	660		24	360	470
68	650		23	350	460
67	650		22	350	450
66	640		21	340	440
65	630		20	330	430
64	620		19	330	420
63	620		18	320	410
62	610		17	310	410
61	600		16	310	400
60	600		15	300	390
59	590	800	14	300	380
58	580	780	13	290	370
57	580	770	12	280	360
56	570	760	11	270	350
55	570	750	10	270	340
54	560	740	9	260	340
53	550	730	8	250	330
52	550	720	7	250	320
51	540	710	6	240	310
50	530	700	5	230	300
49	530	690	4	220	290
48	520	680	3	220	280
47	510	670	2	210	280
46	510	660	1	200	270
45	500	660	0	200	260
44	490	650	−1	200	250
43	490	640	−2	200	240
42	480	630	−3	200	230
41	470	620	−4	200	230
			−5	200	220
			−6 or below	200	200

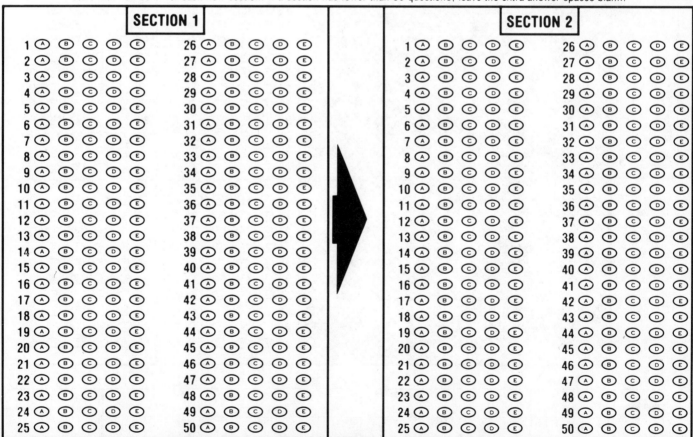

COLLEGE BOARD — SCHOLASTIC APTITUDE TEST
and Test of Standard Written English   Side 1

Use a No. 2 pencil only. Be sure each mark is dark and completely fills the intended oval. Completely erase any errors or stray marks.

1.
YOUR NAME: _____
(Print)   Last   First   M.I.

SIGNATURE: _____   DATE: ___/___/___

HOME ADDRESS: _____
(Print)   Number and Street

_____
City   State   Zip Code

CENTER: _____
(Print)   City   State   Center Number

5. YOUR NAME

First 4 letters of last name | First Init. | Mid. Init.

(A) (B) (C) (D) (E) (F) (G) (H) (I) (J) (K) (L) (M) (N) (O) (P) (Q) (R) (S) (T) (U) (V) (W) (X) (Y) (Z)

IMPORTANT: Please fill in these boxes exactly as shown on the back cover of your test book.

FOR ETS USE ONLY

2. TEST FORM

3. FORM CODE

4. REGISTRATION NUMBER
(Copy from your Admission Ticket.)

6. DATE OF BIRTH

Month	Day	Year
Jan.		
Feb.		
Mar.	0 0	0 0
Apr.	1 1	1 1
May	2 2	2 2
June	3 3	3 3
July	4 4	4 4
Aug.	5 5	5 5
Sept.	6 6	6 6
Oct.	7 7	7 7
Nov.	8	8
Dec.	9	9

Form code columns: 0 1 2 3 4 5 6 7 8 9
(A B C D E F G H I) (J K L M N O P Q) (S T U V W X Y Z)

7. SEX
○ Female
○ Male

8. TEST BOOK SERIAL NUMBER

Start with number 1 for each new section. If a section has fewer than 50 questions, leave the extra answer spaces blank.

SECTION 1

1 (A) (B) (C) (D) (E)   26 (A) (B) (C) (D) (E)
2 (A) (B) (C) (D) (E)   27 (A) (B) (C) (D) (E)
3 (A) (B) (C) (D) (E)   28 (A) (B) (C) (D) (E)
4 (A) (B) (C) (D) (E)   29 (A) (B) (C) (D) (E)
5 (A) (B) (C) (D) (E)   30 (A) (B) (C) (D) (E)
6 (A) (B) (C) (D) (E)   31 (A) (B) (C) (D) (E)
7 (A) (B) (C) (D) (E)   32 (A) (B) (C) (D) (E)
8 (A) (B) (C) (D) (E)   33 (A) (B) (C) (D) (E)
9 (A) (B) (C) (D) (E)   34 (A) (B) (C) (D) (E)
10 (A) (B) (C) (D) (E)   35 (A) (B) (C) (D) (E)
11 (A) (B) (C) (D) (E)   36 (A) (B) (C) (D) (E)
12 (A) (B) (C) (D) (E)   37 (A) (B) (C) (D) (E)
13 (A) (B) (C) (D) (E)   38 (A) (B) (C) (D) (E)
14 (A) (B) (C) (D) (E)   39 (A) (B) (C) (D) (E)
15 (A) (B) (C) (D) (E)   40 (A) (B) (C) (D) (E)
16 (A) (B) (C) (D) (E)   41 (A) (B) (C) (D) (E)
17 (A) (B) (C) (D) (E)   42 (A) (B) (C) (D) (E)
18 (A) (B) (C) (D) (E)   43 (A) (B) (C) (D) (E)
19 (A) (B) (C) (D) (E)   44 (A) (B) (C) (D) (E)
20 (A) (B) (C) (D) (E)   45 (A) (B) (C) (D) (E)
21 (A) (B) (C) (D) (E)   46 (A) (B) (C) (D) (E)
22 (A) (B) (C) (D) (E)   47 (A) (B) (C) (D) (E)
23 (A) (B) (C) (D) (E)   48 (A) (B) (C) (D) (E)
24 (A) (B) (C) (D) (E)   49 (A) (B) (C) (D) (E)
25 (A) (B) (C) (D) (E)   50 (A) (B) (C) (D) (E)

SECTION 2

1 (A) (B) (C) (D) (E)   26 (A) (B) (C) (D) (E)
2 (A) (B) (C) (D) (E)   27 (A) (B) (C) (D) (E)
3 (A) (B) (C) (D) (E)   28 (A) (B) (C) (D) (E)
4 (A) (B) (C) (D) (E)   29 (A) (B) (C) (D) (E)
5 (A) (B) (C) (D) (E)   30 (A) (B) (C) (D) (E)
6 (A) (B) (C) (D) (E)   31 (A) (B) (C) (D) (E)
7 (A) (B) (C) (D) (E)   32 (A) (B) (C) (D) (E)
8 (A) (B) (C) (D) (E)   33 (A) (B) (C) (D) (E)
9 (A) (B) (C) (D) (E)   34 (A) (B) (C) (D) (E)
10 (A) (B) (C) (D) (E)   35 (A) (B) (C) (D) (E)
11 (A) (B) (C) (D) (E)   36 (A) (B) (C) (D) (E)
12 (A) (B) (C) (D) (E)   37 (A) (B) (C) (D) (E)
13 (A) (B) (C) (D) (E)   38 (A) (B) (C) (D) (E)
14 (A) (B) (C) (D) (E)   39 (A) (B) (C) (D) (E)
15 (A) (B) (C) (D) (E)   40 (A) (B) (C) (D) (E)
16 (A) (B) (C) (D) (E)   41 (A) (B) (C) (D) (E)
17 (A) (B) (C) (D) (E)   42 (A) (B) (C) (D) (E)
18 (A) (B) (C) (D) (E)   43 (A) (B) (C) (D) (E)
19 (A) (B) (C) (D) (E)   44 (A) (B) (C) (D) (E)
20 (A) (B) (C) (D) (E)   45 (A) (B) (C) (D) (E)
21 (A) (B) (C) (D) (E)   46 (A) (B) (C) (D) (E)
22 (A) (B) (C) (D) (E)   47 (A) (B) (C) (D) (E)
23 (A) (B) (C) (D) (E)   48 (A) (B) (C) (D) (E)
24 (A) (B) (C) (D) (E)   49 (A) (B) (C) (D) (E)
25 (A) (B) (C) (D) (E)   50 (A) (B) (C) (D) (E)

(Cut here to detach.)

Q1362-04

I.N. 574006—110VV25P3015

Start with number 1 for each new section. If a section has fewer than 50 questions, leave the extra answer spaces blank.

SECTION 3	SECTION 4	SECTION 5	SECTION 6

9. SIGNATURE:

SECTION 5

1 (A) (B) (C) (D) (E)
2 (A) (B) (C) (D) (E)
3 (A) (B) (C) (D) (E)
4 (A) (B) (C) (D) (E)
5 (A) (B) (C) (D) (E)
6 (A) (B) (C) (D) (E)
7 (A) (B) (C) (D) (E)
8 (A) (B) (C) (D) (E)
9 (A) (B) (C) (D) (E)
10 (A) (B) (C) (D) (E)
11 (A) (B) (C) (D) (E)
12 (A) (B) (C) (D) (E)
13 (A) (B) (C) (D) (E)
14 (A) (B) (C) (D) (E)
15 (A) (B) (C) (D) (E)
16 (A) (B) (C) (D) (E)
17 (A) (B) (C) (D) (E)
18 (A) (B) (C) (D) (E)
19 (A) (B) (C) (D) (E)
20 (A) (B) (C) (D) (E)
21 (A) (B) (C) (D) (E)
22 (A) (B) (C) (D) (E)
23 (A) (B) (C) (D) (E)
24 (A) (B) (C) (D) (E)
25 (A) (B) (C) (D) (E)
26 (A) (B) (C) (D) (E)
27 (A) (B) (C) (D) (E)
28 (A) (B) (C) (D) (E)
29 (A) (B) (C) (D) (E)
30 (A) (B) (C) (D) (E)
31 (A) (B) (C) (D) (E)
32 (A) (B) (C) (D) (E)
33 (A) (B) (C) (D) (E)
34 (A) (B) (C) (D) (E)
35 (A) (B) (C) (D) (E)
36 (A) (B) (C) (D) (E)
37 (A) (B) (C) (D) (E)
38 (A) (B) (C) (D) (E)
39 (A) (B) (C) (D) (E)
40 (A) (B) (C) (D) (E)
41 (A) (B) (C) (D) (E)
42 (A) (B) (C) (D) (E)
43 (A) (B) (C) (D) (E)
44 (A) (B) (C) (D) (E)
45 (A) (B) (C) (D) (E)
46 (A) (B) (C) (D) (E)
47 (A) (B) (C) (D) (E)
48 (A) (B) (C) (D) (E)
49 (A) (B) (C) (D) (E)
50 (A) (B) (C) (D) (E)

SECTION 6

1 (A) (B) (C) (D) (E)
2 (A) (B) (C) (D) (E)
3 (A) (B) (C) (D) (E)
4 (A) (B) (C) (D) (E)
5 (A) (B) (C) (D) (E)
6 (A) (B) (C) (D) (E)
7 (A) (B) (C) (D) (E)
8 (A) (B) (C) (D) (E)
9 (A) (B) (C) (D) (E)
10 (A) (B) (C) (D) (E)
11 (A) (B) (C) (D) (E)
12 (A) (B) (C) (D) (E)
13 (A) (B) (C) (D) (E)
14 (A) (B) (C) (D) (E)
15 (A) (B) (C) (D) (E)
16 (A) (B) (C) (D) (E)
17 (A) (B) (C) (D) (E)
18 (A) (B) (C) (D) (E)
19 (A) (B) (C) (D) (E)
20 (A) (B) (C) (D) (E)
21 (A) (B) (C) (D) (E)
22 (A) (B) (C) (D) (E)
23 (A) (B) (C) (D) (E)
24 (A) (B) (C) (D) (E)
25 (A) (B) (C) (D) (E)
26 (A) (B) (C) (D) (E)
27 (A) (B) (C) (D) (E)
28 (A) (B) (C) (D) (E)
29 (A) (B) (C) (D) (E)
30 (A) (B) (C) (D) (E)
31 (A) (B) (C) (D) (E)
32 (A) (B) (C) (D) (E)
33 (A) (B) (C) (D) (E)
34 (A) (B) (C) (D) (E)
35 (A) (B) (C) (D) (E)
36 (A) (B) (C) (D) (E)
37 (A) (B) (C) (D) (E)
38 (A) (B) (C) (D) (E)
39 (A) (B) (C) (D) (E)
40 (A) (B) (C) (D) (E)
41 (A) (B) (C) (D) (E)
42 (A) (B) (C) (D) (E)
43 (A) (B) (C) (D) (E)
44 (A) (B) (C) (D) (E)
45 (A) (B) (C) (D) (E)
46 (A) (B) (C) (D) (E)
47 (A) (B) (C) (D) (E)
48 (A) (B) (C) (D) (E)
49 (A) (B) (C) (D) (E)
50 (A) (B) (C) (D) (E)

TEST 8—FORM CODE 5H

Each question below consists of a word in capital letters, followed by five lettered words or phrases. Choose the word or phrase that is most nearly opposite in meaning to the word in capital letters. Since some of the questions require you to distinguish fine shades of meaning, consider all the choices before deciding which is best.

Example:

GOOD: (A) sour   (B) bad   (C) red   (D) hot   (E) ugly

Ⓐ ● Ⓒ Ⓓ Ⓔ

1. EXCLUDE: (A) admit   (B) review
   (C) harden   (D) make sound
   (E) make happy

2. SUBTERRANEAN: (A) empty
   (B) completed   (C) inaudible
   (D) near water   (E) above ground

3. ELONGATE: (A) melt   (B) wind
   (C) confine   (D) smooth   (E) shorten

4. FOREMOST: (A) vacant   (B) oldest
   (C) motionless   (D) lowest in rank
   (E) impossible to restrain

5. DISINCLINATION: (A) anger
   (B) merriment   (C) eagerness
   (D) humility   (E) trepidation

6. OBSCURE: (A) formal   (B) well-known
   (C) quick-witted   (D) serene   (E) voluntary

7. DISENTANGLE: (A) arouse   (B) donate
   (C) soften   (D) ascend   (E) snarl

8. FISSION: (A) descent   (B) reflection
   (C) saturation   (D) lack of stability
   (E) process of joining

9. SUMPTUOUS: (A) legal   (B) austere
   (C) isolated   (D) gradual   (E) authentic

10. DAUNT: (A) reassure   (B) respect
    (C) simplify   (D) entrap   (E) correct

11. UNREMITTING: (A) subtle   (B) imminent
    (C) sporadic   (D) prodigious   (E) sufficient

12. INDUCEMENT: (A) omission   (B) exposure
    (C) impediment   (D) exaggeration
    (E) misinterpretation

13. PALLIATE: (A) consult   (B) distrust
    (C) rectify   (D) defy   (E) intensify

14. COPIOUS: (A) accidental   (B) obvious
    (C) unpopular   (D) meager   (E) dubious

15. EUPHONY: (A) blasphemy   (B) dissonance
    (C) dispersion   (D) infirmity   (E) autonomy

Each sentence below has one or two blanks, each blank indicating that something has been omitted. Beneath the sentence are five lettered words or sets of words. Choose the word or set of words that, when inserted in the sentence, best fits the meaning of the sentence as a whole.

Example:

Although its publicity has been ----, the film itself is intelligent, well-acted, handsomely produced, and altogether ----.

(A) tasteless. .respectable (B) extensive. .moderate (C) sophisticated. .amateur (D) risqué. .crude (E) perfect. .spectacular

● Ⓑ Ⓒ Ⓓ Ⓔ

16. In their too unwary innocence, the originators of this new methodology did not ---- these difficulties, or doubtless they would have done something to head them off.

    (A) permit   (B) ignore   (C) anticipate
    (D) obliterate   (E) deprecate

17. Designed to resist storms by virtue of their ---- weight, the oil platforms towed into the North Sea were the heaviest objects ever moved by human technology.

    (A) inconsistent   (B) purported
    (C) unstable   (D) random   (E) immense

18. Although of great potential benefit, many existing programs established to deal specifically with relations between police departments and local communities are decidedly ----.

    (A) indispensable   (B) ineffective
    (C) incorrupt   (D) impressive
    (E) unrivaled

19. It may be true that creativity often emerges from struggle, but even so it is surprising that Akhmatova was able to grow so much as a poet while her ---- was ---- by the turmoil of the Russian Revolution.

    (A) existence..enhanced
    (B) innocence..matured
    (C) reason..sacrificed
    (D) life..buffeted
    (E) thought..roused

20. Their conversation was unsettling, for the gravity of their topic contrasted so oddly with the ---- of their tone.

    (A) uniqueness   (B) rapidity   (C) lightness
    (D) precision   (E) reverence

GO ON TO THE NEXT PAGE

221

Each passage below is followed by questions based on its content. Answer the questions following each passage on the basis of what is stated or implied in that passage.

In the world today agriculture is not even tolerably productive unless it incorporates many goods and services produced in or transplanted from cities. Moreover, the most thoroughly urbanized countries are precisely those that produce food most abundantly.

Surges in agricultural productivity follow the growth of cities. Japanese cities began their modern industrial and commercial growth in the latter part of the nineteenth century, and by the Second World War Japan had become a highly urbanized country. Before the war, although Japanese farmers were industrious and used their land efficiently, neither they nor the city populations were well fed. Rice was the staff of life; for many Japanese there was little else except fish from the sea. Yet Japan did not raise enough rice for its own people, and a full quarter of what they consumed had to be imported. It was the custom to ascribe this severe food deficit to Japan's small supply of arable soil.

But after the war and during the 1950's, remarkable changes occurred in Japanese agriculture, changes that cannot be explained by catchwords like "reform"; indeed, the Japanese have made advances that have not been made in countries where reform of agriculture, landholding, and rural life have all been pursued more determinedly and heroically.

For the first time rural Japan began receiving vast amounts of fertilizers, machines, electric power, refrigeration equipment, the results of plant and animal research, and a host of other tangible goods and services developed in cities—the same cities where the richest food markets already lay.

As a result Japanese agriculture rapidly achieved a degree of productivity that had been thought unattainable. In 1960, although the population was twenty-five percent larger than it had been before the war and total consumption of rice had soared, Japanese farms were supplying all of Japan's rice; none had to be imported. Even more interesting, the per capita consumption of rice had dropped a little, but not because of shortages. Like the steady, long-term drop in starch consumption in the United States, the drop was caused by the availability of more abundant and varied food. The farmers, in addition to supplying more rice, were producing so much other food that the Japanese were not only eating more than before, they were eating better. Nowadays, when Japan imports food and pays for it with industrial products, the food imported is meat, not rice.

If modern Japanese cities had waited to grow until a surplus of rural products could support that growth, they would be waiting still. By basing rural productivity on a foundation of urban productivity, Japan accomplished rapidly what can also be done by other nations in both Asia and the rest of the world.

The reading passages in this test are brief excerpts or adaptations of excerpts from published material. The ideas contained in them do not necessarily represent the opinions of the College Board or Educational Testing Service. To make the text suitable for testing purposes, we may in some cases have altered the style, contents, or point of view of the original.

21. Which of the following statements best expresses the main idea of the passage?

    (A) A strong agricultural economy is an important prerequisite to the development of cities.
    (B) Japanese agriculture developed rapidly in the years following the Second World War because of a reduced dependence on rice.
    (C) Urban progress provides a sound foundation for agricultural productivity.
    (D) A decrease in national starch consumption is an indicator of an improved balance of trade.
    (E) Urban industrial centers provide the largest markets for rural agricultural products.

22. Which of the following does the author list among the contributions of the city to agricultural advancement?

    I.   Research
    II. A large labor force
    III. Industrial products

    (A) I only   (B) II only   (C) III only
    (D) I and III only   (E) I, II, and III

23. Which of the following statements about the American diet can be inferred from the passage?

    (A) Starch has not always accounted for as small a share of the American diet as it does today.
    (B) Japanese food is becoming increasingly popular in the United States.
    (C) Urban industry has contributed to the consumption of rice and potatoes in the United States.
    (D) Americans eat a wide variety of foods because of their varied ethnic heritages.
    (E) Agricultural diversity is responsible for the popularity of canned and frozen foods in the United States.

24. Which of the following is NOT cited in the passage as evidence of Japan's agricultural growth?

    (A) A drop in the per capita consumption of rice
    (B) An increase in the amount of rice produced on Japanese farms
    (C) The end of Japan's dependence on imported rice
    (D) The production of foodstuffs other than rice
    (E) The end of Japan's importation of food

25. In the passage, the author makes the central point primarily by

    (A) posing a series of rhetorical questions
    (B) developing fully a single example
    (C) citing statistics from a variety of disciplines
    (D) quoting the ideas of noted economists and historians
    (E) criticizing holders of opposing points of view

GO ON TO THE NEXT PAGE

Mr. and Mrs. Veneering were bran-new people in a bran-new house in a bran-new quarter of London. Everything about the Veneerings was spick and span
Line new. In the Veneering establishment, from the hall-
(5) chairs with the new coat of arms, to the grand piano-forte with the new action, and upstairs again to the new fire-escape, all things were in a state of high varnish and polish. And what was observable in the furniture, was observable in the Veneerings—the
(10) surface smelt a little too much of the workshop and was a trifle sticky.

There was an innocent piece of dinner-furniture that was kept over a livery stableyard in Duke Street, Saint James's, when not in use. The name of this
(15) article was Twemlow. Being first cousin to Lord Snigsworth, he was in frequent requisition, and at many houses might be said to represent the dining-table in its normal state. Mr. and Mrs. Veneering, for example, arranging a dinner, habitually started with
(20) Twemlow, and then put leaves in him, or added guests to him. Sometimes, the table consisted of Twemlow and half-a-dozen leaves; sometimes, of Twemlow and a dozen leaves; sometimes, Twemlow was pulled out to his utmost extent of twenty leaves.
(25) The Veneerings were a source of utter confusion to Twemlow. The abyss to which he could find no bottom, and from which started forth the engrossing and ever-swelling difficulty of his life, was the insoluble question whether he was Veneering's oldest
(30) friend, or newest friend. Twemlow had first known Veneering at his club, where Veneering then knew nobody but the man who made them known to one another, who seemed to be the most intimate friend he had in the world, and whom he had known two
(35) days—the bond of union between their souls, the nefarious conduct of the committee respecting the cookery of a fillet of veal, having been accidentally cemented at that date. Immediately upon this, Twemlow received an invitation to dine with the
(40) man, and dined: Veneering being of the party. At the man's were a Member, an Engineer, a Payer-off of the National Debt, a Poem on Shakespeare, a Grievance, and a Public Office, who all seemed to be utter strangers to Veneering. And yet immediately
(45) after that, Twemlow received an invitation to dine at Veneering's, expressly to meet the Member, the Engineer, the Payer-off of the National Debt, the Poem on Shakespeare, the Grievance, and the Public Office, and, dining, discovered that all of them were
(50) the most intimate friends Veneering had in the world, and that the wives of all of them (who were all there) were the objects of Mrs. Veneering's most devoted affection and tender confidence.

26. By comparing Twemlow to a "piece of dinner-furniture" (line 12), the author creates the impression that
(A) those who invite Twemlow have little regard for him as an individual
(B) the Veneerings and their friends warmly accept Twemlow as a member of their families
(C) the Veneerings feel that Twemlow is socially inferior to them
(D) Twemlow's manner and appearance are stiff and formal
(E) Twemlow is pathetically grateful for the many invitations he receives

27. From the information given in the passage, it can be inferred that the Veneerings were impressed by Twemlow because of
(A) the genuineness of his humility
(B) the wit and intelligence of his conversation
(C) his connection with a socially prestigious person
(D) his loneliness and need for social contact
(E) his appreciation of their efforts on his behalf

28. The author indicates that Twemlow reacts to the Veneerings with
(A) total bewilderment
(B) open appreciation
(C) begrudging admiration
(D) passing curiosity
(E) strong contempt

29. From the information in the passage, which of the following can be inferred about the guests at the dinner party described in lines 44-53 ?
(A) They all worked on similar projects.
(B) They had recently been guests at a party at Twemlow's.
(C) The wives disliked Mrs. Veneering.
(D) They had only recently met the Veneerings.
(E) Their friendship with Twemlow had lasted several years.

30. According to the passage, the friendship between Veneering and the man who introduced Veneering to Twemlow was based on a mutual
(A) regard for each other's accomplishments
(B) interest in fine furniture and interior design
(C) loyalty toward the club to which they belonged
(D) responsibility for overseeing the preparation of food at the club
(E) disapproval of the preparation of certain food at the club

GO ON TO THE NEXT PAGE

Select the word or set of words that <u>best</u> completes each of the following sentences.

31. In order to have ---- the water and then be able to return easily to the surface to breathe, the seal ---- breaks in the ice produced by wind, tides, and currents.

    (A) use of..glides over
    (B) protection from..covers over
    (C) desire for..shrinks from
    (D) freedom from..dives into
    (E) access to..depends on

32. Demographers and anthropologists have corrected the notion that European explorers in North America entered a ---- territory by showing that the land in some areas was already as densely ---- as parts of Europe.

    (A) fertile..settled
    (B) colossal..wooded
    (C) desolate..populated
    (D) valuable..exploited
    (E) hostile..concentrated

33. The first time that I met her, she was so ---- that she seemed more ---- than the alert and vivacious woman she was reputed to be.

    (A) learned..an aesthete
    (B) exultant..a stoic
    (C) abstracted..a somnambulist
    (D) mesmerizing..an activist
    (E) witty..an intellectual

34. All forms of solidarity, insofar as they imply preconceived codes obediently followed, ---- the passion for ---- and freedom inherent in modern artistic creation.

    (A) violate..spontaneity
    (B) expose..fervor
    (C) satisfy..nonchalance
    (D) deny..authority
    (E) kindle..compliance

35. Currently rising temperatures in the Arctic and Antarctic are ---- of a still warmer world that could result from an excess of atmospheric carbon dioxide produced by the burning of oil, gas, and coal.

    (A) polarities   (B) harbingers   (C) vestiges
    (D) counterexamples   (E) aftereffects

Each question below consists of a related pair of words or phrases, followed by five lettered pairs of words or phrases. Select the lettered pair that <u>best</u> expresses a relationship similar to that expressed in the original pair.

Example:

YAWN:BOREDOM :: (A) dream:sleep
(B) anger:madness   (C) smile:amusement
(D) face:expression   (E) impatience:rebellion
Ⓐ Ⓑ ● Ⓓ Ⓔ

36. FLASK:LIQUOR :: (A) cube:ice
(B) pencil:paper   (C) tank:oxygen
(D) bottle:glass   (E) grain:beer

37. PLANET:SOLAR SYSTEM :: (A) sun:star
(B) galaxy:universe   (C) orbit:sky
(D) asteroid:comet   (E) moon:night

38. CHIMNEY:SMOKE :: (A) horn:fog
(B) gate:fence   (C) tinder:fire
(D) gutter:water   (E) bank:snow

39. ORDAIN:MINISTER ::
(A) inaugurate:president
(B) nominate:candidate
(C) esteem:monarch
(D) acquiesce:authority
(E) extol:champion

40. CONTUSION:SKIN :: (A) antiseptic:wound
(B) transfusion:blood   (C) diagnostic:health
(D) contagion:flu   (E) concussion:brain

41. SMORGASBORD:MEAL ::
(A) carousel:child   (B) anthology:book
(C) entrée:menu   (D) collage:artist
(E) article:magazine

42. SLEEP:FITFUL ::
(A) mood:buoyant   (B) performance:erratic
(C) speech:brief   (D) dream:fanciful
(E) knowledge:extensive

43. TACITURN:TALK :: (A) arbitrary:decide
(B) itinerant:journey   (C) indolent:work
(D) imprudent:argue   (E) harmful:injure

44. STUPEFY:TORPOR ::
(A) exhaust:frenzy   (B) perplex:quandary
(C) amuse:convulsion   (D) rescue:jeopardy
(E) condescend:superiority

45. SALVAGE:DESTRUCTION ::
(A) commemorate:value
(B) dismantle:removal
(C) preserve:defense
(D) smuggle:permission
(E) conceal:scrutiny

IF YOU FINISH BEFORE TIME IS CALLED, YOU MAY CHECK YOUR WORK ON THIS SECTION ONLY. DO NOT TURN TO ANY OTHER SECTION IN THE TEST.   **STOP**

SECTION **2** Time—30 minutes
25 Questions

In this section solve each problem, using any available space on the page for scratchwork. Then decide which is the best of the choices given and fill in the corresponding oval on the answer sheet.

The following information is for your reference in solving some of the problems.

Circle of radius r: Area = πr^2; Circumference = $2\pi r$
The number of degrees of arc in a circle is 360.
The measure in degrees of a straight angle is 180.

Definition of symbols:
= is equal to $\leq$ is less than or equal to
$\neq$ is unequal to $\geq$ is greater than or equal to
< is less than $\parallel$ is parallel to
> is greater than $\perp$ is perpendicular to

Triangle: The sum of the measures in degrees of the angles of a triangle is 180.
If $\angle CDA$ is a right angle, then

(1) area of $\triangle ABC = \dfrac{AB \times CD}{2}$

(2) $AC^2 = AD^2 + DC^2$

Note: Figures that accompany problems in this test are intended to provide information useful in solving the problems. They are drawn as accurately as possible EXCEPT when it is stated in a specific problem that its figure is not drawn to scale. All figures lie in a plane unless otherwise indicated. All numbers used are real numbers.

---

1. A letter is defined as being "foldable" if it is symmetric with respect to its horizontal midline. For example, the three letters below are "foldable" because they are symmetric with respect to the midlines shown.

Each of the following letters is "foldable" EXCEPT

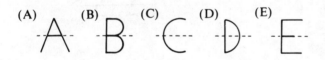

(A) (B) (C) (D) (E)

$$x + y + z = 6$$
$$2y + z = 7$$

2. In the equations above, if $z = 1$, then $x =$

(A) -1 (B) 1   (C) 2   (D) 3   (E) 5

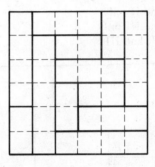

3. In the figure above, twelve rectangles (outlined by solid lines) are arranged to form a 6-by-6 square as shown. If the same rectangles were connected, without overlapping, to form a strip of width 1 unit, the strip would be how many units long?

(A) 12   (B) 18   (C) 24   (D) 30   (E) 36

4. $\dfrac{1}{1,000} + \dfrac{3}{10} + \dfrac{5}{100} =$

(A) 0.135   (B) 0.153   (C) 0.315
(D) 0.351   (E) 0.531

5. If $n = 10$, which of the following has the least value?

(A) $2 - n$ (B) $n - 2$ (C) $\dfrac{2}{n}$

(D) $\dfrac{n}{2}$ (E) $\dfrac{n}{2} - 2$

GO ON TO THE NEXT PAGE

225

6. A certain company makes a total of 96 ski vests a day in sizes small, medium, and large. If the number of vests in the small and large sizes combined is equal to the number of vests in the medium size, what is the daily production of vests in the medium size?

(A) 23
(B) 24
(C) 28
(D) 32
(E) 48

7. On a rectangular coordinate graph, which of the following points would be the same distance from the origin as (2, 0)?

I. (0, 2)
II. (−2, 0)
III. (1, 1)

(A) I only
(B) III only
(C) I and II only
(D) I and III only
(E) I, II, and III

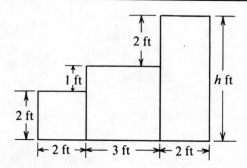

8. The rectangles above represent three cut tree trunks arranged with trunks perpendicular to the ground to form "stairs." What is the value of h, in feet?

(A) 5   (B) 6   (C) 7   (D) 10   (E) 12

9. Of the 35 students in a certain homeroom, 20 joined the math club. Of these 20 students, $\frac{3}{5}$ were females. What was the number of female students in the homeroom?

(A) 12
(B) 15
(C) 18
(D) 21
(E) It cannot be determined from the information given.

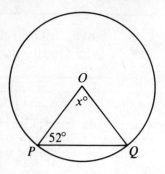

10. In the figure above, if O is the center of the circle, then x =

(A) 70   (B) 72   (C) 74   (D) 76   (E) 78

11. Each of the line segments in the figure above is the perpendicular bisector of the other. If the figure is rotated in the same plane 180° clockwise about the point of intersection of the segments, the resulting figure will look like which of the following?

(A)   (B)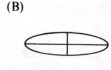

(C)   (D)

(E)

GO ON TO THE NEXT PAGE

12. $(-2a)^3 =$

(A) $-8a$ (B) $8a^3$ (C) $-2a^3$

(D) $-8(-a)^3$ (E) $-8a^3$

13. Which of the following can be expressed as the product of two consecutive even integers?

(A) 24   (B) 36   (C) 42   (D) 60   (E) 72

14. Martin and Alice buy newspapers for $0.20 each and sell them for $0.25 each. If, at the end of one week, Martin made a profit of $12.60 and Alice made a profit of $18.75, how many more papers did Alice sell than Martin?

(A) 125
(B) 123
(C) 63
(D) 62
(E) 43

15. The volume of solid X is $\frac{4}{3}\pi w^3$ and the volume of solid Y is $2\pi w^3$. The volume of solid X is what percent of the volume of solid Y?

(A) $33\frac{1}{3}\%$

(B) 50%

(C) $66\frac{2}{3}\%$

(D) 75%

(E) $133\frac{1}{3}\%$

16. The operation $\triangle$ is defined for particular values a, b, and c by the equations $a \triangle b = 2$ and $2 \triangle c = 5$. For these values of a, b, and c, the expression $(a \triangle b) \triangle c$ is equal to

(A) 3
(B) 4
(C) 5
(D) 7
(E) 10

17. There are 5 locked doors and 3 keys. Each key opens one and only one door, and no two keys open the same door. Sam chooses a key, and tries it on different doors until he opens one. Leaving that door open, he repeats this process with the next key, and then the next, until three doors are open. If x is the total number of attempts, both successful and unsuccessful, to open these doors, what are the minimum and maximum possible values of x?

(A) 3 and 5
(B) 3 and 12
(C) 3 and 15
(D) 5 and 12
(E) 5 and 15

18. If x and y are integers and $\frac{x}{y} = \frac{2}{7}$, then $(x + y)$ could equal each of the following EXCEPT

(A) -9 (B) 27   (C) 45

(D) 56   (E) 117

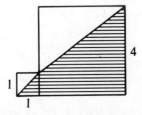

19. In the figure above, a square with side of length 1 and a square with side of length 4 are placed as shown. What is the area of the shaded region?

(A) $8\frac{1}{2}$ (B) 10   (C) $10\frac{1}{4}$ (D) $10\frac{1}{2}$ (E) 12

20. If x is an integer and the product $x(x + 1)(x + 2)$ is negative, then the greatest possible value for x is

(A) -4 (B) -3 (C) -2 (D) -1 (E) 1

GO ON TO THE NEXT PAGE

21. The first two terms in a sequence are 2 and 4. The third term and all successive terms are generated by taking the average (arithmetic mean) of all the preceding terms. For example, the third term is 3, which is the average of 2 and 4. What is the sixth term of the sequence?

(A) $7\frac{1}{2}$

(B) 6

(C) $3\frac{1}{2}$

(D) 3

(E) $2\frac{1}{2}$

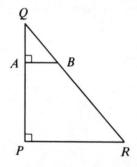

Start   Finish

Note: Figure not drawn to scale.

23. In the figure above, the solid line shows the aerial view of a 15-mile path on which a race is run. If the radius r of the semicircular path is $\frac{2}{\pi}$ miles, how many miles long is the straight portion of the path?

(A) 11 (B) 13 (C) $15 - 2\pi$

(D) $15 - \frac{2}{\pi}$ (E) $15 - \frac{8}{\pi}$

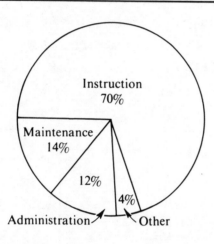

Instruction 70%

Maintenance 14%

12%

4%

Administration   Other

22. The graph above gives the breakdown of expenditures in school district X last year. If the cost of maintenance had been 50 percent less and the amount saved had been applied to instruction, then the increase in the expenditures for instruction would be what percent of the actual expenditures for instruction?

(A) 3.5% (B) 7% (C) 10%

(D) 20% (E) 50%

24. If $n = (11^7 \times 2) + (11^7 \times 4) + (11^7 \times 6)$, which of the following is NOT a whole number?

(A) $\frac{n}{2}$ (B) $\frac{n}{3}$ (C) $\frac{n}{2} - \frac{n}{3}$

(D) $\frac{n^2}{6}$ (E) $\frac{n+6}{12}$

25. In the figure above, the area of $\triangle PQR = 54$. If $AQ = \frac{1}{3}PQ$ and $AB = \frac{1}{3}PR$, what is the area of $\triangle AQB$?

(A) 6 (B) 9 (C) 17 (D) 18

(E) It cannot be determined from the information given.

IF YOU FINISH BEFORE TIME IS CALLED, YOU MAY CHECK YOUR WORK ON THIS SECTION ONLY. DO NOT TURN TO ANY OTHER SECTION IN THE TEST.   **STOP**

5

SECTION 5 — Time—30 minutes / 40 Questions — For each question in this section, choose the best answer and fill in the corresponding oval on the answer sheet.

Each question below consists of a word in capital letters, followed by five lettered words or phrases. Choose the word or phrase that is most nearly opposite in meaning to the word in capital letters. Since some of the questions require you to distinguish fine shades of meaning, consider all the choices before deciding which is best.

Example:

GOOD: (A) sour (B) bad (C) red
(D) hot (E) ugly

Ⓐ ● Ⓒ Ⓓ Ⓔ

1. CONTAMINATE: (A) lubricate
   (B) regulate (C) make pure
   (D) make available (E) make known

2. TURBULENCE: (A) originality
   (B) longevity (C) roundness
   (D) stillness (E) closeness

3. EXQUISITE:
   (A) perishable
   (B) independent
   (C) contemporary
   (D) sudden and unexpected
   (E) crude and unattractive

4. UNDERPLAY:
   (A) emphasize boldly
   (B) overlook accidentally
   (C) reduce temporarily
   (D) compete fairly
   (E) refuse to accept

5. MOROSE: (A) reserved (B) lovable
   (C) virtuous (D) jolly (E) patient

6. RAIL AT: (A) imitate (B) compliment
   (C) assign responsibility (D) alter abruptly
   (E) banish permanently

7. ADAMANCY: (A) effectiveness
   (B) pliancy (C) suspicion
   (D) vitality (E) intricacy

8. EXACTING: (A) indulgent
   (B) false (C) numerous
   (D) beneficial (E) unpopular

9. STASIS: (A) hindrance (B) organization
   (C) fluctuation (D) barrenness
   (E) spaciousness

10. PERFUNCTORY: (A) painstaking
    (B) disconcerting (C) conforming
    (D) penitent (E) artificial

Each sentence below has one or two blanks, each blank indicating that something has been omitted. Beneath the sentence are five lettered words or sets of words. Choose the word or set of words that, when inserted in the sentence, best fits the meaning of the sentence as a whole.

Example:

Although its publicity has been ----, the film itself is intelligent, well-acted, handsomely produced, and altogether ----.

(A) tasteless. .respectable (B) extensive. .moderate
(C) sophisticated. .amateur (D) risqué. .crude
(E) perfect. .spectacular

● Ⓑ Ⓒ Ⓓ Ⓔ

11. Scent glands vary widely in the ---- of their structure, but there is a basic ---- that can be traced in all of them.

    (A) details..pattern
    (B) vividness..consideration
    (C) uniformity..difference
    (D) dimensions..size
    (E) intensity..discrepancy

12. Austin is almost too gentle, too ----, to give his analyses the necessary hard edges and ---- conclusions.

    (A) blunt..forthright
    (B) tentative..firm
    (C) thorough..lukewarm
    (D) creative..imaginative
    (E) uncompromising..predictable

13. She protested that a foreign policy subject to momentary political passions, veering sharply with elections and ---- to overnight repudiation, would be useless because of its ----.

    (A) indifferent..impartiality
    (B) inclined..conservatism
    (C) liable..inflexibility
    (D) immune..inadequacy
    (E) vulnerable..inconsistency

GO ON TO THE NEXT PAGE

5

14. When Voltaire called Shakespeare "barbaric," he was making a criticism that is today often ---- by the English as typical of Voltaire's lack of taste; but most Englishmen in the eighteenth century ---- Voltaire.

    (A) mocked..protested against
    (B) defended..sympathized with
    (C) refuted..contended with
    (D) cited..agreed with
    (E) rejected..scoffed at

15. To refer to the ability to wreak catastrophic destruction and kill hundreds of thousands of people as "nuclear capability" is to indulge in ----.

    (A) invective   (B) didacticism
    (C) hyperbole   (D) euphemism
    (E) pessimism

Each question below consists of a related pair of words or phrases, followed by five lettered pairs of words or phrases. Select the lettered pair that best expresses a relationship similar to that expressed in the original pair.

Example:

YAWN : BOREDOM ::   (A) dream : sleep
(B) anger : madness   (C) smile : amusement
(D) face : expression   (E) impatience : rebellion

 Ⓐ Ⓑ ● Ⓓ Ⓔ

---

16. CHECKMATE:CHESS:: (A) kickoff:football
    (B) serve:tennis   (C) error:baseball
    (D) hurdle:track   (E) knockout:boxing

17. SCAR:INJURY:: (A) ointment:burn
    (B) cut:blood   (C) stain:spill
    (D) cork:bottle   (E) ice:water

18. EPITAPH:TOMBSTONE:: (A) clapper:bell
    (B) mural:wall   (C) parable:moral
    (D) portrait:vista   (E) metaphor:dream

19. ACCOMPLICE:CRIMINAL::
    (A) tenant:landlord
    (B) negotiator:invader
    (C) spectator:daredevil
    (D) passenger:pilot
    (E) colleague:worker

20. THIMBLE:FINGER:: (A) armor:body
    (B) crown:head   (C) torso:waist
    (D) earring:ear   (E) stocking:leg

21. DIRGE:MOURNER:: (A) march:composer
    (B) mercy:hostage   (C) hymn:worshiper
    (D) course:runner   (E) lyric:conductor

22. PINNACLE:LOFTY::
    (A) avalanche:dangerous
    (B) promontory:windy
    (C) plateau:variable
    (D) precipice:steep
    (E) foothill:surmountable

23. PRESUMPTUOUS:CONFIDENCE::
    (A) cunning:bravery
    (B) curious:knowledge
    (C) fanatic:enthusiasm
    (D) tedious:fascination
    (E) tiresome:energy

24. CAUCUS:MEETING::
    (A) platform:convention
    (B) issue:election
    (C) invocation:prayer
    (D) budget:defense
    (E) government:politics

25. IMPECUNIOUS:MONEY::
    (A) talented:effort
    (B) wanton:haste
    (C) clandestine:intention
    (D) despondent:hope
    (E) compulsive:ambition

GO ON TO THE NEXT PAGE

Each passage below is followed by questions based on its content. Answer the questions following each passage on the basis of what is stated or implied in that passage.

Lois Mailou Jones is one example of an answer to the charge that there are no Black or female American artists to include in art history textbooks and classes. Beginning her formal art education at the School of the Museum of Fine Arts in Boston, Lois Jones found herself strongly attracted to design rather than fine arts. After teaching for a while, she went to Paris to study, on the advice of the sculptor Meta Warrick Fuller.

It was in Paris that she first felt free to paint. Following her return to this country in 1938, Jones had an exhibit at the Vose Gallery in Boston, a major breakthrough for a Black artist at that time. Her work during this period consisted of excellent impressionist scenes of Paris. It was not until the early 1940's, after she met the Black aesthetician Alain Locke, that she began to paint works like *Mob Victim*, which explicitly dealt with her own background as a Black American. Later, in the fifties, she went often to Haiti, which had yet another influence on her style. Then a sabbatical leave in Africa again changed her imagery. Indeed, the scope of this distinguished artist's career so well spans the development of twentieth-century art that her work could be a textbook in itself.

26. The passage primarily focuses on the

(A) influence of Lois Jones on other artists
(B) recognition given to Lois Jones for her work
(C) experiences that influenced the work of Lois Jones
(D) obstacles that Lois Jones surmounted in her career
(E) techniques that characterize the work of Lois Jones

27. Which of the following best summarizes the relationship of the first sentence to the rest of the passage?

(A) Assertion followed by supporting evidence
(B) Challenge followed by debate pro and con
(C) Prediction followed by analysis
(D) Specific instance followed by generalizations
(E) Objective reporting followed by personal reminiscences

28. It can be inferred from the passage that Alain Locke encouraged Lois Jones to

(A) exhibit her work at recognized galleries
(B) use her experiences as a Black American in her work
(C) incorporate Haitian imagery in her work
(D) work in art media other than painting
(E) continue her studies abroad

Some of the ridges of beach grass that I saw were planted by the government many years ago to preserve the harbor of Provincetown and the extremity of Cape Cod. My guidebook indicated that, during the spring and summer, beach grass grows about two and a half feet. If the grass is surrounded by naked beach, the storms of autumn and winter heap up the sand on all sides, causing it to rise nearly to the top of the plant. In the spring the grass sprouts anew and is again covered with sand during the winter. Thus a ridge continues to ascend as long as there is a sufficient base to support it, or till the surrounding sand, also covered with beach grass, will no longer yield to the force of the winds.

Sand hills formed in this way are sometimes one hundred feet high, shift continually, and assume many shapes, resembling snowdrifts, or desert tents. The grass is very firmly rooted. When I endeavored to pull some grass up, it usually broke off ten or twelve inches below the surface of the sand, at what had been the surface the year before, as was indicated by the numerous offshoots there. The grass had a straight, round shoot and showed by its length how much sand had accumulated that year. Sometimes the dead stubs of a previous season came up with it from deeper in the sand, with their own more decayed shoot attached. The age of a sand hill, and its annual rate of increase, are recorded by these grass shoots with a fair degree of accuracy.

29. The author's primary purpose in the passage is to

(A) describe the beauty of the Cape Cod sand hills
(B) warn against the danger of allowing sand hills to spread
(C) describe the process by which the Cape Cod sand hills were formed
(D) present an original scientific discovery
(E) complain about the planting of beach grass

30. It can be inferred from the passage that a piece of grass pulled by hand from a sand hill would provide information about which of the following?

I. Length that the grass grew in the previous year
II. Total height of the sand hill
III. Accumulation of sand during the previous year

(A) I only
(B) III only
(C) I and II only
(D) I and III only
(E) I, II, and III

GO ON TO THE NEXT PAGE

31. As described in the passage, the interaction between sand and beach grass is most similar to the interaction between

    (A) wind-blown snow and a fence
    (B) drifting logs and a river
    (C) heavy surf and a concrete jetty
    (D) a stiff breeze and a high cliff
    (E) a sled and a snow-covered hill

32. The author's viewpoint is primarily that of a

    (A) botanist who hopes to identify new plants
    (B) historian who tries to record the past
    (C) sightseer who is mystified by nature
    (D) researcher who seeks to disprove a theory
    (E) visitor who is curious about nature

It would be mistaken, as well as uncharitable, to imagine that the men and women who from time to time carry the banners of anti-intellectualism are
Line
(5) of necessity committed to it as though it were some positive creed or a kind of principle. They are not in most cases wholly dedicated to denying the merit of rational thought; they are not categorically hostile to ideas. To be confronted with a simple and unqualified evil is no doubt a kind of luxury, but
(10) such is not the case here; and if anti-intellectualism has become, as I believe it has, a broadly diffused quality in our civilization, it has become so because it has often been linked to good, or at least defensible, causes. Anti-intellectualism first got its strong
(15) grip on our ways of thinking because it was fostered by an evangelical religion that also purveyed many humane and democratic sentiments. It made its way into our politics because it became associated with our passion for equality. It has
(20) become formidable in our education partly because our educational beliefs are evangelically egalitarian.
    Hence, as far as possible, our anti-intellectualism must be excised from the benevolent impulses upon which it lives by constant and
(25) delicate acts of intellectual surgery. The benevolent impulses themselves must be preserved. Only in this way can anti-intellectualism be checked and contained; I do not say eliminated altogether, for I believe not only that this is beyond our powers but
(30) also that an unbridled passion for the total elimination of this or that evil can be as dangerous as any of the delusions of our time.

33. The author recommends which of the following to those who would control anti-intellectualism?

    (A) Probing self-examination on the part of all citizens
    (B) Gentle suppression of our benevolent impulses
    (C) Elimination of anti-intellectuals from positions of power
    (D) Resigned compromise on the part of intellectuals
    (E) Careful separation of anti-intellectualism from its commendable motives

34. The metaphor used in the second paragraph to describe the author's solution is drawn from

    (A) law
    (B) politics
    (C) medicine
    (D) theology
    (E) athletics

35. It can be inferred that the author believes that confronting a "simple and unqualified evil" (lines 8-9) is a "luxury" because it

    (A) costs society a great price
    (B) provides an obvious and easy target
    (C) is generally alluring at first glance
    (D) is associated with obvious extravagance
    (E) can be afforded by only a very few

GO ON TO THE NEXT PAGE

In the twentieth century, physicists have found explanations for many phenomena that were previously observed but not understood, such as the stability of atoms over millions of years. In turn, the theories that explain these phenomena have also given us important new perspectives on other phenomena that formerly had been thought to be completely understood, such as the behavior of light and the motion of planetary bodies. In addition, physicists have been led by these theories to the discovery of qualitatively new phenomena, such as the transmutation of chemical elements and the creation and annihilation of subatomic particles.

As this progress has taken place, the very ideas that physicists have of nature have been replaced by radical new concepts. Both the quantum theory and the special and general theories of relativity are examples of such new scientific perspectives. Physicists have been led to these new descriptions of phenomena through a combination of experimentation, observation, and mathematical reasoning, and they have come to accept the truth of the descriptions. The new theories, however, have often seemed strange and incomprehensible to nonphysicists, including those who are familiar with the earlier descriptions offered by Newtonian physics. It is perhaps inevitable that in the early stages of any scientific revolution new principles should appear strange to most outsiders. This was the case with Newtonian physics: when it was proposed in the seventeenth century, it was denounced as unreasonable even by other leading physicists such as Gottfried Leibniz. However, more than fifty years have now passed since the quantum theory was given its definitive form—surely a long enough time that novelty should no longer act as a bar to the comprehension of this theory by nonphysicists. By contrast, in the arts, the ideas of fifty years ago, far from being considered too novel to comprehend, are generally thought to be old and hackneyed. Why, then, does a more widespread understanding of modern physics not exist?

One explanation may be that the concepts introduced by physicists to explain phenomena are often quite different from anything that can be deduced from observation of everyday occurrences. According to the theory of relativity, the length of a second as measured by a clock varies with the speed of the clock as it travels through space. This phenomenon is not observable in ordinary experience, and thus it is not surprising that nonphysicists have often found such ideas strange and confusing. In fact, many physicists were slow to accept the relativity theory and the quantum theory when they were first proposed because of the way these theories account for ordinary and extraordinary experiences, and because the new ideas differed so markedly from previously held concepts in physics.

36. According to the passage, before the twentieth century, physicists assumed that they completely understood which of the following?

   I. The behavior of light
   II. The transmutation of chemical elements
   III. The stability of atoms over millions of years

(A) I only
(B) III only
(C) I and II only
(D) I and III only
(E) I, II, and III

37. Which of the following does the author consider to be accomplishments of twentieth-century physics?

   I. Explanations of previously observed phenomena
   II. Clarifications of phenomena previously thought to be completely understood
   III. Discoveries of new phenomena

(A) I only
(B) III only
(C) I and II only
(D) I and III only
(E) I, II, and III

38. According to the author, ideas that were developed in the arts at approximately the same time as the quantum theory was formulated are now considered

(A) trite
(B) prophetic
(C) illogical
(D) classic
(E) eccentric

GO ON TO THE NEXT PAGE

39. In the final paragraph, the author's attitude toward those nonphysicists who fail to understand twentieth-century physics is best described as one of

(A) impatience
(B) disappointment
(C) indifference
(D) perplexed curiosity
(E) sympathetic tolerance

40. Which of the following best states the central idea of the passage?

(A) Twentieth-century physicists have made marvelous strides in discovering explanations for a wide variety of phenomena.
(B) Twentieth-century physics has introduced radically new concepts that are not widely understood.
(C) The important new perspectives of modern physics should be learned by all educated people.
(D) Advances in modern physics are occurring at so rapid a pace that neither physicists nor nonphysicists can understand them.
(E) The evidence supporting Newtonian physics is not encountered in ordinary experience.

IF YOU FINISH BEFORE TIME IS CALLED, YOU MAY CHECK YOUR WORK ON THIS SECTION ONLY. DO NOT TURN TO ANY OTHER SECTION IN THE TEST. **S T O P**

SECTION 6

SECTION 6   Time—30 minutes   In this section solve each problem, using any available space on the page for scratchwork. Then decide which is the best of the choices given and fill in the corresponding oval on the answer sheet.
                35 Questions

The following information is for your reference in solving some of the problems.

Circle of radius r: Area $= \pi r^2$; Circumference $= 2\pi r$
   The number of degrees of arc in a circle is 360.
The measure in degrees of a straight angle is 180.

Definition of symbols:
$=$ is equal to $\leq$ is less than or equal to
$\neq$ is unequal to $\geq$ is greater than or equal to
$<$ is less than $\parallel$ is parallel to
$>$ is greater than $\perp$ is perpendicular to

Triangle: The sum of the measures in degrees of the angles of a triangle is 180.
If $\angle CDA$ is a right angle, then

(1) area of $\triangle ABC = \dfrac{AB \times CD}{2}$

(2) $AC^2 = AD^2 + DC^2$

Note: Figures that accompany problems in this test are intended to provide information useful in solving the problems. They are drawn as accurately as possible EXCEPT when it is stated in a specific problem that its figure is not drawn to scale. All figures lie in a plane unless otherwise indicated. All numbers used are real numbers.

1. $2(9 + 6) - 4(10 \div 2) =$

   (A) 10   (B) 5   (C) 4   (D) -5 (E) -10

2. How many revolutions are made in 5 minutes by a fan that makes 30 revolutions per second?

   (A) 900   (B) 1,500   (C) 1,800
   (D) 5,400   (E) 9,000

3. A baker's dozen contains 13 items. A normal dozen contains 12 items. How many normal dozens contain as many items as 12 baker's dozens?

   (A) 12   (B) $12\frac{1}{2}$ (C) 13

   (D) 14   (E) $15\frac{1}{3}$

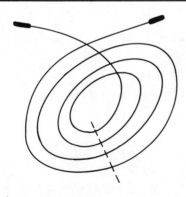

4. A rope is coiled 4 times as shown in the figure above. If a cut is made through the rope along the dotted line segment shown, into how many pieces will the rope be cut?

   (A) Two   (B) Four   (C) Five
   (D) Six   (E) Eight

5. If the average (arithmetic mean) of four numbers is 37 and the average of two of these numbers is 33, what is the average of the other two numbers?

   (A) 35
   (B) 39
   (C) 40
   (D) 41
   (E) 43

6. Which of the following is NOT equal to $\frac{1}{2}$ of an integer?

   (A) $\frac{1}{4}$ (B) $\frac{1}{2}$ (C) 1   (D) $\frac{3}{2}$ (E) 2

7. In the figure above, $ABCD$ is a parallelogram. What is the value of x?

   (A)   50
   (B)   60
   (C)   70
   (D)   80
   (E)   110

GO ON TO THE NEXT PAGE

Questions 8-27 each consist of two quantities, one in Column A and one in Column B. You are to compare the two quantities and on the answer sheet fill in oval

A if the quantity in Column A is greater;
B if the quantity in Column B is greater;
C if the two quantities are equal;
D if the relationship cannot be determined from the information given.

AN E RESPONSE WILL NOT BE SCORED.

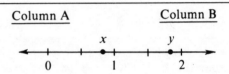

	EXAMPLES		
	Column A	Column B	Answers
E1.	2×6	$2 + 6$	● ⓑ ⓒ ⓓ ⓔ
E2.	$180 - x$	y	ⓐ ⓑ ● ⓓ ⓔ
E3.	$p - q$	$q - p$	ⓐ ⓑ ⓒ ● ⓔ

Notes:

1. In certain questions, information concerning one or both of the quantities to be compared is centered above the two columns.
2. In a given question, a symbol that appears in both columns represents the same thing in Column A as it does in Column B.
3. Letters such as x, n, and k stand for real numbers.

	Column A	Column B
8.	The price of 1 dozen apples	The price of a 3 pound bag of apples

$$S = \{1, 2, 3, 4, 5, 6, 7, 8, 9\}$$

	Column A	Column B
9.	The product of the even integers in S	The product of the odd integers in S

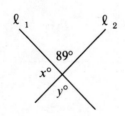

	Column A	Column B
10.	x	y

There are 22 boys and 21 girls in a class of 43 students.

	Column A	Column B
11.	The ratio of the number of girls to the number of boys	The ratio of the number of boys to the number of girls

Questions 12-13 refer to the following definition of $[a, b, c]$ for all real numbers a, b, and c.

$$[a, b, c] = (a - b)(a - c)(b - c)$$

	Column A	Column B
12.	$[1, 1, 1]$	$[2, 2, 2]$
13.	$[a, 2, 1]$	$a^2 - 3a - 2$

	Column A	Column B

x and y are points on the number line.

	Column A	Column B
14.	xy	2

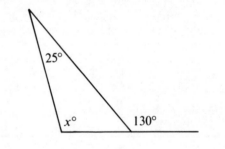

	Column A	Column B
15.	x	110

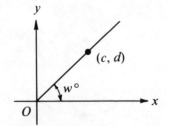

Note: Figure not drawn to scale.

$$c \neq d$$

	Column A	Column B
16.	w	45

GO ON TO THE NEXT PAGE ⟶

Column A	Column B
17. $(3 + 5)^2$	$3^2 + 5^2$

×	P	Q	R
P	1	6	
Q	6		18
R			

An incomplete multiplication table for positive integers P, Q, and R is shown.

18. The number of blank squares for which products can be calculated — 5

If a certain number n is reduced by 3, the result equals $\frac{1}{2}$ the value of n.

19. n — 5

A ————————— B ——— C

Segment AC represents a ribbon $15\frac{3}{4}$ inches long. The length of AB equals $\frac{2}{3}$ of the length of AC.

20. The length of BC — 5 inches

$xy = 8$ and $yz = 12$.

21. $\dfrac{8}{x}$ — $\dfrac{12}{z}$

22. The volume of a cube if the area of one of its faces is 36 square inches — The volume of a rectangular solid if its edges are 3 inches, 7 inches, and 10 inches

Column A	Column B

$x + (4 - y) = 10$

23. $x + y$ — $x - y$

The fraction $\frac{1}{7}$ can be written as the repeating decimal 0.142857142857 . . . where the block of digits 142857 repeats.

24. The 610th digit following the decimal point — 5

a and b are positive numbers.

25. $a \cdot b$ — $\dfrac{a}{b}$

$b + c = a$
$b + a = d$
$c + c = d$

26. $2b$ — $c + 1$

$y = 4 - (2 + x)^2$

27. The greatest possible value of y — 4

GO ON TO THE NEXT PAGE

Solve each of the remaining problems in this section using any available space for scratchwork. Then decide which is the best of the choices given and fill in the corresponding oval on the answer sheet.

28. If x and y are positive integers and $x - \dfrac{1}{y} = \dfrac{7}{2}$, then $x =$

(A) 3   (B) 4   (C) 6   (D) 7   (E) 8

29. Mary has $(m + 17)$ apples, Scott has $(m + 8)$ apples, and John has $(m + 5)$ apples. All of these apples are put into 3 empty boxes so that each box contains exactly x apples. What is the value of x in terms of m?

(A) $m + 10$
(B) $3m + 10$
(C) $3m + 30$
(D) $10m$
(E) $11m$

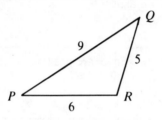

30. In $\triangle PQR$ above, if point S (not shown) is on QR between Q and R, then the length of segment PS could be any number between

(A) 7 and 10   (B) 6 and 9   (C) 5 and 11
(D) 1 and 9   (E) 1 and 15

31. 5 percent of 6 percent is

(A) 0.11%   (B) 0.3%   (C) 3%
(D) 11%   (E) 30%

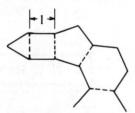

32. When the figure above is completed, it will consist of six regular polygons, each having sides of length 1 and each having one side in common with each of its adjacent polygons. If the two polygons that complete the figure have 8 and 10 sides, respectively, what will be the perimeter of the completed figure?

(A) 24   (B) 26   (C) 30   (D) 31   (E) 36

33. If a bus averages 55 miles per hour on a certain trip, it will arrive at the terminal 2 hours early. If the bus averages 35 miles per hour, it will arrive 2 hours late. What is the length, in miles, of the trip?

(A) 9   (B) 90   (C) 125
(D) 385   (E) 550

34. Gina has exactly $39 in $10, $5, and $1 bills in her purse. If she has more $1 than $5 bills and more $5 than $10 bills, how many different combinations containing at least one of each type could she have?

(A) Two
(B) Three
(C) Four
(D) Five
(E) Six

35. If a rectangular piece of paper is cut into exactly three pieces by making two straight cuts, which of the following could be the total number of edges on the three pieces?
     I.   9
     II. 11
     III. 12

(A) I only   (B) III only   (C) I and III only
(D) II and III only   (E) I, II, and III

Correct Answers for Scholastic Aptitude Test
Form Code 5H

VERBAL		MATHEMATICAL	
Section 1	Section 5	Section 2	Section 6
1. A	1. C	1. A	1. A
2. E	2. D	2. C	2. E
3. E	3. E	3. E	3. C
4. D	4. A	4. D	4. C
5. C	5. D	5. A	5. D
6. B	6. B	6. E	6. A
7. E	7. B	7. C	7. C
8. E	8. A	8. A	*8. D
9. B	9. C	9. E	*9. B
10. A	10. A	10. D	*10. A
11. C	11. A	11. A	*11. B
12. C	12. B	12. E	*12. C
13. E	13. E	13. A	*13. A
14. D	14. D	14. B	*14. B
15. B	15. D	15. C	*15. B
16. C	16. E	16. C	*16. D
17. E	17. C	17. B	*17. A
18. B	18. B	18. D	*18. C
19. D	19. E	19. D	*19. A
20. C	20. A	20. B	*20. A
21. C	21. C	21. D	*21. C
22. D	22. D	22. C	*22. A
23. A	23. C	23. B	*23. D
24. E	24. C	24. E	*24. A
25. B	25. D	25. A	*25. D
26. A	26. C		*26. B
27. C	27. A		*27. C
28. A	28. B		28. B
29. D	29. C		29. A
30. E	30. D		30. B
31. E	31. A		31. B
32. C	32. E		32. B
33. C	33. E		33. D
34. A	34. C		34. C
35. B	35. B		35. E
36. C	36. A		
37. B	37. E		
38. D	38. A		
39. A	39. E		
40. E	40. B		
41. B			
42. B			
43. C			
44. B			
45. E			

*Indicates four-choice questions. (All of the other questions are five-choice.)

239

The Scoring Process

Machine-scoring is done in three steps:

- *Scanning.* Your answer sheet is "read" by a scanning machine and the oval you filled in for each question is recorded on a computer tape.

- *Scoring.* The computer compares the oval filled in for each question with the correct response. Each correct answer receives one point; omitted questions do not count toward your score. For each wrong answer, a fraction of a point is subtracted to correct for random guessing. For questions with five answer choices, one-fourth of a point is subtracted for each wrong response; for questions with four answer choices, one-third of a point is subtracted for each wrong response. The SAT-verbal test has 85 questions with five answer choices each. If, for example, a student has 44 right, 32 wrong, and 9 omitted, the resulting raw score is determined as follows:

$$44 \text{ right} - \frac{32 \text{ wrong}}{4} = 44 - 8 = 36 \text{ raw score points}$$

Obtaining raw scores frequently involves the rounding of fractional numbers to the nearest whole number. For example, a raw score of 36.25 is rounded to 36, the nearest whole number. A raw score of 36.50 is rounded upward to 37.

- *Converting to reported scaled score.* Raw test scores are then placed on the College Board scale of 200 to 800 through a process that adjusts scores to account for minor differences in difficulty among different editions of the test. This process, known as equating, is performed so that a student's reported score is not affected by the edition of the test taken nor by the abilities of the group with whom the student takes the test. As a result of placing SAT scores on the College Board scale, scores earned by students at different times can be compared. For example, an SAT-verbal score of 400 on a test taken at one administration indicates the same level of developed verbal ability as a 400 score obtained on a different edition of the test taken at another time.

How to Score the Test

SAT-Verbal Sections 1 and 5

Step A: Count the number of correct answers for *section 1* and record the number in the space provided on the worksheet on the next page. Then do the same for the incorrect answers. (Do not count omitted answers.) To determine subtotal A, use the formula:

$$\text{number correct} - \frac{\text{number incorrect}}{4} = \text{subtotal A}$$

Step B: Count the number of correct answers and the number of incorrect answers for *section 5* and record the numbers in the spaces provided on the worksheet. To determine subtotal B, use the formula:

$$\text{number correct} - \frac{\text{number incorrect}}{4} = \text{subtotal B}$$

Step C: To obtain C, add subtotal A to subtotal B, keeping any decimals. Enter the resulting figure on the worksheet.

Step D: To obtain D, your raw verbal score, round C to the nearest whole number. (For example, any number from 44.50 to 45.49 rounds to 45.) Enter the resulting figure on the worksheet.

Step E: To find your reported SAT-verbal score, look up the total raw verbal score you obtained in step D in the conversion table on page 242. Enter this figure on the worksheet.

SAT-Mathematical Sections 2 and 6

Step A: Count the number of correct answers and the number of incorrect answers for *section 2* and record the numbers in the spaces provided on the worksheet. To determine the subtotal A, use the formula:

$$\text{number correct} - \frac{\text{number incorrect}}{4} = \text{subtotal A}$$

Step B: Count the number of correct answers and the number of incorrect answers for the *five-choice questions (questions 1 through 7 and 28 through 35) in section 6* and record the numbers in the spaces provided on the worksheet. To determine the subtotal B, use the formula:

$$\text{number correct} - \frac{\text{number incorrect}}{4} = \text{subtotal B}$$

Step C: Count the number of correct answers and the number of incorrect answers for the *four-choice questions (questions 8 through 27) in section 6* and record the numbers in the spaces provided on the worksheet. To determine the subtotal C, use the formula:

$$\text{number correct} - \frac{\text{number incorrect}}{3} = \text{subtotal C}$$

Step D: To obtain D, add subtotal A, subtotal B, and subtotal C, keeping any decimals. Enter the resulting figure on the worksheet.

Step E: To obtain E, your raw mathematical score, round D to the nearest whole number. (For example, any number from 44.50 to 45.49 rounds to 45.) Enter the resulting figure on the worksheet.

Step F: To find your reported SAT-mathematical score, look up the total raw mathematical score you obtained in E in the conversion table on page 242. Enter this figure on the worksheet.

SAT SCORING WORKSHEET

SAT-Verbal Sections

A. Section 1:   _____ − ¼ (_____) = _____
                         no. correct   no. incorrect   subtotal A

B. Section 5:   _____ − ¼ (_____) = _____
                         no. correct   no. incorrect   subtotal B

C. Total unrounded raw score   _____
   (Total A + B)   C

D. Total rounded raw score   _____
   (Rounded to nearest whole number)   D

E. SAT-verbal reported scaled score
   (See the conversion table on page 242.)

                                                          SAT-verbal
                                                             score

SAT-Mathematical Sections

A. Section 2:   _____ − ¼ (_____) = _____
                         no. correct   no. incorrect   subtotal A

B. Section 6:
   Questions <u>1 through 7</u> and   _____ − ¼ (_____) = _____
   <u>28 through 35</u> (5-choice)   no. correct   no. incorrect   subtotal B

C. Section 6:
   Questions <u>8 through 27</u>   _____ − ⅓ (_____) = _____
   (4-choice)   no. correct   no. incorrect   subtotal C

D. Total unrounded raw score   _____
   (Total A + B + C)   D

E. Total rounded raw score   _____
   (Rounded to nearest whole number)   E

F. SAT-mathematical reported scaled score
   (See the conversion table on page 242.)

                                                          SAT-math
                                                             score

Score Conversion Table
Scholastic Aptitude Test
Form Code 5H

Raw Score	College Board Reported Score		Raw Score	College Board Reported Score	
	SAT-Verbal	SAT-Math		SAT-Verbal	SAT-Math
85	800		40	460	600
84	780		39	450	590
83	760		38	440	580
82	750		37	440	570
81	740		36	430	560
80	730		35	420	550
79	720		34	420	540
78	710		33	410	530
77	700		32	400	520
76	690		31	400	510
75	680		30	390	500
74	680		29	380	490
73	670		28	380	480
72	660		27	370	480
71	660		26	360	470
70	650		25	350	460
69	640		24	350	450
68	640		23	340	440
67	630		22	330	430
66	620		21	330	420
65	620		20	320	410
64	610		19	310	400
63	600		18	300	400
62	600		17	300	390
61	590		16	290	380
60	590	800	15	280	370
59	580	790	14	280	360
58	570	780	13	270	350
57	570	770	12	260	350
56	560	760	11	250	340
55	550	750	10	250	330
54	550	740	9	240	320
53	540	730	8	230	310
52	540	720	7	230	300
51	530	710	6	220	290
50	520	700	5	210	290
49	520	690	4	200	280
48	510	680	3	200	270
47	500	670	2	200	260
46	500	660	1	200	250
45	490	650	0	200	240
44	480	640	−1	200	230
43	480	630	−2	200	230
42	470	620	−3	200	220
41	460	610	−4	200	210
			−5 or below	200	200

COLLEGE BOARD — SCHOLASTIC APTITUDE TEST
and Test of Standard Written English   Side 1

Use a No. 2 pencil only. Be sure each mark is dark and completely fills the intended oval. Completely erase any errors or stray marks.

(Cut here to detach.)

1.

YOUR NAME: _____
(Print)   Last   First   M.I.

SIGNATURE: _____   DATE: __/__/__

HOME ADDRESS: _____
(Print)   Number and Street

_____
City   State   Zip Code

CENTER: _____
(Print)   City   State   Center Number

IMPORTANT: Please fill in these boxes exactly as shown on the back cover of your test book.

FOR ETS USE ONLY

2. TEST FORM

_____

3. FORM CODE

4. REGISTRATION NUMBER
(Copy from your Admission Ticket.)

5. YOUR NAME

First 4 letters of last name | First Init. | Mid. Init.

(Ⓐ–Ⓩ ovals grid)

6. DATE OF BIRTH

Month	Day	Year
Jan.		
Feb.		
Mar.	⓪ ⓪	⓪ ⓪
Apr.	① ①	① ①
May	② ②	② ②
June	③ ③	③ ③
July	④	④
Aug.	⑤ ⑤	⑤
Sept.	⑥ ⑥	⑥
Oct.	⑦ ⑦	⑦
Nov.	⑧	⑧
Dec.	⑨	⑨

Form Code columns:
Ⓞ Ⓐ Ⓙ Ⓢ
① Ⓑ Ⓚ Ⓣ
② Ⓒ Ⓛ Ⓤ
③ Ⓓ Ⓜ Ⓥ
④ Ⓔ Ⓝ Ⓦ
⑤ Ⓕ Ⓞ Ⓧ
⑥ Ⓖ Ⓟ Ⓨ
⑦ Ⓗ Ⓠ Ⓩ
⑧ Ⓘ Ⓡ
⑨

Registration Number columns: ⓪–⑨

7. SEX
Ⓞ Female
Ⓞ Male

8. TEST BOOK SERIAL NUMBER

_____

Start with number 1 for each new section. If a section has fewer than 50 questions, leave the extra answer spaces blank.

SECTION 1

1 Ⓐ Ⓑ Ⓒ Ⓓ Ⓔ   26 Ⓐ Ⓑ Ⓒ Ⓓ Ⓔ
2 Ⓐ Ⓑ Ⓒ Ⓓ Ⓔ   27 Ⓐ Ⓑ Ⓒ Ⓓ Ⓔ
3 Ⓐ Ⓑ Ⓒ Ⓓ Ⓔ   28 Ⓐ Ⓑ Ⓒ Ⓓ Ⓔ
4 Ⓐ Ⓑ Ⓒ Ⓓ Ⓔ   29 Ⓐ Ⓑ Ⓒ Ⓓ Ⓔ
5 Ⓐ Ⓑ Ⓒ Ⓓ Ⓔ   30 Ⓐ Ⓑ Ⓒ Ⓓ Ⓔ
6 Ⓐ Ⓑ Ⓒ Ⓓ Ⓔ   31 Ⓐ Ⓑ Ⓒ Ⓓ Ⓔ
7 Ⓐ Ⓑ Ⓒ Ⓓ Ⓔ   32 Ⓐ Ⓑ Ⓒ Ⓓ Ⓔ
8 Ⓐ Ⓑ Ⓒ Ⓓ Ⓔ   33 Ⓐ Ⓑ Ⓒ Ⓓ Ⓔ
9 Ⓐ Ⓑ Ⓒ Ⓓ Ⓔ   34 Ⓐ Ⓑ Ⓒ Ⓓ Ⓔ
10 Ⓐ Ⓑ Ⓒ Ⓓ Ⓔ   35 Ⓐ Ⓑ Ⓒ Ⓓ Ⓔ
11 Ⓐ Ⓑ Ⓒ Ⓓ Ⓔ   36 Ⓐ Ⓑ Ⓒ Ⓓ Ⓔ
12 Ⓐ Ⓑ Ⓒ Ⓓ Ⓔ   37 Ⓐ Ⓑ Ⓒ Ⓓ Ⓔ
13 Ⓐ Ⓑ Ⓒ Ⓓ Ⓔ   38 Ⓐ Ⓑ Ⓒ Ⓓ Ⓔ
14 Ⓐ Ⓑ Ⓒ Ⓓ Ⓔ   39 Ⓐ Ⓑ Ⓒ Ⓓ Ⓔ
15 Ⓐ Ⓑ Ⓒ Ⓓ Ⓔ   40 Ⓐ Ⓑ Ⓒ Ⓓ Ⓔ
16 Ⓐ Ⓑ Ⓒ Ⓓ Ⓔ   41 Ⓐ Ⓑ Ⓒ Ⓓ Ⓔ
17 Ⓐ Ⓑ Ⓒ Ⓓ Ⓔ   42 Ⓐ Ⓑ Ⓒ Ⓓ Ⓔ
18 Ⓐ Ⓑ Ⓒ Ⓓ Ⓔ   43 Ⓐ Ⓑ Ⓒ Ⓓ Ⓔ
19 Ⓐ Ⓑ Ⓒ Ⓓ Ⓔ   44 Ⓐ Ⓑ Ⓒ Ⓓ Ⓔ
20 Ⓐ Ⓑ Ⓒ Ⓓ Ⓔ   45 Ⓐ Ⓑ Ⓒ Ⓓ Ⓔ
21 Ⓐ Ⓑ Ⓒ Ⓓ Ⓔ   46 Ⓐ Ⓑ Ⓒ Ⓓ Ⓔ
22 Ⓐ Ⓑ Ⓒ Ⓓ Ⓔ   47 Ⓐ Ⓑ Ⓒ Ⓓ Ⓔ
23 Ⓐ Ⓑ Ⓒ Ⓓ Ⓔ   48 Ⓐ Ⓑ Ⓒ Ⓓ Ⓔ
24 Ⓐ Ⓑ Ⓒ Ⓓ Ⓔ   49 Ⓐ Ⓑ Ⓒ Ⓓ Ⓔ
25 Ⓐ Ⓑ Ⓒ Ⓓ Ⓔ   50 Ⓐ Ⓑ Ⓒ Ⓓ Ⓔ

SECTION 2

1 Ⓐ Ⓑ Ⓒ Ⓓ Ⓔ   26 Ⓐ Ⓑ Ⓒ Ⓓ Ⓔ
2 Ⓐ Ⓑ Ⓒ Ⓓ Ⓔ   27 Ⓐ Ⓑ Ⓒ Ⓓ Ⓔ
3 Ⓐ Ⓑ Ⓒ Ⓓ Ⓔ   28 Ⓐ Ⓑ Ⓒ Ⓓ Ⓔ
4 Ⓐ Ⓑ Ⓒ Ⓓ Ⓔ   29 Ⓐ Ⓑ Ⓒ Ⓓ Ⓔ
5 Ⓐ Ⓑ Ⓒ Ⓓ Ⓔ   30 Ⓐ Ⓑ Ⓒ Ⓓ Ⓔ
6 Ⓐ Ⓑ Ⓒ Ⓓ Ⓔ   31 Ⓐ Ⓑ Ⓒ Ⓓ Ⓔ
7 Ⓐ Ⓑ Ⓒ Ⓓ Ⓔ   32 Ⓐ Ⓑ Ⓒ Ⓓ Ⓔ
8 Ⓐ Ⓑ Ⓒ Ⓓ Ⓔ   33 Ⓐ Ⓑ Ⓒ Ⓓ Ⓔ
9 Ⓐ Ⓑ Ⓒ Ⓓ Ⓔ   34 Ⓐ Ⓑ Ⓒ Ⓓ Ⓔ
10 Ⓐ Ⓑ Ⓒ Ⓓ Ⓔ   35 Ⓐ Ⓑ Ⓒ Ⓓ Ⓔ
11 Ⓐ Ⓑ Ⓒ Ⓓ Ⓔ   36 Ⓐ Ⓑ Ⓒ Ⓓ Ⓔ
12 Ⓐ Ⓑ Ⓒ Ⓓ Ⓔ   37 Ⓐ Ⓑ Ⓒ Ⓓ Ⓔ
13 Ⓐ Ⓑ Ⓒ Ⓓ Ⓔ   38 Ⓐ Ⓑ Ⓒ Ⓓ Ⓔ
14 Ⓐ Ⓑ Ⓒ Ⓓ Ⓔ   39 Ⓐ Ⓑ Ⓒ Ⓓ Ⓔ
15 Ⓐ Ⓑ Ⓒ Ⓓ Ⓔ   40 Ⓐ Ⓑ Ⓒ Ⓓ Ⓔ
16 Ⓐ Ⓑ Ⓒ Ⓓ Ⓔ   41 Ⓐ Ⓑ Ⓒ Ⓓ Ⓔ
17 Ⓐ Ⓑ Ⓒ Ⓓ Ⓔ   42 Ⓐ Ⓑ Ⓒ Ⓓ Ⓔ
18 Ⓐ Ⓑ Ⓒ Ⓓ Ⓔ   43 Ⓐ Ⓑ Ⓒ Ⓓ Ⓔ
19 Ⓐ Ⓑ Ⓒ Ⓓ Ⓔ   44 Ⓐ Ⓑ Ⓒ Ⓓ Ⓔ
20 Ⓐ Ⓑ Ⓒ Ⓓ Ⓔ   45 Ⓐ Ⓑ Ⓒ Ⓓ Ⓔ
21 Ⓐ Ⓑ Ⓒ Ⓓ Ⓔ   46 Ⓐ Ⓑ Ⓒ Ⓓ Ⓔ
22 Ⓐ Ⓑ Ⓒ Ⓓ Ⓔ   47 Ⓐ Ⓑ Ⓒ Ⓓ Ⓔ
23 Ⓐ Ⓑ Ⓒ Ⓓ Ⓔ   48 Ⓐ Ⓑ Ⓒ Ⓓ Ⓔ
24 Ⓐ Ⓑ Ⓒ Ⓓ Ⓔ   49 Ⓐ Ⓑ Ⓒ Ⓓ Ⓔ
25 Ⓐ Ⓑ Ⓒ Ⓓ Ⓔ   50 Ⓐ Ⓑ Ⓒ Ⓓ Ⓔ

COLLEGE BOARD — SCHOLASTIC APTITUDE TEST
and Test of Standard Written English   Side 2

Use a No. 2 pencil only. Be sure each mark is dark and completely fills the intended oval. Completely erase any errors or stray marks.

Start with number 1 for each new section. If a section has fewer than 50 questions, leave the extra answer spaces blank.

9. SIGNATURE:

SECTION 3
(Questions 1–50, each with answer options A B C D E)

SECTION 4
(Questions 1–50, each with answer options A B C D E)

SECTION 5
(Questions 1–50, each with answer options A B C D E)

SECTION 6
(Questions 1–50, each with answer options A B C D E)

TEST 9—FORM CODE 6E

SECTION 1   Time—30 minutes   For each question in this section, choose the best answer and fill in
40 Questions   the corresponding oval on the answer sheet.

Each question below consists of a word in capital letters, followed by five lettered words or phrases. Choose the word or phrase that is most nearly opposite in meaning to the word in capital letters. Since some of the questions require you to distinguish fine shades of meaning, consider all the choices before deciding which is best.

Example:

GOOD: (A) sour   (B) bad   (C) red
(D) hot   (E) ugly

Ⓐ ● Ⓒ Ⓓ Ⓔ

1. SELF-SUFFICIENT: (A) impolite
   (B) helpless   (C) careful
   (D) faulty   (E) extreme

2. SURGE: (A) sudden decrease
   (B) loud noise   (C) unusual color
   (D) destructive agent   (E) negative reaction

3. EXACTNESS:
   (A) sentimentality   (B) imprecision
   (C) ignorance   (D) lack of originality
   (E) resistance to change

4. RANT: (A) plan carefully
   (B) speak peaceably   (C) request promptly
   (D) defend bravely   (E) convince wholly

5. LAPSE: (A) calculation   (B) revelation
   (C) final decision   (D) ample allowance
   (E) continued improvement

6. DEFUNCT: (A) financial   (B) accurate
   (C) existing   (D) colorful   (E) saturated

7. INSENTIENT: (A) generous
   (B) productive   (C) permanent
   (D) unable to hope   (E) capable of feeling

8. EMBROIL: (A) determine provisionally
   (B) accuse falsely   (C) handle ineffectually
   (D) beautify   (E) extricate

9. AMBIVALENCE: (A) valuable skill
   (B) lack of strength   (C) honesty
   (D) certainty   (E) success

10. TINGE: (A) recommend   (B) conform
    (C) soothe   (D) revise   (E) blanch

Each sentence below has one or two blanks, each blank indicating that something has been omitted. Beneath the sentence are five lettered words or sets of words. Choose the word or set of words that, when inserted in the sentence, best fits the meaning of the sentence as a whole.

Example:

Although its publicity has been ----, the film itself is intelligent, well-acted, handsomely produced, and altogether ----.

(A) tasteless. .respectable (B) extensive. .moderate
(C) sophisticated. .amateur (D) risqué. .crude
(E) perfect. .spectacular

● Ⓑ Ⓒ Ⓓ Ⓔ

11. Because she has a great need for ----, she loathes the public appearances demanded of her as a leading literary figure.

(A) luxury   (B) privacy   (C) reward
(D) devotion   (E) distraction

12. Barbara McClintock's systematic examination of corn demonstrated the transposition of genes, a finding that overturned entrenched beliefs and proved that ---- study may produce brilliant insights and ---- change.

(A) haphazard..radical
(B) inherent..controversial
(C) improvised..startling
(D) methodical..revolutionary
(E) derivative..gradual

13. Sympathetic from the start, the faculty committee listened to the students' grievances with ---- and then set out to ---- the conditions that caused them.

(A) alarm..exacerbate
(B) remorse..enumerate
(C) disdain..improve
(D) concern..rectify
(E) enthusiasm..restate

GO ON TO THE NEXT PAGE ⟩

14. Ms. Fergusson's main criticism of the artist's rendering of the ancient mammal's physical appearance is that, unsupported by even a ---- of fossil evidence, the image is bound to be ----.

   (A) modicum..speculative
   (B) particle..supplemented
   (C) perusal..substantiated
   (D) fabrication..obsolete
   (E) recapitulation..exhausted

15. Even as the danger of an epidemic has ----, there has risen, paradoxically, ---- the adoption and implementation of proven preventative measures.

   (A) diminished..apathy about
   (B) intensified..interest in
   (C) increased..resistance to
   (D) spread..encouragement for
   (E) evaporated..understanding of

Each question below consists of a related pair of words or phrases, followed by five lettered pairs of words or phrases. Select the lettered pair that best expresses a relationship similar to that expressed in the original pair.

Example:

YAWN : BOREDOM :: (A) dream : sleep
(B) anger : madness (C) smile : amusement
(D) face : expression (E) impatience : rebellion

Ⓐ Ⓑ ● Ⓓ Ⓔ

---

16. SOIL:EARTHWORM :: (A) sky:star
   (B) skin:mosquito   (C) field:tree
   (D) water:fish   (E) grass:cow

17. BLINDFOLD:SEEING ::
   (A) microphone:hearing
   (B) smudge:writing
   (C) tongue:tasting
   (D) muzzle:biting
   (E) tingle:feeling

18. CARPENTER:WOOD :: (A) artist:palette
   (B) gardener:hoe   (C) mason:stone
   (D) surgeon:scalpel   (E) writer:plot

19. ABBREVIATION:WORD ::
   (A) signature:name   (B) sentence:paragraph
   (C) survey:poll   (D) shortcut:route
   (E) bypass:issue

20. HAZE:LANDSCAPE ::
   (A) subtlety:bluntness   (B) sand:desert
   (C) maze:psychology   (D) veil:face
   (E) confusion:conciseness

21. PRIEST:SEMINARY ::
   (A) pilot:aviary
   (B) soldier:maneuver
   (C) artist:exhibit
   (D) comedian:amphitheater
   (E) musician:conservatory

22. REPROBATE:CONDEMNATION ::
   (A) prodigal:wealth
   (B) outcast:exclusion
   (C) renegade:conformity
   (D) turncoat:nationality
   (E) upstart:consequence

23. CRITERION:DECISION ::
   (A) duplicate:adaptation
   (B) standard:comparison
   (C) resolution:antagonism
   (D) sample:purchase
   (E) shame:justice

24. PRECARIOUS:PERCH ::
   (A) risky:investment
   (B) preconceived:notion
   (C) injurious:plunge
   (D) premature:opinion
   (E) pretentious:display

25. LABYRINTHINE:ARGUMENT ::
   (A) discordant:music
   (B) convoluted:pattern
   (C) exotic:cuisine
   (D) symmetrical:proportion
   (E) comprehensive:plan

GO ON TO THE NEXT PAGE →

Each passage below is followed by questions based on its content. Answer the questions following each passage on the basis of what is stated or implied in that passage.

While governments wrangled over future canals to the Pacific, the shipwrights of New York and New England were engaged in cutting down the time of ocean passage around Cape Horn. In one month of 1850, thirty-three sailing vessels from New York and Boston entered San Francisco Bay after an average passage of 159 days. Then there came booming through the Golden Gate the clipper ship Sea Witch of New York, 97 days out. At once the cry went up for more clippers.

This type of full-rigged sailing vessel was characterized by great length in proportion to breadth of beam, an enormous sail area, and long concave bows ending in a gracefully curved cutwater. Sea Witch, built for the China-New York tea trade, now proved the new type's value for the California trade. But, as California then afforded no return cargo except gold dust, the Yankee clippers sailed in ballast to China where they came into competition with the British merchant marine. Crack ships of the British East India Company waited for a cargo weeks on end, while one American clipper after another sailed with a cargo of tea at double the ordinary freight.

These clipper ships were built of wood in shipyards from Maine to Baltimore. Their architects obeyed what wind and wave had taught them and created the noblest of all sailing vessels. These were our Gothic cathedrals, our Parthenon; but monuments carved from snow. For a few brief years they flashed their splendor around the world, then disappeared with the finality of the wild pigeon.

26. The main purpose of the passage is to

(A) compare British and American sailing ships
(B) discuss the China-New York tea trade in the 1850's
(C) describe and celebrate the clipper ship
(D) explain why the clipper ship disappeared
(E) demonstrate the superiority of American ingenuity to British tradition

27. In the first paragraph of the passage, the author implies that

(A) American shipwrights acted more effectively than governments did
(B) the New York to San Francisco route was too long to be commercially viable
(C) the Sea Witch had an unfair advantage over other sailing ships
(D) sailing ships of any type would soon be outdated
(E) only a canal could significantly reduce the time of ocean passage between New York and San Francisco

28. In the passage, the author does NOT state or imply that the clipper ships were

(A) graceful   (B) costly   (C) profitable
(D) short-lived   (E) swift

GO ON TO THE NEXT PAGE →

However people may be enraptured by Shakespeare's works, whatever merits they may attribute to them, it is certain that he was not an artist. Without a sense of proportion there could never be an artist.

"But to judge Shakespeare one must allow for the times when he wrote," say his admirers. "It was a time of coarse manners, a time of elaborate and artificial speech, a time of life strange to us. In Homer also there is much that is strange to us, but this does not prevent our valuing the beauties of Homer."

But when one compares Shakespeare with Homer, the infinite distance separating true poetic art from its imitation emerges vividly. However alien to us may be the events Homer describes, he believes in what he says and speaks seriously of what he is describing, and therefore he never exaggerates and the sense of measure never deserts him. We can, then, without the slightest effort transport ourselves into the life he describes. But it is not so with Shakespeare. From his first words exaggeration is seen: of events, of feeling, of expression. It is at once evident that he does not believe in what he is saying, that he has devised his characters merely for the stage, to please the public; and so we do not believe either in the actions or in the sufferings of his characters.

29. The author implies that Homer's works are characterized by which of the following?

    I. Plausible characters
    II. A sense of proportion
    III. Sincere expression of feelings

(A) II only   (B) I and II only
(C) I and III only   (D) II and III only
(E) I, II, and III

30. According to the author, Shakespeare's admirers refer to the times in which Shakespeare lived in order to

(A) praise his use of exaggerated speech
(B) justify the lack of proportion in his writing
(C) emphasize what is most fascinating about his writing
(D) verify the realism of the strange events he describes
(E) establish a standard by which all poetic art should be judged

31. According to the author, Shakespeare's goal in writing was to

(A) imitate the art of Homer
(B) provide an outlet for his inner feelings
(C) immortalize the people of his times
(D) portray significant contemporary issues
(E) find favor with the theater audiences of his day

GO ON TO THE NEXT PAGE →

Prostaglandins are short-lived hormonelike substances made by most cells in the body after injury or shock. They are responsible for a number of physiological reactions. Prostaglandins have been shown to influence blood pressure, muscle contraction, and blood coagulation and are involved in producing pain, fever, and inflammation. When released from platelets—minute discs in the blood—a prostaglandin derivative called thromboxane makes the platelets clump together and thus initiates clotting.

In 1971, John Vane, a British researcher, discovered that aspirin interferes with the synthesis of prostaglandins. Scientists now know that aspirin relieves pain by inactivating cyclooxygenase, an enzyme that aids in initiating the synthesis of prostaglandins. When scientists realized that aspirin can also interfere with clotting, they began to wonder whether it could help prevent heart attacks and strokes, which are often caused by blood clots that block arteries in the chest or neck. Studies now indicate that low daily doses of aspirin can cut the risk of a second heart attack by about twenty percent and the risk of a second stroke by nearly half. It seems logical to assume that if the drug can prevent second heart attacks, it can also ward off an attack the first time around. Therefore, many doctors recommend an aspirin tablet every other day to inhibit excessive platelet clumping among people who have high blood pressure or other symptoms that increase the risk of heart attacks.

32. According to the passage, prostaglandins play a role in all of the following EXCEPT the

   (A) clotting of blood
   (B) sensation of pain
   (C) contraction of muscles
   (D) manufacture of platelets
   (E) inflammation of tissue

33. The passage suggests that which of the following would be most likely to initiate the production of prostaglandins?

   (A) Taking an aspirin
   (B) Spraining an ankle
   (C) Climbing stairs
   (D) Flexing a muscle
   (E) Running a fever

34. It can be inferred from the passage that when the production of prostaglandins is impeded, which of the following occur(s)?

   I. Blood coagulation is slowed.
   II. Pain is reduced.
   III. Inflammation increases.

   (A) I only   (B) II only   (C) I and II only
    (D) II and III only   (E) I, II, and III

35. It can be inferred from the passage that aspirin helps prevent heart attacks by

   (A) interfering with the production of
        thromboxane
   (B) lowering blood pressure
   (C) easing muscular contractions
   (D) initiating the production of cyclooxygenase
   (E) widening the arteries

GO ON TO THE NEXT PAGE

This free, joking way of Bartley's was one of the things that made him popular; he passed the time of day, and was give and take right along, as his
Line admirers expressed it, from the first, in a community
(5) where his smartness had that honor which gives us more smart men to the square mile than any other country in the world. The fact of his smartness had been affirmed and established in the strongest manner by the authorities of the college at which he was
(10) graduated, in answer to the reference he made to them when negotiating with the committee in charge for the place he now held as editor of the Equity Free Press. The faculty spoke of the solidity and variety of his acquirements, and the distinction with which he
(15) had acquitted himself in every branch of study he had undertaken. They added that he deserved the greater credit because his early disadvantages as an orphan, dependent on his own exertions for a livelihood, had been so great that he had entered college with diffi-
(20) culty, and with heavy conditions. This turned the scale with a committee who had all been poor boys themselves, and justly feared the encroachments of hereditary aristocracy. They perhaps had their misgivings when the young man, in his well-blacked
(25) boots, his gray trousers neatly fitting over them, and his diagonal coat buttoned high with one button, stood before them with his thumbs in his waistcoat pockets, and looked down over his mustache at the floor with sentiments concerning their wisdom which
(30) they could not explore; they must have resented the fashionable keeping of everything about him, for Bartley wore his one suit as if it were but one of many; but when they understood that he had come by everything through his own unaided smartness,
(35) they could no longer hesitate. One, indeed, still felt it a duty to call attention to the fact that the college authorities said nothing of the young man's moral characteristics in a letter dwelling so largely upon his intellectual qualifications. The others referred this
(40) point by a silent look to Squire Gaylord.
"I don't know," said the Squire, "as I ever heard that a great deal of morality was required by a newspaper editor." The rest laughed at the joke, and the Squire continued: "But I guess if he worked his own
(45) way through college, as they say, that he haint had time to be up to a great deal of mischief. You know it's for idle hands that the Devil provides, doctor."
"That's true, as far as it goes," said the doctor. "But it isn't the whole truth. The Devil provides for some busy hands, too."

36. According to the passage, Bartley is presently employed as a

(A) college professor　(B) research scholar
(C) newspaper editor　(D) medical doctor
(E) business executive

37. The tone of the phrase "in a community . . . the world" (lines 4-7) is best described as one of

(A) seriousness and concern
(B) bitterness and reproach
(C) indifference and detachment
(D) enthusiasm and admiration
(E) irony and amusement

38. All of the following factors helped Bartley in his candidacy for the position for which he was considered EXCEPT

(A) his amiable personality
(B) his intellectual achievements at college
(C) his fashionable attire
(D) the letter of recommendation from the college he attended
(E) the selection committee's prejudice against those with inherited wealth

39. All of the following statements about Squire Gaylord may be inferred from the passage EXCEPT:

(A) He has the respect of the other committee members.
(B) He displays a sense of humor.
(C) He values the virtue of work.
(D) He is certain Bartley is of unimpeachable character.
(E) He claims some knowledge of newspaper editors.

40. According to the passage, the one observation about Bartley that impresses Squire Gaylord the most is that Bartley

(A) also has an aristocratic background
(B) attended a prestigious university
(C) has been energetic and hardworking
(D) displays a fine moral character
(E) is the favorite of influential citizens

IF YOU FINISH BEFORE TIME IS CALLED, YOU MAY CHECK YOUR WORK ON THIS SECTION ONLY. DO NOT TURN TO ANY OTHER SECTION IN THE TEST. **STOP**

In this section solve each problem, using any available space on the page for scratchwork. Then decide which is the best of the choices given and fill in the corresponding oval on the answer sheet.

The following information is for your reference in solving some of the problems.

Circle of radius r: Area $= \pi r^2$; Circumference $= 2\pi r$
    The number of degrees of arc in a circle is 360.
The measure in degrees of a straight angle is 180.

Definition of symbols:
$=$ is equal to $\leq$ is less than or equal to
$\neq$ is unequal to $\geq$ is greater than or equal to
$<$ is less than $\parallel$ is parallel to
$>$ is greater than $\perp$ is perpendicular to

Triangle: The sum of the measures in degrees of the angles of a triangle is 180.
If $\angle CDA$ is a right angle, then

(1) area of $\triangle ABC = \dfrac{AB \times CD}{2}$

(2) $AC^2 = AD^2 + DC^2$

Note: Figures that accompany problems in this test are intended to provide information useful in solving the problems. They are drawn as accurately as possible EXCEPT when it is stated in a specific problem that its figure is not drawn to scale. All figures lie in a plane unless otherwise indicated. All numbers used are real numbers.

1. If $3x + 5 = 15 - 2x$, then $x =$

(A) -2
(B) 2
(C) 4
(D) 10
(E) 20

2. In the figure above, what is the degree measure of the smaller angle formed by the hour and minute hands of the clock?

(A) 240°
(B) 120°
(C) 80°
(D) 75°
(E) 60°

3. The scale of a certain map is 1 centimeter equals 1 kilometer. On this map 1.5 centimeters would represent how many meters? (1 kilometer = 1,000 meters)

(A) 100.5
(B) 150
(C) 1,000.5
(D) 1,500
(E) 15,000

GO ON TO THE NEXT PAGE

4. Which of the following is equal to a number greater than 1 ?

(A) $\frac{1}{2} \div \frac{1}{3}$

(B) $\frac{1}{2} \times \frac{1}{3}$

(C) $\frac{1}{2} - \frac{1}{3}$

(D) $\frac{1}{2} + \frac{1}{3}$

(E) $\frac{1}{3} \div \frac{1}{2}$

5. If $\frac{x}{3} = \frac{12}{y}$ and $y - 2 = 2$, then $x =$

(A) 3
(B) 4
(C) 6
(D) 9
(E) 12

x	y
2	6
3	8
4	10
5	12

6. The table above gives four sets of values for the ordered pair (x, y). Which of the following could be an equation for y in terms of x ?

(A) $y = \frac{x}{2}$ (B) $y = \frac{5x}{2}$ (C) $y = 2x + 2$

(D) $y = 2x - 6$ (E) $y = x + 4$

7. If n is an odd integer, which of the following is an even integer?

(A) $\frac{n}{2}$

(B) $n + 2$

(C) $2n + 1$

(D) n^2

(E) $n(n + 1)$

GO ON TO THE NEXT PAGE

Questions 8-27 each consist of two quantities, one in Column A and one in Column B. You are to compare the two quantities and on the answer sheet fill in oval

A if the quantity in Column A is greater;
B if the quantity in Column B is greater;
C if the two quantities are equal;
D if the relationship cannot be determined from the information given.

AN E RESPONSE WILL NOT BE SCORED.

	EXAMPLES		
	Column A	Column B	Answers
E1.	2×6	$2 + 6$	● ⑧ © ⑩ ⑤
E2.	$180 - x$	y	ⓐ ⑧ ● ⑩ ⑤
E3.	$p - q$	$q - p$	ⓐ ⑧ © ● ⑤

Notes:

1. In certain questions, information concerning one or both of the quantities to be compared is centered above the two columns.
2. In a given question, a symbol that appears in both columns represents the same thing in Column A as it does in Column B.
3. Letters such as x, n, and k stand for real numbers.

Column A	Column B

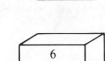

Solid I   Solid II

8. The volume of rectangular solid I | The volume of rectangular solid II

9. $3^2 \times 5^3$ | $3 \times 4 \times 5 \times 6 \times 7$

10. The number of gumdrops John has after eating 3 | The number of gumdrops Ann has after eating 2

11. $2 \cdot 3 + (24 \div 6)(2)$ | 14

A cube has each face painted a different one of the colors—red, blue, yellow, orange, green, and black. The cube is evenly balanced and is rolled across a flat surface.

12. The chance of the cube stopping with a face other than yellow on top | The chance of the cube stopping with the yellow face on top

Column A	Column B

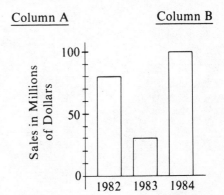

13. Sales for 1982 | Average (arithmetic mean) sales per year for the 2-year period 1983-1984

$$\frac{n^a}{n^b} = 1 \text{ and } n > 1$$

14. a | b

Machine A can do a certain job in 7 seconds. Machine B can do the same job in 9 seconds. Both machines operate at constant rates.

15. The fraction of the job done by machine A in 1 second | The fraction of the job done by machine B in 1 second

16. 0.0009×10^3 | 900×10^{-3}

GO ON TO THE NEXT PAGE ➡

Column A   Column B

$$\begin{cases} x = 2 \\ x + y = -2 \\ x + y + z = -6 \end{cases}$$

17. y z

Lines ℓ_1 and ℓ_2 lie in the same plane and have no points in common. Another line, ℓ_3, also lies in this plane.

18. The number of points   1
of intersection formed
by pairs of these three
lines

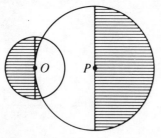

O is the center of the small circle with radius 3 and P is the center of the large circle with radius 6.

19. Four times the area   The area of the
of the shaded portion   shaded portion of
of the small circle   the large circle

The least prime factor of the integer k is 7.
The least prime factor of the integer n is 7.

20. k n

On a certain trip, Ms. Waters traveled part of the distance at an average speed of 45 miles per hour and the remainder at an average speed of 55 miles per hour.

21. Ms. Waters' average   50
speed, in miles per
hour, for the entire
trip

Column A   Column B

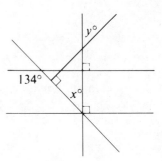

22. x y

The ratio of $\frac{1}{3}$ to $\frac{1}{2}$ is equal to the ratio of $\frac{1}{2}$ to w.

23. w $\frac{2}{3}$

x is a positive integer.

24. The value of the   9
units' digit of 2^x

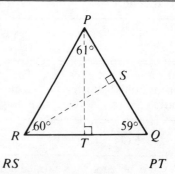

25. RS PT

For any number x, let $\lceil x \rceil$ be equal to the least integer greater than or equal to x.

26. $\lceil -3.5 \rceil$ -3

$$x^2 + x - 2 = 0$$

27. x 0

GO ON TO THE NEXT PAGE

Solve each of the remaining problems in this section using any available space for scratchwork. Then decide which is the best of the choices given and fill in the corresponding oval on the answer sheet.

28. If $80^2 = n(40^2)$, then $n =$

(A) 2
(B) 4
(C) 8
(D) 16
(E) 20

29. Of 300 high school students in a gymnasium, which of the following must be true?

   I.   At least 2 were born in the same year.
   II. At least 2 have the same birthday.
   III. At least 1 was born at midnight.

(A) I only
(B) II only
(C) III only
(D) I and II only
(E) I, II, and III

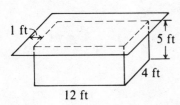

12 ft

30. The figure above shows a rectangular piece of tin laid on a rectangular box. If the tin extends uniformly 1 foot over each edge as shown, what is the area, in square feet, of the top surface of the tin?

(A) 65
(B) 70
(C) 78
(D) 84
(E) 98

31. If $\overset{a}{\underset{b-c}{\wedge}}$ is defined to be $ab + ac - bc$, for what value of x will $\overset{3}{\underset{4-x}{\wedge}}$ equal zero?

(A) 12
(B) 7
(C) 5
(D) −7
(E) −12

32. If x is 3 less than $\frac{n}{2}$, which of the following gives n in terms of x?

(A) $\dfrac{x+3}{2}$

(B) $2(x+3)$

(C) $2x+3$

(D) $2(x-3)$

(E) $2(3-x)$

GO ON TO THE NEXT PAGE

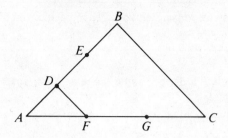

33. In the figure above, D and E divide side AB into three equal parts and F and G divide side AC into 3 equal parts. The ratio

$\dfrac{\text{area of } \triangle ADF}{\text{area of } \triangle ABC}$ is

(A) $\dfrac{1}{3}$

(B) $\dfrac{1}{6}$

(C) $\dfrac{1}{8}$

(D) $\dfrac{1}{9}$

(E) $\dfrac{1}{12}$

34. If the sum of n consecutive integers is zero, which of the following must be true?

I. The product of the n consecutive integers is zero.
II. The average (arithmetic mean) of the n consecutive integers is zero.
III. n is an odd number.

(A) I only
(B) II only
(C) III only
(D) I and II only
(E) I, II, and III

35. In 1970, the price of a certain antique car was 30 percent greater than in 1965. In 1975, the price of the same car was 50 percent greater than in 1970. The price of the car was what percent greater in 1975 than in 1965 ?

(A) 40%
(B) 45%
(C) 80%
(D) 90%
(E) 95%

IF YOU FINISH BEFORE TIME IS CALLED, YOU MAY CHECK YOUR WORK ON THIS SECTION ONLY. DO NOT TURN TO ANY OTHER SECTION IN THE TEST. **STOP**

SECTION 3   Time—30 minutes
45 Questions

For each question in this section, choose the best answer and fill in the corresponding oval on the answer sheet.

Each question below consists of a word in capital letters, followed by five lettered words or phrases. Choose the word or phrase that is most nearly <u>opposite</u> in meaning to the word in capital letters. Since some of the questions require you to distinguish fine shades of meaning, consider all the choices before deciding which is best.

Example:

GOOD: (A) sour   (B) bad   (C) red
(D) hot   (E) ugly

Ⓐ ● Ⓒ Ⓓ Ⓔ

1. FARFETCHED: (A) tranquil   (B) probable
   (C) monotonous   (D) exposed to danger
   (E) readily changed

2. CRUMPLE: (A) confine   (B) smooth
   (C) stifle   (D) rub together
   (E) make clearer

3. SUCCULENT: (A) dry   (B) unmusical
   (C) unfriendly   (D) lumpy   (E) sore

4. TOPPLE: (A) identify   (B) stabilize
   (C) combine   (D) improve   (E) increase

5. HILARITY: (A) detachment   (B) diligence
   (C) gloominess   (D) meekness
   (E) patience

6. KINDLE: (A) slash   (B) pull   (C) bend
   (D) douse   (E) scatter

7. EXPENDABLE: (A) irreconcilable
   (B) irreplaceable   (C) extensive
   (D) elaborate   (E) innovative

8. ACCORD: (A) pleasure   (B) curiosity
   (C) sluggishness   (D) disharmony
   (E) insensitivity

9. CAUSTIC: (A) soothing   (B) rash
   (C) toxic   (D) flexible   (E) effective

10. REPUDIATE: (A) exaggerate   (B) distract
    (C) adopt   (D) finesse   (E) deceive

11. OPULENCE: (A) weariness   (B) symmetry
    (C) meagerness   (D) flattery   (E) despair

12. TAWDRY: (A) significant   (B) responsive
    (C) talkative   (D) melodious   (E) refined

13. INUNDATE: (A) release   (B) drain
    (C) balance   (D) brighten   (E) ascend

14. IGNOMINY: (A) honor   (B) understanding
    (C) solemnity   (D) tranquillity
    (E) sincerity

15. ARABLE: (A) dormant   (B) disreputable
    (C) unreliable   (D) sloping   (E) untillable

GO ON TO THE NEXT PAGE →

Each sentence below has one or two blanks, each blank indicating that something has been omitted. Beneath the sentence are five lettered words or sets of words. Choose the word or set of words that, when inserted in the sentence, best fits the meaning of the sentence as a whole.

Example:

Although its publicity has been ----, the film itself is intelligent, well-acted, handsomely produced, and altogether ----.

(A) tasteless..respectable (B) extensive..moderate
(C) sophisticated..amateur (D) risqué..crude
(E) perfect..spectacular

● Ⓑ Ⓒ Ⓓ Ⓔ

16. Strobe light (pulses of light rather than ---- illumination) makes it possible for photographers to capture events that occur too ---- for the human eye to see.

(A) artificial..subtly
(B) continuous..rapidly
(C) unfocused..recently
(D) brilliant..casually
(E) local..prominently

17. Food can be ---- element in family life, bringing us together in times of trouble and in times of joy.

(A) an additive   (B) a conflicting
(C) a unifying   (D) a residual
(E) an inconsistent

18. Arthur lost his cynical attitude toward the study of economics and began to ---- the major contributions of giants in the field.

(A) initiate   (B) recant   (C) duplicate
(D) recognize   (E) authorize

19. Our view of ---- rulers is like our view of stars in the sky: great distances may actually ---- them, but they appear close to each other.

(A) despotic..imprison
(B) famous..denigrate
(C) ancient..separate
(D) legendary..conceal
(E) popular..exaggerate

20. Many of the misconceptions about Queen Victoria were created by those who ---- her most; in their efforts to ---- her as a model of all virtues, they lost sight of the real woman.

(A) esteemed..discredit
(B) idolized..disparage
(C) challenged..delineate
(D) admired..depict
(E) censured..represent

21. Before the introduction of the fur trade, hunting patterns among Native Americans living in the area encouraged the conservation of game, since hunting was a means of ---- for the group, not profit.

(A) experimentation   (B) subsistence
(C) continuity   (D) domestication
(E) collaboration

22. In contrast to many social science writers who become ---- obfuscating jargon, Welch ---- political concepts in a book suitable for general readers as well as social science classes.

(A) free of..elucidates
(B) mired in..demystifies
(C) enhanced by..camouflages
(D) evasive about..circumvents
(E) ensnared by..eclipses

23. Physical laws do not, of course, in themselves force bodies to behave in a certain way, but merely ---- how, as a matter of fact, they do behave.

(A) determine   (B) preclude
(C) counteract   (D) describe
(E) commend

24. Public education is regarded in America as the pathway to social salvation, a ---- for secular difficulties.

(A) panacea   (B) scapegoat   (C) prototype
(D) criterion   (E) fountainhead

25. After closely observing the remarkable responsiveness of newborn infants to their environment, scientists are revising a long-held belief that infants are primarily ---- creatures.

(A) innocent   (B) passive   (C) inquisitive
(D) timid   (E) sensitive

GO ON TO THE NEXT PAGE

258

Each passage below is followed by questions based on its content. Answer the questions following each passage on the basis of what is stated or implied in that passage.

Folklorist Willis James has identified and traced through its various stages what he theorizes to be the basis of Afro-American music: the "cry." The "cry" is the dominant element of Afro-American music that has greatly influenced much of American music.

James contends that the element of the "cry" accounts for the great pull this music has had on people in this country and in Europe: "... White people have been trying to find a cause of Afro-American musical uniqueness somewhere in Africa when the cause was always present with us Black people by their side, suffering and struggling for existence."

Based on many years of thoughtful study, James's analysis of Afro-American music proposes that the "cry" is the oldest form of vocal expression and is heard in uninhibited and spontaneous vocalizations that, in the manner of folk music, evolved from oral tradition. "Cries" may be articulate in regard to speech or inarticulate in regard to musical requirements, making possible only the barest type of musical notation. According to James, "cries" of a musical nature are only representations heard at a given moment, since improvisation and originality prevent a "cry" from being vocalized the same way twice. "Cries" that are articulate musically but inarticulate in terms of speech are perhaps older than song, if we are to consider song the "wedding of words to notes." James suggests it is the use of microtones in "cries," particularly at the end of phrases, that brings African and Afro-American music closest together. Also, the use of microtones makes notation more difficult in the Western system of notation.

James divides "cries" into three musical categories, each of which is compared to the European song style of the Gregorian chant: (1) plain cries, the simplest in form and structure, employ one note or tone per word or syllable, and are described as "syllabic"; (2) florid cries, the most prevalent and favored, employ several notes or tones to a word, similar to the "neumatic" treatment in chants; and (3) coloratura cries, which represent one of the most remarkable vocal feats in music, are restricted in use because of their great complexity. The coloratura "cry" is compared with the melismatic treatment in chants in which many notes adorn a single word or syllable.

Aside from James's reputation as a musicologist, the fact that Gregorian chants, too, were handed down from one generation to another and evolved from an oral tradition seems to add credibility to the use of European musical descriptions in the analysis of "cries."

26. The main purpose of the passage is to

(A) discuss a study
(B) revive a tradition
(C) dispel a notion
(D) describe a procedure
(E) refute a theory

27. According to the passage, "cries" and Gregorian chants have in common the fact that both

(A) are difficult for Westerners to appreciate
(B) are equally recognizable styles of music
(C) evolved from oral tradition
(D) created unique systems of musical notation
(E) resulted from cross-cultural contacts

28. The author apparently considers James's comparison of "cries" with Gregorian chants to be

(A) contradictory   (B) restrictive
(C) ironic   (D) valid   (E) novel

29. According to the passage, which of the following is true of both coloratura cries and melismatic chants?

(A) They have been a major influence in American music.
(B) They are musically inarticulate.
(C) They may be described as syllabic.
(D) They are spontaneous vocalizations.
(E) They use many notes to vocalize a single word or syllable.

30. Which of the following best states the central idea of the passage?

(A) The "cry" is a legitimate form of American folk music.
(B) The Gregorian chant is the European counterpart of Afro-American music.
(C) Afro-American music has more European than African elements.
(D) The basis of Afro-American music is an improvisational vocal style.
(E) Afro-American music has evolved through both an oral and a recorded tradition.

GO ON TO THE NEXT PAGE

(This passage was written in 1958.)

In the sixteenth century, Galileo's contemporaries rejected his report that he had seen spots on the face of the Sun. His *Letters on the Solar Spots*, they said,
Line were heretically contrary to the dogma that "this most
(5) lucid body" must be without blemish. But knowledge of the existence of sunspots was inescapable. Centuries before Galileo, sky-watchers in China had beheld sunspots with unaided eyes. Galileo's successors in astronomy brought the Sun under close surveillance,
(10) and after two or three centuries established that the spots fluctuate in number in a regular cycle. Observation showed this cycle to be synchronized with a fluctuation in the number of displays of the aurora borealis. Observers began to suspect that the sunspots
(15) might exert further effects on our planet. It was discovered that the passage of spots across the face of the Sun is associated with violent storms in the Earth's magnetic field; with the arrival of radio it was found that these storms were accompanied by
(20) widespread blackouts of radio communication.

Now we are at the beginning of the next significant advance in knowledge of the Sun. Though the statistical coincidence of solar activity and geomagnetic storms is conclusive, physicists have been unable to
(25) describe a process connecting events on the solar surface with the Earth's upper atmosphere. The storms that disturb the ionized layers of our atmosphere require a source of high-energy radiation and highly energetic particles. Obviously the Sun is this source.
(30) But just as the Earth's atmosphere shelters us from the hard radiation and cosmic particles raining on it, so the Sun's atmosphere absorbs and blocks the radiations of short wavelength and the particles that radiate from the solar surface. Recent advances in
(35) instrumentation, however, have made it possible for solar astronomers to turn from the face of the Sun to investigate the solar corona.

For many years astronomers who wanted to observe the Sun's atmosphere had to wait for the
(40) infrequent opportunity of a solar eclipse. At other times the dazzling light of the photosphere (the Sun's surface seen in ordinary light) overwhelms the faint light radiated by the gases in the atmosphere. Today, thanks to the genius of Bernard Lyot, astronomers are
(45) able to keep a day-to-day watch on the Sun's atmosphere. Lyot invented a coronagraph to make an artificial eclipse. This specialized telescope cuts out the light of the Sun's surface with an occulting disk and employs an elaborate train of optics to get rid of
(50) scattered light. Lyot also devised a filter that selectively admits narrow regions of the spectrum; with the coronagraph and filter together, we can observe the processes that go on in the solar atmosphere.

31. It can be inferred that the author would describe Galileo's contemporaries as

(A) apathetic   (B) narrow-minded
(C) irresponsible   (D) hypocritical
(E) unconventional

32. According to the passage, the Earth's atmosphere and the Sun's atmosphere are alike in which of the following ways?

I.   Each protects the surface beneath it from hard radiation.
II. Each is subject to cyclical disturbances.
III. Each protects the surface of the Earth from some radiation from the solar surface.

(A) I only   (B) II only   (C) I and III only
(D) II and III only   (E) I, II, and III

33. The author's statement that solar astronomers can now "turn from the face of the Sun" (line 36) means that they can

(A) study phenomena in the solar atmosphere
(B) study the photosphere in greater detail
(C) view the Sun's disk without suffering harmful effects
(D) determine the sources of solar radiation
(E) prevent communication blackouts caused by solar radiation

34. The passage suggests answers to all of the following questions EXCEPT:

(A) What is a source of high-energy radiation that bombards the Earth's atmosphere?
(B) Why are special instruments needed to observe the Sun's atmosphere?
(C) How are high-energy particles from the solar surface able to penetrate the solar atmosphere?
(D) What is the nature of the evidence that links sunspots and geomagnetic storms?
(E) Why are astronomers interested in studying the Sun's atmosphere?

35. Which of the following first indicated to astronomers that sunspots have an effect on the Earth?

(A) Sunspots appear to occur at regular intervals.
(B) Atmospheric storms cause blackouts of radio communication.
(C) Magnetic storms originate in the Earth's high atmosphere.
(D) Sunspots are so large that they are visible to the unaided eye.
(E) The activity of sunspots coincides with the activity of the aurora borealis.

GO ON TO THE NEXT PAGE →

Each question below consists of a related pair of words or phrases, followed by five lettered pairs of words or phrases. Select the lettered pair that best expresses a relationship similar to that expressed in the original pair.

Example:

YAWN : BOREDOM ::   (A) dream : sleep
(B) anger : madness   (C) smile : amusement
   (D) face : expression   (E) impatience : rebellion

Ⓐ Ⓑ ● Ⓓ Ⓔ

36. HEADLINE : ARTICLE ::
   (A) portrait : painting   (B) index : summary
   (C) encore : performance   (D) title : book
   (E) footnote : thesis

37. PEBBLE : SLINGSHOT ::   (A) knuckle : fist
   (B) clapper : bell   (C) nail : hammer
   (D) powder : rifle   (E) arrow : bow

38. SYNCHRONIZE : MOVEMENTS ::
   (A) sublimate : goals   (B) realize : dreams
   (C) prolong : intervals   (D) remit : payments
   (E) harmonize : voices

39. BULLETIN : INFORMATION ::
   (A) editorial : opinion
   (B) journal : instruction
   (C) clue : interpretation
   (D) report : confidence
   (E) rumor : publicity

40. VULGARIAN : TASTE ::
   (A) mystic : credibility
   (B) stoic : forbearance
   (C) scoundrel : conduct
   (D) hypochondriac : sensitivity
   (E) penitent : deficiency

41. ABSOLVE : OBLIGATION ::
   (A) accept : invitation
   (B) liberate : bondage
   (C) verify : testimony
   (D) condemn : property
   (E) negotiate : victory

42. CHATTERBOX : GARRULOUS ::
   (A) killjoy : merry
   (B) volunteer : heedless
   (C) fussbudget : dissatisfied
   (D) autocrat : didactic
   (E) soothsayer : reassuring

43. INTUITIVE : DELIBERATION ::
   (A) arduous : hazard
   (B) inevitable : logic
   (C) ponderous : decision
   (D) consecutive : order
   (E) spontaneous : planning

44. SOPORIFIC : SLEEP ::
   (A) appetizing : hunger
   (B) excruciating : relief
   (C) prominent : surprise
   (D) instantaneous : time
   (E) incoherent : order

45. SCUTTLE : SHIP ::
   (A) reject : voter
   (B) protest : cause
   (C) subvert : government
   (D) annoy : irritant
   (E) confiscate : possession

IF YOU FINISH BEFORE TIME IS CALLED, YOU MAY CHECK YOUR WORK ON THIS SECTION ONLY. DO NOT TURN TO ANY OTHER SECTION IN THE TEST.   **S T O P**

SECTION **4**   Time—30 minutes
25 Questions

In this section solve each problem, using any available space on the page for scratchwork. Then decide which is the best of the choices given and fill in the corresponding oval on the answer sheet.

The following information is for your reference in solving some of the problems.

Circle of radius r: Area $= \pi r^2$; Circumference $= 2\pi r$
The number of degrees of arc in a circle is 360.
The measure in degrees of a straight angle is 180.

Definition of symbols:
$=$ is equal to $\leq$ is less than or equal to
$\neq$ is unequal to $\geq$ is greater than or equal to
$<$ is less than $\parallel$ is parallel to
$>$ is greater than $\perp$ is perpendicular to

Triangle: The sum of the measures in degrees of the angles of a triangle is 180.
If $\angle CDA$ is a right angle, then

(1) area of $\triangle ABC = \dfrac{AB \times CD}{2}$

(2) $AC^2 = AD^2 + DC^2$

Note: Figures that accompany problems in this test are intended to provide information useful in solving the problems. They are drawn as accurately as possible EXCEPT when it is stated in a specific problem that its figure is not drawn to scale. All figures lie in a plane unless otherwise indicated. All numbers used are real numbers.

---

1. $(5 \times 0.5) + 0.5 =$

    (A) 1.5
    (B) 3.0
    (C) 5.0
    (D) 5.5
    (E) 6.0

Row 1 ⟶ • • •
     • • • •
     • • • • •

2. If the pattern of dots shown above is continued so that each row after row 1 contains 1 dot more than the row immediately above it, how many dots will row 8 contain?

    (A) Seven
    (B) Eight
    (C) Nine
    (D) Ten
    (E) Twelve

3. A store offers to reupholster old sofas at a price of $200 per sofa plus $50 extra for every loose cushion. If every sofa to be reupholstered has at least one loose cushion, what is the maximum number of sofas, including loose cushions, that can be reupholstered for $1,150 ?

    (A) 6
    (B) 5
    (C) 4
    (D) 3
    (E) 2

4. In his closet Lewis has 12 garments, all of which are shirts or trousers. If 75 percent of the garments are shirts, how many of the garments are trousers?

    (A) Three
    (B) Four
    (C) Five
    (D) Nine
    (E) Ten

5. When 6 is added to some number n and this sum is divided by 6, the result is a whole number. Which of the following could be n ?

    (A) 33,333
    (B) 44,444
    (C) 55,555
    (D) 66,666
    (E) 77,777

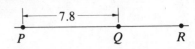

6. In the figure above, if the average (arithmetic mean) of the lengths of segments PQ and QR is 6.5, what is the length of QR ?

    (A) 3.9
    (B) 4.2
    (C) 4.7
    (D) 5.2
    (E) 5.9

GO ON TO THE NEXT PAGE ⟹

7. Two integers have a sum of 53 and a difference of 11. The greater of the two integers is

(A) 22
(B) 25
(C) 28
(D) 31
(E) 32

8. On a certain day the temperature rose 8° between 6 a.m. and 10 a.m., and it rose 7° between 10 a.m. and 2 p.m. It fell 6° between 2 p.m. and 6 p.m. If the temperature at 6 p.m. was 5°, what was the temperature at 6 a.m. that day?

(A) −16°
(B) −4°
(C) 10°
(D) 14°
(E) 26°

9. Alex estimates that if he lies in the sun for k hours it will take him $(10 + 10k)$ minutes to get to sleep at night because of sunburn pain. If Alex wants to get as much sun as possible without taking more than a half-hour to get to sleep, how many <u>hours</u> can he lie in the sun?

(A) $\frac{1}{2}$

(B) 1

(C) 2

(D) $2\frac{1}{2}$

(E) 3

10. If the sum of p and r is 18 and if $s = 12$, what is the average (arithmetic mean) of p, r, and s?

(A) 6
(B) 9
(C) 10
(D) 15
(E) 30

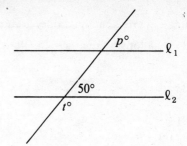

11. In the figure above, if $\ell_1 \parallel \ell_2$, what is the value of $p + t$?

(A) 180
(B) 150
(C) 130
(D) 100
(E) It cannot be determined from the information given.

12. A square piece of paper measuring 5 inches on a side is cut along one of its diagonals. Of the following, what is the closest approximation, in inches, to the perimeter of one of the resulting paper triangles?

(A) 15
(B) 17
(C) 20
(D) 27
(E) 30

$$S = 1 - \frac{1}{3} + \frac{1}{5} - \frac{1}{7} + \frac{1}{9} - \frac{1}{11}$$
$$T = 1 - \frac{1}{3} + \frac{1}{5} - \frac{1}{7}$$

13. For the expressions above, S is how much greater than T?

(A) $\frac{2}{99}$

(B) $\frac{1}{11}$

(C) $\frac{1}{10}$

(D) $\frac{1}{7}$

(E) $\frac{1}{2}$

GO ON TO THE NEXT PAGE

14. How many quarts of a liquid does it take to make $84\frac{1}{2}$ gallons? (4 quarts = 1 gallon)

(A) $21\frac{1}{8}$

(B) $21\frac{1}{2}$

(C) 336

(D) $336\frac{1}{2}$

(E) 338

15. If x, y, and z are different integers and $x + y + z = 3$, what is the <u>least</u> possible value of z ?

(A) -3
(B) 1
(C) 2
(D) 3
(E) It cannot be determined from the information given.

16. In a circle graph showing world production of aluminum, what is the measure of the central angle of the sector representing a country that produces $\frac{4}{15}$ of the total world production of aluminum?

(A) 26°
(B) 60°
(C) 85°
(D) 92°
(E) 96°

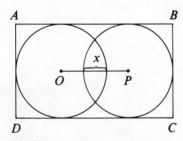

17. In the figure above, the circles with centers O and P each have a radius of 2. If $x = 1$, then the perimeter of rectangle $ABCD$ is

(A) 10
(B) 18
(C) 20
264 (D) 22
(E) 24

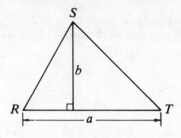

Note: Figure not drawn to scale.

18. If the area of triangle RST above is 46, which of the following values can be determined?

(A) a

(B) b

(C) ab

(D) $a + b$

(E) $\frac{a}{b}$

19. If the sum of the positive integers x and y is 12, then x can be equal to all of the following EXCEPT

(A) $5y$
(B) $4y$
(C) $3y$
(D) $2y$
(E) y

20. If segments are drawn to join points $A(-1, 0)$, $B(5, 0)$, and $C(2, -4)$, which of the following statements is true?

(A) $AC < BC$
(B) $AC > BC$
(C) $AB = BC$
(D) $AC = BC$
(E) $AC = AB$

GO ON TO THE NEXT PAGE

21. If a rectangle has area 72, width w, and perimeter p and if $w = \frac{p}{6}$, then $w =$

   (A)   4
   (B)   6
   (C)   8
   (D)   9
   (E)   12

22. If $p = \frac{a}{a+b}$, then $1 - p =$

   (A) $\frac{b}{a+b}$

   (B) $\frac{1-a}{a+b}$

   (C) $\frac{1-a}{1-(a+b)}$

   (D) $-a$

   (E)   0

$$\begin{array}{r} A\,1\,5 \\ \times\, B\,5 \\ \hline \end{array}$$

23. In the multiplication problem above, A and B are two different digits. In terms of A and B, which of the following is the product?

   (A) $100AB + 10B + 25$
   (B) $100AB + 50B + 25$
   (C) $100AB + 500A + 150B + 75$
   (D) $1,000AB + 10B + 75$
   (E) $1,000AB + 500A + 150B + 75$

24. The two legs of a right triangle are a and $a - d$, and the hypotenuse is $a + d$. In terms of a, what is the value of d?

   (A) $\frac{1}{4}a$

   (B) $\frac{1}{3}a$

   (C) $\frac{1}{2}a$

   (D) $\frac{2}{3}a$

   (E) $\frac{3}{4}a$

25. At the end of each week, the price of a garment was reduced by 25 percent of its price during that week. If p was the price of the garment at the beginning of the first week, then, in terms of p, what was the price of the garment at the beginning of the 5th week?

   (A) $\frac{p}{256}$

   (B) $\frac{3p}{256}$

   (C) $\frac{9p}{256}$

   (D) $\frac{27p}{256}$

   (E) $\frac{81p}{256}$

IF YOU FINISH BEFORE TIME IS CALLED, YOU MAY CHECK YOUR WORK ON THIS SECTION ONLY. DO NOT TURN TO ANY OTHER SECTION IN THE TEST.   **STOP**

Correct Answers for Scholastic Aptitude Test
Form Code 6E

VERBAL		MATHEMATICAL	
Section 1	Section 3	Section 4	Section 2
1. B	1. B	1. B	1. B
2. A	2. B	2. D	2. B
3. B	3. A	3. C	3. D
4. B	4. B	4. A	4. A
5. E	5. C	5. D	5. D
6. C	6. D	6. D	6. C
7. E	7. B	7. E	7. E
8. E	8. D	8. B	*8. C
9. D	9. A	9. C	*9. B
10. E	10. C	10. C	*10. D
11. B	11. C	11. A	*11. C
12. D	12. E	12. B	*12. A
13. D	13. B	13. A	*13. A
14. A	14. A	14. E	*14. C
15. C	15. E	15. E	*15. A
16. D	16. B	16. E	*16. C
17. D	17. C	17. D	*17. C
18. C	18. D	18. C	*18. D
19. D	19. C	19. B	*19. A
20. D	20. D	20. D	*20. D
21. E	21. B	21. B	*21. D
22. B	22. B	22. A	*22. B
23. B	23. D	23. E	*23. A
24. A	24. A	24. A	*24. B
25. B	25. B	25. E	*25. A
26. C	26. A		*26. C
27. A	27. C		*27. D
28. B	28. D		28. B
29. E	29. E		29. A
30. B	30. D		30. D
31. E	31. B		31. A
32. D	32. D		32. B
33. B	33. A		33. D
34. C	34. C		34. E
35. A	35. E		35. E
36. C	36. D		
37. E	37. E		
38. C	38. E		
39. D	39. A		
40. C	40. C		
	41. B		
	42. C		
	43. E		
	44. A		
	45. C		

*Indicates four-choice questions. (All of the other questions are five-choice.)

The Scoring Process

Machine-scoring is done in three steps:

- *Scanning.* Your answer sheet is "read" by a scanning machine and the oval you filled in for each question is recorded on a computer tape.

- *Scoring.* The computer compares the oval filled in for each question with the correct response. Each correct answer receives one point; omitted questions do not count toward your score. For each wrong answer, a fraction of a point is subtracted to correct for random guessing. For questions with five answer choices, one-fourth of a point is subtracted for each wrong response; for questions with four answer choices, one-third of a point is subtracted for each wrong response. The SAT-verbal test has 85 questions with five answer choices each. If, for example, a student has 44 right, 32 wrong, and 9 omitted, the resulting raw score is determined as follows:

$$44 \text{ right} - \frac{32 \text{ wrong}}{4} = 44 - 8 = 36 \text{ raw score points}$$

Obtaining raw scores frequently involves the rounding of fractional numbers to the nearest whole number. For example, a raw score of 36.25 is rounded to 36, the nearest whole number. A raw score of 36.50 is rounded upward to 37.

- *Converting to reported scaled score.* Raw test scores are then placed on the College Board scale of 200 to 800 through a process that adjusts scores to account for minor differences in difficulty among different editions of the test. This process, known as equating, is performed so that a student's reported score is not affected by the edition of the test taken nor by the abilities of the group with whom the student takes the test. As a result of placing SAT scores on the College Board scale, scores earned by students at different times can be compared. For example, an SAT-verbal score of 400 on a test taken at one administration indicates the same level of developed verbal ability as a 400 score obtained on a different edition of the test taken at another time.

How to Score the Test

SAT-Verbal Sections 1 and 3

Step A: Count the number of correct answers for *section 1* and record the number in the space provided on the worksheet on the next page. Then do the same for the incorrect answers. (Do not count omitted answers.) To determine subtotal A, use the formula:

$$\text{number correct} - \frac{\text{number incorrect}}{4} = \text{subtotal A}$$

Step B: Count the number of correct answers and the number of incorrect answers for *section 3* and record the numbers in the spaces provided on the worksheet. To determine subtotal B, use the formula:

$$\text{number correct} - \frac{\text{number incorrect}}{4} = \text{subtotal B}$$

Step C: To obtain C, add subtotal A to subtotal B, keeping any decimals. Enter the resulting figure on the worksheet.

Step D: To obtain D, your raw verbal score, round C to the nearest whole number. (For example, any number from 44.50 to 45.49 rounds to 45.) Enter the resulting figure on the worksheet.

Step E: To find your reported SAT-verbal score, look up the total raw verbal score you obtained in step D in the conversion table on page 270. Enter this figure on the worksheet.

SAT-Mathematical Sections 4 and 2

Step A: Count the number of correct answers and the number of incorrect answers for *section 4* and record the numbers in the spaces provided on the worksheet. To determine the subtotal A, use the formula:

$$\text{number correct} - \frac{\text{number incorrect}}{4} = \text{subtotal A}$$

Step B: Count the number of correct answers and the number of incorrect answers for the *five-choice questions (questions 1 through 7 and 28 through 35)* in section 2 and record the numbers in the spaces provided on the worksheet. To determine the subtotal B, use the formula:

$$\text{number correct} - \frac{\text{number incorrect}}{4} = \text{subtotal B}$$

Step C: Count the number of correct answers and the number of incorrect answers for the *four-choice questions (questions 8 through 27)* in section 2 and record the numbers in the spaces provided on the worksheet. To determine the subtotal C, use the formula:

$$\text{number correct} - \frac{\text{number incorrect}}{3} = \text{subtotal C}$$

Step D: To obtain D, add subtotal A, subtotal B, and subtotal C, keeping any decimals. Enter the resulting figure on the worksheet.

Step E: To obtain E, your raw mathematical score, round D to the nearest whole number. (For example, any number from 44.50 to 45.49 rounds to 45.) Enter the resulting figure on the worksheet.

Step F: To find your reported SAT-mathematical score, look up the total raw mathematical score you obtained in E in the conversion table on page 270. Enter this figure on the worksheet.

SAT SCORING WORKSHEET

SAT-Verbal Sections

A. Section 1: _____ − ¼ (_____) = _____
   no. correct   no. incorrect   subtotal A

B. Section 3: _____ − ¼ (_____) = _____
   no. correct   no. incorrect   subtotal B

C. Total unrounded raw score
   (Total A + B)   _____
                                                          C

D. Total rounded raw score
   (Rounded to nearest whole number)   _____
                                                          D

E. SAT-verbal reported scaled score
   (See the conversion table on page 270.)   _____

                                                     SAT-verbal
                                                       score

SAT-Mathematical Sections

A. Section 4: _____ − ¼ (_____) = _____
   no. correct   no. incorrect   subtotal A

B. Section 2:
   Questions 1 through 7 and   _____ − ¼ (_____) = _____
   28 through 35 (5-choice)   no. correct   no. incorrect   subtotal B

C. Section 2:
   Questions 8 through 27   _____ − ⅓ (_____) = _____
   (4-choice)   no. correct   no. incorrect   subtotal C

D. Total unrounded raw score
   (Total A + B + C)   _____
                                                          D

E. Total rounded raw score
   (Rounded to nearest whole number)   _____
                                                          E

F. SAT-mathematical reported scaled score
   (See the conversion table on page 270.)   _____

                                                     SAT-math
                                                       score

Score Conversion Table
Scholastic Aptitude Test
Form Code 6E

Raw Score	College Board Reported Score SAT-Verbal	College Board Reported Score SAT-Math	Raw Score	College Board Reported Score SAT-Verbal	College Board Reported Score SAT-Math
85	800		40	440	590
84	780		39	440	590
83	760		38	430	580
82	750		37	420	570
81	740		36	420	560
80	730		35	410	550
79	720		34	400	540
78	710		33	400	530
77	700		32	390	520
76	690		31	390	520
75	680		30	380	510
74	680		29	370	500
73	670		28	370	490
72	660		27	360	480
71	650		26	350	470
70	640		25	350	460
69	630		24	340	450
68	630		23	330	440
67	620		22	330	430
66	610		21	320	430
65	600		20	310	420
64	600		19	310	410
63	590		18	300	400
62	580		17	300	390
61	570		16	290	380
60	570	800	15	280	370
59	560	780	14	280	370
58	550	760	13	270	360
57	550	750	12	260	350
56	540	740	11	260	340
55	530	730	10	250	330
54	530	720	9	240	330
53	520	710	8	240	320
52	510	700	7	230	310
51	510	690	6	230	300
50	500	680	5	220	300
49	500	670	4	210	290
48	490	660	3	210	280
47	480	650	2	200	270
46	480	650	1	200	270
45	470	640	0	200	260
44	470	630	−1	200	250
43	460	620	−2	200	240
42	450	610	−3	200	230
41	450	600	−4	200	230
			−5	200	220
			−6	200	210
			−7 or below	200	200

COLLEGE BOARD — SCHOLASTIC APTITUDE TEST
and Test of Standard Written English Side 1

Use a No. 2 pencil only. Be sure each mark is dark and completely fills the intended oval. Completely erase any errors or stray marks.

1.

YOUR NAME: _____
(Print) Last   First   M.I.

SIGNATURE: _____ DATE: ___/___/___

HOME ADDRESS: _____
(Print) Number and Street

_____
City   State   Zip Code

CENTER: _____
(Print) City   State   Center Number

IMPORTANT: Please fill in these boxes exactly as shown on the back cover of your test book.

FOR ETS USE ONLY

5. YOUR NAME

First 4 letters of last name | First Init | Mid Init

A B C D E F G H I J K L M N O P Q R S T U V W X Y Z

2. TEST FORM
_____

3. FORM CODE

0 A J S
1 B K T
2 C L U
3 D M V
4 E N W
5 F O X
6 G P Y
7 H Q Z
8 I R
9

4. REGISTRATION NUMBER
(Copy from your Admission Ticket.)

0 1 2 3 4 5 6 7 8 9

6. DATE OF BIRTH

Month	Day	Year
Jan.		
Feb.		
Mar.	0 0 0 0	
Apr.	1 1 1 1	
May	2 2 2 2	
June	3 3 3 3	
July	4 4 4	
Aug.	5 5 5	
Sept.	6 6 6	
Oct.	7 7 7	
Nov.	8 8	
Dec.	9 9	

7. SEX
○ Female
○ Male

8. TEST BOOK SERIAL NUMBER
_____

Start with number 1 for each new section. If a section has fewer than 50 questions, leave the extra answer spaces blank.

SECTION 1

1 A B C D E   26 A B C D E
2 A B C D E   27 A B C D E
3 A B C D E   28 A B C D E
4 A B C D E   29 A B C D E
5 A B C D E   30 A B C D E
6 A B C D E   31 A B C D E
7 A B C D E   32 A B C D E
8 A B C D E   33 A B C D E
9 A B C D E   34 A B C D E
10 A B C D E   35 A B C D E
11 A B C D E   36 A B C D E
12 A B C D E   37 A B C D E
13 A B C D E   38 A B C D E
14 A B C D E   39 A B C D E
15 A B C D E   40 A B C D E
16 A B C D E   41 A B C D E
17 A B C D E   42 A B C D E
18 A B C D E   43 A B C D E
19 A B C D E   44 A B C D E
20 A B C D E   45 A B C D E
21 A B C D E   46 A B C D E
22 A B C D E   47 A B C D E
23 A B C D E   48 A B C D E
24 A B C D E   49 A B C D E
25 A B C D E   50 A B C D E

SECTION 2

1 A B C D E   26 A B C D E
2 A B C D E   27 A B C D E
3 A B C D E   28 A B C D E
4 A B C D E   29 A B C D E
5 A B C D E   30 A B C D E
6 A B C D E   31 A B C D E
7 A B C D E   32 A B C D E
8 A B C D E   33 A B C D E
9 A B C D E   34 A B C D E
10 A B C D E   35 A B C D E
11 A B C D E   36 A B C D E
12 A B C D E   37 A B C D E
13 A B C D E   38 A B C D E
14 A B C D E   39 A B C D E
15 A B C D E   40 A B C D E
16 A B C D E   41 A B C D E
17 A B C D E   42 A B C D E
18 A B C D E   43 A B C D E
19 A B C D E   44 A B C D E
20 A B C D E   45 A B C D E
21 A B C D E   46 A B C D E
22 A B C D E   47 A B C D E
23 A B C D E   48 A B C D E
24 A B C D E   49 A B C D E
25 A B C D E   50 A B C D E

(Cut here to detach.)

Q1362-04

I.N. 574006—110VV25P3015

COLLEGE BOARD — SCHOLASTIC APTITUDE TEST
and Test of Standard Written English Side 2

Use a No. 2 pencil only. Be sure each mark is dark and completely fills the intended oval. Completely erase any errors or stray marks.

Start with number 1 for each new section. If a section has fewer than 50 questions, leave the extra answer spaces blank.

SECTION 3	SECTION 4	SECTION 5	SECTION 6

SECTION 5

1 (A) (B) (C) (D) (E)
2 (A) (B) (C) (D) (E)
3 (A) (B) (C) (D) (E)
4 (A) (B) (C) (D) (E)
5 (A) (B) (C) (D) (E)
6 (A) (B) (C) (D) (E)
7 (A) (B) (C) (D) (E)
8 (A) (B) (C) (D) (E)
9 (A) (B) (C) (D) (E)
10 (A) (B) (C) (D) (E)
11 (A) (B) (C) (D) (E)
12 (A) (B) (C) (D) (E)
13 (A) (B) (C) (D) (E)
14 (A) (B) (C) (D) (E)
15 (A) (B) (C) (D) (E)
16 (A) (B) (C) (D) (E)
17 (A) (B) (C) (D) (E)
18 (A) (B) (C) (D) (E)
19 (A) (B) (C) (D) (E)
20 (A) (B) (C) (D) (E)
21 (A) (B) (C) (D) (E)
22 (A) (B) (C) (D) (E)
23 (A) (B) (C) (D) (E)
24 (A) (B) (C) (D) (E)
25 (A) (B) (C) (D) (E)
26 (A) (B) (C) (D) (E)
27 (A) (B) (C) (D) (E)
28 (A) (B) (C) (D) (E)
29 (A) (B) (C) (D) (E)
30 (A) (B) (C) (D) (E)
31 (A) (B) (C) (D) (E)
32 (A) (B) (C) (D) (E)
33 (A) (B) (C) (D) (E)
34 (A) (B) (C) (D) (E)
35 (A) (B) (C) (D) (E)
36 (A) (B) (C) (D) (E)
37 (A) (B) (C) (D) (E)
38 (A) (B) (C) (D) (E)
39 (A) (B) (C) (D) (E)
40 (A) (B) (C) (D) (E)
41 (A) (B) (C) (D) (E)
42 (A) (B) (C) (D) (E)
43 (A) (B) (C) (D) (E)
44 (A) (B) (C) (D) (E)
45 (A) (B) (C) (D) (E)
46 (A) (B) (C) (D) (E)
47 (A) (B) (C) (D) (E)
48 (A) (B) (C) (D) (E)
49 (A) (B) (C) (D) (E)
50 (A) (B) (C) (D) (E)

SECTION 6

1 (A) (B) (C) (D) (E)
2 (A) (B) (C) (D) (E)
3 (A) (B) (C) (D) (E)
4 (A) (B) (C) (D) (E)
5 (A) (B) (C) (D) (E)
6 (A) (B) (C) (D) (E)
7 (A) (B) (C) (D) (E)
8 (A) (B) (C) (D) (E)
9 (A) (B) (C) (D) (E)
10 (A) (B) (C) (D) (E)
11 (A) (B) (C) (D) (E)
12 (A) (B) (C) (D) (E)
13 (A) (B) (C) (D) (E)
14 (A) (B) (C) (D) (E)
15 (A) (B) (C) (D) (E)
16 (A) (B) (C) (D) (E)
17 (A) (B) (C) (D) (E)
18 (A) (B) (C) (D) (E)
19 (A) (B) (C) (D) (E)
20 (A) (B) (C) (D) (E)
21 (A) (B) (C) (D) (E)
22 (A) (B) (C) (D) (E)
23 (A) (B) (C) (D) (E)
24 (A) (B) (C) (D) (E)
25 (A) (B) (C) (D) (E)
26 (A) (B) (C) (D) (E)
27 (A) (B) (C) (D) (E)
28 (A) (B) (C) (D) (E)
29 (A) (B) (C) (D) (E)
30 (A) (B) (C) (D) (E)
31 (A) (B) (C) (D) (E)
32 (A) (B) (C) (D) (E)
33 (A) (B) (C) (D) (E)
34 (A) (B) (C) (D) (E)
35 (A) (B) (C) (D) (E)
36 (A) (B) (C) (D) (E)
37 (A) (B) (C) (D) (E)
38 (A) (B) (C) (D) (E)
39 (A) (B) (C) (D) (E)
40 (A) (B) (C) (D) (E)
41 (A) (B) (C) (D) (E)
42 (A) (B) (C) (D) (E)
43 (A) (B) (C) (D) (E)
44 (A) (B) (C) (D) (E)
45 (A) (B) (C) (D) (E)
46 (A) (B) (C) (D) (E)
47 (A) (B) (C) (D) (E)
48 (A) (B) (C) (D) (E)
49 (A) (B) (C) (D) (E)
50 (A) (B) (C) (D) (E)

9. SIGNATURE:

FOR ETS USE ONLY	VTR	VTFS	VRR	VRFS	VVR	VVFS	WER	WEFS	M4R	M4FS	M5R	M5FS	MTFS	
	VTW	VTCS	VRW	VRCS	VVW	VVCS	WEW	WECS	M4W		M5W		MTCS	

TEST 10—FORM CODE 6G

SECTION **1**   Time—30 minutes   In this section solve each problem, using any available space on the
                35 Questions   page for scratchwork. Then decide which is the best of the choices
                                   given and fill in the corresponding oval on the answer sheet.

The following information is for your reference in solving some of the problems.

Circle of radius r: Area = πr^2; Circumference = $2\pi r$
   The number of degrees of arc in a circle is 360.
The measure in degrees of a straight angle is 180.

Definition of symbols:
= is equal to $\leq$ is less than or equal to
$\neq$ is unequal to $\geq$ is greater than or equal to
< is less than $\parallel$ is parallel to
> is greater than $\perp$ is perpendicular to

Triangle: The sum of the measures in
   degrees of the angles of a
   triangle is 180.
If $\angle CDA$ is a right angle, then

(1) area of $\triangle ABC = \dfrac{AB \times CD}{2}$

(2) $AC^2 = AD^2 + DC^2$

Note: Figures that accompany problems in this test are intended to provide information useful in solving the problems.
They are drawn as accurately as possible EXCEPT when it is stated in a specific problem that its figure is not drawn
to scale. All figures lie in a plane unless otherwise indicated. All numbers used are real numbers.

---

1. Bob makes 720 telephone calls each year. What
   is the average (arithmetic mean) number of calls
   that Bob makes per month?

   (A) 60
   (B) 70
   (C) 80
   (D) 100
   (E) 120

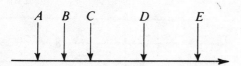

2. On the number line above, if the numbers 3, −1,
   5, 0, and 1 are indicated by the arrows, which
   arrow indicates 0 ?

   (A) A (B) B (C) C (D) D (E) E

---

3. If $3 + x = 2x + 1$, then $x =$

   (A) $\dfrac{2}{3}$

   (B) 1

   (C) $\dfrac{4}{3}$

   (D) 2

   (E) 4

---

4. $\sqrt{25 \times 64} =$

   (A) 1,600   (B) 400   (C) 80
   (D) 40   (E) 13

---

5. A beach umbrella was rented each day for one
   week at the rate of $8 per day on days that were
   sunny and $3 per day on days that were not
   sunny. If the total rental charge for that week
   was $46, what was the number of sunny days in
   that week?

   (A) 6
   (B) 5
   (C) 4
   (D) 3
   (E) 2

---

6. If $\dfrac{N \times N}{N + N} = 1$, then $N =$

   (A) $\dfrac{1}{4}$ (B) $\dfrac{1}{2}$ (C) 1   (D) 2   (E) 4

---

7. A square and an equilateral triangle have sides
   of lengths x and y, respectively. The sum of
   their perimeters can be represented by

   (A) $x + y$ (B) $3x + 4y$ (C) $4x + 3y$
   (D) $7(x + y)$ (E) $x^2 + y^2$

GO ON TO THE NEXT PAGE

Questions 8-27 each consist of two quantities, one in Column A and one in Column B. You are to compare the two quantities and on the answer sheet fill in oval

A if the quantity in Column A is greater;
B if the quantity in Column B is greater;
C if the two quantities are equal;
D if the relationship cannot be determined from the information given.

AN E RESPONSE WILL NOT BE SCORED.

EXAMPLES

	Column A	Column B	Answers
E1.	2×6	$2 + 6$	● Ⓑ Ⓒ Ⓓ Ⓔ

E2.	$180 - x$	y	Ⓐ Ⓑ ● Ⓓ Ⓔ
E3.	$p - q$	$q - p$	Ⓐ Ⓑ Ⓒ ● Ⓔ

Notes:

1. In certain questions, information concerning one or both of the quantities to be compared is centered above the two columns.
2. In a given question, a symbol that appears in both columns represents the same thing in Column A as it does in Column B.
3. Letters such as x, n, and k stand for real numbers.

	Column A	Column B
8.	The least positive integer divisible by 2, 3, and 4	24

$n > 0$

	Column A	Column B
9.	40% of n	20% of $2n$

Parallel lines ℓ_1 and ℓ_2 are 2 inches apart. P is a point on ℓ_1 and Q is a point on ℓ_2.

10.	Length of PQ	3 inches

11.	The sum of 3 consecutive integers if the middle integer is 8	The sum of 4 consecutive integers if the least integer is 5

$x = 3$

12.	$(4x)^5$	$4x^5$

$k + k + k + k = 8$
$3(m + 2m) = 18$

13.	k	m

$x + y + z = 6$

	Column A	Column B
14.	$2x + 2y + 2z$	14

$x < y$

15.	$3x$	$2y$

Point R (not shown) is between P and T on line segment PT. The length of RT is 9.

16.	Length of RM	2

x and y are different even integers greater than 2.

17.	The number of odd integers between x and y	The number of prime numbers between x and y

$$\frac{2}{3} = \frac{4}{x} = \frac{8}{y}$$

18.	$x + y$	18

GO ON TO THE NEXT PAGE

274

	Column A	Column B

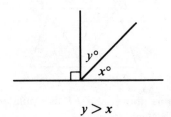

$$y > x$$

| 19. | x | 45 |

| 20. | $\dfrac{1}{2-\frac{1}{2}}$ | $\dfrac{1}{2-\frac{1}{2-\frac{1}{2}}}$ |

The three angles of a triangle are $x°$, $x°$, and $\dfrac{x°}{2}$.

| 21. | x | 60 |

$$x = y \neq 0$$

| 22. | xy | 0 |

<u>Questions 23-25</u> refer to the following definition of

$\widehat{a,\ b,\ c}$ for all real numbers a, b, and c.

$$\widehat{a,\ b,\ c} = (a-b)(b-c)$$

| 23. | $\widehat{1,\ 1,\ x}$ | $\widehat{2,\ 2,\ x}$ |

| 24. | $\widehat{0,\ 1,\ x}$ | $\widehat{1,\ 0,\ x}$ |

| 25. | $\widehat{x,\ 2,\ 1}$ | $x - 3$ |

	Column A	Column B
26.	$2^{10} - 2^9$	2^9

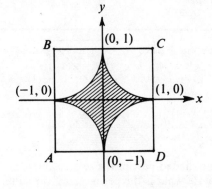

Quadrilateral $ABCD$ is a square with sides parallel to the axes. The shaded region is bounded by arcs of circles with radii 1 and centers A, B, C, and D.

| 27. | The area of the shaded region | 1 |

GO ON TO THE NEXT PAGE

Solve each of the remaining problems in this section using any available space for scratchwork. Then decide which is the best of the choices given and fill in the corresponding oval on the answer sheet.

28. Suppose that angles of geometric figures were measured in "bleeps" instead of in degrees. If the sum of the measures of the angles of a triangle were 12 bleeps, what would be the sum of the measures of the angles of a rectangle, in bleeps?

(A) 6
(B) 12
(C) 16
(D) 24
(E) 36

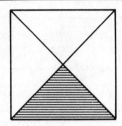

29. If the shaded part of the square above has area 16, what is the perimeter of the square?

(A) 4 (B) 8 (C) 16 (D) 32 (E) 64

30. On a number line, if point A has coordinate $3\frac{1}{2}$ and point B has coordinate $-1\frac{1}{2}$, what is the coordinate of the point equidistant from A and B?

(A) $\frac{1}{2}$ (B) $\frac{3}{4}$ (C) 1 (D) $1\frac{1}{2}$ (E) 2

31. A total of $24.00 is to be divided among three children in amounts proportional to their ages. If the children's ages are 9, 12, and 15 years, how much money will the youngest child receive?

(A) $2.00 (B) $3.00 (C) $4.00
(D) $5.00 (E) $6.00

32. If the product of two positive integers r and s is 7,240, which of the following must be true?

    I. Both r and s are even numbers.
    II. Either r or s is a multiple of 10.
    III. Either r or s is a multiple of 5.

(A) None (B) I only (C) II only
(D) III only (E) I, II, and III

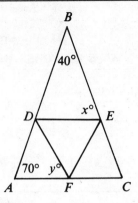

33. In the figure above, $\triangle DEF$ is equilateral. If $DE \parallel AC$, then $x - y =$

(A) 0 (B) 5 (C) 10 (D) 15 (E) 20

34. If x multiplied by $\frac{11}{2}$ gives the same result as x subtracted from $\frac{11}{2}$, what is the value of x?

(A) $\frac{11}{13}$ (B) 1 (C) $\frac{11}{9}$ (D) $\frac{11}{3}$ (E) $\frac{11}{2}$

35. If Sue is not on the Planning Committee, from which of the following statements can it be determined whether Sue is on the Rules Committee?

(A) Everyone on the Planning Committee is on the Rules Committee.
(B) Everyone on the Rules Committee is on the Planning Committee.
(C) Some people not on the Planning Committee are also not on the Rules Committee.
(D) Anyone not on the Rules Committee is not on the Planning Committee.
(E) No one is on both the Planning Committee and the Rules Committee.

IF YOU FINISH BEFORE TIME IS CALLED, YOU MAY CHECK YOUR WORK ON THIS SECTION ONLY. DO NOT TURN TO ANY OTHER SECTION IN THE TEST.   **STOP**

SECTION 2 Time—30 minutes 40 Questions

For each question in this section, choose the best answer and fill in the corresponding oval on the answer sheet.

Each question below consists of a word in capital letters, followed by five lettered words or phrases. Choose the word or phrase that is most nearly <u>opposite</u> in meaning to the word in capital letters. Since some of the questions require you to distinguish fine shades of meaning, consider all the choices before deciding which is best.

Example:

GOOD: (A) sour (B) bad (C) red
(D) hot (E) ugly

Ⓐ ● Ⓒ Ⓓ Ⓔ

1. FRISKY: (A) tiny (B) perfect (C) alone
(D) sluggish (E) flexible

2. PROPEL: (A) indent (B) expose
(C) dismount (D) hold back
(E) put together

3. SQUABBLE: (A) permit (B) agree
(C) avoid (D) add to (E) gloss over

4. KINDLE: (A) distribute (B) extinguish
(C) make poisonous (D) cause rigidity
(E) mix vigorously

5. AWESOME: (A) unfamiliar (B) uniform
(C) insignificant (D) inconvenient
(E) misleading

6. CONVERGE: (A) remain silent
(B) grow weaker (C) despair
(D) resume (E) separate

7. PLAUSIBLE: (A) symmetrical
(B) unbelievable (C) randomly chosen
(D) unclearly stated (E) extremely long

8. INSTIGATION: (A) inhibition
(B) insulation (C) intuition
(D) abstraction (E) jubilation

9. CONTENTIOUS:
(A) eager to please
(B) ready to leave
(C) anxious to intervene
(D) afraid of danger
(E) suspicious of flattery

10. DERISION: (A) conclusion (B) applause
(C) safety (D) gradual decline
(E) sudden return

Each sentence below has one or two blanks, each blank indicating that something has been omitted. Beneath the sentence are five lettered words or sets of words. Choose the word or set of words that, when inserted in the sentence, <u>best</u> fits the meaning of the sentence as a whole.

Example:

Although its publicity has been ----, the film itself is intelligent, well-acted, handsomely produced, and altogether ----.

(A) tasteless. .respectable (B) extensive. .moderate
(C) sophisticated. .amateur (D) risqué. .crude
(E) perfect. .spectacular

● Ⓑ Ⓒ Ⓓ Ⓔ

11. The ---- of trees in East Africa has caused the number of native antelopes to ---- sharply because they can live only where the forest is most dense.

(A) planting. .decline
(B) destruction. .grow
(C) felling. .decrease
(D) abundance. .dip
(E) protection. .drop

12. The speaker stated that progress in the civil rights movement would be ---- unless organizations move beyond ---- the problems of the times to developing strategies for solving them.

(A) comprehensive. .sustaining
(B) minimal. .defining
(C) painstaking. .rejuvenating
(D) trivial. .eradicating
(E) overwhelming. .analyzing

13. Even though the task of editing the series seems to become increasingly ---- with each volume, Donna feels compelled to ---- the project until others can take over the responsibility.

(A) creative. .enlarge
(B) inspiring. .publicize
(C) feasible. .malign
(D) monotonous. .relinquish
(E) demanding. .continue

GO ON TO THE NEXT PAGE ⇒

14. The committee's report was entirely ----; those who ---- it did so with the deliberate intent of damaging my reputation.

   (A) erroneous..expunged
   (B) legitimate..perused
   (C) infallible..endorsed
   (D) spontaneous..compiled
   (E) malicious..circulated

15. As a scientific work, the paper is flawed by the inclusion of many ---- details that are not sufficiently ---- to the overall thesis.

   (A) picayune..alien
   (B) verifiable..contradictory
   (C) ancillary..germane
   (D) integral..incidental
   (E) inconspicuous..detrimental

Each question below consists of a related pair of words or phrases, followed by five lettered pairs of words or phrases. Select the lettered pair that best expresses a relationship similar to that expressed in the original pair.

Example:

YAWN : BOREDOM ::   (A) dream : sleep
(B) anger : madness   (C) smile : amusement
   (D) face : expression   (E) impatience : rebellion

ⓐ ⓑ ● ⓓ ⓔ

---

16. VEAL:CALF ::   (A) egg:chicken
   (B) lamb:goat   (C) milk:cow
    (D) pork:pig   (E) duck:goose

17. RESTRAIN:IMMOBILIZE ::
   (A) hinder:prevent
   (B) forbid:defy
   (C) camouflage:substitute
   (D) excuse:resent
   (E) store:misplace

18. SOLDIER:INFANTRY ::
   (A) salesperson:convention
   (B) musician:rhythm
   (C) athlete:team
   (D) sprinter:marathon
   (E) violinist:solo

19. SENTINEL:PROTECTION ::
   (A) adversary:relief
   (B) arbitrator:domination
   (C) interpreter:translation
   (D) idler:reminiscence
   (E) nominee:election

20. SHARD:POTTERY ::   (A) tack:metal
   (B) chip:stone   (C) slab:meat
    (D) varnish:wood   (E) flask:water

21. DISCONTENTED:MOROSE ::
   (A) successful:vain
   (B) proud:arrogant
   (C) nonchalant:tense
   (D) helpful:useful
   (E) jovial:unpopular

22. UNPRECEDENTED:PREVIOUS OCCURRENCE ::
   (A) obvious:conformity
   (B) peerless:equal
   (C) untimely:irregularity
   (D) unique:exception
   (E) erratic:mobility

23. MOUNTAIN:RANGE ::   (A) lake:ocean
   (B) glacier:snow   (C) island:archipelago
    (D) sand:dune   (E) surf:beach

24. DULCET:HEARING ::
   (A) wishful:realizing   (B) savory:tasting
    (C) sincere:speaking   (D) sobbing:weeping
     (E) inquisitive:learning

25. HIDEBOUND:INFLEXIBILITY ::
   (A) suspicious:guilt
   (B) audacious:reserve
   (C) compassionate:sympathy
   (D) successful:admiration
   (E) extravagant:elegance

GO ON TO THE NEXT PAGE →

Each passage below is followed by questions based on its content. Answer the questions following each passage on the basis of what is <u>stated</u> or <u>implied</u> in that passage.

In most of the truest and most fully satisfying fiction written in the United States after the Second World War, the newborn or self-sustaining or orphaned hero is plunged again and again, for his or her own good and for ours, into the spurious, disruptive rituals of the actual world. We may mention especially *Invisible Man*, by Ralph Ellison; J. D. Salinger's *The Catcher in the Rye*; and *The Adventures of Augie March*, by Saul Bellow—novels in which the heroes are willing, with marvelously inadequate equipment, to take on as much of the world as is available to them, without ever fully submitting to any of the world's determining categories. Ellison's hero is a nameless Black, Salinger's an unstable adolescent, Bellow's a rebellious Chicago Jew. But they share in their common aloneness an odd aura of moral priority over the waiting world. Each of them struggles tirelessly, sometimes unwittingly, and often absurdly, to realize the full potentialities of the classic type each represents—the Emersonian "simple genuine self against the whole world." These characters are clearly indebted to the great innocents of nineteenth-century American fiction, but their creators are also able to engender from within their work the hopeful and vulnerable sense of life that makes experience and so makes narrative action possible. To test that sense of life by irony and drama they must create it from within, for they can scarcely find it any longer in the historic world about them.

26. This passage is primarily concerned with
   (A) defining the nature of the hero in certain contemporary fiction
   (B) criticizing the lack of originality in popular twentieth-century fiction
   (C) giving examples of the instability of modern society
   (D) prescribing the direction that fiction should take
   (E) satirizing the inadequate heroes of recent fiction

27. The author suggests that all of the characters discussed share the quality of being
   (A) sophisticated   (B) defeatist   (C) naïve
   (D) impulsive   (E) intellectual

28. The author's attitude toward the fictional characters mentioned seems to be
   (A) neutral   (B) contemptuous
   (C) despairing   (D) reverent   (E) admiring

GO ON TO THE NEXT PAGE ⇨

Both living and nonliving things interact with their environments across their surfaces. The nature of the surface greatly affects the kinds of interactions that
Line can occur. As a rule, a smooth surface has less func-
(5) tional surface area per square meter than a rough or wrinkled one, and a larger ratio of surface area to volume will permit more rapid interaction of materials. Finely granulated sugar, for instance, dissolves more rapidly in a cup of coffee than a lump of sugar
(10) does.

During the course of evolution, modification of surface area has been an important adaptation of organisms to the environment. The wall of the human small intestine, for example, is layered with microvilli
(15) that provide greater surface area for absorption of food. Similarly, in plant roots epidermal cells have extensions (root hairs) that increase a plant's ability to take in water and minerals from the soil.

Unlike the interchanges that occur at the surfaces
(20) of most nonliving substances (such as the sugar cube), exchanges of materials in living cells occur through cell membranes that are selectively permeable. Cell membranes regulate the movement of most substances in and out of the cell, allowing passage of
(25) some substances and blocking others.

Cell membranes, however, appear unable to regulate the movement of water. Over the millenia, organisms have evolved many strategies to conserve water. Cactus plants have adapted to their hot, dry
(30) environment by developing thickened leaves with relatively reduced surface area. In areas where the lack of water is not so severe, most plants have leaves with smaller volumes and larger surface areas. Broad-leaved plants such as beech and maple trees lose water
(35) rapidly through transpiration and thrive where moisture is abundant and temperatures are moderate.

29. This passage primarily discusses

(A) the difference between the surfaces of living things and the surfaces of nonliving things
(B) how the roughness of an object's surface affects its permeability
(C) in what manner various living things have adapted to their environment
(D) why cell membranes are unable to control the absorption and release of water
(E) how the surface area of living and nonliving things affects their interaction with their environment

30. In lines 13-18, the author mentions microvilli in human intestines and root hairs on plant roots as illustrations of adaptations that

(A) decrease the cells' dependence on water
(B) increase the absorptive ability of the organism
(C) retard the exchange of material between the cells and the environment
(D) maintain the flexibility of the cellular walls
(E) decrease the surface area of the cellular walls

31. According to information in the passage, "most substances" (lines 23-24) would include which of the following?

    I. Food
   II. Water
  III. Minerals

(A) II only   (B) III only   (C) I and II only
(D) I and III only   (E) I, II, and III

32. It can be inferred from the passage that the surface of which of the following is LEAST conducive to rapid interaction of materials?

(A) A prune   (B) A sponge
(C) A piece of cake   (D) A balloon
(E) A tree root

GO ON TO THE NEXT PAGE

Many years later, he was to remember that distant afternoon with his father, Arcadio. The world was so recent that many things lacked names, and in order to indicate them it was necessary to point. Every year during the month of March a family of gypsies would set up their tents near the village, and with a great uproar of pipes and kettledrums they would display new inventions. First they brought the magnet. A heavy man with an untamed beard and sparrow hands, who introduced himself as Melquiades, put on a bold public demonstration of what he himself called the eighth wonder of the learned alchemists of Macedonia. He went from house to house dragging two metal ingots and everybody was amazed to see pots, pans, tongs, and braziers tumble down from their places and beams creak from the desperation of nails and screws trying to emerge. Arcadio, whose unbridled imagination always went beyond the genius of nature and even beyond miracles and magic, thought that it would be possible to make use of that useless invention to extract gold from the bowels of the earth. Melquiades, who was an honest man, warned him: "It won't work for that." But Arcadio at that time did not believe in the honesty of Melquiades, so he traded his mule and a pair of goats for the two magnetized ingots. He explored every inch of the region, even the riverbed, dragging the two iron ingots along and reciting Melquiades' incantation aloud. The only thing he succeeded in doing was unearthing a rusted suit of fifteenth-century armor.

33. The passage focuses primarily on

    (A) a man's desire to relive the past
    (B) a childhood incident as it is later recalled
    (C) an account of a day in the life of a traveler
    (D) an invention and its impact on a rural village
    (E) the poverty of a man's childhood environment

34. It can be inferred that the speaker refers to things lacking names (line 3) in order to suggest the

    (A) whimsical quality of the relationship between the speaker and his father
    (B) importance of technological advances in remote areas of the world
    (C) overwhelming interest in the gypsies' visit
    (D) recency of the establishment of the village
    (E) freshness of childhood perceptions

35. Which of the following best expresses Arcadio's reaction to the metal ingots?

    (A) He was frightened by their magical power.
    (B) He suspected all along that they were inherently worthless.
    (C) He resented the way they were used to exploit the villagers.
    (D) He remained aloof from all the commotion they caused.
    (E) He was determined to find a profitable application for them.

The study of ethics is perhaps most commonly conceived as being concerned with the questions, "What sort of actions ought people to perform?"
Line and "What sort of actions ought they to avoid?"
(5) As a result, the study of ethics is usually regarded as the practical study, to which all others may be opposed as theoretical; the good and the true are spoken of as independent kingdoms, the former belonging to ethics, the latter to science.
(10)   This view, however, is doubly defective. In the first place, it overlooks the fact that the object of ethics is to discover true propositions about virtuous and vicious conduct and that these are just as much a part of truth as true propositions about oxygen or the
(15) multiplication table. The aim is not practice, but propositions about practice; and propositions about practice are not themselves practical, any more than propositions about gases are gaseous. One might as well maintain that botany is vegetable or zoology
(20) animal. Thus the study of ethics is not something outside science and coordinate with it: it is one among sciences.
    In the second place, the view in question unduly limits the province of ethics. When we are told that
(25) actions of certain kinds ought to be performed or avoided, as for example that we ought to speak the truth, we may always legitimately ask for a reason, and this reason will be concerned not only with the actions themselves, but also with the goodness or
(30) badness of the consequences likely to follow from such actions. We shall be told that truth-speaking generates mutual confidence and facilitates the dispatch of business, and hence increases the wealth of the society that practices it. If we ask why we should
(35) aim at increasing mutual confidence or increasing the wealth of society, we may be told that obviously these things are good or that they lead to happiness and happiness is good. If we still ask why, the ordinary person will probably feel irritation and will reply that

GO ON TO THE NEXT PAGE

(40) no one knows.

However, it is the business of the student of ethics to ask for reasons as long as reasons can legitimately be demanded and to register the propositions which give the most ultimate reasons that are attainable.

(45) Since a proposition can be proven only by means of other propositions, it is obvious that not all propositions can be proven, for proofs can begin only by assuming something. The first step in ethics, therefore, is to be quite clear as to what we assume when we

(50) conceive of "good" and "bad." Only then can we begin to formulate propositions about conduct and ask how right conduct is related to the production of good and the avoidance of evil.

36. In the passage, the author is primarily concerned with

   (A) proving that ethics is a practical study
   (B) disputing the claim that ethics is a scientific discipline
   (C) challenging common notions about the province of ethics
   (D) proving the basic assumptions of ethics
   (E) defining what is meant by good and evil

37. The author most probably includes the questions in lines 3-4 in order to do which of the following?

   (A) Emphasize the narrowness of ethical concerns
   (B) Provide an example of a practical and a theoretical issue
   (C) Allude to recent changes in the study of ethics
   (D) Emphasize the conflicting objectives of ethics
   (E) Illustrate what ethics is usually thought to encompass

38. The "view in question" (line 23) refers to the view that

   (A) propositions about actions should be evaluated in terms of the goodness or badness of their consequences
   (B) propositions about actions are based on unproven assumptions
   (C) ethics deals exclusively with the good and science exclusively with the true
   (D) ethics deals with the discovery of true propositions about actions
   (E) ethics is not independent of science but merely one of its disciplines

39. According to the author, some propositions cannot be proven because

   (A) the number of possible true propositions is unlimited
   (B) propositions about conduct require knowledge of human motives
   (C) the ultimate consequences of a proposition cannot always be foreseen
   (D) the truth of propositions can be determined only through other propositions
   (E) the goodness or badness of some propositions is self-evident

40. The author most probably refers to the increase in wealth promoted by the practice of truth-speaking (lines 31-34) in order to

   (A) prove that good actions are those that benefit a large group of people
   (B) suggest that the process of evaluating the consequences of an action can never end
   (C) imply that actions that appear to be good may have questionable consequences
   (D) show how an action that is neither bad nor good can have beneficial consequences
   (E) illustrate how one can begin to evaluate an action in terms of its consequences

---

IF YOU FINISH BEFORE TIME IS CALLED, YOU MAY CHECK YOUR WORK ON THIS SECTION ONLY. DO NOT TURN TO ANY OTHER SECTION IN THE TEST. **STOP**

SECTION 5 Time—30 minutes 25 Questions

In this section solve each problem, using any available space on the page for scratchwork. Then decide which is the best of the choices given and fill in the corresponding oval on the answer sheet.

The following information is for your reference in solving some of the problems.

Circle of radius r: Area = πr^2; Circumference = $2\pi r$
The number of degrees of arc in a circle is 360.
The measure in degrees of a straight angle is 180.

Definition of symbols:
= is equal to   ≤ is less than or equal to
≠ is unequal to   ≥ is greater than or equal to
< is less than   ∥ is parallel to
> is greater than   ⊥ is perpendicular to

Triangle: The sum of the measures in degrees of the angles of a triangle is 180.

If $\angle CDA$ is a right angle, then

(1) area of $\triangle ABC = \dfrac{AB \times CD}{2}$

(2) $AC^2 = AD^2 + DC^2$

Note: Figures that accompany problems in this test are intended to provide information useful in solving the problems. They are drawn as accurately as possible EXCEPT when it is stated in a specific problem that its figure is not drawn to scale. All figures lie in a plane unless otherwise indicated. All numbers used are real numbers.

1. If $a = -1$ and $b = 2$, then $a^2 + b =$

   (A) -1
   (B) 0
   (C) 1
   (D) 3
   (E) 4

2. The cost to construct a fence 10 meters long is $350. At this rate, what is the cost to construct a fence 15 meters long?

   (A) $400
   (B) $420
   (C) $500
   (D) $525
   (E) $1,750

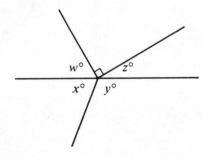

3. In the figure above, $w + x + y + z =$

   (A) 360
   (B) 300
   (C) 270
   (D) 240
   (E) 180

4. Each of the following two-digit numbers has one digit covered. Which of these five numbers is the only possible multiple of 12 ?

   (A) ▨9
   (B) ▨5
   (C) ▨3
   (D) 3▨
   (E) 5▨

5. When $2x$ is multiplied by $3x$, the product is

   (A) 5
   (B) $5x$
   (C) $6x$
   (D) $5x^2$
   (E) $6x^2$

6. If the fraction $\dfrac{x}{7}$ is between 2 and 3, which of the following numbers is a possible value of x ?

   (A) 10
   (B) 12
   (C) 16
   (D) 22
   (E) 26

GO ON TO THE NEXT PAGE

7. $(6 \div 3) \div 5 =$

(A) 0.4   (B) 0.6   (C) 1.0
(D) 2.5   (E) 10.0

8. A rectangle with length 12 and width 8 has an area equal to the sum of the areas of how many squares each with side of length 4 ?

(A) 3
(B) 6
(C) 8
(D) 24
(E) 96

9. Mary ran 6 kilometers in 30 minutes. What was her average speed in kilometers per <u>hour</u>?

(A) 5
(B) 10
(C) 12
(D) 15
(E) 30

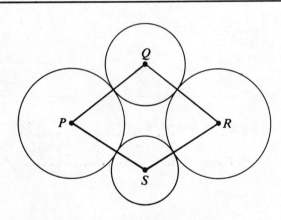

10. In the figure above, the circles with centers P and R have radius 8, the circle with center Q has radius 6, and the circle with center S has radius 5. If the circles are tangent as shown, what is the perimeter of quadrilateral $PQRS$?

(A) 27   (B) 38   (C) 44   (D) 50   (E) 54

11. If a department store offers an item originally priced at $8.00 at a reduced price of $6.00, by what percent is the original price reduced?

(A) 10%

(B) $12\frac{1}{2}\%$

(C) 20%

(D) 25%

(E) $33\frac{1}{3}\%$

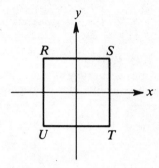

12. In the figure above, the center of square $RSTU$ is at the origin and the sides of the square are parallel to the x- and y-axes. If the square is rotated through 180° about the y-axis and then rotated through 180° about the x-axis, the vertices will be in which of the following positions?

(A) T U

    S R

(B) T S

    U R

(C) R U

    S T

(D) U R

    T S

(E) S T

    U R

GO ON TO THE NEXT PAGE ⟹

13. The number 0.253 is how much greater than $\frac{1}{4}$?

(A) $\frac{1}{3}$ (B) $\frac{3}{10}$ (C) $\frac{3}{25}$

(D) $\frac{3}{100}$ (E) $\frac{3}{1,000}$

14. Segments AB, CD, and EF lie in the same plane. If AB and CD are perpendicular bisectors of each other and if CD is perpendicular to and bisects EF at point D, which of the following statements must be true?

   I. Segment AB is parallel to segment EF.
  II. Segment AB is a perpendicular bisector of segment EF.
 III. Segment AB and segment EF have the same length.

(A) I only   (B) II only   (C) III only

(D) I and III   (E) II and III

Questions 15-17 refer to the following definition.

For any integer n, define $\boxed{n}$ by the equation
$$\boxed{n} = (n+1)n - (n-1)(n-2).$$

15. $\boxed{5} =$

(A) 18
(B) 16
(C) 14
(D) 12
(E) 10

16. If $\boxed{n} = 30$, then $n =$

(A) 6
(B) 7
(C) 8
(D) 9
(E) 10

17. $\boxed{n+1} - \boxed{n-1} =$

(A) 1
(B) 2
(C) 3
(D) 4
(E) 8

GO ON TO THE NEXT PAGE

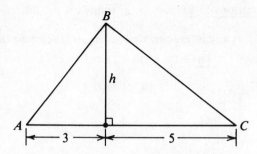

Note: Figure not drawn to scale.

18. If the area of $\triangle ABC$ above is 30, what is the value of h?

(A) 3.75
(B) 6
(C) 7.5
(D) 10
(E) It cannot be determined from the information given.

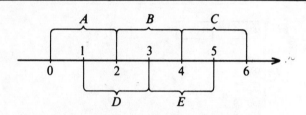

19. A portion of a number line has intervals labeled as shown in the figure above. If a number x is in interval A and a number y is in interval D, then the number $\frac{1}{2}(x + y + 1)$ must be in interval

(A) A (B) B (C) C (D) D (E) E

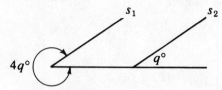

Note: Figure not drawn to scale.

20. If $s_1 \parallel s_2$ in the figure above, what is the value of q?

(A) 36
(B) 60
(C) 72
(D) 90
(E) 120

21. A piece of wire 0.002 meter long is cut off from a wire 0.2 meter long. The remaining piece is how many times as long as the piece that was cut off?

(A) 40
(B) 99
(C) 100
(D) 198
(E) 1,000

GO ON TO THE NEXT PAGE

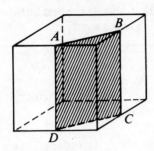

22. In the figure above, A, B, C, and D are midpoints of four edges of the cube. If the length of an edge of the cube is x, what is the area of rectangle $ABCD$?

(A) $\dfrac{x^2}{2}$

(B) x^2

(C) $\dfrac{x^2\sqrt{2}}{2}$

(D) $x^2\sqrt{2}$

(E) $2x^2$

23. If $\frac{1}{2}n + 2 = A$, then $2n + 2 =$

(A) $2A$
(B) $2A - 2$
(C) $4A$
(D) $4A - 2$
(E) $4A - 6$

24. If the present time is x minutes past y o'clock, where $0 \leqq x < 60$ and y is a positive integer less than 12, in how many <u>seconds</u> will it be $(y + 1)$ o'clock?

(A) $1 - x$ (B) $60 - x$ (C) $60(1 - x)$
(D) $60(60 - x)$ (E) $60x$

25. If the average (arithmetic mean) of ten consecutive integers arranged in increasing order is $15\frac{1}{2}$, what is the average of the first five of these integers?

(A) $15\frac{1}{2}$

(B) 13

(C) $10\frac{1}{2}$

(D) 9

(E) $7\frac{3}{4}$

SECTION 6	Time—30 minutes 45 Questions	For each question in this section, choose the best answer and fill in the corresponding oval on the answer sheet.

Each question below consists of a word in capital letters, followed by five lettered words or phrases. Choose the word or phrase that is most nearly <u>opposite</u> in meaning to the word in capital letters. Since some of the questions require you to distinguish fine shades of meaning, consider all the choices before deciding which is best.

Example:

GOOD: (A) sour   (B) bad   (C) red
(D) hot   (E) ugly

Ⓐ ● Ⓒ Ⓓ Ⓔ

1. INFLATE: (A) fail   (B) deny   (C) evade
(D) expose   (E) flatten

2. MISHAP:
   (A) fortunate event
   (B) thorough understanding
   (C) useful object
   (D) wealthy person
   (E) sincere apology

3. LENIENT: (A) stern   (B) gross
(C) superior   (D) unlucky   (E) mature

4. SUPPRESS: (A) reveal   (B) await
(C) receive   (D) repent   (E) influence

5. DIEHARD: (A) heartbreaker   (B) pushover
(C) simpleton   (D) spoilsport
(E) scatterbrain

6. UNDERMINE: (A) entangle   (B) parch
(C) overwork   (D) enter   (E) support

7. ZANY: (A) active   (B) content
(C) generous   (D) reasonable
(E) talkative

8. REPUGNANT: (A) orderly   (B) appealing
(C) languorous   (D) haughty   (E) defensive

9. INEPTNESS: (A) importance
(B) eagerness   (C) heaviness
(D) expertise   (E) novelty

10. CLANDESTINE: (A) swift   (B) open
(C) odorless   (D) reassuring
(E) conceivable

11. IMPROVIDENCE: (A) foresight
(B) sentiment   (C) courage
(D) eloquence   (E) authority

12. TRANSIENT: (A) enduring   (B) indisposed
(C) endangered   (D) internal   (E) scornful

13. CENSORIOUS: (A) adaptable
(B) attentive   (C) complimentary
(D) sluggish   (E) suspicious

14. ROTUND: (A) immoral   (B) placid
(C) gaunt   (D) astute   (E) solitary

15. CURSORY: (A) meticulous   (B) approving
(C) educated   (D) confusing   (E) delayed

GO ON TO THE NEXT PAGE →

Each sentence below has one or two blanks, each blank indicating that something has been omitted. Beneath the sentence are five lettered words or sets of words. Choose the word or set of words that, when inserted in the sentence, best fits the meaning of the sentence as a whole.

Example:

Although its publicity has been ----, the film itself is intelligent, well-acted, handsomely produced, and altogether ----.

(A) tasteless..respectable (B) extensive..moderate
(C) sophisticated..amateur (D) risqué..crude
(E) perfect..spectacular ●Ⓑ Ⓒ Ⓓ Ⓔ

16. Although the sociologist thought she would ---- the explanation with her charts and graphs, they actually caused additional ----.

(A) magnify..details
(B) clarify..benefits
(C) simplify..complications
(D) deprecate..problems
(E) illustrate..particulars

17. By relying on deductive reasoning, mathematicians have obtained results that would be very difficult or even ---- to obtain by other methods.

(A) essential   (B) effortless   (C) logical
(D) desirable   (E) impossible

18. Although Helena's life was both ---- and painful, it was not without ----, for she had accomplished many of her goals.

(A) defiant..strife
(B) tragic..frustration
(C) gratifying..reward
(D) arduous..satisfaction
(E) purposeful..ambition

19. The economic landscape of the 1920's was overrun with amateur firefighters, each clutching what was believed to be a magic formula for ---- the spreading fire of inflation.

(A) fanning   (B) inciting   (C) quenching
(D) refueling   (E) purifying

20. In the fifteenth century, ancient authority and empirical investigation were ----; not until the seventeenth century was a system created by which the two might be reconciled.

(A) unorthodox   (B) incompatible
(C) inadequate   (D) unintelligible
(E) interchangeable

21. The test of truth is not ----, for we have often felt firmly convinced of many things that were not so.

(A) implication   (B) certitude
(C) originality   (D) impartiality
(E) moderation

22. Although there is not a great deal we can do to prevent storage of information about ourselves in computer data banks, we are not entirely ----.

(A) indispensable   (B) anonymous
(C) neglectful   (D) helpless
(E) remorseless

23. Although Chester has his ----, he is no one's ----, for he has his own style of thinking and it is not derivative.

(A) detractors..critic
(B) followers..exemplar
(C) competitors..rival
(D) forerunners..compatriot
(E) predecessors..disciple

24. The tone of this autobiography becomes ---- as the author ---- the applause, the accolades, and the prizes that his labors have earned him.

(A) sullen..revels in
(B) smug..basks in
(C) boastful..atones for
(D) humble..exaggerates
(E) irresolute..relishes

25. The argument that science periodicals neither acknowledge nor ---- fraud in the scientific community is belied by this leading scientific journal's investigation of fabricated research and corrupt methodology.

(A) indulge   (B) exploit   (C) allow
(D) police   (E) perpetrate

GO ON TO THE NEXT PAGE ⇒

Each passage below is followed by questions based on its content. Answer the questions following each passage on the basis of what is stated or implied in that passage.

One of the most serious violations of civil liberties in the United States was the treatment of Japanese-Americans during the Second World War. In 1942 the army removed all persons of Japanese descent from coastal areas of three West Coast states and moved them inland to "relocation camps" in which conditions were far from satisfactory. The justification given for this drastic step was that it was necessary to prevent spy activities and sabotage in an essential military zone. But two-thirds of those detained were American citizens. In 1944 the Supreme Court finally ruled on the legal issues involved, holding that the mass evacuation had been legal under the war powers of the President, but that American citizens against whom no charge had been filed and whose loyalty was not questioned could not be detained after removal from the military zone. In the meantime, the War Department repealed its ban against the return of loyal citizens to the coast, but certain elements of the public in the West bitterly opposed the return of the Japanese-Americans and no less than fifty-nine acts of violence were committed in attempts to terrorize them. Although the majority of the people on the West Coast condemned such tactics, many of the Japanese-Americans decided to find new homes in parts of the country where they would encounter less prejudice.

In Hawaii between thirty and forty percent of the population was of Japanese ancestry; hence, it was not possible to remove those persons to the mainland, as was actually suggested, without completely disrupting the economic life of the islands. Therefore, Japanese-Americans in Hawaii were not relocated, but the political rights of all citizens, regardless of their race, color, or nationality, were almost completely abolished during the war. Military law replaced civilian government, and army officers discharged the duties normally assigned to judges and police magistrates. Regulations that might have had meaning right after the 1941 Japanese bombing of Pearl Harbor in Hawaii were enforced with military ruthlessness long after the reasons for their adoption had disappeared.

In spite of the violence and wholesale discrimination against Japanese-Americans, thousands of Hawaiian and mainland Americans of Japanese ancestry served with the United States armed services. Japanese-American battle units had outstanding records in the European theater of war to which they were assigned. No Japanese-American was convicted of either sabotage or espionage on the mainland or in Hawaii before or during the war.

26. It can be inferred from the passage that, according to the 1944 Supreme Court decision, it was legal for the United States government to do which of the following?

   I. Remove all people of Japanese ancestry from coastal areas of three West Coast states

   II. Detain in relocation camps people of Japanese ancestry who were not American citizens

   III. Detain in relocation camps American citizens of Japanese ancestry whose loyalty to the United States was questioned

(A) III only   (B) I and II only
(C) I and III only   (D) II and III only
   (E) I, II, and III

27. The author would be most likely to agree with which of the following statements about the enforcement of strict military regulations in Hawaii?

(A) It was justified as long as a state of war existed.
(B) It was reasonable immediately after Pearl Harbor was bombed.
(C) It was defensible if the rules were applied to only certain elements of the population.
(D) It was necessary because Hawaii was economically important.
(E) It was unavoidable because Hawaii was so politically unstable.

GO ON TO THE NEXT PAGE ▶

28. According to the passage, Japanese-Americans were not removed from Hawaii during the Second World War because

   (A) the military authorities on Hawaii were able to detain them in relocation camps
   (B) Hawaii was under attack from the Japanese
   (C) there was little resentment against them in Hawaii
   (D) they were important to the economic life of Hawaii
   (E) the distance between Hawaii and the relocation camps on the mainland was too great

29. The passage suggests that which of the following statements about American soldiers of Japanese ancestry during the Second World War is true?

   (A) They were not involved in combat.
   (B) They were under stricter military regulations than other soldiers.
   (C) They were in segregated battalions.
   (D) They could enlist but they were not drafted.
   (E) They were kept in relocation camps unless they volunteered for overseas service.

30. Which of the following would be the best title for the passage?

   (A) The Role of Japanese-Americans in Hawaii and on the West Coast of the United States
   (B) Hostility Toward Japanese-Americans During the Second World War
   (C) The Second World War: The Japanese-American Response
   (D) American Attitudes During the Second World War
   (E) Military Intervention in Hawaii During the Second World War

GO ON TO THE NEXT PAGE

In February 1902 Lee De Forest wrote, "I shall move all heaven and earth to put in at once a broad fundamental patent on telephony without wires by hertzian waves." As a graduate student at Yale, he had specialized in the study of electromagnetic waves, a phenomenon discovered by Heinrich Hertz in 1887. His subsequent work focused on the inadequacies of the Branly coherer, a device designed to detect these waves and a critical link in Marconi's system of wireless telegraphy. Despite research and invention that had spanned a number of years, De Forest's plans remained unrealized until a completely reliable detector was found to replace the Branly coherer.

The solution at last appeared, thanks to an observation Edison made in 1883 when he put a metal-wire electrode with a positive charge into his light bulb and found that electricity flowed from the glowing filament to the new electrode across the space between them. Twenty years later John Fleming discovered that the "Edison effect" bulb could detect hertzian waves in a completely new way. This was the first radio vacuum tube, the diode.

De Forest began experimenting with a simple detector that contained a gas flame instead of an electric filament. In addition, he used a telephone receiver—with a battery of its own—and clearly heard the dot-dash wireless signals from a distant transmitter. He added these two items to Fleming's diode and later tried a zigzag grid of wire between the filament and a metal-plate electrode to carry the incoming signal. De Forest named this first triode (patented in 1907) the "Audion" and much later called it "the granddaddy of all the vast progeny of electric tubes that have come into existence since."

But the progeny were not immediately forthcoming, partly because no one fully understood how the Audion really worked. Some gases remained in the tube's partial vacuum. To De Forest, it seemed that the current could only flow from filament to plate through a transporting medium—the ionized gases. It was an obvious explanation—but incorrect. By 1912 it had become clear that a transporting medium was unnecessary. The filament emitted electrons—particles with a negative charge—and the plate with its positive charge attracted them. High-vacuum tubes would be far more efficient than the "soft" gassy tubes used by De Forest until then.

De Forest also discovered that by feeding part of the output of his triode vacuum tube back into its grid, he could cause a self-regenerating oscillation in the circuit. The signal from this circuit was far more powerful and effective than that of the crude transmitters then generally employed. When appropriately modified, this single invention was capable of transmitting, receiving, or amplifying radio signals and it was not surpassed until the invention of the transistor in 1947.

31. According to the passage, the first triode could best be described as

(A) a rudimentary device that was later refined and improved
(B) a simple structure that functioned as efficiently as does a transistor
(C) a complex machine that ultimately proved too intricate to be practical
(D) an ill-conceived design that was quickly superseded by the work of other inventors
(E) a controversial apparatus that stunned scientists of the time

32. De Forest's statements quoted in the passage reveal which of the following attitudes?

(A) Impatience and modesty
(B) Idealism and detachment
(C) Determination and pride
(D) Fascination and awe
(E) Hostility and defiance

33. According to the passage, De Forest's explanation of how his original Audion functioned was incorrect because he misunderstood the

(A) role of electrons in ionized gases
(B) means by which electrons travel in a vacuum tube
(C) rate at which electricity is absorbed by the plate
(D) composition of the partial vacuum inside the tube
(E) necessity for both a filament and a plate

34. It can be inferred from the passage that De Forest's triode was capable of which of the following?

I. Intensification of the strength of the signal produced by a transmitter
II. Production of supplementary electrical power
III. Amplification of incoming signals in the receiver

(A) II only   (B) III only   (C) I and II only
(D) I and III only   (E) I, II, and III

35. Which of the following titles is most suitable for the passage?

(A) Founders of Modern Electronics
(B) Personalities of Early Radio
(C) The Discovery of Hertzian Waves
(D) How to Use the High-Vacuum Tube
(E) A Pioneer in Radio Technology

GO ON TO THE NEXT PAGE

Each question below consists of a related pair of words or phrases, followed by five lettered pairs of words or phrases. Select the lettered pair that best expresses a relationship similar to that expressed in the original pair.

Example:

YAWN : BOREDOM ::   (A) dream : sleep
(B) anger : madness   (C) smile : amusement
(D) face : expression   (E) impatience : rebellion

Ⓐ Ⓑ ● Ⓓ Ⓔ

36. WOODS : TREES ::   (A) lawn : grass
(B) ocean : rocks   (C) forest : paths
(D) shore : lake   (E) valley : stream

37. CROCODILE : REPTILE ::   (A) frog : pond
(B) bridge : gorge   (C) tornado : storm
(D) dawn : day   (E) spring : flower

38. IMPOSE : BESTOW ::   (A) stroll : walk
(B) leave : depart   (C) demand : ask
(D) praise : honor   (E) estimate : calculate

39. BOGUS : DECEIVE ::
(A) prudish : offend
(B) perilous : neglect
(C) listless : enliven
(D) mysterious : perplex
(E) threatening : safeguard

40. SHIRK : OBLIGATION ::
(A) desert : correction
(B) penalize : mistake
(C) recognize : authority
(D) default : payment
(E) blame : accusation

41. STRATUM : EARTH ::   (A) seat : theater
(B) story : building   (C) sequence : event
(D) trademark : company   (E) stalk : plant

42. INTERLOPER : INTRUSION ::
(A) witness : interrogation
(B) actor : intermission
(C) recluse : interference
(D) mediator : intercession
(E) orator : interruption

43. PNEUMATIC : AIR ::   (A) electric : light
(B) insulated : cold   (C) galvanized : iron
(D) hydraulic : liquid   (E) inorganic : solid

44. HABITABLE : DWELLERS ::
(A) literate : editors
(B) hospitable : combatants
(C) passable : travelers
(D) invulnerable : aggressors
(E) indestructible : developers

45. DIORAMA : SCENE ::   (A) prologue : play
(B) effigy : person   (C) cartoon : movie
(D) tableau : stage   (E) drama : cast

IF YOU FINISH BEFORE TIME IS CALLED, YOU MAY CHECK YOUR WORK ON THIS SECTION ONLY. DO NOT TURN TO ANY OTHER SECTION IN THE TEST.   **S T O P**

Correct Answers for Scholastic Aptitude Test
Form Code 6G

VERBAL		MATHEMATICAL	
Section 2	Section 6	Section 5	Section 1
1. D	1. E	1. D	1. A
2. D	2. A	2. D	2. B
3. B	3. A	3. C	3. D
4. B	4. A	4. D	4. D
5. C	5. B	5. E	5. B
6. E	6. E	6. C	6. D
7. B	7. D	7. A	7. C
8. A	8. B	8. B	*8. B
9. A	9. D	9. C	*9. C
10. B	10. B	10. E	*10. D
11. C	11. A	11. D	*11. B
12. B	12. A	12. A	*12. A
13. E	13. C	13. E	*13. C
14. E	14. C	14. A	*14. B
15. C	15. A	15. A	*15. D
16. D	16. C	16. C	*16. B
17. A	17. E	17. E	*17. D
18. C	18. D	18. C	*18. C
19. C	19. C	19. D	*19. B
20. B	20. B	20. C	*20. B
21. B	21. B	21. B	*21. A
22. B	22. D	22. C	*22. A
23. C	23. E	23. E	*23. C
24. B	24. B	24. D	*24. D
25. C	25. D	25. B	*25. A
26. A	26. E		*26. C
27. C	27. B		*27. B
28. E	28. D		28. D
29. E	29. C		29. D
30. B	30. B		30. C
31. D	31. A		31. E
32. D	32. C		32. D
33. B	33. B		33. C
34. E	34. D		34. A
35. E	35. E		35. B
36. C	36. A		
37. E	37. C		
38. C	38. C		
39. D	39. D		
40. E	40. D		
	41. B		
	42. D		
	43. D		
	44. C		
	45. B		

*Indicates four-choice questions. (All of the other questions are five-choice.)

The Scoring Process

Machine-scoring is done in three steps:

- *Scanning.* Your answer sheet is "read" by a scanning machine and the oval you filled in for each question is recorded on a computer tape.

- *Scoring.* The computer compares the oval filled in for each question with the correct response. Each correct answer receives one point; omitted questions do not count toward your score. For each wrong answer, a fraction of a point is subtracted to correct for random guessing. For questions with five answer choices, one-fourth of a point is subtracted for each wrong response; for questions with four answer choices, one-third of a point is subtracted for each wrong response. The SAT-verbal test has 85 questions with five answer choices each. If, for example, a student has 44 right, 32 wrong, and 9 omitted, the resulting raw score is determined as follows:

$$44 \text{ right} - \frac{32 \text{ wrong}}{4} = 44 - 8 = 36 \text{ raw score points}$$

Obtaining raw scores frequently involves the rounding of fractional numbers to the nearest whole number. For example, a raw score of 36.25 is rounded to 36, the nearest whole number. A raw score of 36.50 is rounded upward to 37.

- *Converting to reported scaled score.* Raw test scores are then placed on the College Board scale of 200 to 800 through a process that adjusts scores to account for minor differences in difficulty among different editions of the test. This process, known as equating, is performed so that a student's reported score is not affected by the edition of the test taken nor by the abilities of the group with whom the student takes the test. As a result of placing SAT scores on the College Board scale, scores earned by students at different times can be compared. For example, an SAT-verbal score of 400 on a test taken at one administration indicates the same level of developed verbal ability as a 400 score obtained on a different edition of the test taken at another time.

How to Score the Test

SAT-Verbal Sections 2 and 6

Step A: Count the number of correct answers for *section 2* and record the number in the space provided on the worksheet on the next page. Then do the same for the incorrect answers. (Do not count omitted answers.) To determine subtotal A, use the formula:

$$\text{number correct} - \frac{\text{number incorrect}}{4} = \text{subtotal A}$$

Step B: Count the number of correct answers and the number of incorrect answers for *section 6* and record the numbers in the spaces provided on the worksheet. To determine subtotal B, use the formula:

$$\text{number correct} - \frac{\text{number incorrect}}{4} = \text{subtotal B}$$

Step C: To obtain C, add subtotal A to subtotal B, keeping any decimals. Enter the resulting figure on the worksheet.

Step D: To obtain D, your raw verbal score, round C to the nearest whole number. (For example, any number from 44.50 to 45.49 rounds to 45.) Enter the resulting figure on the worksheet.

Step E: To find your reported SAT-verbal score, look up the total raw verbal score you obtained in step D in the conversion table on page 298. Enter this figure on the worksheet.

SAT-Mathematical Sections 5 and 1

Step A: Count the number of correct answers and the number of incorrect answers for *section 5* and record the numbers in the spaces provided on the worksheet. To determine the subtotal A, use the formula:

$$\text{number correct} - \frac{\text{number incorrect}}{4} = \text{subtotal A}$$

Step B: Count the number of correct answers and the number of incorrect answers for the *five-choice questions (questions 1 through 7 and 28 through 35) in section 1* and record the numbers in the spaces provided on the worksheet. To determine the subtotal B, use the formula:

$$\text{number correct} - \frac{\text{number incorrect}}{4} = \text{subtotal B}$$

Step C: Count the number of correct answers and the number of incorrect answers for the *four-choice questions (questions 8 through 27) in section 1* and record the numbers in the spaces provided on the worksheet. To determine the subtotal C, use the formula:

$$\text{number correct} - \frac{\text{number incorrect}}{3} = \text{subtotal C}$$

Step D: To obtain D, add subtotal A, subtotal B, and subtotal C, keeping any decimals. Enter the resulting figure on the worksheet.

Step E: To obtain E, your raw mathematical score, round D to the nearest whole number. (For example, any number from 44.50 to 45.49 rounds to 45.) Enter the resulting figure on the worksheet.

Step F: To find your reported SAT-mathematical score, look up the total raw mathematical score you obtained in E in the conversion table on page 298. Enter this figure on the worksheet.

SAT SCORING WORKSHEET

SAT-Verbal Sections

A. Section 2:
$$\underline{\hspace{4cm}} - \tfrac{1}{4} \ (\underline{\hspace{4cm}}) = \underline{\hspace{4cm}}$$
no. correct — no. incorrect — subtotal A

B. Section 6:
$$\underline{\hspace{4cm}} - \tfrac{1}{4} \ (\underline{\hspace{4cm}}) = \underline{\hspace{4cm}}$$
no. correct — no. incorrect — subtotal B

C. Total unrounded raw score
(Total A + B)

C

D. Total rounded raw score
(Rounded to nearest whole number)

D

E. SAT-verbal reported scaled score
(See the conversion table on page 298.)

SAT-verbal
score

SAT-Mathematical Sections

A. Section 5:
$$\underline{\hspace{4cm}} - \tfrac{1}{4} \ (\underline{\hspace{4cm}}) = \underline{\hspace{4cm}}$$
no. correct — no. incorrect — subtotal A

B. Section 1:
Questions 1 through 7 and
28 through 35 (5-choice)
$$\underline{\hspace{4cm}} - \tfrac{1}{4} \ (\underline{\hspace{4cm}}) = \underline{\hspace{4cm}}$$
no. correct — no. incorrect — subtotal B

C. Section 1:
Questions 8 through 27
(4-choice)
$$\underline{\hspace{4cm}} - \tfrac{1}{3} \ (\underline{\hspace{4cm}}) = \underline{\hspace{4cm}}$$
no. correct — no. incorrect — subtotal C

D. Total unrounded raw score
(Total A + B + C)

D

E. Total rounded raw score
(Rounded to nearest whole number)

E

F. SAT-mathematical reported scaled score
(See the conversion table on page 298.)

SAT-math
score

Score Conversion Table
Scholastic Aptitude Test
Form Code 6G

Raw Score	College Board Reported Score		Raw Score	College Board Reported Score	
	SAT-Verbal	SAT-Math		SAT-Verbal	SAT-Math
85	800		40	450	580
84	780		39	450	570
83	760		38	440	570
82	740		37	430	560
81	730		36	430	550
80	720		35	420	540
79	710		34	410	530
78	700		33	410	520
77	690		32	400	510
76	690		31	390	500
75	680		30	390	490
74	670		29	380	480
73	660		28	380	480
72	650		27	370	470
71	650		26	360	460
70	640		25	360	450
69	630		24	350	440
68	630		23	340	430
67	620		22	330	420
66	610		21	330	420
65	600		20	320	410
64	600		19	310	400
63	590		18	310	390
62	580		17	300	390
61	580		16	290	380
60	570	800	15	290	370
59	570	780	14	280	360
58	560	760	13	270	350
57	550	750	12	270	350
56	550	740	11	260	340
55	540	730	10	250	330
54	540	720	9	250	330
53	530	710	8	240	320
52	520	700	7	230	310
51	520	690	6	230	300
50	510	680	5	220	300
49	510	670	4	210	290
48	500	660	3	200	280
47	490	650	2	200	270
46	490	640	1	200	270
45	480	630	0	200	260
44	480	620	−1	200	250
43	470	610	−2	200	240
42	460	600	−3	200	240
41	460	590	−4	200	230
			−5	200	220
			−6	200	210
			−7	200	210
			−8 or below	200	200

Notes

Notes

Notes

Notes

Notes

Notes